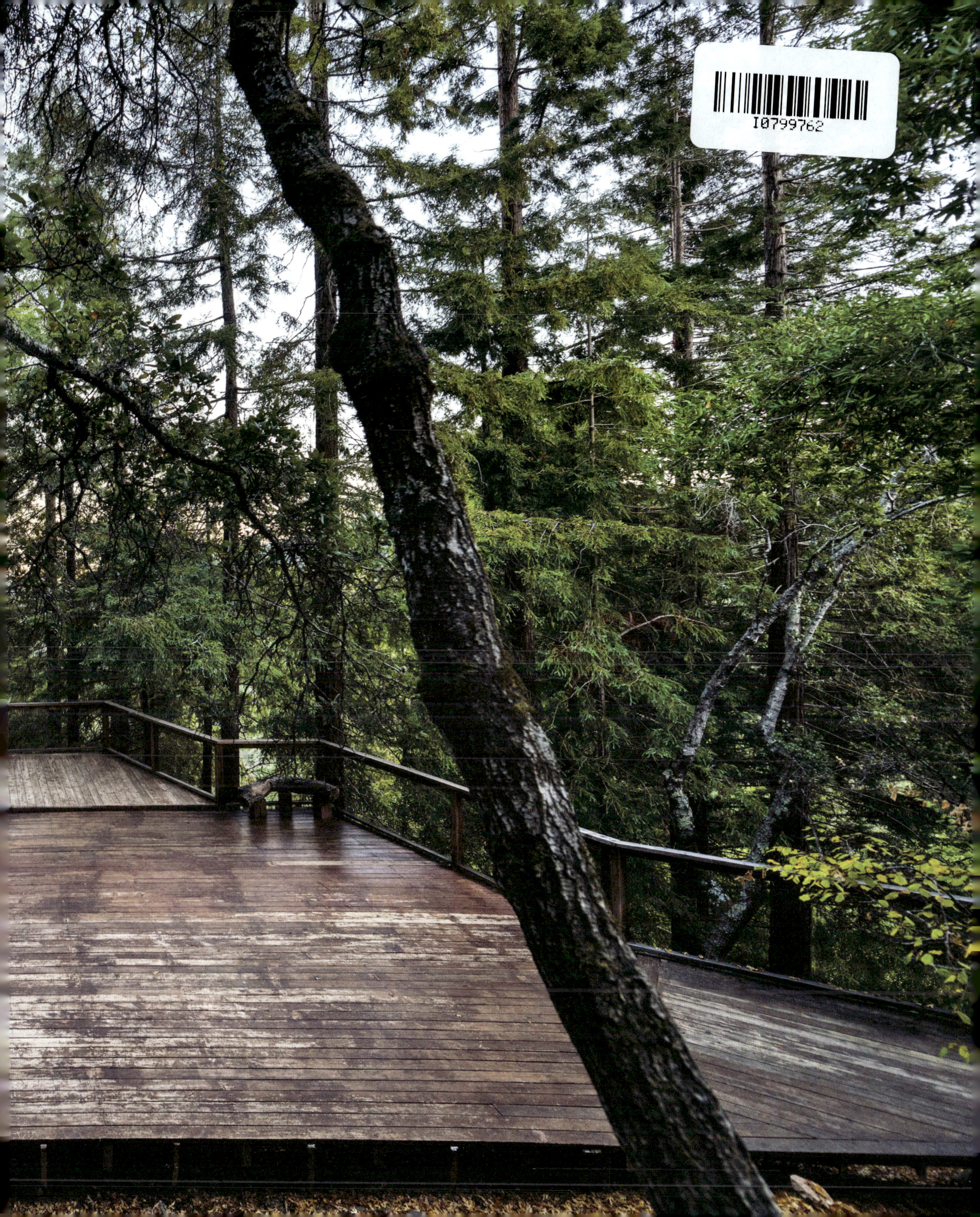

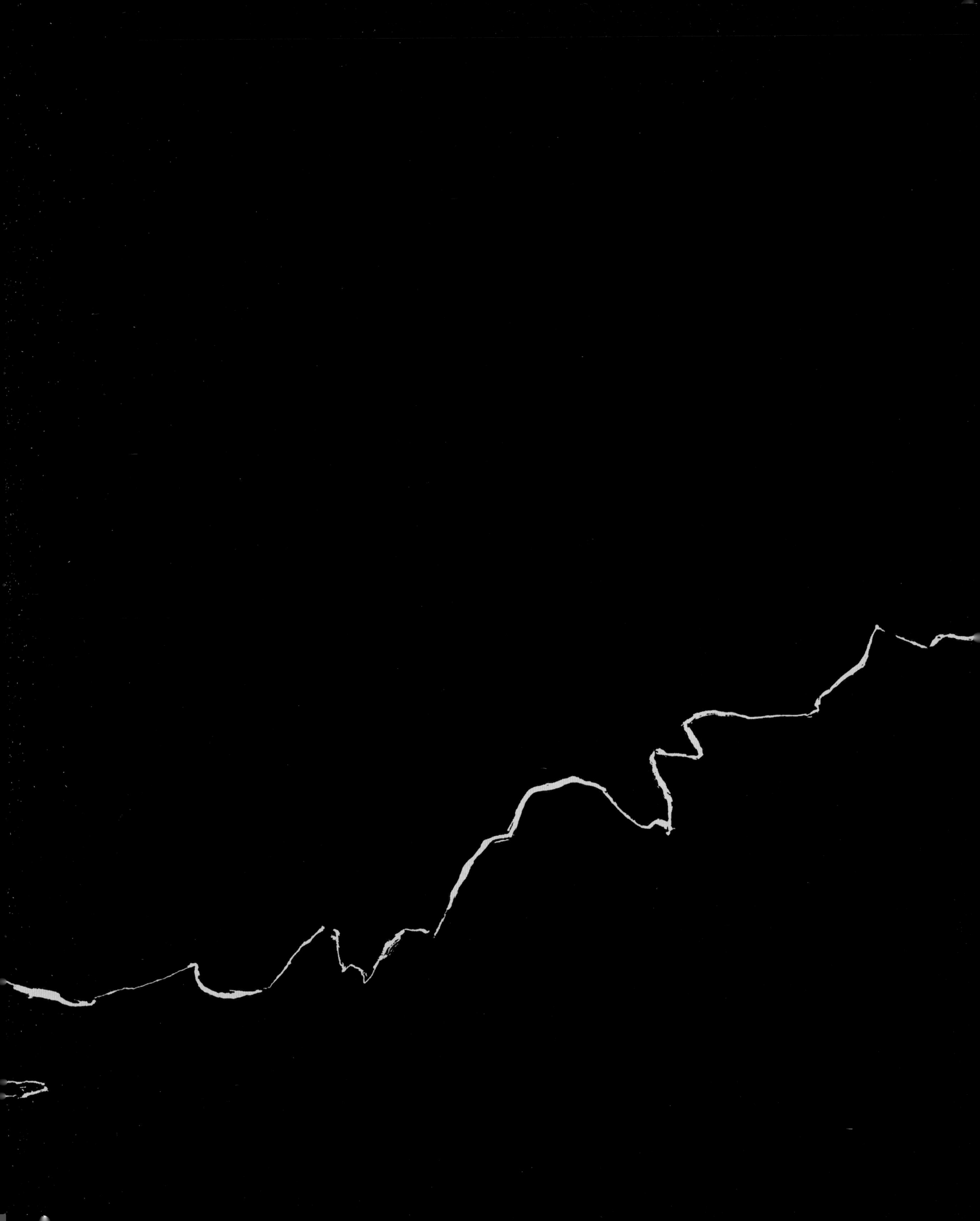

JANINE ANTONI   ANNA HALPRIN   STEPHEN PETRONIO

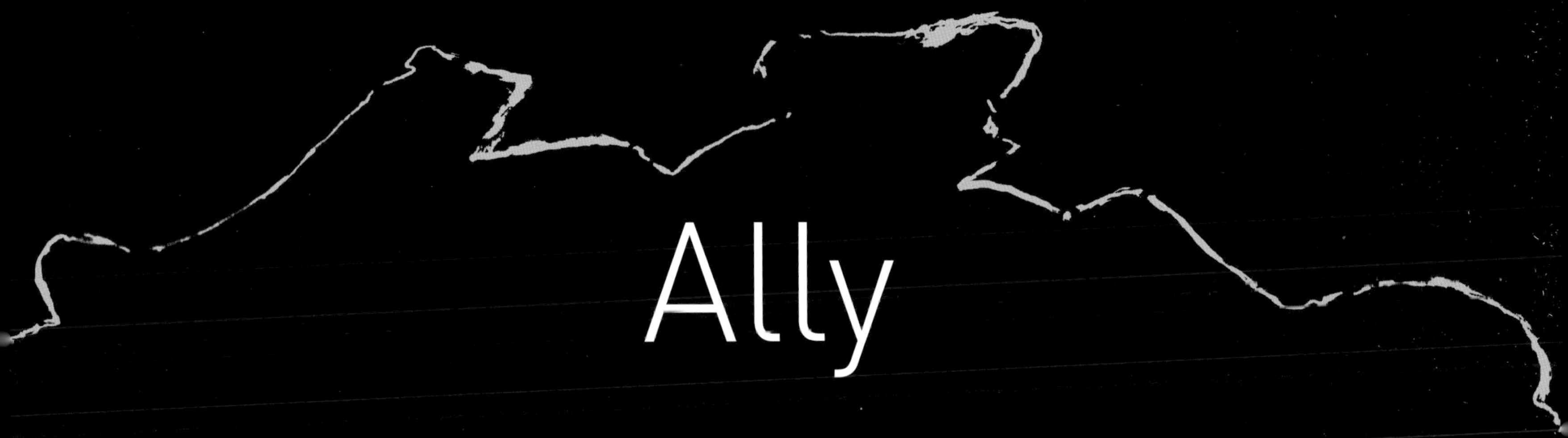

Ally

EDITED BY ADRIAN HEATHFIELD

PUBLISHED BY THE FABRIC WORKSHOP AND MUSEUM & HIRMER PUBLISHERS

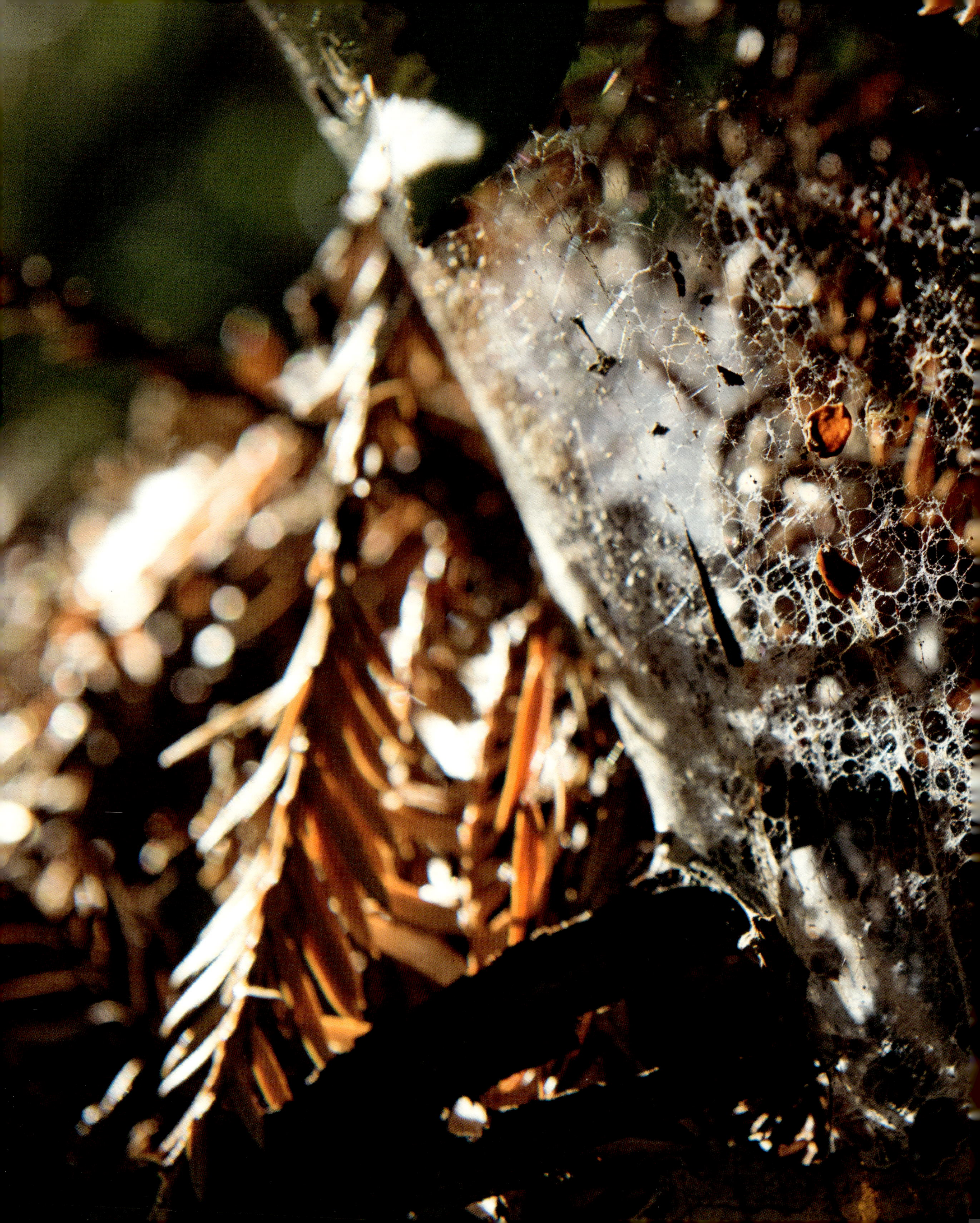

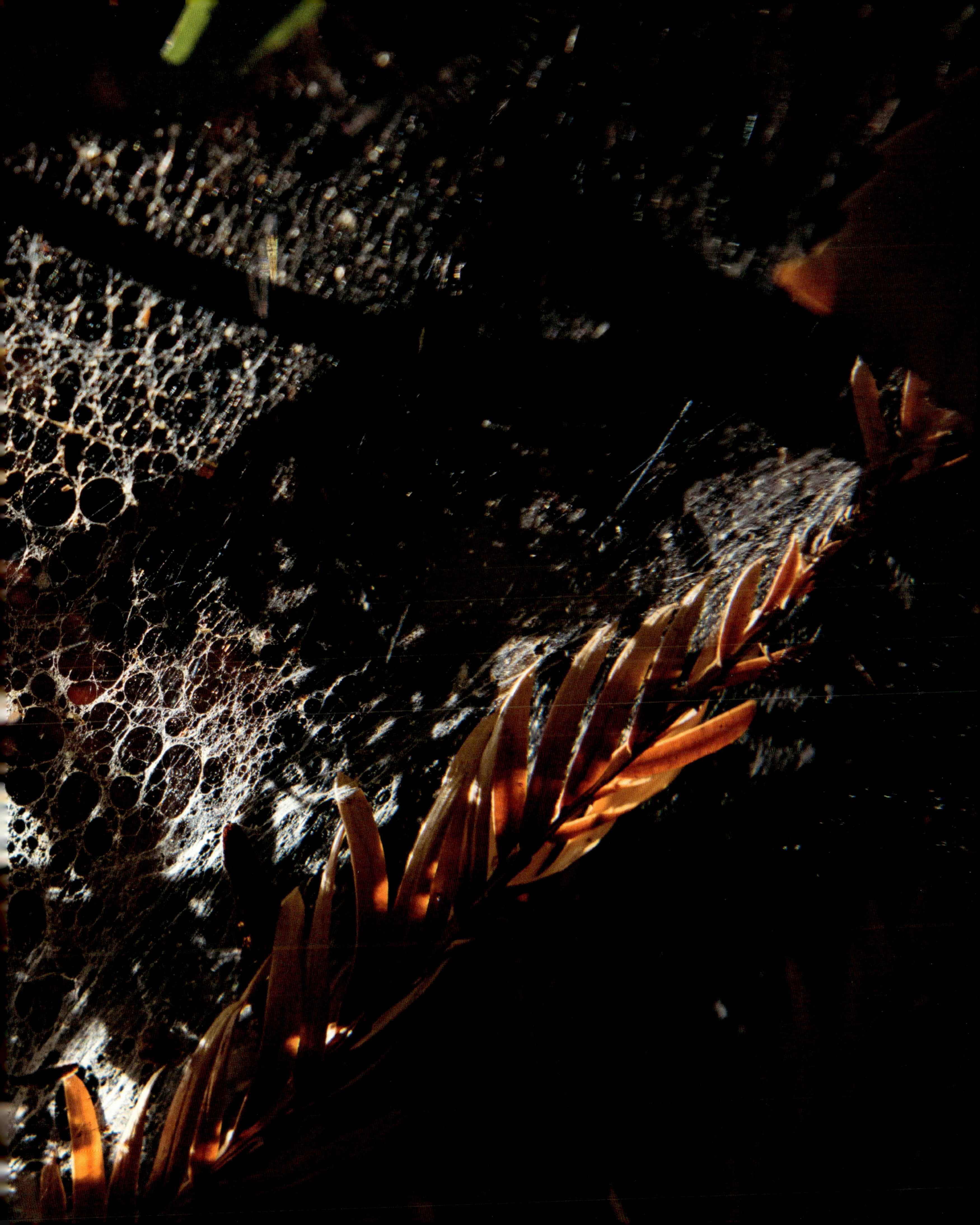

CONTENTS

PREFACE

Janine Antoni's artist residency at The Fabric Workshop and Museum was initially to culminate with a career retrospective — presented, however, through the lens of dance and movement. An object maker and performance artist, Antoni invited choreographer Stephen Petronio and exploratory movement pioneer Anna Halprin to join her and as their concept evolved, they thought more and more about the notion of connection. Petronio described their process as "three distinct artistic languages coming together to meet in the gap between art and dance." And together, they created four multi-layered and interrelated pieces involving movement, installation, sculpture, sound and video that they called *Ally*. The title spoke to a bond between artists of different generations and disciplines working as collaborators.

The live dances all originated with Halprin, either as re-workings of her earlier compositions or, in the case of *Rope Dance*, as a newly conceived piece for Antoni and Petronio. When *Rope Dance* was performed at The Fabric Workshop and Museum, the artists invited audience members to interact with them, a rope, and a wall-sized video of Halprin's face as she responded to an early iteration of the piece. *Paper Dance*, enacted solely by Antoni, was the realization of a new work, with Halprin's seminal *Parades and Changes* (1964) as its foundation. Each performance of *Paper Dance* began with the act of uncrating one artwork from Antoni's archive after re-crating the work revealed the previous week. Slowly, over the course of twenty-one performances, Antoni scrolled through her artistic output offering a retrospective of sorts. Halprin also worked with Petronio to reimagine her solo piece, *The Courtesan and the Crone* (first performed in 1999, when she was seventy-nine years old). With Petronio as a middle-aged courtesan, masked and cloaked in a golden robe created by museum staff, the work took on new meaning. As he disrobed, his sultry dance addressed not only age, but gender as well.

Ally often took the artists outside their comfort zones, challenging them to present movement and dance in a museum setting while creating artworks that could stand alone when no performances were scheduled. *Swallow*, an immersive sound and sculptural installation devoid of live performers, documented an act of communion between Petronio and Antoni, as described on digital recordings from ten invited witnesses. As in *Paper Dance*, the concept was fully revealed with the passing of time. Moth larvae slowly ate through an image of the act — printed on hand-woven cloth — during the course of the project.

Three years in the making, *Ally* looked both forward and back, inspired by Halprin's groundbreaking oeuvre and the desire of all three artists to expand their individual practices. Since its founding in 1977, The Fabric Workshop and Museum has encouraged experimentation and its founder, Marion "Kippy" Stroud always embraced innovation. From early on, performance had a place in an evolving program, and when Antoni posed the notion of *Ally* to Stroud, she immediately saw the creative potential of a project with this level of ambition.

I thank the artists first and foremost for these extraordinary works. It took true allies to create a production of this breadth and scope. The realization of their concept also owes a debt to independent curator and writer Adrian Heathfield who contributed to the exhibition in innumerable ways and also served as editor and essayist for this book.

A venture of this magnitude could not have been realized without our generous funders. I would like to thank The Pew Center for Arts & Heritage led by Paula Marincola (Executive Director) who, with her colleague Bill Bissell (Director of Performance), had the foresight to see the early promise of this project and to provide major support for its realization. *Ally* also received critical underwriting from the National Endowment for the Arts whose funding has sustained this organization. Thanks are due as well to the LLWW Foundation; Harvey S. Shipley Miller and the Shipley Miller Foundation and Creative Capital, who made an early grant to Antoni for *Ally*'s development. Major support for The Fabric Workshop and Museum is provided by the Marion Boulton "Kippy" Stroud Foundation.

I wish to recognize the museum staff whose dedication and cooperative spirit helped to make *Ally* a reality. Particular thanks go to Director of Studio Operations, Nami Yamamoto; Project Technician, Paige Fetchen and our entire Studio staff, as well as Exhibitions Manager, Alexander Unkovic. I add my appreciation to Antoni's gallery, Luhring Augustine. Witnesses to *Swallow* gave their time and insights and I thank Stephanie Berger; Winston Cheng; Sam Gregory; Kristen, Viva and Felix Johnson; Tim Kilker; Susan Klein; Dr. Michael Vincent Miller; and Greg Pardlo.

The publication of this book could not have been accomplished without the guidance of Heathfield and the contributions of the other authors: Jacquelynn Baas, Carol Becker and Richard Move. Their essays bring new insights to a complex group of works that many readers may not have experienced in their original form. I am also grateful to Hélène Cixous whose memoir extract complements and extends these writings and artworks. Finally, I wish to thank Associate Director for Administration, Stephanie Greene who coordinated all aspects of this publication; and designer David Caines.

The help of many staff, consultants and contractors impacted *Ally's* realization. A full list of participants is included in the end pages and I am grateful for their expertise.

Ally was not completed until after Kippy Stroud's death, but it stands as a testament to her vision. I was privileged to play a role in its presentation.

Susan Lubowsky Talbott
Executive Director

REMEMBERING AIR

Adrian Heathfield

Composed from shards of time, perceptions and speculations, this essay looks back on the processes of the *Ally* collaboration. I am a participant-observer, a researcher, an interlocutor, a curator, a dramaturge, an archivist and creative respondent in different passages of these processes. As an intermediary, then, I can only speak hesitantly from the middle of things. I cannot be the artists' voice. I attempt to write closely, beside the emergent qualities of the artworks. The words that have fallen and have been wrestled onto this page slide out of these distinct practices into a weave. I travel with the process and take in the local air. If it is not caught, can gossamer at least be carried?

Late-April, 2015, Brooklyn, New York. Janine Antoni gives me a loan: an object for contemplation and discussion. I will spend some time with it. Perhaps it will unlock new insights into the ongoing *Ally* collaboration with which I have become critically embroiled. The object is a multicolored wool yarn on a spool, pinned to a small sample of crochet work. It feels long kept. Antoni tells me that the yarn belonged to her grandmother Maria Rosario De Medina: a woman whose interest in craft was matched by her ability to fabricate spellbinding spoken tales. The young Antoni had given the yarn to her ailing grandmother, but had later found the attached unfinished crochet work beside the matriarch's deathbed. Compelled to save the thing as a memento, the adult Antoni became aware of its singular force as a "sculptural object." Its incompletion, its carriage of a certain interruption seemed to speak powerfully to Antoni's aesthetics, often concerned with presenting traces of charged actions in everyday materials. Her dilemma: should she exhibit the spool and crochet as a found work, or transform it into another object of her own making? Antoni had kept the thing for some time, wanting to answer its call, but was unable to resolve the conundrum of how to work with it. What would art add to (or subtract from) its force, and was it not already a resonant and complete aesthetic thing? How to draw on the potentials of a lost relation? How to re-weave the singularities of Maria Rosario De Medina and her unfinished labor into a meaningful work in the present?

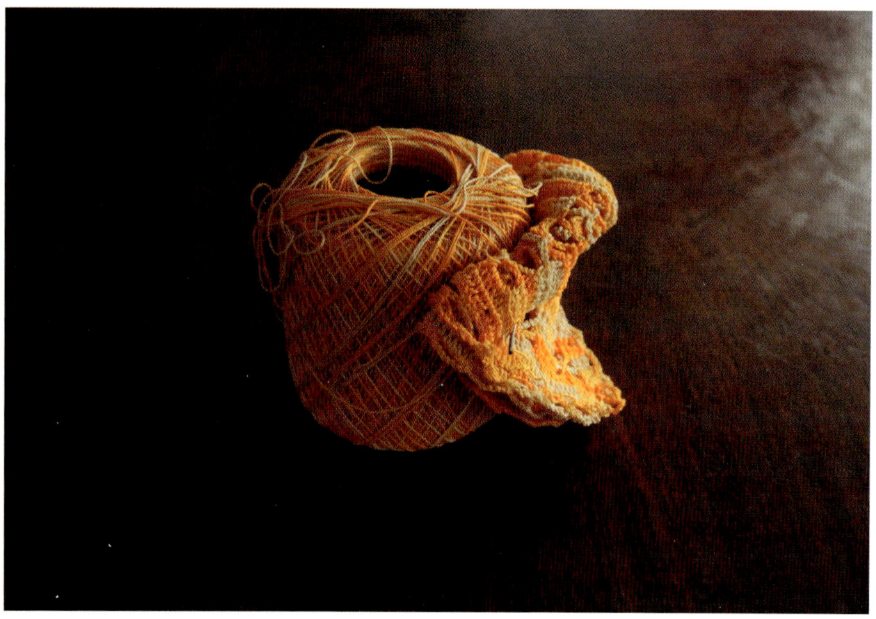

Granny Maina's yarn. Photo: Holli McEntegart. © Janine Antoni. Courtesy of the artist.

I had heard of De Medina before: as Granny Maina. Antoni had recalled two of her stories in a small catalogue marking the showing of *Loving Care* (1993) and *Butterfly Kisses* (1993) at the Wadsworth Atheneum.[1] Each is a work on feminine caress, bodily extremities and arduous labor. Both stories involved Maina in compulsive acts of hair cutting (her own and her husband's while he slept) as assertions of her desires in disputes of love.[2] And so I was aware of the symbolism of the cutting of threads for Antoni: a sign of male power, or in Granny Maina's case, its contestation. By using the hair on her head (*Loving Care*) or the blink of her eyelashes (*Butterfly Kisses*) to create action paintings, Antoni continued Maina's audacity in relation to restrictive convention, but found a space of somatic expression that exceeded her subjection. Likewise the unbroken woven threads, fabrics and ropes that recur throughout Antoni's oeuvre are symbols and valuations of female autonomy, power and labor. So, what to do with Granny Maina's unfinished yarn? An interruption of a braided line is not quite the same as a cut, which is absolute and irreversible. Maina's death was a cut, but her yarn promised a matrilineal continuation of spirited actions. Interruptions simply invite recommencement, restoration or diversion. Where might Antoni take the line that connects her grandmother's desire to her own, and what might this course say about the changed relations between female desire and labor, or the labors of love?

The fate of Granny Maina's yarn intrigued me because, holding it, I was aware that it intensified something characteristic of all human subject-object relations. I felt it before I knew the provenance of the object. Its thingness reminded me of what Peter Schwenger has called "the tears of things": a melancholy aspect that underlies relations between lasting material objects and people.[3] Things evoke a sense of loss because, while they remain inseparable from our perception of them, they also disclose that they are ultimately inaccessible, fundamentally distant and unpossessable. Their indifference reminds us that they will outlive us. These qualities of objects have long been discussed in key philosophical and psychoanalytical writings, and more recently in the profusion of theories within object studies, new materialism and speculative realism.[4] But what interests me here in relation to the entwining of Antoni's practices with those of Anna Halprin and Stephen Petronio in *Ally* are certain qualities of *thingness* that persist through Antoni's work and become vectors of affinity within these current collaborations and makings. I understand thingness as an affective quality of matter that perturbs definition and naming. Some associate thingness with an object's dysfunction, others with its instability, ambiguity, uncanny animation or vitality.[5] My tendency is to see the thingly as a rupture of objecthood that discloses an anterior amorphous state within the physical world: an emergence of formlessness in form.[6]

Many years before the realization of *Ally*, curators had requested that Antoni consider a retrospective of her body of sculptures and photographs. But she was wary of this exhibition genre whose function is to trace an individual artist's trajectory from the past into the present, accumulating weighted understandings and new perspectives through the act of overviewing an oeuvre. She distrusted its self-consolidations, internal coherence, its narrative and teleological tendencies. Moreover, she was preoccupied with surfacing a dimension of her previous labor: its resource of somatic practices, and its subtle deployment of gesture and choreographic arrangements. Antoni decided that instead of retrospecting she would rather regenerate or transform her existing works, pass them through the bodies or visions of others. In this way, the identitarian, historiographical and scopic traditions of retrospection would be put in question. The past would not be closed, but used as a forge for new works, cast into unknown futures. She began to seek out dance collaborators and took a workshop with the preeminent choreographer, theater maker and community activist Anna Halprin. An elder of American postmodern dance working since the early 1940s, Halprin is known for her radical experimentation with theatrical form, the use of improvisation in transdisciplinary works, and the melding of actional or task-based activities with choreographic and dramatic materials. Working for much of her career on an elevated outdoor dance deck in a forest in Marin County built by her life-partner landscape architect Lawrence Halprin, her work championed the abandonment of performance enclosures for site-specific movement interventions in city streets and the countryside. With Lawrence Halprin she developed radical redeterminations of the practice of scoring within artistic creation. Her early work in community oriented processes, often concerned with racism and the politics of sexuality and health, in later years has turned toward pedagogic initiatives, large scale public rituals, and practices of conciliation, attunement and acceptance in relation to social division, ecology and mortality.

Though she had been aware of Halprin's oeuvre for over twenty years, their first physical encounter was in Antoni's late-forties when Halprin was already in her nineties. Antoni's subsequent envelopment in Halprin's practice and ethos has formed a vital axis of *Ally*. When I asked Antoni what motivated this new phase of her work she replied, "One question: how can we meet each other in the past?" This aspiration to cross over into other histories and forms of expression was also an impetus in Antoni's collaborations with the pioneering New York-based choreographer Stephen Petronio. She was invited to create scenography for his dance work *Like Lazarus Did* (2013), a choreographic assemblage on sacrifice and transformation. In this piece Antoni inserted a sculptural constellation and her body, prone and suspended, into the theatre architecture. Challenging the proscenium division and its spectatorial regime, she described this work as a meditation and a "living set." The radical polarities of Petronio and Antoni's sensibilities were much in evidence. Petronio's choreography is built from frenetic energy. His early collaborations with Michael Clark were marked by the sliding postures of a punk classicism. However, his individual choreographic language was already composed of rapid propulsions and postural stops, where bodies weave around and over each other and limbs scissor and slice in rotations and immediate counter-pulsions. In *Like Lazarus Did* the acceleration and dense formality of this movement contrasts with Antoni's investment in simple corporeal presence and stillness. But a shared ground emerged in their testing of physiological limits and their investment in the intense and excessive forces of the passions. For Petronio the next boundary to cross was to step outside of the theater and into a visual arts terrain through further collaborations. Shedding his choreographic language in order to make this journey in *Ally*, Petronio would also need to return to some older coordinates of his aesthetic development. As a pupil of Steve Paxton, and as a Trisha Brown dancer, he was schooled in the techniques of dance improvisation. In working collaboratively with Halprin, he would engage with a teacher of his teachers and with an ethos, language and environment, which is a root of much contemporary dance experimentation. Antoni had set a complex alliance in motion.

Late-November, 2014, Marin County, California. Antoni, Petronio and I are down on the Kentfield deck. For Petronio and I it is the first time that we have worked in this historic space, and its charms are immediately evident. As we sweep leaves from the boards on to the forest floor, we both speculate on the bodies that have moved through this space, and the acts that have been witnessed here in the sixty years that have passed since its completion. Places remember. Every action, however mundane, feels carried by this virtual accompaniment. A light breeze plays through the surrounding trees and the faint drone of a far-off plane fringes our conversation for a time. Wooded quiet. The space is a secluded opening, a clearing and a private window that lets all manner of others in. In the photographs I had seen of the early days of the deck, three Madrone trees pierced its surface, creating the sense that the architectural plane had found space within the forest, worked around its existent structures. Such accommodations were part of environmental architect Lawrence Halprin's ethos, where responsiveness to natural forms was prized and human imposition eschewed. Those trees have now gone and the plane is uninterrupted, though no less accommodating of its living companions. Natural growth has also curtained its back line, partially obscuring the vista beyond Mount Tamalpais across the San Francisco Bay. The forest and the deck are still learning to be with each other in their own durations. For Halprin and his collaborator on the project, the theater architect and designer Arch Lauterer, architectural form was a negotiation with shifting environmental facts and, one might add, a conciliation between potential antagonisms. One such clash, as Janice Ross makes clear in her comprehensive book on Anna Halprin, was the insistent social conflict for women at the time, between mothering and working.[7] For the Halprins, the institution of the deck was a means to sidestep a normative cut between life and art that would have traditionally accompanied Anna Halprin's raising of a family. As Lawrence Halprin put it, his intervention on the land was a means "to enrich the living environment of my family," a phrasing that assumes an ecological understanding of family itself.[8] His family is his environment.

Sitting here, watching bodies warm up and be with the elements, it is clear there is something natal about the deck. Perhaps it arises from the deck's infrastructural demand for the co-existence of entities, for symbiosis. As theater architecture all four of its walls are "transparent" (not just "the fourth wall") and so the strict boundary between on and off, micro- and macro-world, one and another, becomes highly porous.[9] The horizontal plane must be with the mountain's fall, and bodies must be with trees and sky. The trapezoid of the main space is extended to the back and left by slightly elevated "wings" giving the plane an irregular many-sided shape suggesting the possibility of multiple places from which to look, the re-orientation of the gaze. Lawrence Halprin, thinking beside Anna Halprin's practice, understood the deck as a non-object that was becoming landscape: it moved around.[10] But it was Anna Halprin who most acutely identified a relational dimension of this architectural intervention that, unbeknownst to her, was to become definitional of the art and performance of the era:

> Since there is ever changing form and texture and light around you, a certain drive develops toward constant experimentation and change in dance itself. There develops a certain sense of exchange between oneself and one's environment and movement develops which must be organic or it seems false. Movement within a moving space, I have found, is different than movement within a static cube.[11]

In a language marked by emergence, Halprin notes that the environmental opening of the deck is simultaneously an opening of the performing body and of performance aesthetics to the complex restlessness of nature itself. An imperative, a kinetic demand, is transmitted in this meeting: to move with the outside in conditions of continuous differentiation. An experimental ethos and the practice of improvisation are inherently linked to a recognition of, and attunement to, the kinetic and autopoetic dimensions of nature. As Halprin comes to take her place beside me on the bleachers, to sit where she has sat for over sixty years watching people perform, it is clear to me that she too is part of the environmental architecture. What if these ghostings of bodies, acts and lives long past, were not counter-posed with the material here and now, but seen as constitutive of them? Spirited matter thus becomes a principle of ecological relations. What if these present natal relations between the immaterial and the substantive, between the organic and the inorganic, were understood as vital infrastructures of art making?

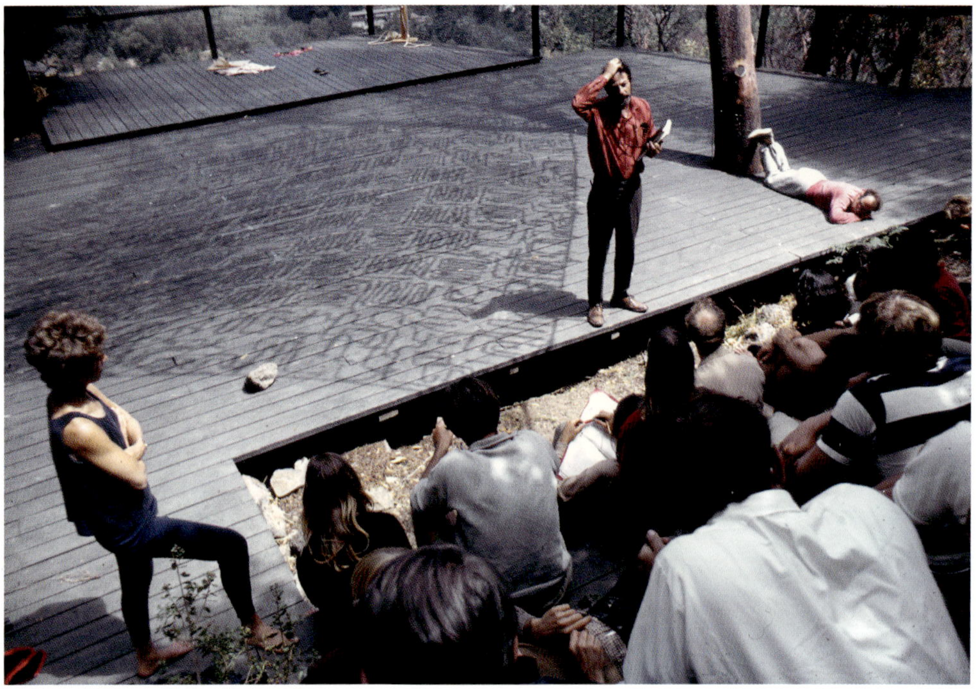

Anna Halprin (left) and Lawrence Halprin (center) on the dance deck, Kentfield, California, 1966.

Five or six days later, November 2014, on the Kentfield deck. Halprin is creating a choreographic experiment with Antoni and Petronio. Her scenario: white ropes are laid somewhat randomly across the boards. They act as an instantaneous scoring device, marking out trajectories in space along which Antoni and then Petronio will move blindfolded. Traversing the rope seems at once ridiculous and impossible. The tightrope act figuration looks redundant since the line is grounded, but the rope's ridging against the floor makes it hard to stay on. Performers move in a constant state of disequilibrium and vulnerability: walking a line becomes a continuous navigation of falling. The ground is ungrounded. Halprin's simple scenario prompts a delicate, found choreography. It is full of narrative tension and potential: two bodies are traveling a course without sight or knowledge of each other. How and when will they meet? The blindfold is an impediment that re-orients the senses, forcing hearing and touch to the foreground and sensualizing movement by alerting the whole skin, attuning it to its environmental outside. This phenomenal reality constantly interferes with the firm symbolism of the blindfold, which marks the subject's incapacity to see, orient, know, judge, to be "fully present" to the other. Halprin has used the rope as a tool to create equivalence between Antoni and Petronio. Both are dance improvisers but Petronio's habituated movement language trusts in formalization and is strongly centered in its torques and swoons, while Antoni's movement tends toward a freestyle viscerality and actional realism. On the rope both stylizations fall away: much of the movement here is found in the attempt to stay upright and on course, to steady and locate oneself, or in the recovery from having slipped or lost your way. In this space of largely involuntary, gravitational movement a different gestural quality is found infused with hesitancy and receptivity. Walking as suspended falling is strangely doubled here on the Halprin deck, where all acts take place in a ground above ground, an architectural suspension between earth and sky. The more the performers practice of course, the more they re-attune to this altered condition of movement, discovering its inner stabilities and possibilities.

An axial moment in the evolving dramaturgy arises when Antoni and Petronio meet: the sensuous "blind" encounter is filled with a tender estrangement. Solitary wanderings re-route into the complex task of traveling together with divergent senses and impulses. Petronio finds ways to burrow his head into Antoni's body, turning their enfolding into precarious lifts. Odd limbs flail out of a fused body. Halprin morphs the performance from this point on: it is conducted without blindfolds, and tumbles into passages of extended play where the ropes are taken up and the performers dance while entangled in multiple lines. The two figures are quickly bound together. Power over and influence upon the other — previously implicit — becomes an active subject. As a performer it is evidently hard to judge the consequences of your actions or movements, which create restraints and dynamics at a distance, at the other ends of ropes. The medium of the rope — a symbolic line of affinity and control — is a material for resistance. Active and passive identifications are in flux. But the performance takes on a formal quality derived from the many lines of rope, an angular graphing of theatrical space. For Halprin, scenography and the kinesthetic meet in this experiment and dancing becomes live choreographing, a way to draw in space. The lines do not literalize energetic connection, but they are fluid vectors, abstractions of inter-subjective dynamisms. Toward the close of this performance, Halprin invites others who have previously only spectated to join in the entanglement, socializing, multiplying and making ever more complex the kinesthetic experiment.

November 22, 2015: the home of Antoni's parents, New York. After discovering the cleansing practice of Vastra Dhauti, one of the six Shatkarmas of Hatha Yoga, Antoni and Petronio took advice and training from Yogi Charu. This physiologically difficult technique involves the swallowing and removal of a long ribbon of cloth. Antoni and Petronio have conceived a performance that will see this usually solitary therapeutic practice transformed into an act of visceral communion between them. They have mostly developed their swallowing in isolation, but today they will perform together — once only — consuming either end of a cloth woven for the occasion by Nami Yamamoto at The Fabric Workshop and Museum. Having swallowed their way along its path, their materially connected bodies will briefly meet and then part. The cloth with its residues of interiors will be retained. The performance is taking place in the privacy of Antoni's family home and a small number of witnesses have been invited from specific walks of life, whose testimonies I will immediately elicit and record. A photographer is one of the witnesses and she will take a single still image of the act, which will form its documentation, alongside the cloth and spoken reports. I will not see the performance in keeping with the concepts of its exposure, which deliberately mirror the limited public conditions and iconic distribution of many downtown loft performances in the late 1950s and 60s. I will be displaced from my now habitual role as participant observer, into a situation more like that of an historian, posed in the exteriority of the aftermath, sifting through multiple versions to read and narrate the event. My absence from the performance creates a confessional and testimonial drive in each relation to a witness: they are eager to say what they saw. I am eager to hear.

Listening to the array of perspectives, it is immediately evident that this short, simple, private act is a scene of contesting visions and experiences, a prodigious narrative generator whose reality will always be in question. Witness is an apt term for the spectators here, since the event remains an "unclaimed experience" in its retelling.[12] The act returns through language in a condition of unknowable excess. Versions proliferate and while they share a ground of agreement in action, the readings of meanings, consequences, motivating psychology, affective tonalities and material

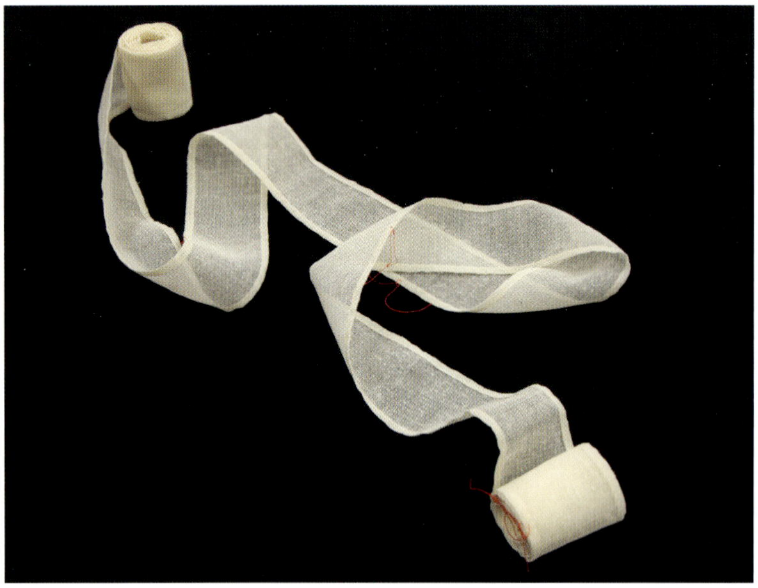

Swallowing cloth. Photo: Carlos Avendaño, 2016. © Janine Antoni and Stephen Petronio. Courtesy of the artists and FWM.

content often diverge. The telling of the event becomes a scene of projections and of other rich subjective disclosures but also a means for the witnesses to question the nature of their own seeing. Phenomenological detail is clearly consuming and seemingly infinite in these narrations; the flesh of each witness has been enfolded into the performers' entwining. Observation turns granular. A genuine accident within the live performance — the smashing of an opaque glass of water — ricochets through the retellings: within every event there is some other purer event, more vibrant and more real and more urgently told. These micro-events — elevated in perception — seem to suggest that the act of communal swallowing itself was securitized by its occurrence as a privately received ritual. Home sanctions such risks. Rhythm and tempo are recurrent witness' concerns, and the description of the performers' parting seems over too quickly for many. The freight of this separation — for some too much to countenance — is sadness at the withdrawal from a state of interconnectedness and visceral proximity, which has quickly accrued idealization. The affinity between Antoni and Petronio troubles articulation, and cannot be mapped onto familiar dyads of romantic investment or artistic collaboration. In each telling there is always a punctum, a small observed detail that becomes a conduit for a stream of realizations. I ask each witness what they will remember of the act, and here in the very process of the archival capture of that memory lives the most hesitation, doubt and ingenuity of response. In conceiving the act as destined to disappear, the artists have also given it potential, animated its afterlives through a social discourse whose plurality will drive its continued retelling.

One late afternoon in the last week of November 2015, Antoni performs *Paper Dance* for Halprin on the dance deck. It is a year since our last weeklong visit to Kentfield, and over three years since Antoni began to carefully entangle her work with Halprin's. Although she improvises the performance on each occasion, Antoni has accumulated a repertoire of gestural images and sculptural possibilities from her earlier labors with the paper. Physical fragments will be played out, differentiating themselves in the unfolding of the event. Before dusk falls, Hugo Glendinning will shoot the first full video recording of the work, stabilizing it in time in wholly other ways. Since our last visit, Antoni's *Paper Dance* has grown in length and detail through numerous discussions and re-workings. A flexible dramaturgy is emerging where specific image-events are sequenced in relation to the developing state of the paper around which Antoni's actions are focused. From Halprin's gift of an open score, Antoni is now making an hour-long solo work that substantially departs from the communal use of paper in *Parades and Changes* (1965). We are working in an echo chamber, a site of inaugural rituals, and as Antoni begins the performance, it is impossible not to think of the specific bodies (past and now present) that have performed in this clearing, with this material, under Halprin's vigilant gaze for over fifty years.

In the "original" scene a mixed group of performers slowly peeled off their clothes before laying out numerous large sheets of brown paper.[13] Quietly lifting, touching, tearing and enfolding themselves into the material, they formed an animate, rustling, skinny, cloud-like assemblage. The sensuousness of Antoni's *Paper Dance* is not as deliberative as that of the first performers who collectively produced a delicate and reverential affective field. Her solo action does not focus on slow time ripping and listening, but on a driven and sustained manipulation of the material that shapes and exhausts its sculptural potential. The performance begins with Antoni using the paper roll as a "telescope" to spy the environment and its spectators: doubling the scopic frame, letting us know that we are looking at intensified looking. Moving through serial acts in which the paper is unrolled, stressed, scrunched, wrapped, unfolded and remolded, Antoni uses all of her body to play with the plasticity of this material and the potential relations between paper and flesh. She is habituated with the paper and the performance has the air of a public intimacy. Antoni creates a series of gestural-sculptural assemblages of body-paper forms that momentarily hold space as propositions and are visibly thought through by their maker. This is an actional-choreographic test in an experimental laboratory: a questioning of material forms. The paper appears as a second skin, wrapping around and sometimes extending Antoni's body in planes and folds that interrogate the dialogic relation between the two "skins." The theater of material affects found in *Parades and Changes* is here turned into a singular test of body-matter relations.

In contrast with the ceremonial undressing of *Parades and Changes*, Antoni's shedding of clothes takes place gradually and often under cover of the paper, without ever seeming deliberately hidden, so that it is barely noted as a subject, or it is noticed only after it happens. Nonetheless we understand that what is taking place is an exposure, a bringing into visibility of things unseen, a play of veils and disclosing surfaces. The baring of Antoni's skin is unforced and de-eroticized; the labor of image making, the transformation of gestures and materials are the main energetic preoccupation. To be bare here seems simply a question of entering affective conditions of equality through which flesh and paper can speak. The dialogue between surfaces, if not mutual, certainly sees the paper displaying "actant" qualities. Its unwieldy scale makes it somewhat uncontrollable: it evidently resists manipulation. The paper's absorption and release of energies as it contracts from pressures and autonomously expands when let go, its occasional animation by the breeze playing across the deck lend it animate qualities. Moreover, every shape the paper finds itself in arises responsively from its previous formings, asking "questions" of the body that makes it.

If Antoni's *Paper Dance* were understood as re-do, then it would already be a radical re-interpretation of its "source," in which faithfulness to the past is not a matter of appearance but of spirit. But the past and its retrospection return to the piece in other unexpected ways. On seeing an earlier version of the work, Chris Sollars, a friend of Antoni, asked her if she was deliberately reiterating figurations from her previous sculptures. Sifting through photographs of this nascent version Antoni was surprised to see that she had been unconsciously performing many postures that were the gestural basis of earlier "static" works. Unconscious production disclosed somatic realities that were then knowingly put to work. This iteration of figurations became a conscious modality and means of creative investigation within the performance. In previous "static" works Antoni had used an object's

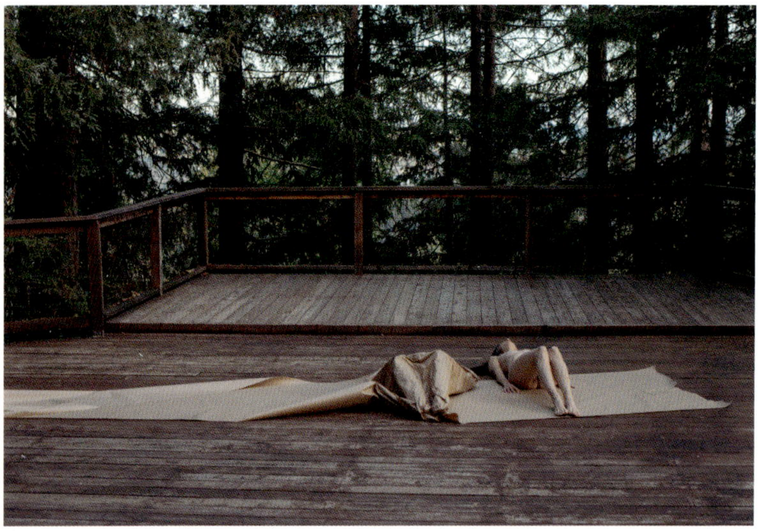

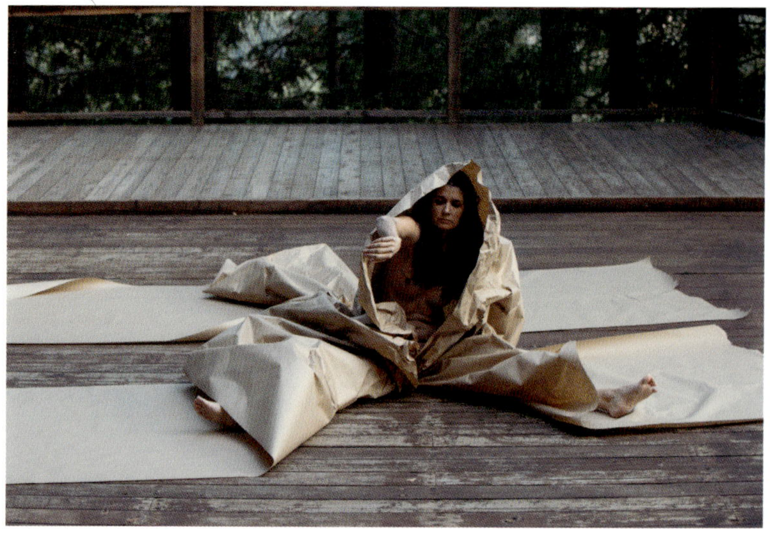

Janine Antoni rehearsing *Paper Dance* in collaboration with Anna Halprin, 2015.
Photo: © Hugo Glendinning, 2015. Courtesy of the artists.

formal relation to a resounding event to question its nature and status. In works such as *Behold* (2014), *Umbilical* (2000), *Cradle* (1999), *Slumber* (1993), *Lick and Lather* (1993) and *Eureka* (1993), object indeterminacy arises from an unresolved relation to a time of action: is the object a tool or prop for future use, a trace impression, document or relic of a past activity or event, or perhaps simply its waste residue? In *Paper Dance* a similar uncertainty is deployed, but realized in the live witnessed relation between Antoni's flesh and the paper thing. The performance moves through a sequence of relations in which the paper's function is itself morphing: from prosthetic to tool, from abstract sculpture to mimetic body-mold, from costume to scenography, from personified object to discarded matter. In the process, Antoni's psychic relations with, and power over, the thing are experienced in states of flux. She is apparently compelled to be with and shape the paper, though her relation with it oscillates between intimacy and distance, scopic evaluation and immersion, care and disregard, affection and violence. In *Paper Dance* the volatile morphology of the performer-thing is both phenomenologically and psychologically charged. But the psyche-soma relation to objects is rather distinct from its formations in Antoni's previous sculpture and performance works. It takes place here — in the space of Halprin's dance deck — through a consciously entwined female genealogy and within environmental conditions that inform and complicate its meanings.

Antoni became renowned for sculptures and actions in a feminist lineage that enacted critiques of patriarchal orders of representation as they were manifested in Abstract Expressionism, Minimalism and realist portraiture. In major works such as *Gnaw* (1992), *Loving Care* (1993) and *Lick and Lather* (1993), she pursued formal dialogues with masculine constructions that humorously marked gender difference through laborious acts of subjection and carnal engagement with mundane materials. These works have been distinguished from those of her 1970s predecessors in this lineage — Carolee Schneemann, Ana Mendieta, Mierle Laderman Ukeles, Hannah Wilke — as more paradoxical in their treatment of ideals of female emancipation, embedded in the intimate realities of female subjectivity, and committed to exploring the psychological ramifications of complicity with power through irony and self-disidentification.[14] If Antoni's early works were dialogically oriented toward male visual power and negotiated spaces of difference in relation with its formal coordinates, her work here with Halprin immerses her in the flows of a female genealogy, in which the labor of dialogue and differentiation

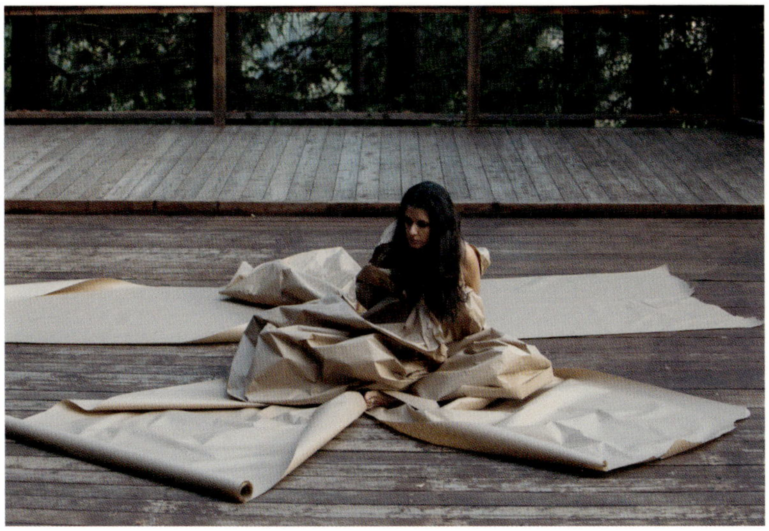

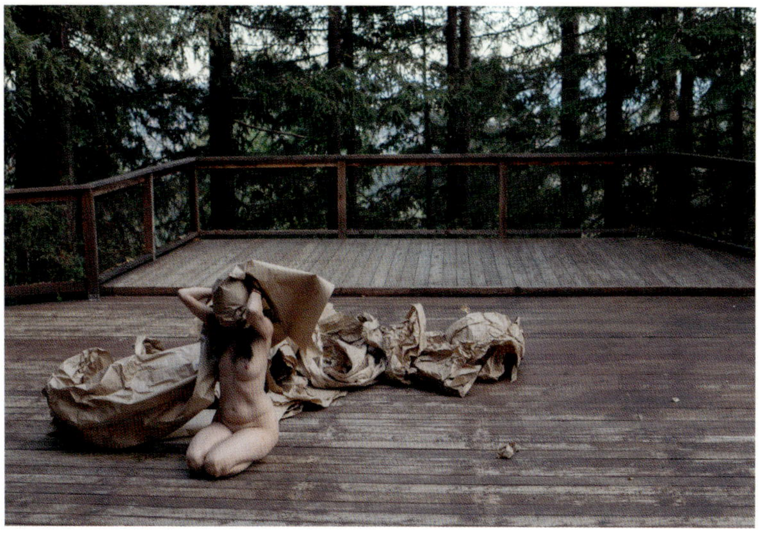

is intensely sustained and collaborative. The matrilineal concerns of works such as *Momme* (1995), *Umbilical* (2000), *If I Die Before I Wake* (2004) and *One Another* (2008) involving Antoni's mother and daughter and testing the nature of fleshly connection have jumped "outside" of her biological family scene, and into a broader feminist artistic sphere. The relational works of *Ally* allow Antoni to explicitly mine what had long been implicit in her use of touch and visceral engagements: sensual relation as a scene of paradoxical *choreographic* forces. Antoni's quest in *Paper Dance* is an evolving improvisational choreography of relations between the female body and sculptural material, navigated through the entwining of her histories and visual languages with those of a living female predecessor.

The sun is fading behind the deck and the darkness that accompanies the surrounding trees creeps into the scene. Antoni separates herself once more from the remnants of the paper she has been sculpting and sits at the side of the deck, looking on from afar. She reinserts herself as a fetal skin-stone amidst an array of globular paper deposits: one small further becoming and counterpoint in the tireless movement of the performance between abstract forms and figurations. Relaying the surfaces of skin and paper, involuting, entwining and enfolding them, Antoni becomes the impetus and carriage of radical indeterminations: between a subject and an object, between a living body and inorganic material, between a monadic and dispersed entity. In its thought-filled spacings, its slow-morphologies of lingering actions, its waiting for decision in relation, the performance refuses the stubborn descent of action into meaning, body into identity, material into objecthood. These indeterminations vibrate with environmental co-actants: every human action-event on this deck is qualified by its being in an architectural suspension between earth and sky, its sounding within the sonosphere of plant and animal life, its opening to the contingencies of weather. Anthropomorphism is tested and discarded. Non-human forces abound. The paper is experienced as insubstantial substance — held by airs — with prodigious capacities of formation. The sustenance of forms, their remaining here in moments of articulation and resonance, is shown as dependent upon the life of these material aerations. Antoni makes herself otherwise: pressing her flesh into multiple extensions and ecstatic creations, implicit and explicit births of things.[15] She oscillates between connection with, and separation from, her makings. Her performance constantly attunes to immaterial movements — opens itself to their ever-present happenings. It becomes apparent that without this connective and unceasing fabric of existence, no

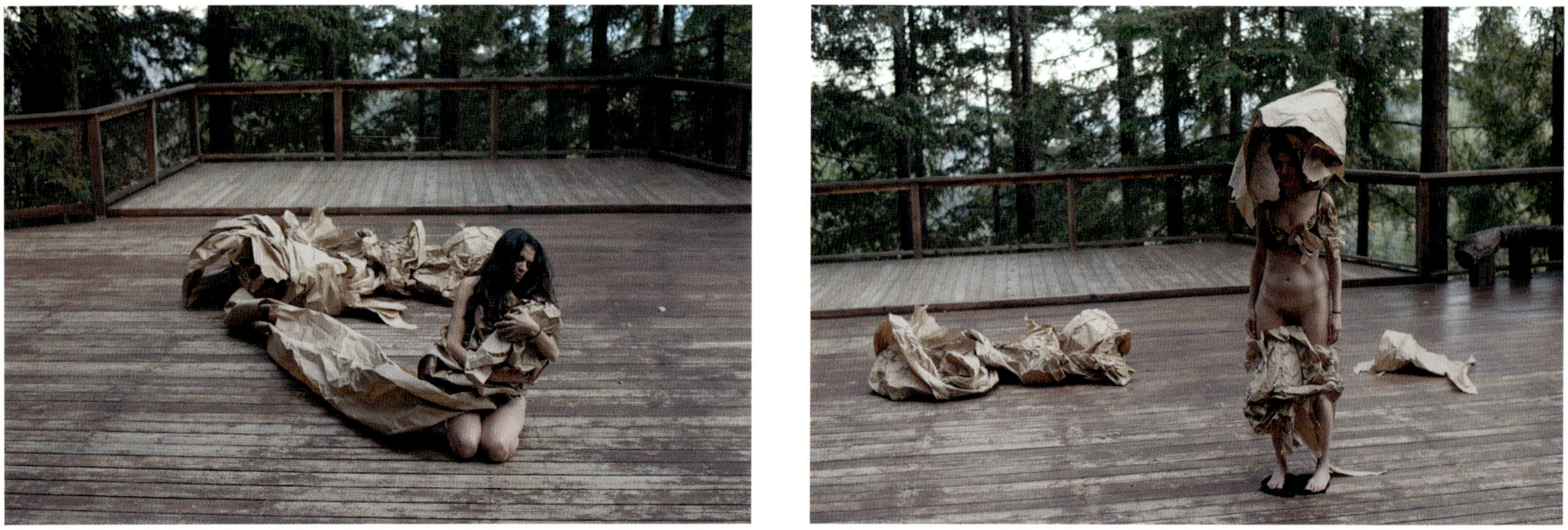

Janine Antoni rehearsing *Paper Dance* in collaboration with Anna Halprin, 2015.
Photo: © Hugo Glendinning, 2015. Courtesy of the artists.

form would form. At stake here is a radical ecological aesthetic of indeterminate entities, where body and material re-enfold to invent new forms of expressive life. The struggle with the matter of things is a making of fresh capacities of relation with materials, a testing of their givenness and its limits, but also an attempt to become more than one with things. In this regard Antoni proceeds in a long line of feminist artists whose goal is self-actualization through differentiation. *Paper Dance* can also be read as an experimental practice of freedom, where freedom is not a property of a subject but an unfolding encounter in the making.[16]

January 2016, Sydney, Australia: writing alone, from afar. What is being surfaced and furthered in Antoni and Halprin's relation is a feminist genealogy of art making, enacted through a trans-generational cross-form dialogue. But the nature of this genealogy's emergence in particular ecological conditions and its engagement with materials makes me want to rethink its cultural and historical force. Such a genealogy is composed of the entwined discursive filaments of artists and their works. Affinity here is not just "influence," not a simple identification between present subjects: when thought historically and materially it folds absent figures and immaterial forces into itself. None of the persons or articulations in such genealogies is an originary or unitary influence; rather they are carriers of investments, intensities and expressions. These spirited affinities, of which the Antoni-Halprin relation is just one intensification, cross historical epochs, distinct cultures and belief systems, and come in and out of critical currency and visibility at different times. Nonetheless, they act as sustaining forces in the fostering of new lives and work. What I am calling spirited affinity is not necessarily passing through institutional validation, systems of knowledge or even conscious recognition on the part of participants, though it may have contact with these powers. Above all, it is not a correspondence of likeness, but a kind of empathy across and within different and differentiating situations that generates a habitat of making. In this regard a genealogy of spirited affinity might be thought as constituted by a trans-historical (or in the Antoni-Halprin case a trans-generational) "ecology of practices," to use a term coined by Isabelle Stengers.[17] These are shared habitats of thinking-doing-feeling that foster and challenge their participants, creating new techniques of making. An ecology of practices is an open set of mobile relations between heterogeneous ways of doing: a manifestation of belonging and communion in divergence that respects the singularity of its inhabitant practices. Interconnectedness, in this context, while attendant to social obligation, is not oriented toward or founded on identities, but is forged through what participants or things may become. In this regard Stengers describes a different ecological relation between subjects and knowledge-making; as in ritual, she says, "it is no longer I, as a subject, as meant to belong to nobody but myself, who thinks and feels."[18] Consequently, such ecologies are hosts of critical social self-transformation: "a decision without a decision-maker ... is making the maker."[19]

To think these spirited affinities as infrastructural to art and performance making involves a divestment of habitual ways of conceiving infrastructure within the arts. Infrastructure is traditionally thought of as constructed, substantive and instrumental, hence its common understanding as architecture and technology. Notions of social and cultural infrastructure, of the support apparatuses of life and of creativity, have formed through rigid distinctions between culture and nature, between the immaterial and the material. Infrastructure has been seen as furthering human power over things, as an exploitation and forging of natural resources, and as a necessary but somehow neutral foundation or cultivated ground for activity. Matter here is inert, stable, and passive, it is put to work, worked on in order to make things happen. Social and cultural activities — embodied practices — though just as material, are rarely seen as infrastructural in and of themselves. But as with Lawrence Halprin's ecological thought of environmental architecture, and with the practical life of the deck he created, there is another, symbiotic way to think the infrastructural. Like Lawrence's deck, this thinking ungrounds its grounds, animates its stolidity and immaterializes it — not a dematerialization, but an expansion of the terms of its mattering. What if every substantive structure or technology is inseparable from its enmeshment within fleeting or sustained living practices, mobile enfleshings that define and shape its social and aesthetic force? The infrastructural, then, becomes complex living relations between social activity and other material structures and technologies. Such an infrastructure is an agency in and of itself, always in flux (however invisible), always self-generative, and connected to other active material forces and agencies that it channels, resists and transforms.

An infrastructure of spirited affinity is close to what urbanist and ethnographer AbdouMaliq Simone terms "relational infrastructure," though perhaps somewhat more ghosted through its historical and communal dimensions. A relational infrastructure is constituted through practices of inhabitation, exchange and attention that model material engagements for others and foster new ways of being.[20] For Simone, "They are vehicles of movement and becoming, ways of mediating the constantly oscillating intersections of various times, spaces, economies, constraints and possibilities."[21] Writing from within the precarious realities of several postcolonial urban contexts in the global South, Simone identifies these infrastructures of relationality, these makings of worlds, in active resistance to the operations of global capital and its governance and regulation of urban space. As such, relational infrastructures are oriented not just toward survival, but also to living well: "the circumvention of domination and the keeping open of many different trajectories of what life could be all at once."[22] For these reasons some relational infrastructures must remain deliberately illegible and invisible, in order to prevent their suppression or assimilation, to sustain their minoritarian force. The mnemonic and historical dimension of infrastructures of spirited affinity necessarily involves the carriage in the present of past inhabitations and material relations, as a continued resource for processes of self-transformation within community and for political actions of resistance. I think of the Halprins and the numerous lived enmeshments arising with that plane jutting out of the wooded fall, the lineaments of these inventions across sixty years of dance, art and performance history, passing in and out of visibility and recognition.

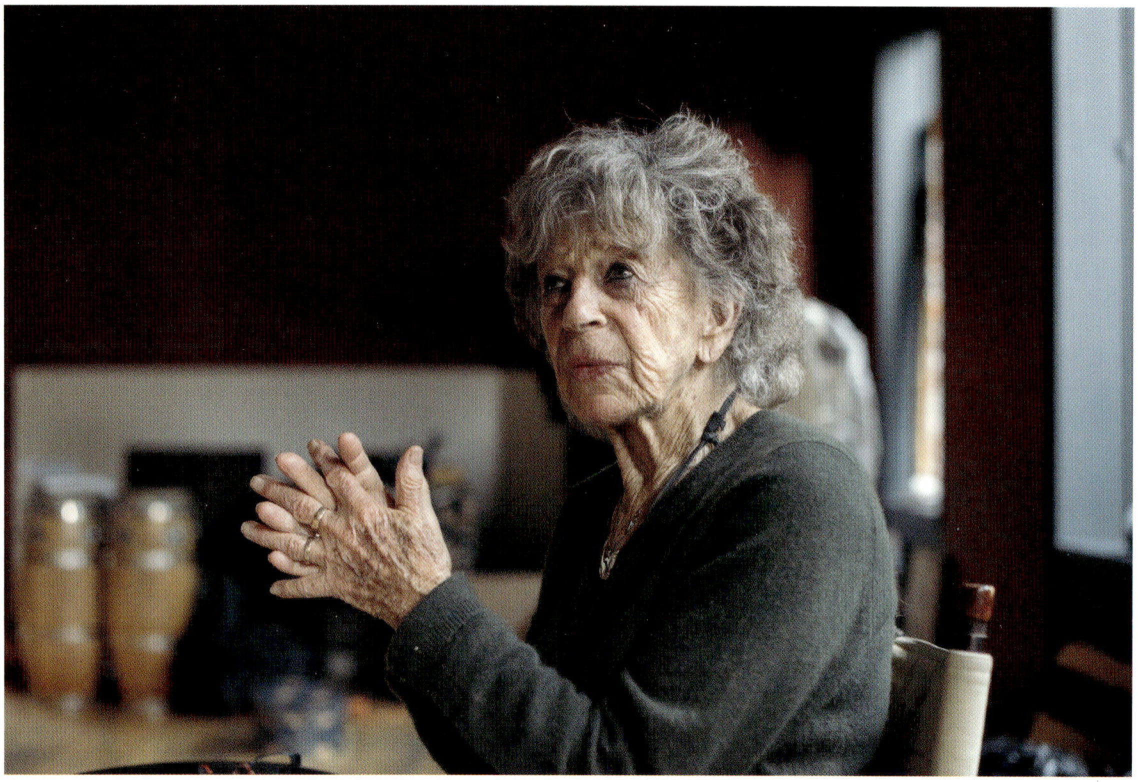

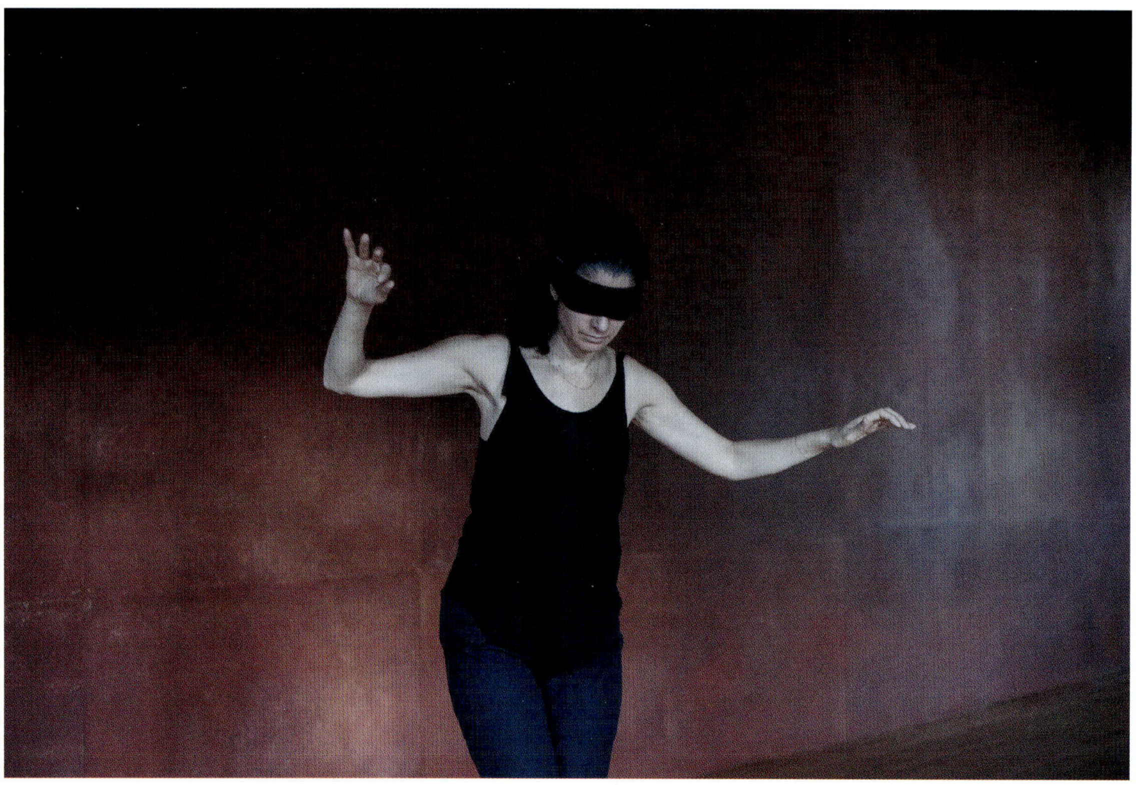

Top: Anna Halprin rehearsing *Rope Dance*, 2015. Photo: © Hugo Glendinning, 2015. Courtesy of the artist and FWM.
Bottom: Janine Antoni rehearsing *Rope Dance*, 2015. Photo: © Hugo Glendinning, 2015. Courtesy of the artist and FWM.

The enunciation of the word spirit in the phrase spirited affinity may seem odd to some ears, especially those conditioned by specific modes of secular thought, or those who adhere to a strict materialism. Odd too, because the artists I am discussing as bearing such affinities do not hold particular religious systems of belief in common. However, it aptly describes the immaterial and affective forces moving through and between these subjects and their works: passages from, to and with outsides. This outside — encapsulated in the surrealist poet Paul Eluard's proclamation "there is another world, and it is in this one" — is immanent, not purely transcendent. As William E. Connolly succinctly states, in speaking for a range of new materialist and process philosophers: "The outside is multiple, active and real, it is merely not, to us, divine. We also construe transcendence as that which is coming into being rather than a Being beyond being."[23] Here the absolute antithesis between matter and spirit falls into redundancy. If the non-human and inorganic are constitutive exteriorities of material lives then a different space for thinking the relation between the phenomena of matter, the senses and spirit is opened: a materialist sense of spirit emerges. This exteriority for many writers in these traditions is thought in relation to cosmic and non-human forces of creation and destruction that far exceed human powers, metamorphosing in temporalities beyond human perception and cognition. Such volatile forces evidently surpass but are also within the human estate: they are found all around us in what was once called the natural world. Spirited affinity: a communion in differentiation, a mutual inclination toward earthly exteriorities, a being together with singular unknowns.

If collaborations such as those of Antoni and Halprin are instances within a genealogy of spirited affinity, and if those affinities are infrastructural for the historical persistence and rejuvenation of performance, there are implications for the ethos of curatorial practice. What role might the curator play in the sustenance of that genealogy? How might curation be rethought, not just as a way of "constellating relations," but also as a labor of caretaking the passage of such affinities between spirits, people and things? The curator is reimagined, then, as an inheritor, temporary custodian and re-animator of spirited affinities. This definition feels closer to my current material engagements with *Ally*.

Mid-April, 2016: The Fabric Workshop and Museum, Philadelphia. The personal testimonies of the *Swallow* witnesses are transformed into a low-level collective whisper as the visitor enters the darkened space of the installation. A human murmur floats above a series of softly lit twin chairs stationed along a carpeted aisle. At the near end of this aisle a large vitrine is bathed in red light, whilst at the other end a glistening object emanates an allure. The sound of each testimony is located above each chair, so that visitors who sit may face each other and listen, perhaps encountering strangers in an unusual intimacy convened by the twinned seats. Visitors compose their own collage of voices depending on their attention within each station: they create a synthetic version of the "absent" event. The environment is church-like, if a strange mixture of Puritan pine and high Catholic glamour. This is a scene of indeterminate faith where the past performance becomes a sought truth. Each station is assigned an archetypal name — for instance the listener, the healer, and the poet — somewhat general categories with a mythic air of authority which cuts against the singularity of the speaker's voice. A congregation is assembled. On close inspection the gleaming object is a perverse monstrance, the vessel used in Catholicism to carry consecrated material or the relics of saints. Clearly visible within its bulbous glass orb, sits the rolled cloth from the *Swallow* performance. The cloth makes irises and pupils in the glass eyeballs: the thing looks back. Monstrances are usually spectacularly solar, radiating out, but this peculiar form, declarative in its showing, is also strangely interior. Its gold and glass shapes mirror the human internal structures of the diaphragm, two trachea, the lungs and the vocal folds: not just those parts associated with the act of swallowing, but with breath. Organs that remind the visitor

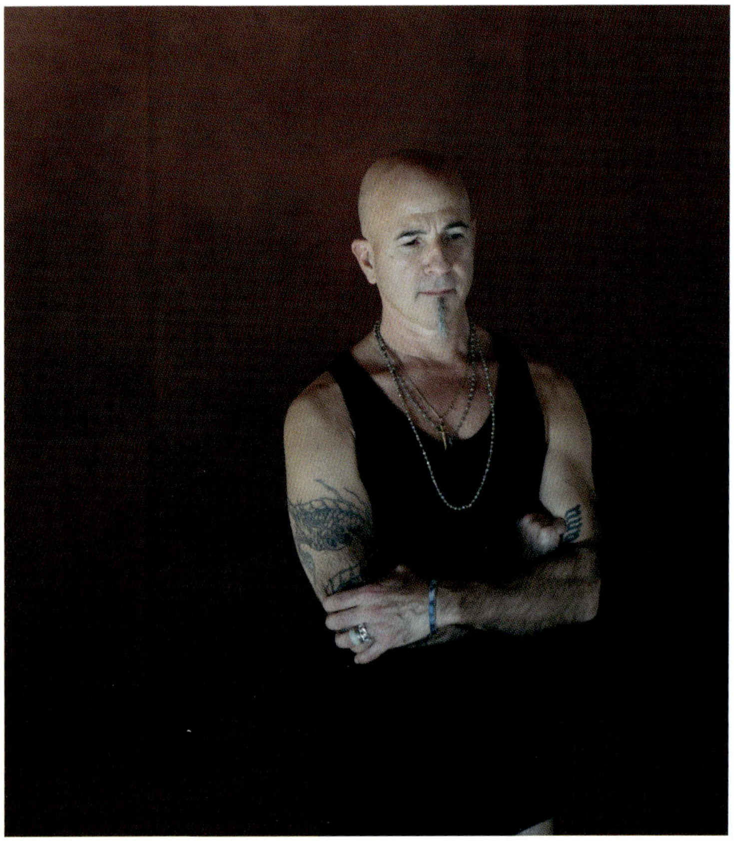

Stephen Petronio rehearsing *Rope Dance*, 2015.
Photo: © Hugo Glendinning, 2015. Courtesy of the artist and FWM.

of that other connective and binding material that carries testaments into the space. The baroque splendor of these reorganized organs — a twisted physiognomy — recalls the elaborate torques of Petronio's choreography. Looking down through the polished and pearled vocal folds, a magnifying lens gives access to the micro-detail of the rolled cloth. The fabric of things. Organic symmetry is found everywhere in this space, not least in this vessel where the immaculate repetitions of the different-same suggest a glorious and monstrous queer body.

At the other extreme, the conserving vessel does not belong to the institution of the church (however queer) but to that other contemporary place of worship: the art museum. The vitrine holds the single photograph of Antoni and Petronio's bodies, joined by the swallowed cloth and printed on wool with their mingled saliva. Sacrilege here is twofold: the vitrine is filled with active colonies of moths that are slowly consuming the material. They flutter and crawl and get on with their work in the warm bath of an artificial night. The moth is the nemesis of this particular institution dedicated to fabric, but a new species of ally for the artists. Their de-fabrications are simultaneously acts of creation and destruction: the scene is teeming, a complex choreography of life and death. Larvae growing in the wool will feed off the image particularly as they are drawn to human excretions. The contained risk of the moths in the museum is liberated by the unpredictable course and duration of this process. Performance returns otherwise. Antoni and Petronio do not know what will become of their image in aesthetic terms, but what is certain is that it will have passed into other bodies, just as it did in the initial event. This animal metamorphosis sits in dialogue with the meanings and resonances of the murmurs of the human animals, and with the promise of transubstantiation carried in a monstrance. The true vessel of faith here is of course the human body — the material within which a life subsists. When it is turned inside out, anatomized before our eyes, joined on the material plane with other bodies, a certain animal reality is disclosed. Material bodies exist within cycles of consumption and excretion, life is entwined with death, and the energetic continuance of this process and its utter indifference to us qualifies all human investments.

Late-April, 2016, Philadelphia. The installation of *Rope Dance* at The Fabric Workshop and Museum — the singular collaboration between Antoni, Halprin and Petronio — is another modulation of relations between the live event of performance and its translation into durable forms in exhibition time. An improvised dance with blindfolds and ropes, on which we worked sporadically for two years, now becomes an absent-presence, inflected through variant live and mediated forms. Visitors are given headphones before entering the gallery, immediately tuning them to an exterior reality — the environs of Halprin's dance deck — preceding the encounter with the work. On their entrance, the gallery appears empty except for a large-scale projection on one side, which is then seen as synchronous with the sound. Facing it: a simple row of chairs. The looped thirty-minute film, a locked-off extreme close-up of Halprin's ninety-four-year-old face, looms over the evacuated space. This is a beautifully weathered, delighted and thoughtful face. It is doing a lot of responsive looking and evaluating: gripped by a quizzical attention to something behind the imagined visual point of the camera. The visitor experiences the sounds of her environment through the intimacy and personalization of the headphones: Halprin's continuous breath, occasional whispered half-thoughts and involuntary articulations are heard in close proximity. In the background, distant sounds punctuate the scene — dogs barking, light planes flying overhead, the screams of children playing, the buzzing of a fly, the caws of crows — but all remain unseen. Mountain song. As the film plays out it becomes evident that in one reality (the time of the film) Halprin is watching a dynamic performance. This artwork (once again) is firmly withdrawn from visibility. But the visitor hears the beats of many footsteps, exclamations, murmurs; they sense the energetics of unfolding acts off-screen.

In fact, Halprin is watching the improvisation-rehearsal in November 2014 I spoke of earlier, with Antoni and Petronio working with blindfolds and ropes: the duration of the film being the exact length of this "original" performance. The empty floor of the gallery offers itself as the new ground of this absent-present event. A virtual actual, time-space conjunction gives the visitor the sense that although it is nowhere apparent, an intense performance is continuously taking place, with and without bodies. Who or what is performing here? In the visitors' reality (the hybrid past-present time of their watching of the film) Halprin is looking "directly" at them, as if they were dancing. Under the sway of her gaze, the visitor becomes a performing object and is forced to consider their spontaneous actions as the possible source of Halprin's response, as a choreography that she is seeing. At the same time the visitor knows this not to be the case, and marks the disjunction between their own moves and the "absent" performance resonating through Halprin's face. The visitor experiences a disjointed time in their passage through the space, in the simultaneous coincidence and de-synchronization of the virtual-actual event. In this continuous overlaying of times, the present time is many times and is infused with kinetic potential. It's as if Halprin is entreating the visitor to dance, compelling them to take up the ropes and make a performance in this space. In this respect the installation of the film succinctly expresses the activist, participatory and communitarian principles that have animated Halprin's work in life. The installation is an open invitation to move without judgment.

Another powerful paradox is in play. Halprin's face is over-scaled (not life-size) and is seen in an intimacy beyond that available to everyday close scrutiny — one might say, following Lacan's phraseology, an extimacy — a deep inside on the exterior. This is a vision of Halprin that we do not normally have access to, even as close collaborators. It is also an intensely craved projection that every performer seeks: clear evidence of the palpable impact of one's action in others. The surface (screen and face) as boundary dissolves into the coursing relay of affects in and from the "absent" performance — through and from Halprin as a receptor-transmitter — to the receptive visitor. And yet the visitor becomes painfully aware that this extimacy, this unprecedented access to the author-choreographer, cannot identify with any certainty the very objects it discloses: Halprin's thoughts and perceptions remain profoundly inaccessible. An enduring presence, Halprin's face is a fluid micro-choreography of flashes of tangible feelings but invisible thoughts. What is she thinking? The visitor can only guess. Yet the quality of this giving over of her self, so redolent with an open acceptance that comes with aging, speaks to the ethos of hospitality and generosity through which Halprin's creative life is lived.

Staying with the film in its full duration, as many do, reveals further emotive paradoxes. Whatever it is that Halprin is watching, it is a chain of events and it evidently has a narrative structure of sorts: things happen one after the other. But they are only available to us through sonic clues and the unfolding, volatile and flickering emotions of Halprin's face. Together with the visitor, she is in the grip of an implicit but continuing story: one readable only through a sensual accrual. Over thirty minutes, Halprin moves through passages of gentle appreciation, intensive curiosity, tension and anxiety, doubt, mild disapproval, assurance, exasperation, confusion, astonishment, fear, tiredness, consternation, excitement, pride, myriad amusements, trepidation, pain, slight boredom and utter joy. A panoptic procession of life's emotions is registered in the surfaces of her face, its liquid glimmering affects. The visitor comes to recognize that this human trajectory (again a story of sorts) whilst utterly singular and specific to the unseen event is simultaneously general, that it could apply to any happening. The peculiar nature of extimacy becomes clear: it is at once personal and impersonal, singular and common. Is this a story of an artistic life, spent in the thick of collaboration, spent looking at and facing others? Perhaps this face is simply the subject of the work itself — there is no "absent" performance. Rather, a facing — with any face and this face in particular — *is the event* that the visitor has come to be in. This event of the witnessing of the witness — the means through which performance has an afterlife — is the definitive aspect of its recursive and transitory nature. Echo of echoes, performance crosses times, spaces, bodies and forms, and in so doing lives again.

Antoni and Petronio do perform live within this gallery on several occasions throughout the duration of the exhibition. But on these occasions the film is absent once they begin, and is reinstated when they close. Instead of presenting a completed work, the performance is returned to a nascent state: an open workshop-performance in which the materials and actions that once constituted the *Rope Dance* are explored collectively with participants. Visitors experience the somatic and choreographic potentials of working and moving while dynamically bound with the shifting vectors of the rope. This hybrid format returns the work to its pedagogic and experiential principles, rather than crystallizing it into a resolved form.

One afternoon in mid-April 2016, Antoni is preparing to perform the first enactment of *Paper Dance* within its completed installation. In curating the work for an interior we have created spatial and temporal divisions in the long gallery of The Fabric Workshop and Museum. On entering the gallery, visitors encounter a slowly growing pile of tattered and discarded brown paper — the by-product of Antoni's previous renditions of the dance — defining this initial space as archival, a holding place of remnants. Ahead of them a wooden dance floor demarcates a larger area and upon it an oval arena of sealed crated artworks. Playing across one of the crates is a projected filmic fragment of Halprin's

Parades and Changes: the "original" scene from which this whole work is partially derived. While gallery lighting picks out the crates as displayed objects — each marked with the name of its contents and shipping restrictions — theatrical lights create a warm wash over this constructed clearing: a hybrid space for present events and display. Beyond the dance floor, a third space sees a series of twenty-two paper rolls leaning and arrayed across an exhibition wall. Each roll is labeled with the date on which it will be used; this area has the qualities of an antechamber, a waiting room for materials. Antoni will perform twenty-two times over the fifteen-week duration of the exhibition, each time altering and rearranging the relation between the *Parades and Changes* projection, and the visible and invisible sculptures and photographs held within the crates. The gallery appears "unfinished," as if the visitors have walked in to an installation in progress.

Each performance will begin with Antoni unpacking and displaying one or more of the crated pieces and will continue as an improvisation with, for and beside the assembly of the presented and hidden artworks. In the periods between performances the chosen works remain on display until one or more of them is re-packed at the beginning of the next performance and new work is revealed. The aesthetic relations between displayed artworks and their sequencing across the fifteen weeks are carefully curated, making dynamic counterpoints in the development of Antoni's oeuvre that shift from week to week. By showing but largely withdrawing her works from view, Antoni makes a powerful address to the exhibition format of the retrospective. Her previous works form a gathering around her — a council of present but largely invisible things — accompanying and reverberating with her many acts of invention within the space. The installation in progress becomes an occasional workshop and performance arena where display is always subject to a durational morphology. A slow-time retrospective, then, but one in which the subject's artwork is barely visible, intermittent, inflected differently on a weekly basis by repeated performances. For Antoni, the self-seeing and self-evaluation implied in these acts is triggered by, and accessed through, the work of another — Halprin — whose history touches but far exceeds her own. The repeated reinvention of the performance in relation to fresh aspects of Antoni's history, arranged differently in relation to Halprin's "original" work, suggests that disclosure of an oeuvre is a constant renegotiation through and with others. Antoni seats her spectators on top of her crated work with packing blankets. Sedentary forms dialogue with their aerated friends. The assembly here is not just the council of artworks, but also the gathering of individuals, who take their place within and upon them. The installation echoes the circling of trees that surrounds the clearing of Lawrence Halprin's dance deck: the mountain top wood has become a gathering of presences, a human-thing assemblage, visible and invisible historical objects intermingling with a present public.

As the visitors gather to spectate, finding a place to sit amongst the crates, Antoni is already unpacking an artwork. Once the location of artworks and spectators is settled she walks to take up the first paper roll. After three years of working with this material, the improvisation is assured and specific image-actions have solidified into a temporal line within a dramaturgy. Fragments of this temporal structure remain in my memory. The paper is thrown out and rolls along the length of the dance floor. Antoni attempts to draw it back toward her in violent spasms that presage the energetics of the actions to come. Unruly matter. Far from her reach, the paper rucks and contorts in unexpected ways. Antoni closely molds a portion around her legs, then extracts herself and places these limbs in counterpoint with the empty mold, as if the quest of the performance were simply to see a singular body outside of itself, to create a duplicate of the self (in constitutive parts). Antoni rolls the length of the stage, wrapping herself in the entire surface; her torso is bound in a funnel of paper that rises above her head. The makeshift phallus is immediately precarious. She takes this towering tube for a blind walk across the stage, her bare legs protruding from its bottom. Audience members protect themselves from this advancing comic shape: a semi-human chimera moving "dangerously" without vision or apparent purpose. Later, Antoni is immersed in a tangled swathe of paper, which seems to form one aggregate amorphous body from which odd limbs emerge. This becoming inorganic mass with living human parts — a golem or monstrous figure — is superseded by an image-action which is its chimeric inverse: Antoni, standing bare, scrunches the whole roll of paper up to her head and holds it there. She has a swollen sphere for a face, erasing her identity but not her sex: a female Atlas fused with the world she carries on her shoulders. A cloud-headed woman: weathered being.

Still later, Antoni seems to become the wind itself. Spinning like a dizzy child, she takes up the tattered remnants of the roll, which fly and flail beside her. The body here, simultaneously radiating and veiling itself, becomes material caught in the eye of a tornado, a half-present spectacle of vulnerable acceleration. Antoni's discarded clothing is reincorporated into her sculptural aspirations: she inverts her long-sleeved top using it as pants, and manically begins to stuff the whole volume of paper into a rapidly expanding belly. Paper begins to extrude from the head hole between her legs, which at first she tries to contain, whilst simultaneously continuing to stuff herself. Now, coming onto her back as she struggles with her belly-load, the image of pregnancy shifts into a disturbing and seemingly unending birth of uncontrollable material. Antoni tries to re-gather the extrusion into a graspable whole, making another body, but it is over-scaled, and her rocking and nursing gestures eventually succumb to the grand pile of material in which she is subsumed. Loss morphs into an erotics of immersion. Later, she re-rolls herself along the ragged length of the paper, winding up at the feet of the seated spectators. She is imprisoned in this tight cocoon, and births herself by violently flaying the paper skin, until her bare flesh is released. She lies still for a while in the residue of this frenetic escape, listening to and gently moving with the barely audible expansions of compacted and distressed paper. Marsyas is lying beside her future. This second (animal) birth, in which *the performer* is "reborn," seems to mark a final escape from the paper as constraint. Still attending to and thinking through her paper strewings across the space as a residual installation, she gathers the ragged remains and takes them off, throwing them into the slow-growing heap at the entrance to the space.

In *Parades and Changes* Halprin brought the outside — the obscene — into the theater through a communal encounter with paper and flesh. Antoni draws from Halprin's architecturally embedded re-attunements of movement practice to elemental conditions: the openness to the flows of air, clouds, the woods, to the sounds of plant and animal life that are found in the clearing of the deck. This incorporation extends beyond her performance action into her sculptural practice itself. She regenerates her own material engagements through these environmental openings, returning the exteriorizations of her sculptural practice to the inside of the gallery space. In comparison to her previous works these temporary sculptures in paper seem insubstantial, but they carry what I would call, after David Abram, the "remembering of air."[24] They hold, move and rustle with that element so sensually encountered on Halprin's elevated deck, that element invisible yet palpable, in which human life and plant life are symbiotically immersed. The unseen common medium through which we co-exist and breathe: the source of *inspiration*. Abram's understanding that an altered awareness of air would lead to new forms of relational creative thought and practice is resonating through Antoni's work:

> As we become conscious of the unseen depths that surround us, the inwardness or interiority that we have come to associate with the personal psyche begins to be encountered in the world at large: we feel ourselves enveloped, immersed, caught up *within* the sensuous world. This breathing landscape is no longer just a passive backdrop against which human history

> unfolds, but a potentialized field of intelligence in which our actions participate ... as we awaken to the air, and to the multiplicitous Others that are implicated, with us, in its generative depths, the shapes around us seem to awaken, to come alive ...

In the transplantation of this aerated performance into the gallery, the new environment is the residual material of Antoni and Haplrin's creative histories, encountered within the contiguity of a public assembly. Serial improvised performances act as the entwining of the two histories in the present, subjecting their materials to a persistent morphology. However, this is not a smooth matrilineal continuum, but a continuous cleaving, a gathering and a parting, a continuation without continuity. In Halprin's "original" work both naked bodies and paper are given an essential natural affinity, as they emerge in a reverential atmosphere from a cacophony of mediated human noise. For Antoni the paper is radically malleable, a synthetic processed material used to create a series of body molds, second skins, momentary images and symbolizations destined for discard or recycling. This non-living material has an uncanny life itself, it breathes and moves, and Antoni constantly re-attunes her performance to that thingness, de-naturing her nature, calling into question the distinction between

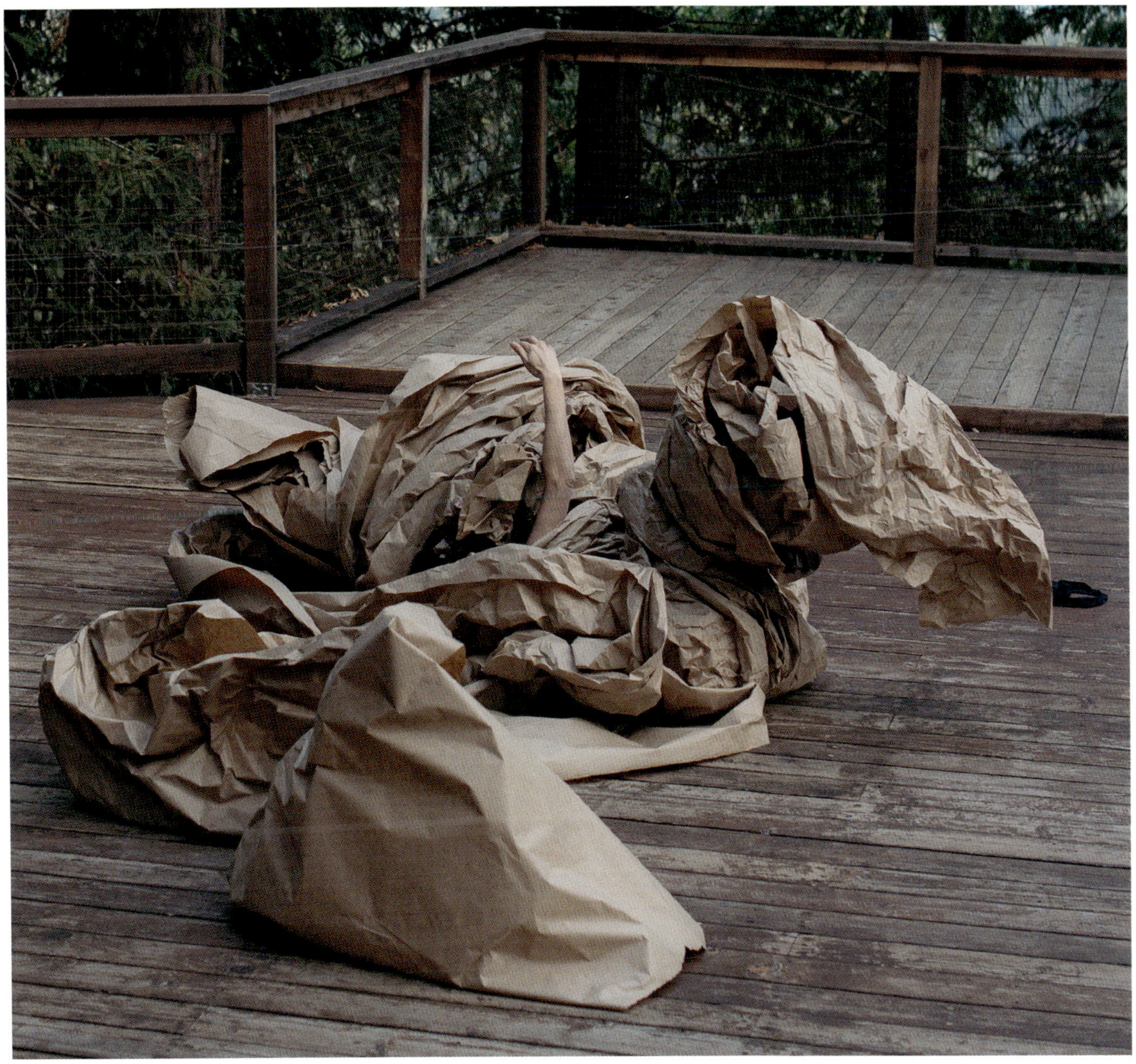

Janine Antoni rehearsing *Paper Dance* in collaboration with Anna Halprin, 2015.
Photo: © Hugo Glendinning, 2015. Courtesy of the artists.

the source and the trace, flesh and paper, body part and its mimetic rendition. The relation between paper and flesh appears autopoetic, one thing leads to another, and it is impossible to decide where the agency of image generation resides.

August 2016. Looking back over the *Ally* exhibition at its close, it is hard to locate its origins. My engagement began with Antoni's invitation to become (in her words) a "critical witness" in new collaborations. But the work could be drawn back to Antoni's decision to detour retrospection through the lives of others and the medium of dance. Was its seeding in Antoni's initial workshop with Halprin at the Esalen Institute, California, 2011, or her first meeting with Petronio at the Armory, New York, 2012? Or perhaps *Ally* was inaugurated in some unknowable moments in 1953 when Anna and Lawrence Halprin first dreamed into existence a deck in the woods of Mount Tamalpais? Many beginnings. Nonetheless, the project makes manifest some valuable imperatives of retrospection: for artists it may act as a means to turn outward, articulate their interconnectedness with numerous others and re-branch their paths, and for performance itself it may operate as a lens through which it can be revivified and persist in time. *Ally*'s curatorial frame treats the life and afterlife of performance as an affair of translation and multiplicity. Performance recurs in many forms in the duration of the exhibition: as a secluded and inaccessible object approached through pluralized testimonies, strange reliquaries and transmogrifying documents; as an absent event presenced through the face of its witness or translated back into its own nascent propositions in participatory workshops; as an iterative improvised occasion moving through a long duration of material engagements with objects and histories; or as an occasionally recovered fleeting act glossed through differences of age, sex and sensibility.

These lives and afterlives of performance, in their promiscuous transits, can be distinguished from the more common modalities of performance exhibition in museums over the last fifteen years. In *Ally*, when a live performance is absent from the gallery at any given time, its withdrawal is marked conceptually and linked to its recurrence in other forms. The "missing" event becomes a film of a face, a relic and monstrance, audio testimonies or a document in the process of re-absorption into other bodies. The default museum modality of documentary video and photographic display — with its attendant archival aesthetic common in performance's first revaluation by visual arts institutions — is circumvented.[25] If absolute absence, other than that transformed through documentary realism is challenged in this way, so too is the mode of continuous durational presence within exhibition time that has been widely deployed by artists such as Marina Abramović, Tino Sehgal and Xavier Le Roy.[26] In these contexts, an aesthetics of duration tends to conform to institutional scheduling: the work is present while the museum is open and stops once it closes. Such acts of "continuous" visible presence often frame the performer as a museal laborer and deploy modes of delegated action.[27] The reliance on the artist's presence in *Ally* is not, however, a simple return to a "valorized live presence and immediacy," nor a disavowal of performance as labor, but rather an attendance to the singularities of performance's occurrence in many forms and durations.[28] Bodies and their actions appear, disappear and reappear: they find translation into different media in accordance with their expressive necessities. Moreover, *Ally* places the many durations of performance materials and forms into an active dialogue. The performativities of documentary and sculptural materials are carried through occasions of live performance: gatherings within which they may mutually resonate and differentiate. For the visitor, the demand of *Ally* is to witness performance as transit and transformation, to think and feel the differences of its passages through multiple lives. Retrospection emerges as something other than an individual endeavor. Looking back is a way to turn inside out, to propose once discrete bodies of work as pre- and re-entwined. In so doing futures are remade.

Notes

1. Janine Antoni, *Matrix 129*, Wadsworth Atheneum, Hartford, Connecticut, January 7 – April 28, 1996.
2. "She told me of the time that my grandfather (Barto) had grown a finely groomed mustache, of which he was very proud. My grandmother, however, thought it looked ridiculous. She begged him to get rid of it, but he paid no attention. One night while he was sleeping, my grandmother shaved off half of the mustache. The next morning my grandfather was horrified when he saw his reflection in the mirror. The second story has a similar theme. Barto told my grandmother that he loved her for her long, beautiful hair. He warned her, however, that if she ever cut her braids he would no longer love her. This enraged my grandmother. After he had left the house that day, she grabbed her two braids — which reached down to her hips — and snipped them off at the ears. She then tacked them in a crucifix form above their bed." Ibid.
3. See Peter Schwenger, *The Tears of Things: Melancholy and Physical Objects* (Minneapolis: University of Minnesota Press, 2006).
4. See Martin Heidegger, "The Thing" in *Poetry, Language, Thought* (New York: Harper Collins: 1975 [1971]), 161–184 and Jacques Lacan, *The Seminar of Jacques Lacan, Book VII: The Ethics of Psychoanalysis, 1959–1960,* ed. Jacques-Alain Miller, trans. Dennis Porter (New York: Norton 1992).
5. See Jane Bennett, "The Force of Things" in *Vibrant Matter: A Political Ecology of Things*, (Durham: Duke University Press, 2010), 1–19.
6. See Bill Brown, "Thing Theory" in *Critical Inquiry*, vol. 28, Autumn, 2001, 1–16.
7. See Janice Ross, *Anna Halprin: Experience as Dance* (Berkeley: University of California Press, 2007) 119–122.
8. Lawrence Halprin, "Structure and Garden Spaces Related in Sequence," *Progressive Architecture*, May 1958, 96–104. For an important discussion of this kind of futural, ecological thinking see Timothy Morton, *The Ecological Thought* (Cambridge: Harvard University Press, 2010).
9. Arch Lauterer, quoted in Ross, 105.
10. Lawrence Halprin, quoted in Ross, 104.
11. Anna Halprin, quoted in Ross, 106.
12. On the voice of the witness see Cathy Caruth, *Unclaimed Experience: Trauma, Narrative, and History* (Baltimore: John Hopkins University Press, 1996).
13. Anna Halprin notes that this scene is itself derived from another improvised performance she gave in a Fritz Perls workshop in which she confronted a suited male participant by taking off all her clothes. See Ross, 175–176.
14. See Ewa Lajer-Burcharth, "Antoni's Difference," in *Janine Antoni* (Küsnacht: Ink Tree, 2000), 42–75.
15. For a fuller discussion of mothering and birthing focused on Antoni's early work see Amy Cappellazzo, "Mother Lode," in *Janine Antoni* (Küsnacht: Ink Tree, 2000), 102–121.
16. For a discussion of the philosophical heritage of such a practice in feminist thought see Elizabeth Grosz, "Feminism, Materialism and Freedom," in *Realism, Materialism, Art*, eds. C. Cox, J. Jaskey, S. Malik (Berlin: Sternberg Press, 2015), 47–60.
17. See Isabelle Stengers, "An Ecology of Practices" in *Cultural Studies Review*, vol. 11 no. 1, March 2005, 183–196.
18. Ibid., 195.
19. Ibid., 185.
20. See AbdouMaliq Simone "Relational Infrastructures in Postcolonial Urban Worlds" in *Infrastructural Lives*, eds. Steve Graham and Colin McFarlane, (New York: Routledge, 2014), 17–38.
21. Ibid., 18.
22. Ibid.
23. William E. Connolly, *The Fragility of Things: Self-Organizing Processes, Neoliberal Fantasies and Democratic Activism*, (Durham: Duke University Press, 2013), 141.
24. See David Abram, "The Forgetting and Remembering of the Air," in *The Spell of the Sensuous* (New York: Vintage Books, 1996), 225–260.
25. See Boris Groys, "Art in the Age of Biopolitics: From Artwork to Art Documentation" in *Perform, Repeat, Record,* eds. Amelia Jones and Adrian Heathfield, (London: Intellect, 2012), 209–218.
26. *Marina Abramović Presents,* Manchester International Festival, Whitworth Art Gallery, Manchester, 3 – 19 July 2009. Tino Sehgal, *These Associations*, 24 July – 28 October 2012. Xavier Le Roy, *Retrospective*, MoMA PS1, 2 October – 1 December 2014.
27. See Claire Bishop, "Delegated Performance: Outsourcing Authenticity" in *October*, Spring 2012, 91–112.
28. Ibid., 91.

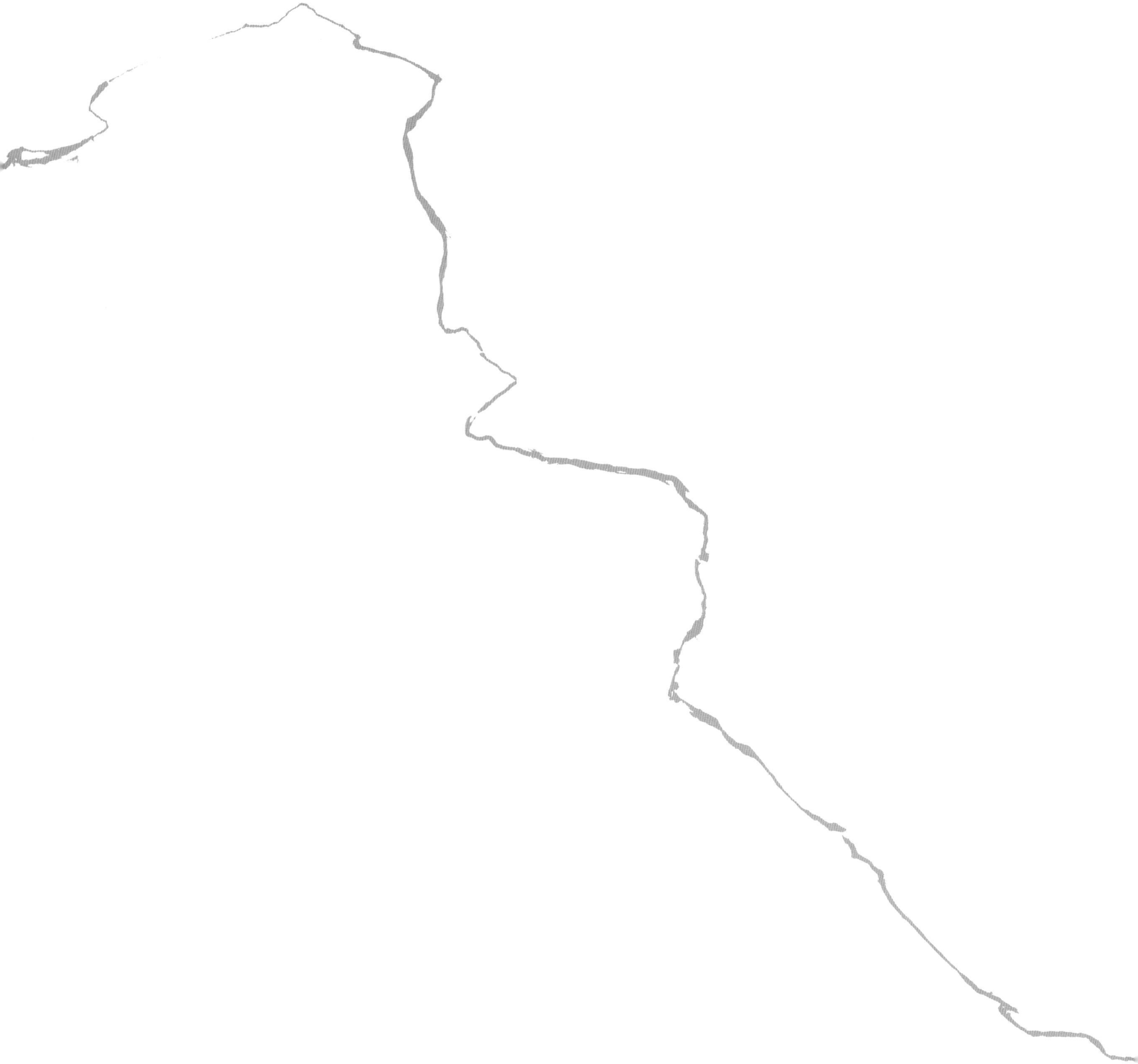

PAPER DANCE

Janine Antoni, Anna Halprin

In 2013 Janine Antoni and Anna Halprin began working on a performance derived from a scene in Halprin's influential theater work *Parades and Changes* (1965). Antoni improvised with long rolls of brown paper, making temporary shapes in the material with her body that echoed many of her previous sculptural works. Translated into a gallery setting, the performance evolved over fifteen weeks, taking place weekly amidst an assembly of crated objects. Antoni would unpack some of her artworks at the beginning of each performance, installing a slow-time retrospective. A fragment of the fifty-one-year-old film of *Parades and Changes* was projected amidst the artworks in between live performances. Together the artists asked how their creative histories could entwine and regenerate themselves.

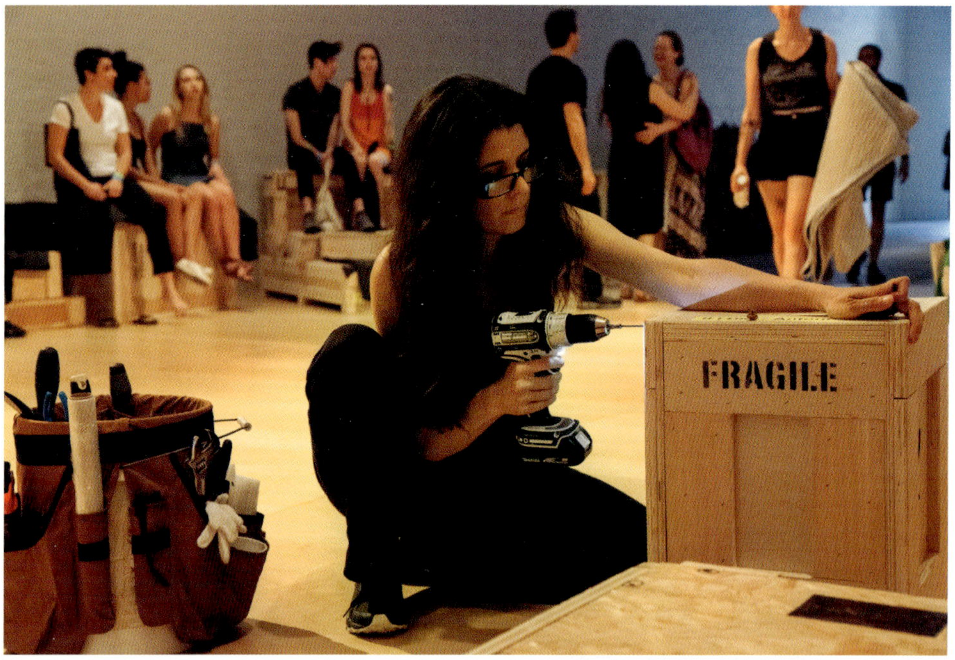
FRAGILE

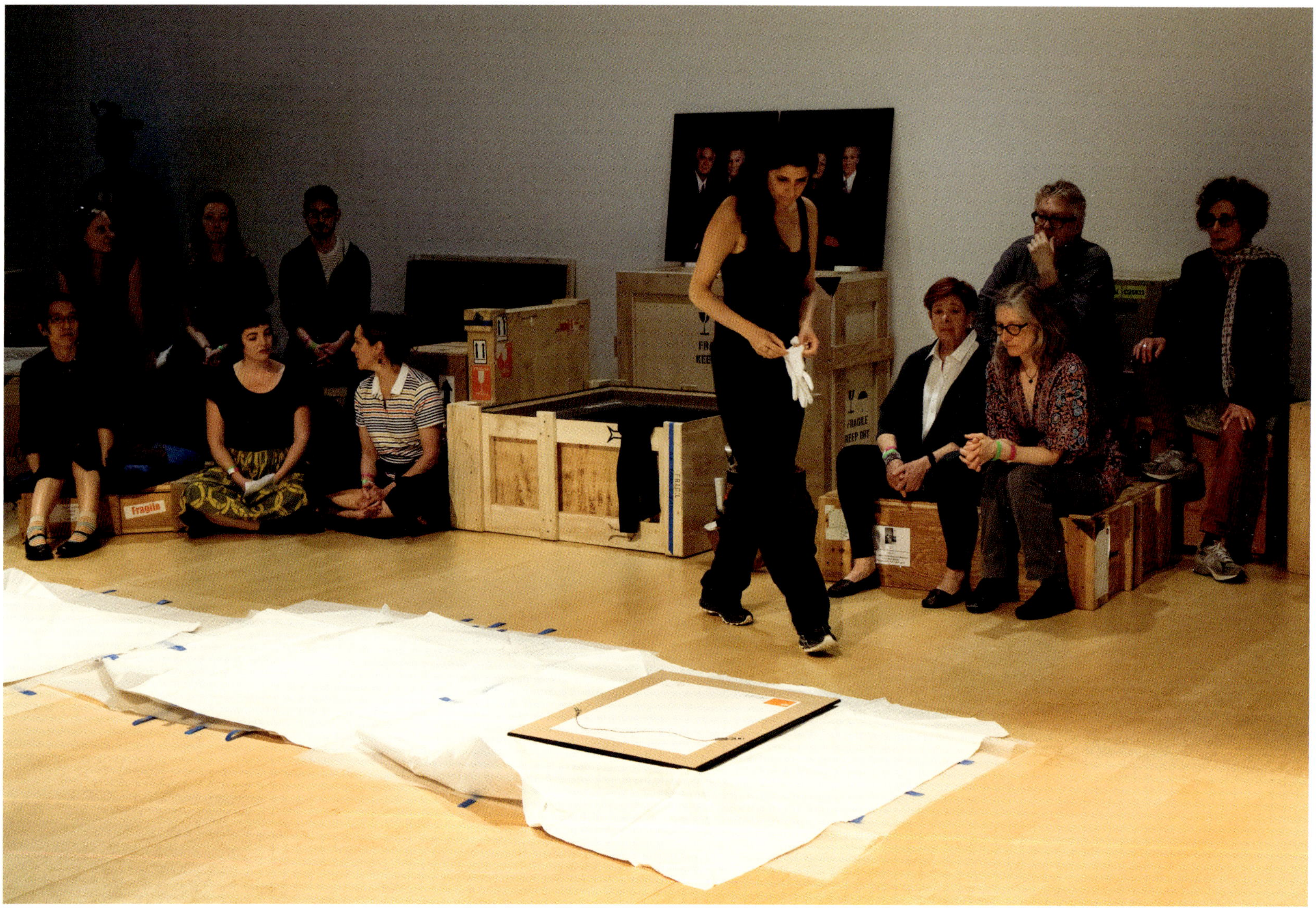
Fragile

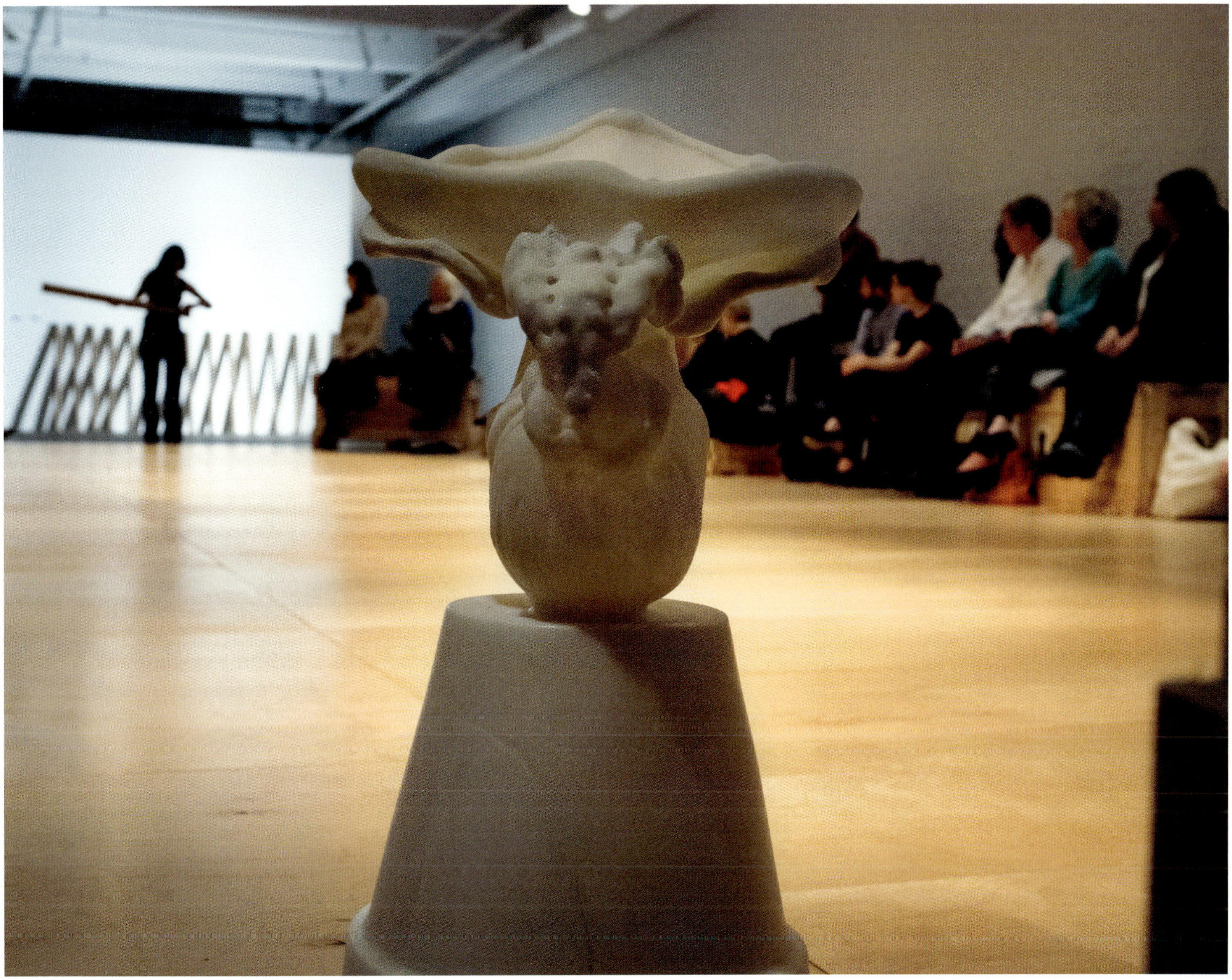

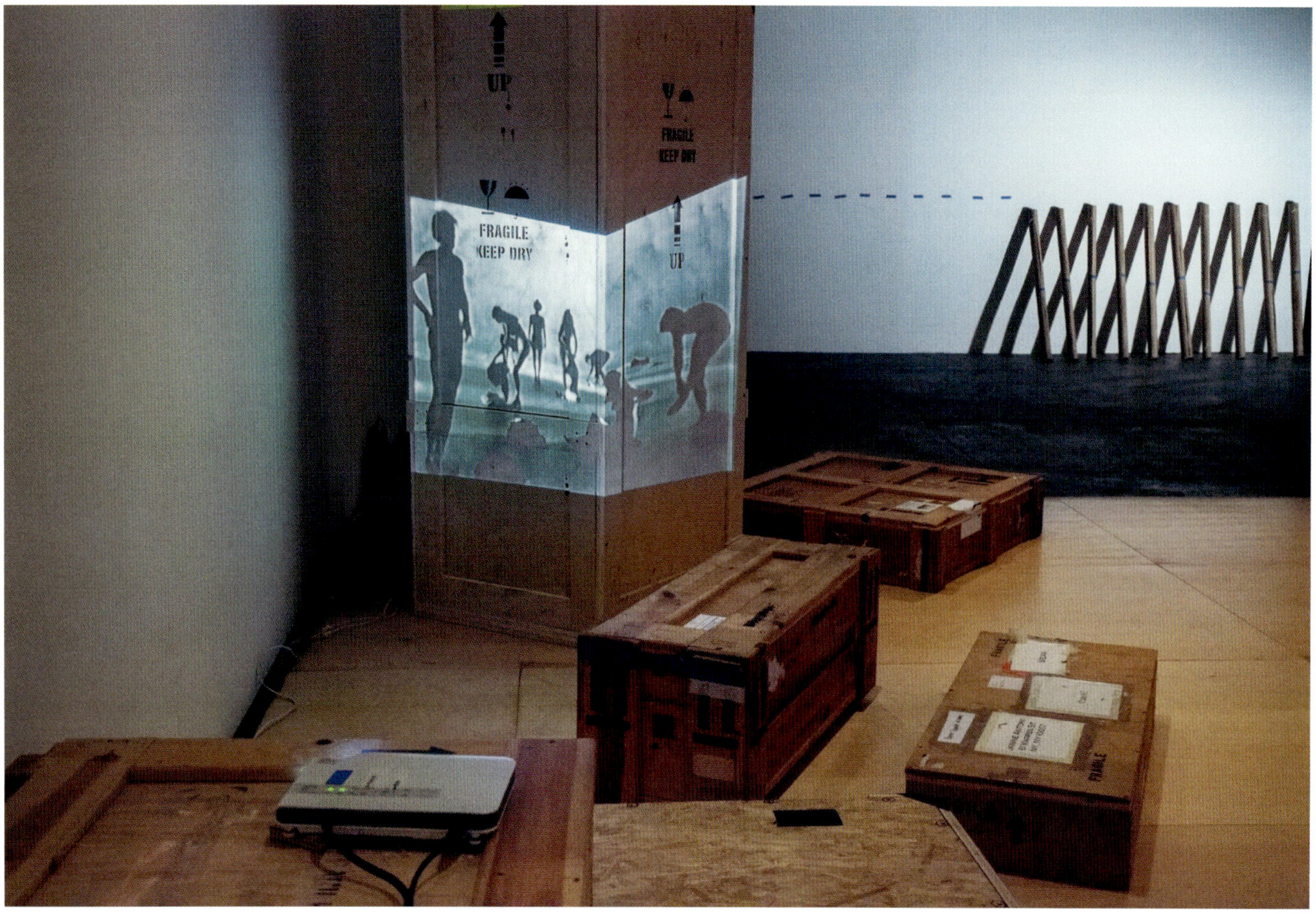
UP
FRAGILE
KEEP DRY
FRAGILE
KEEP DRY
UP
FRAGILE

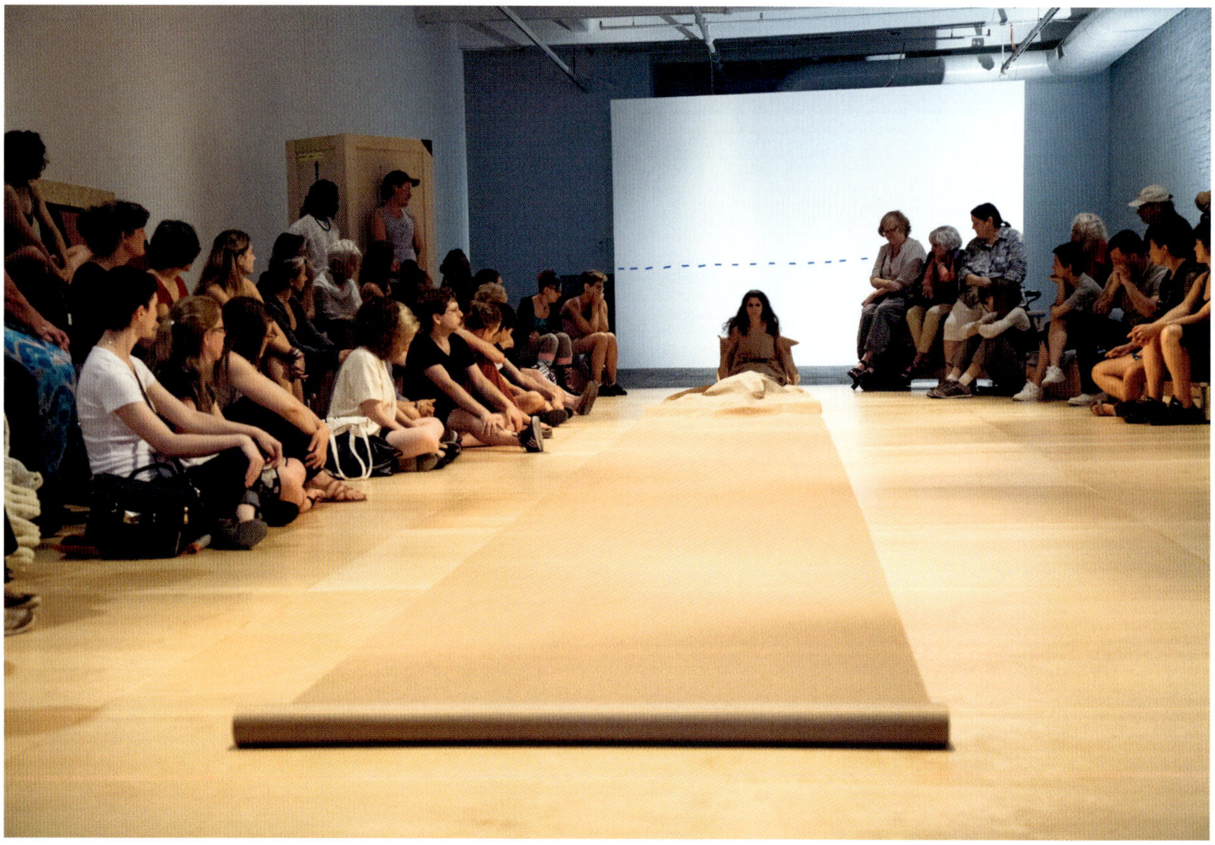

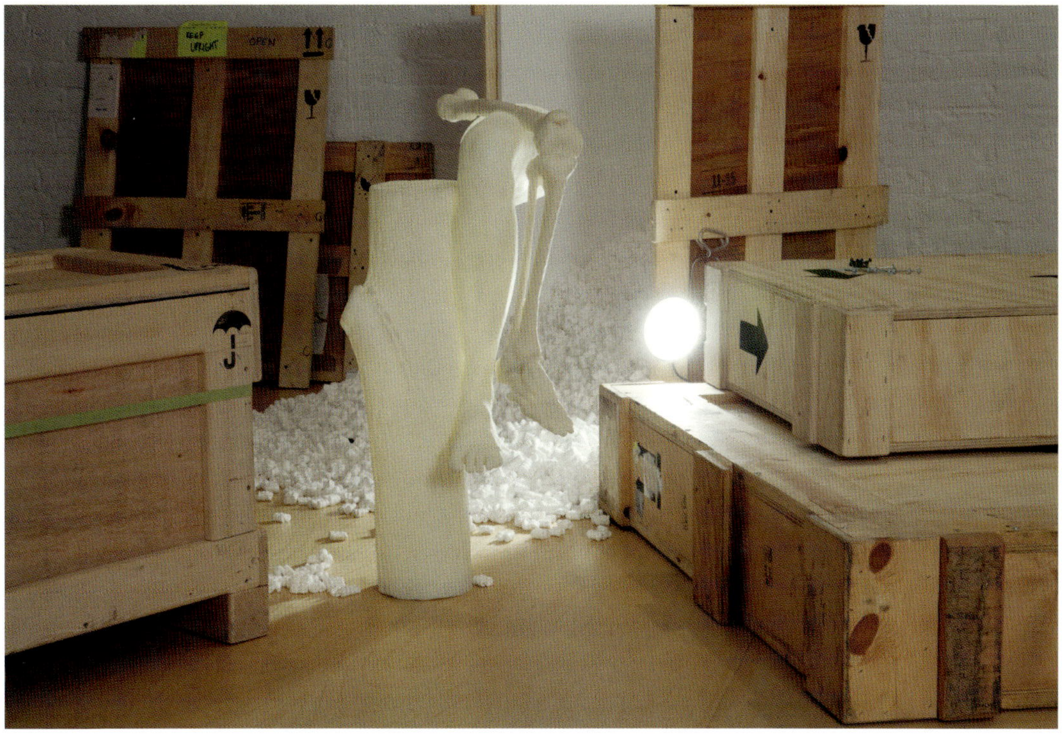

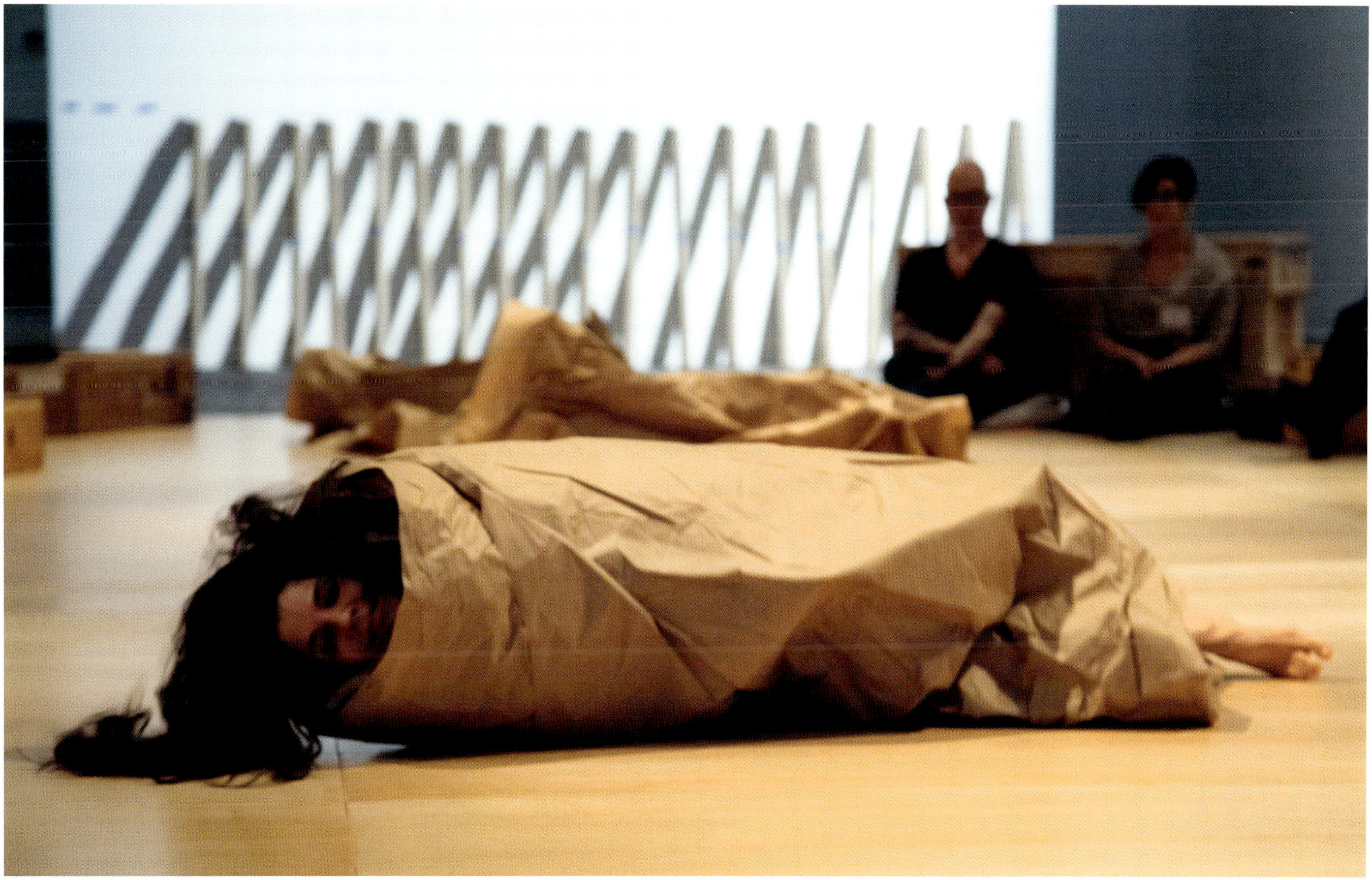

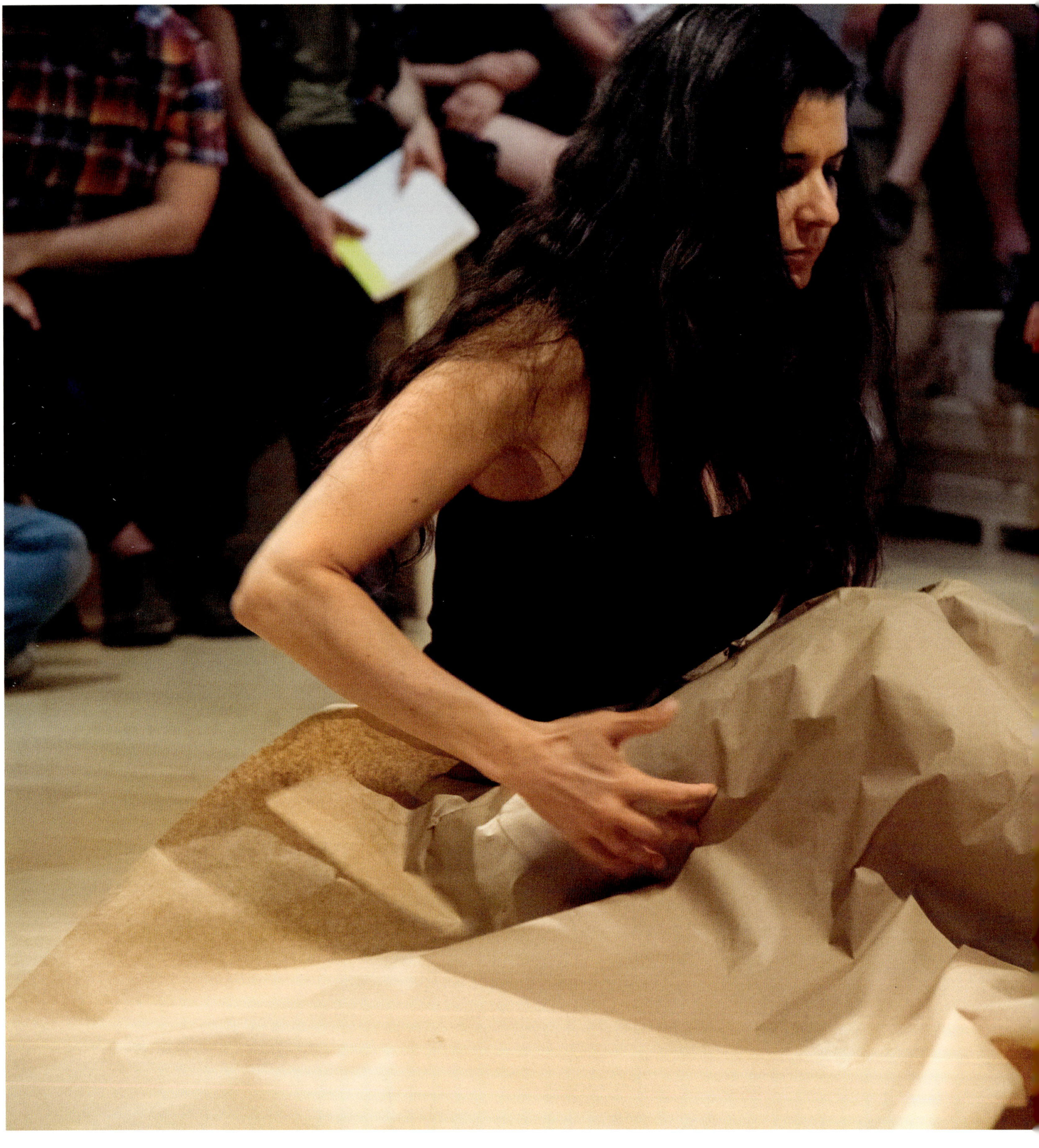

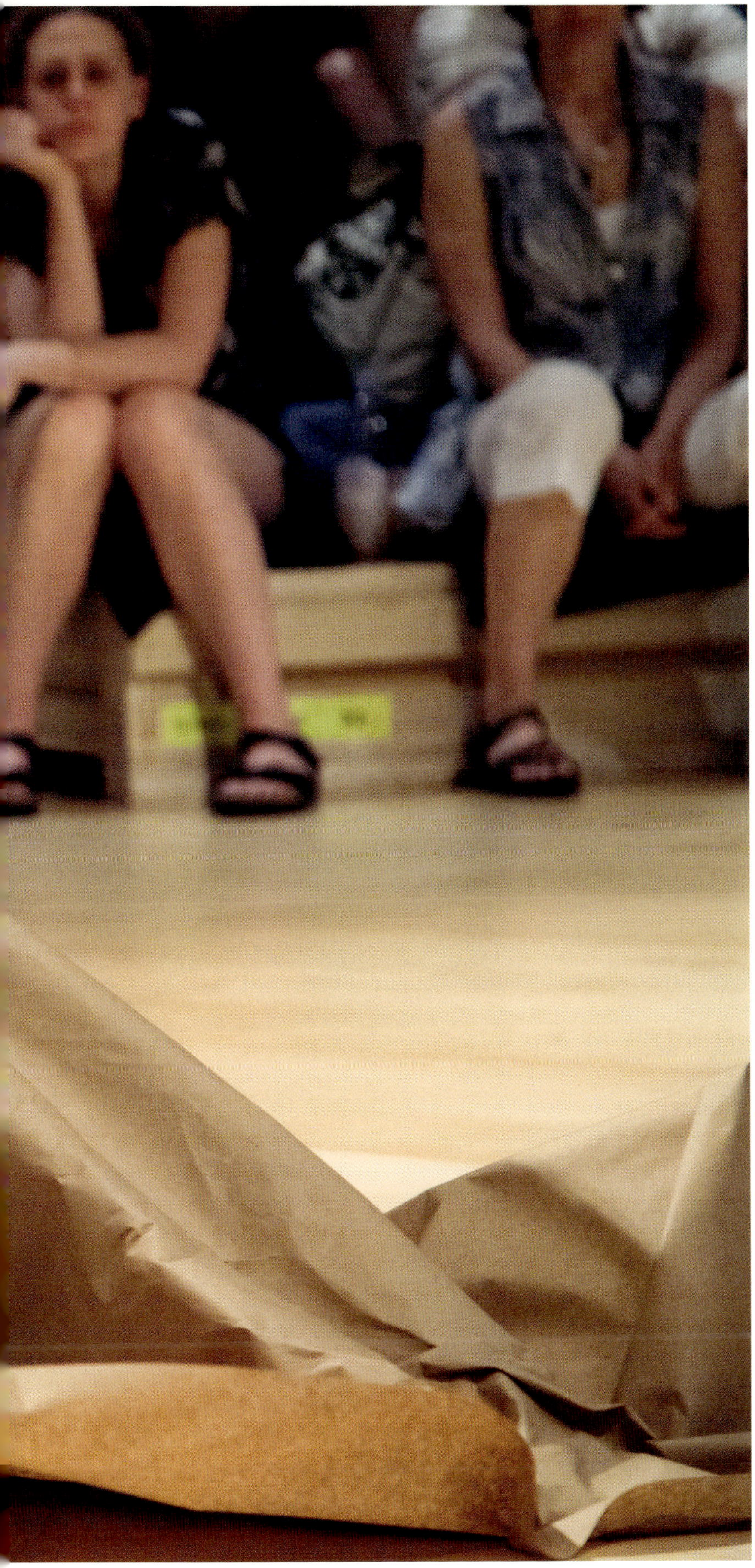

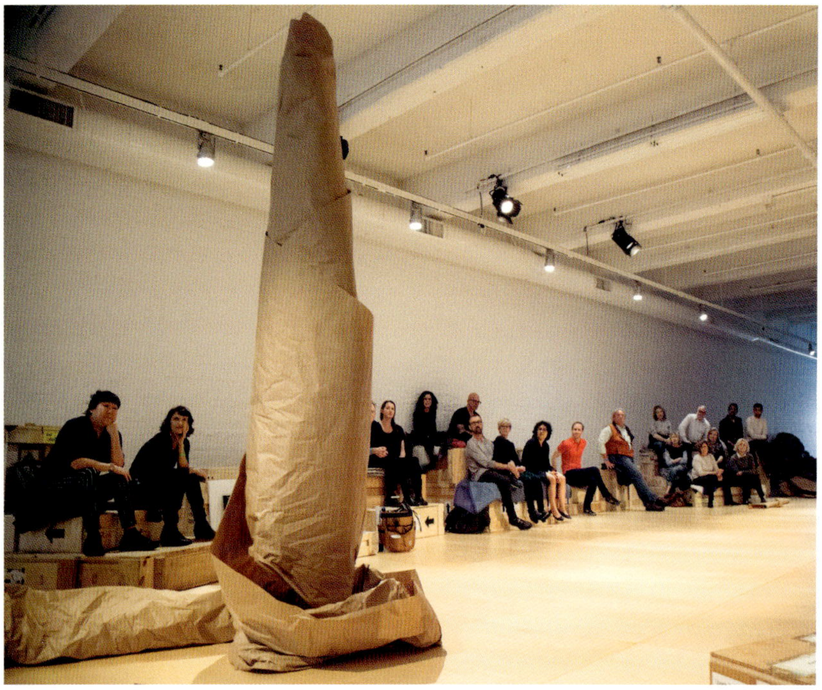

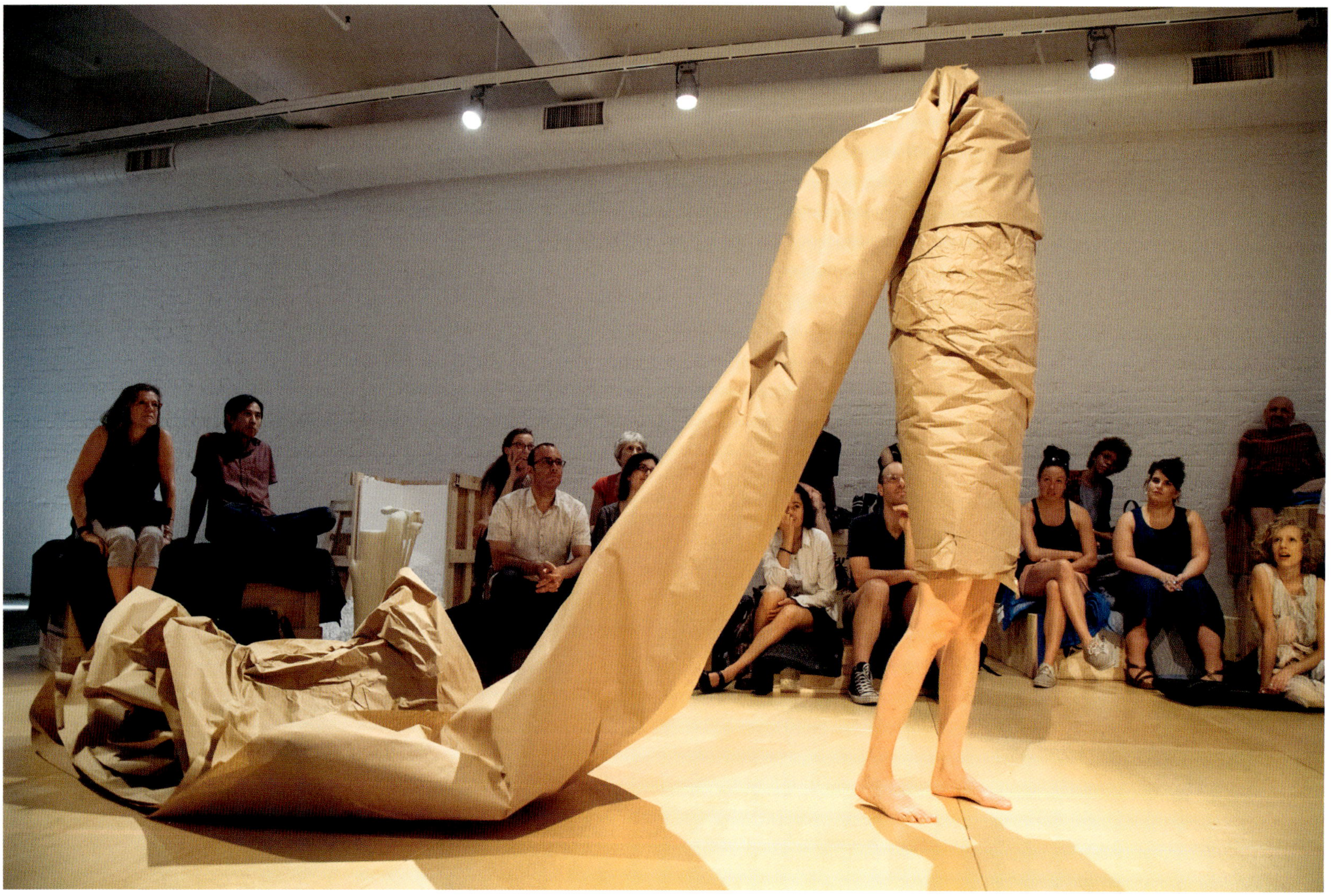

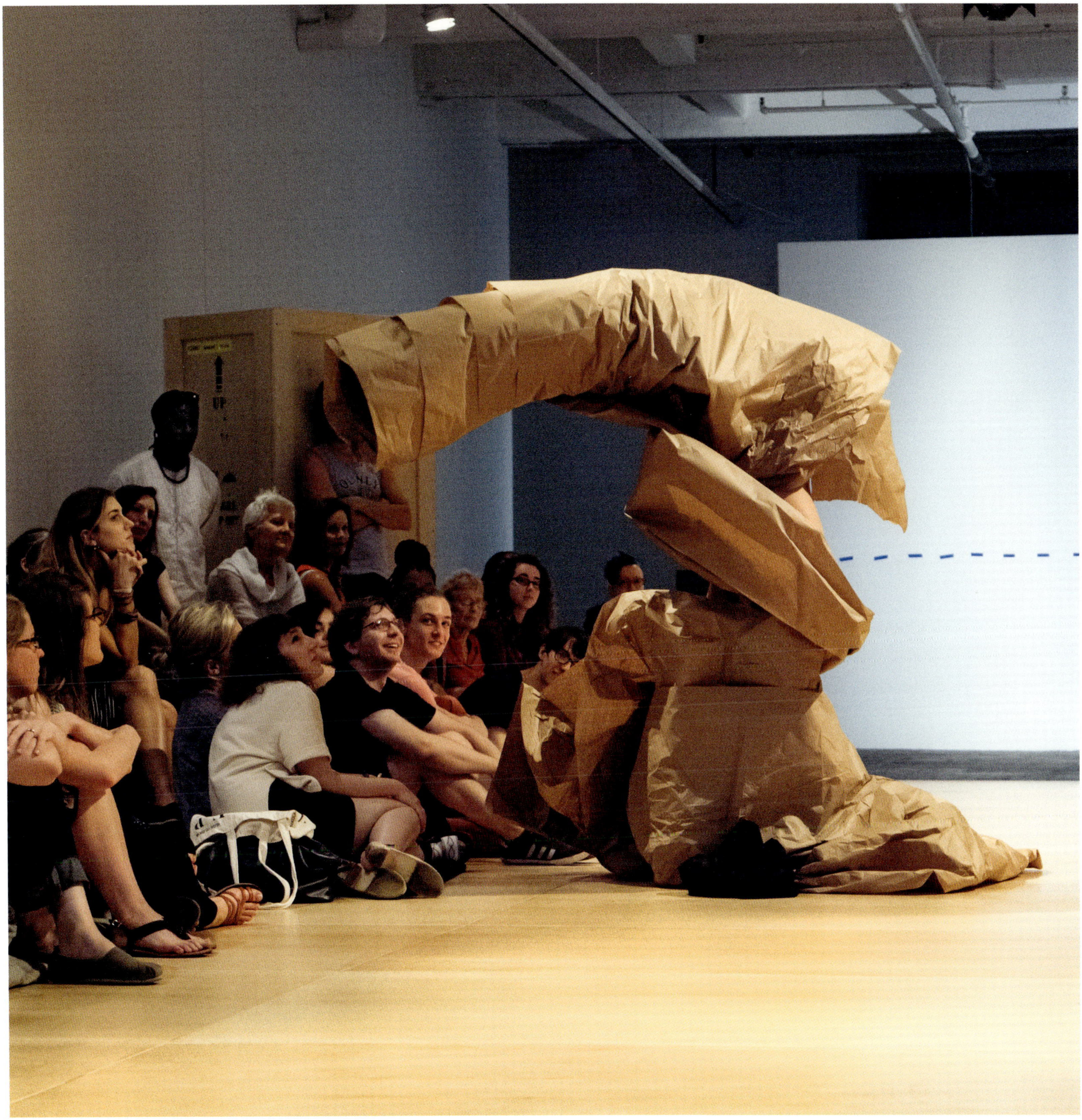

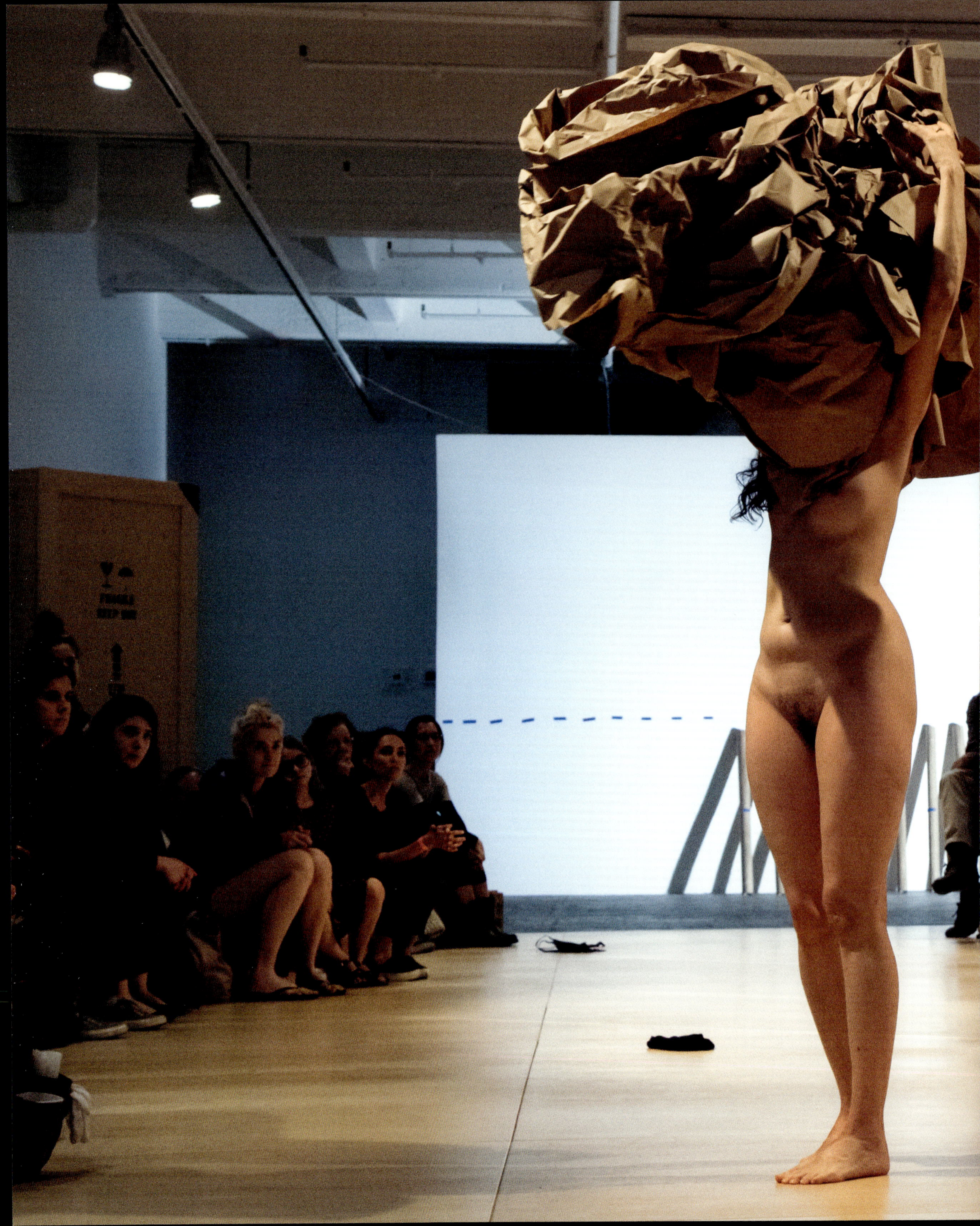

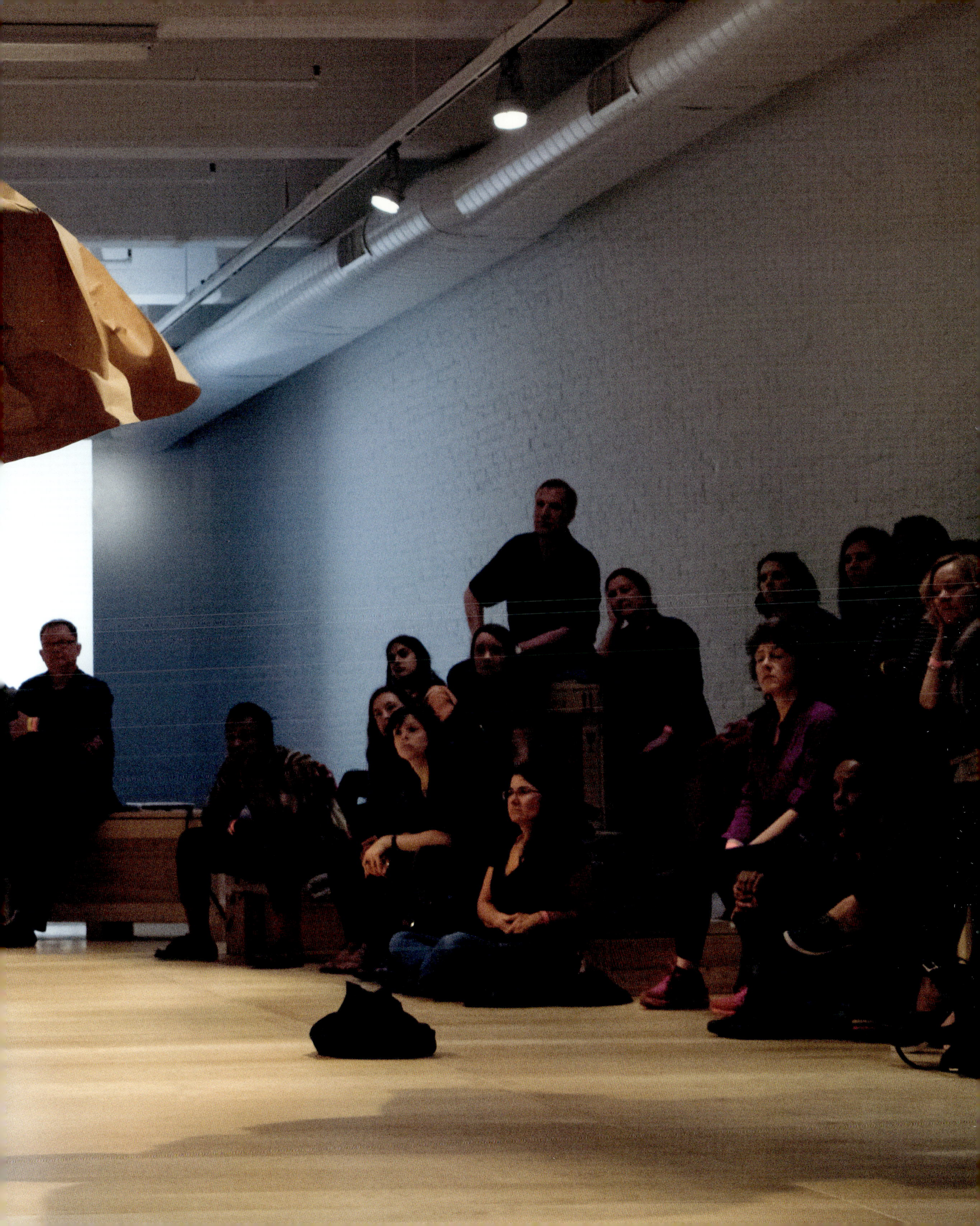

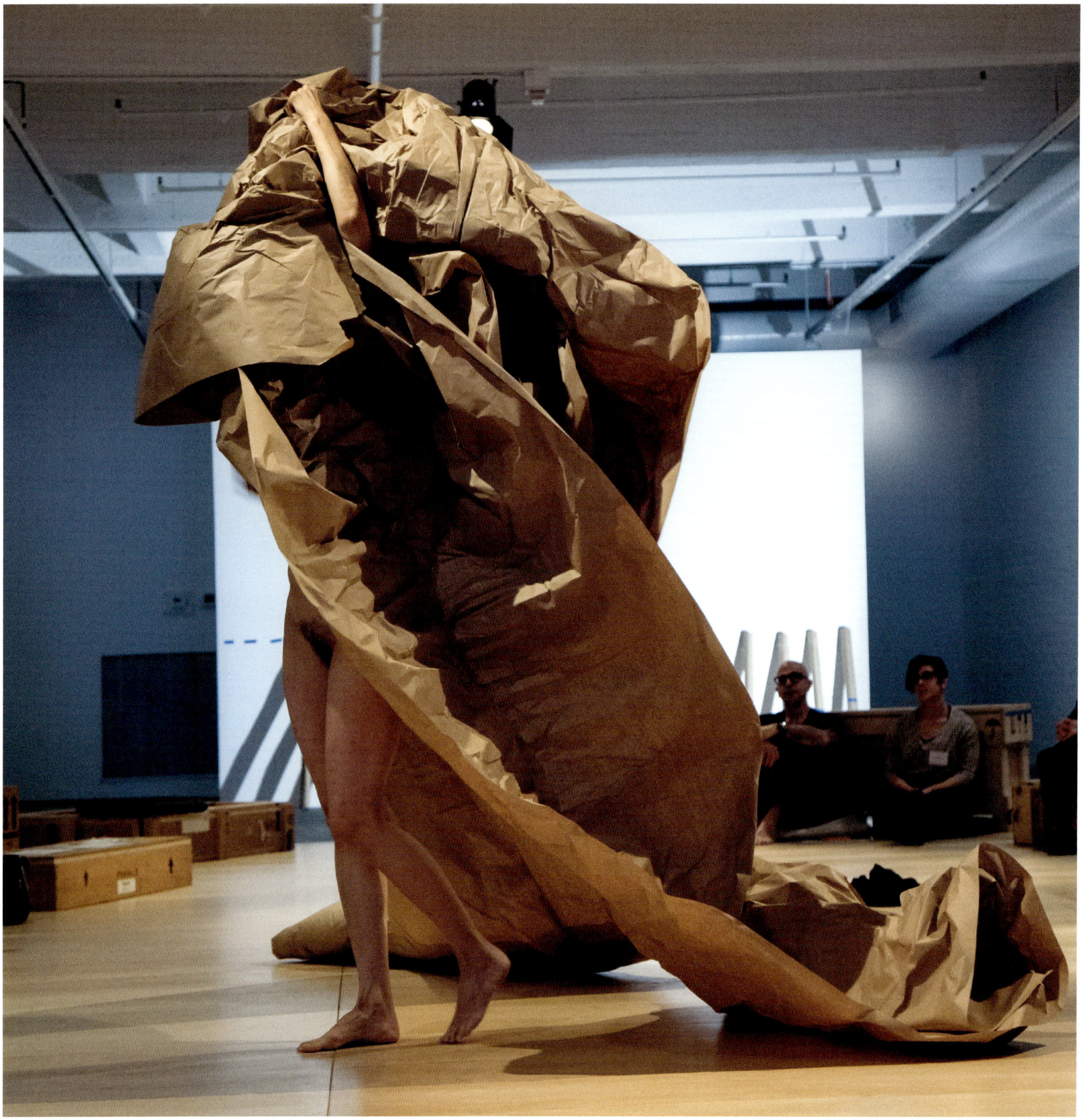

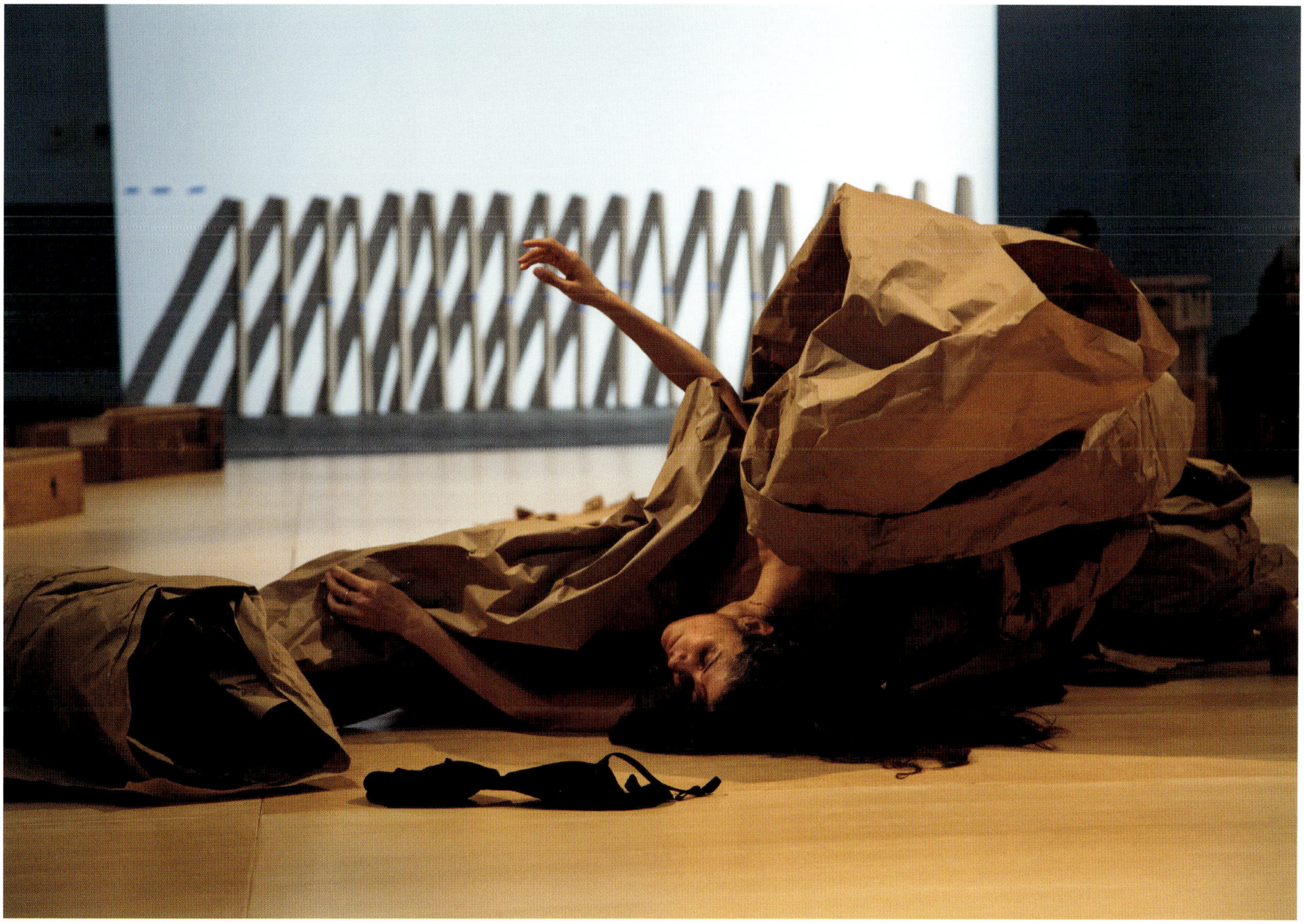

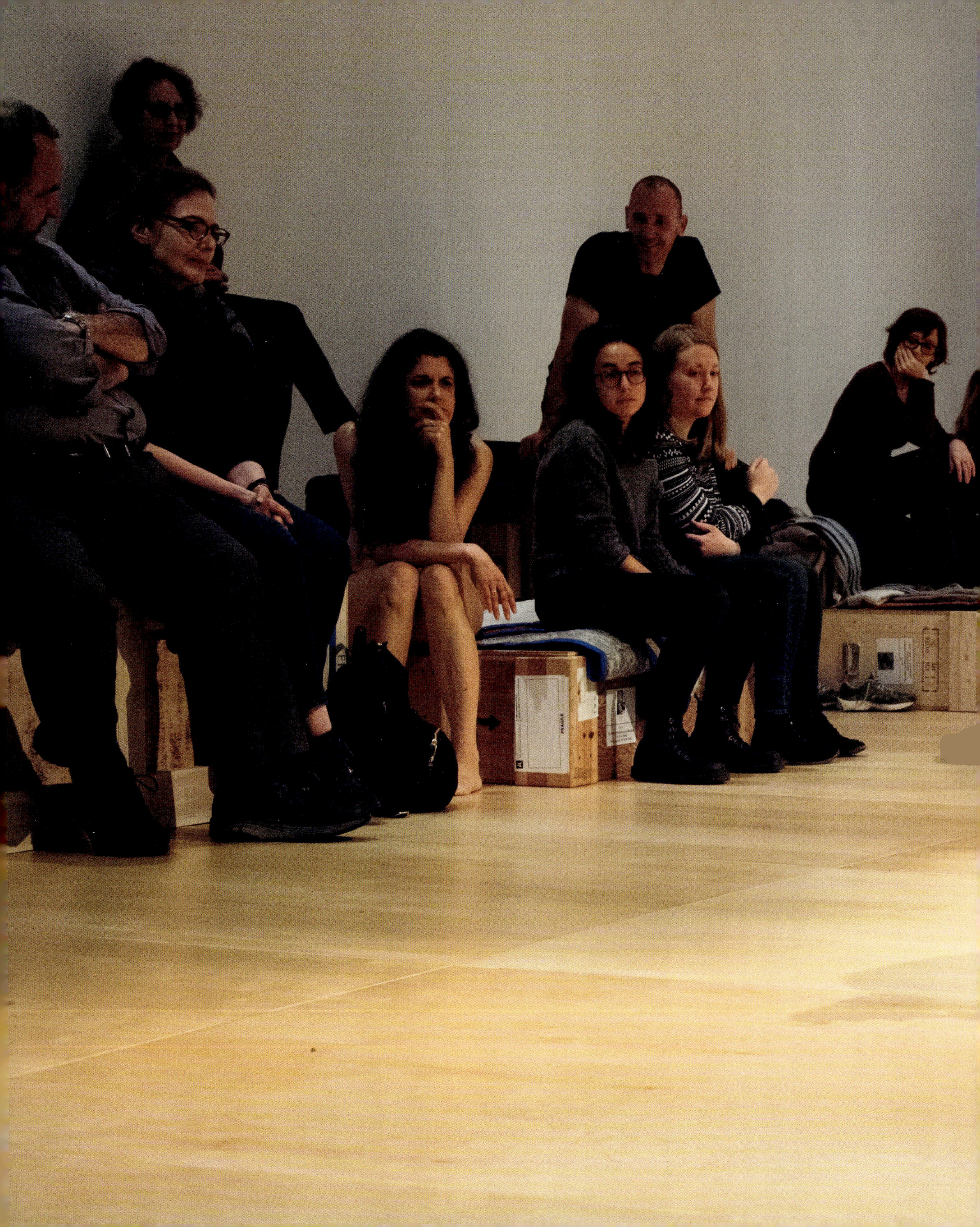

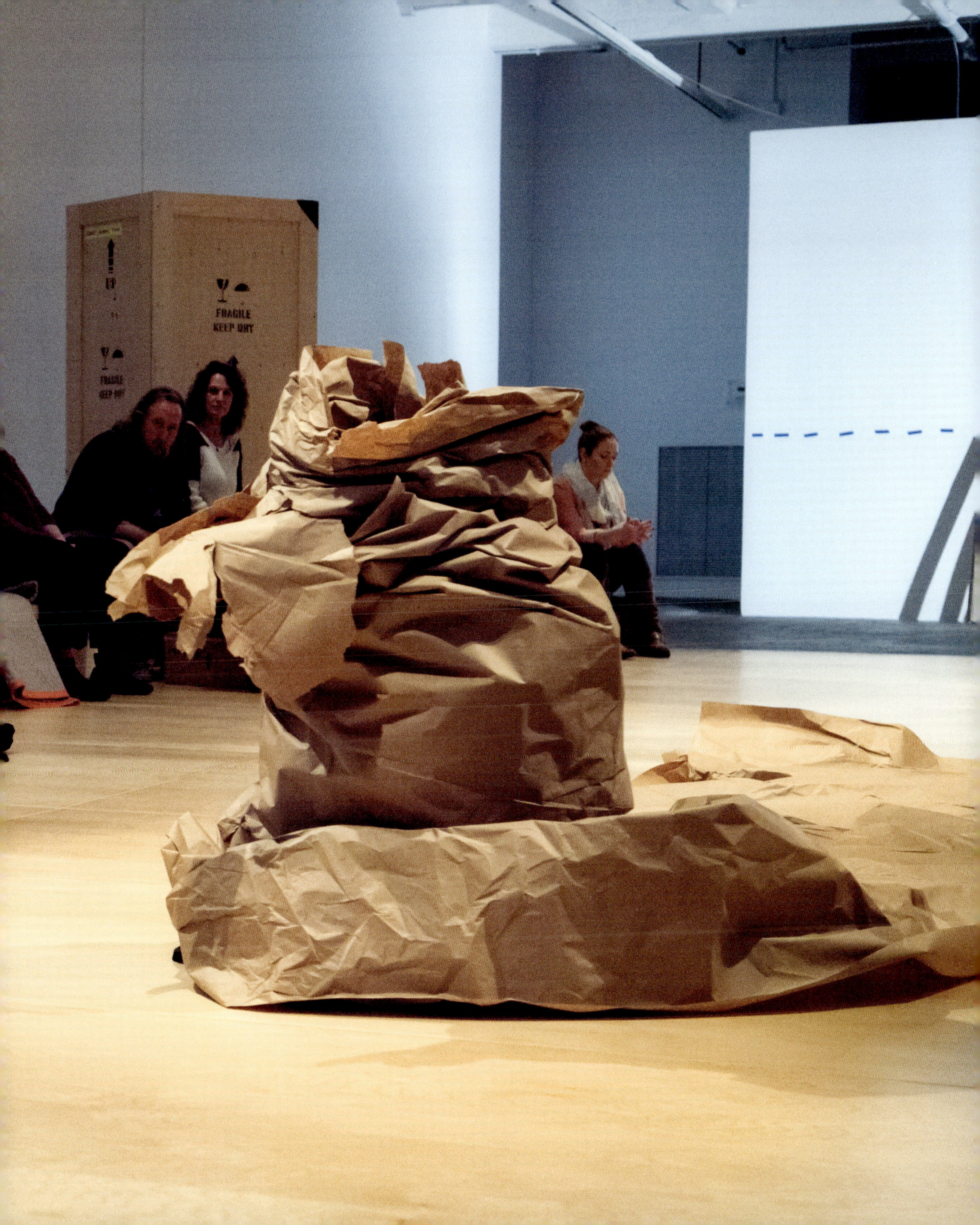
FRAGILE
KEEP DRY

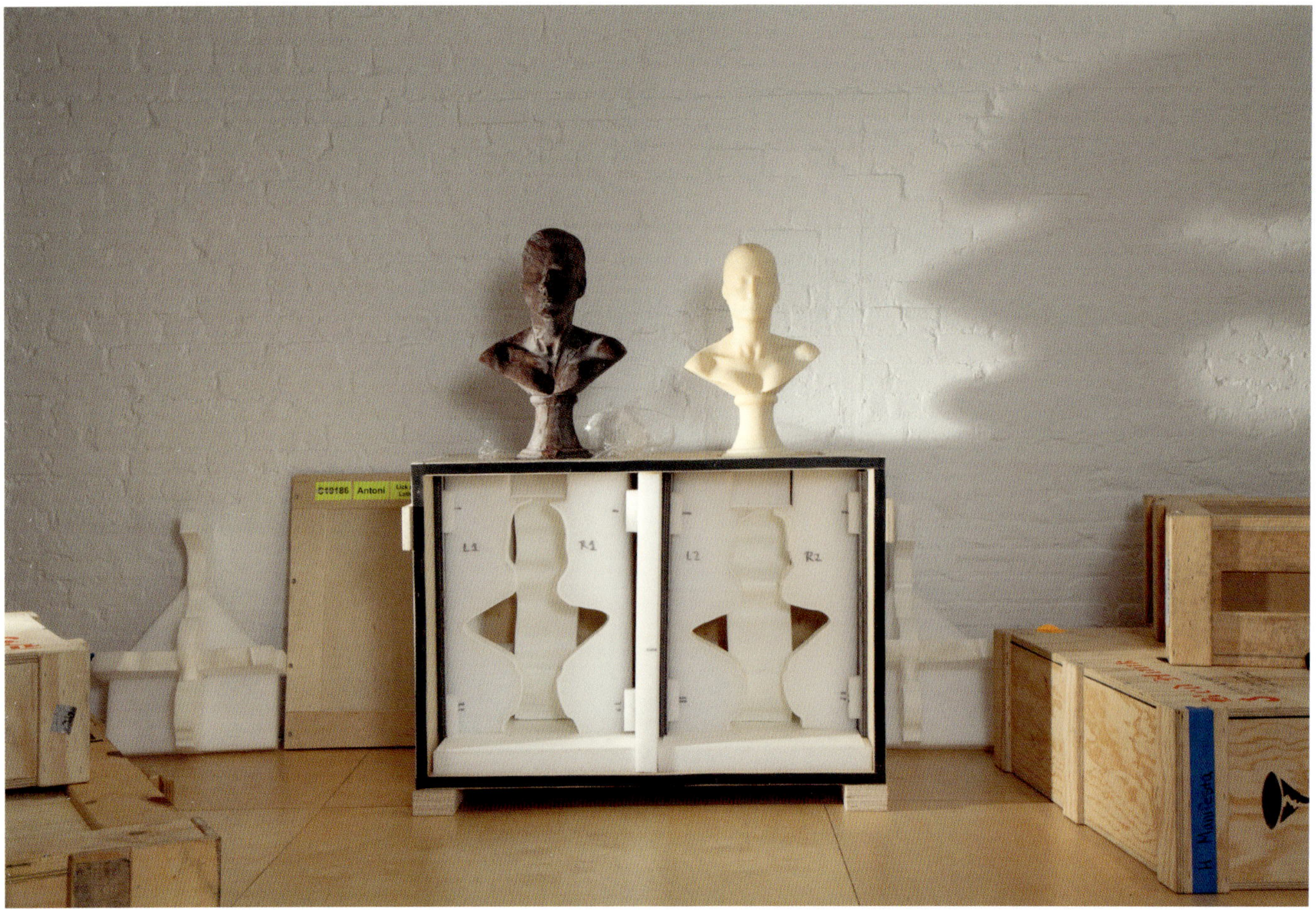
Antoni
L1
R1
L2
R2

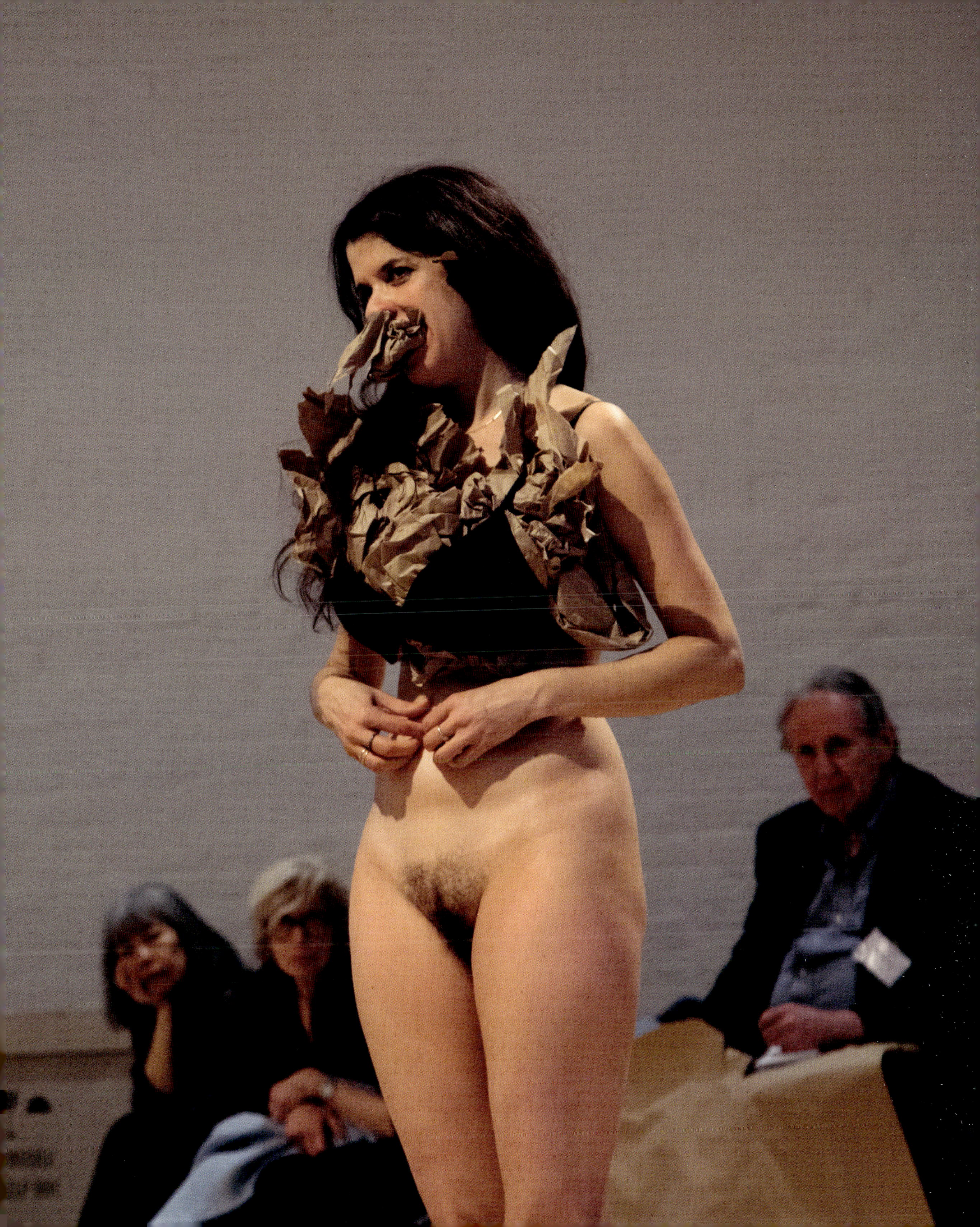

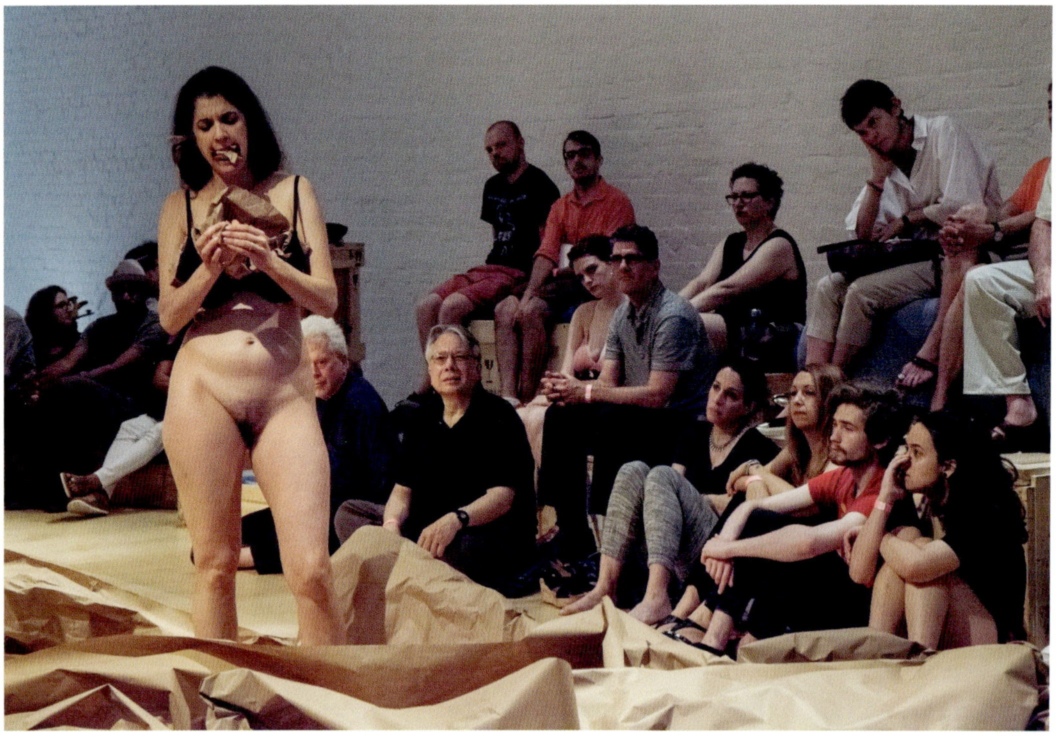

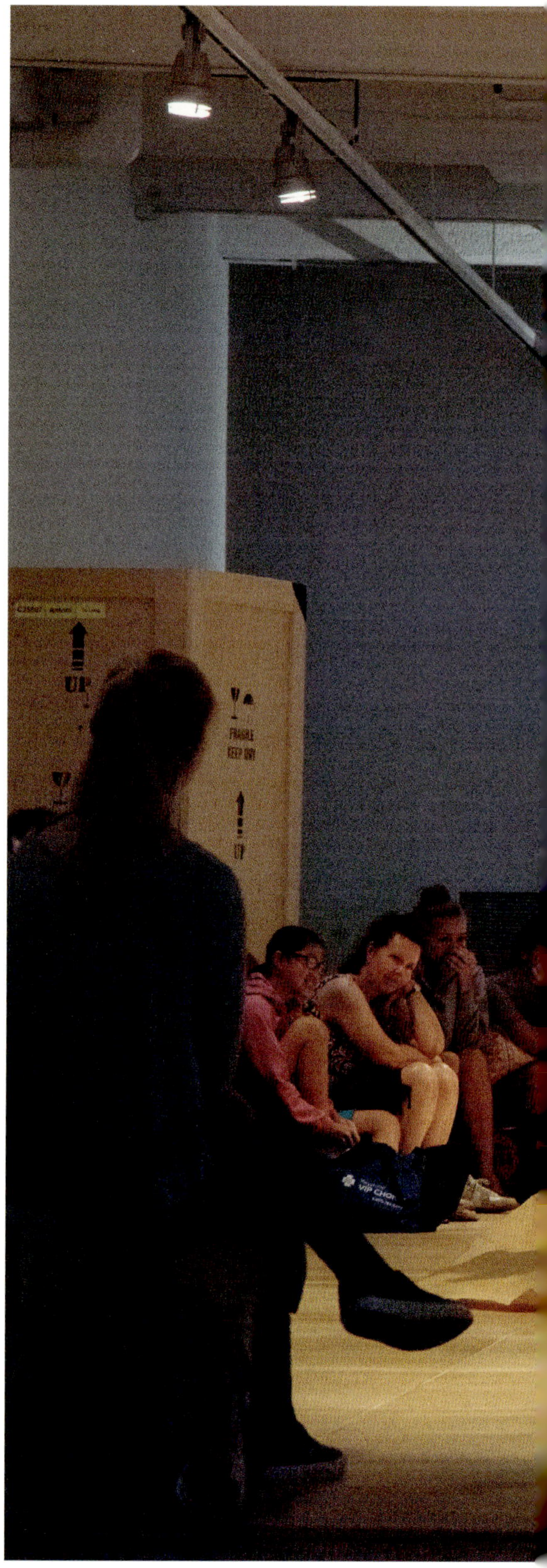

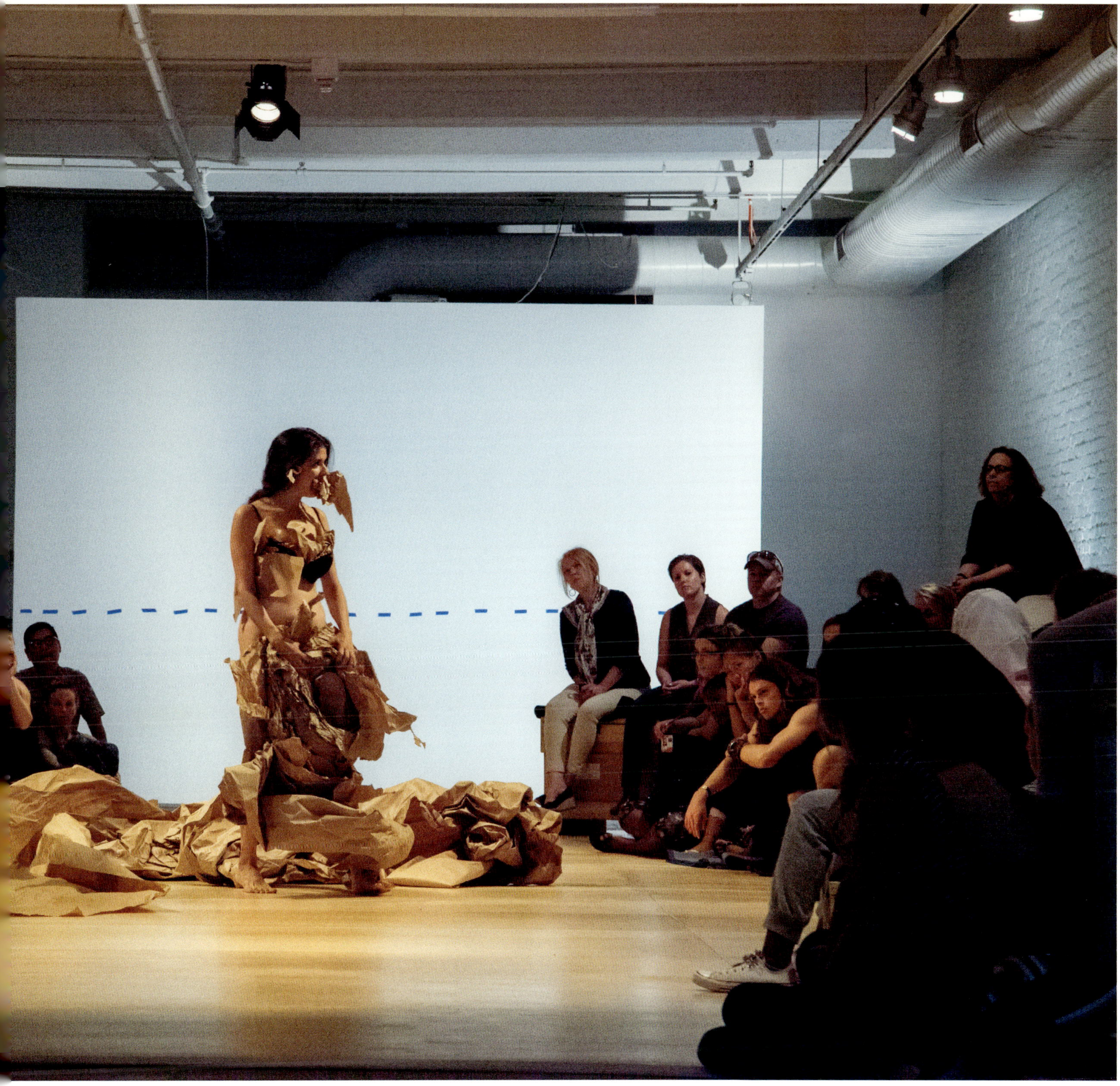

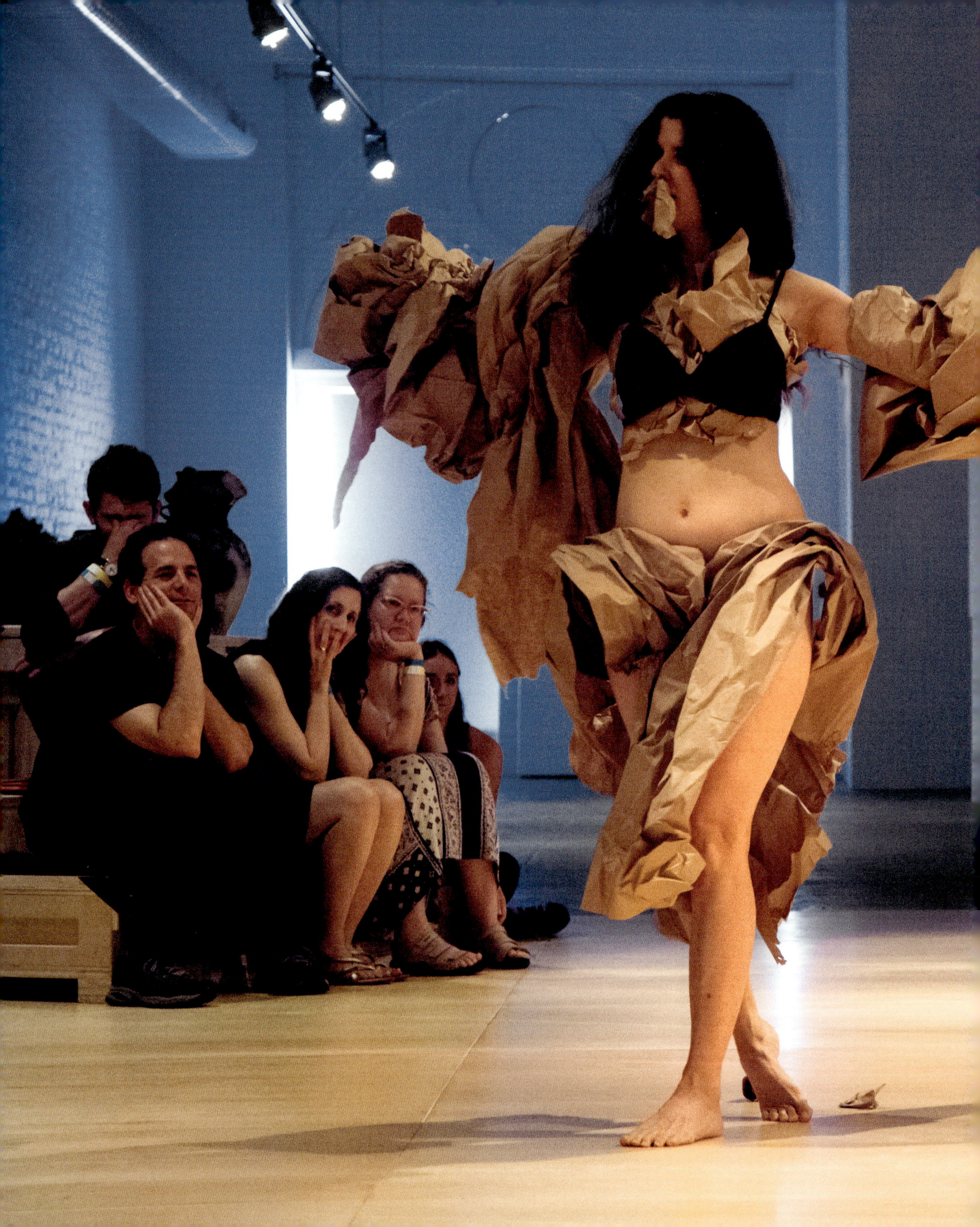

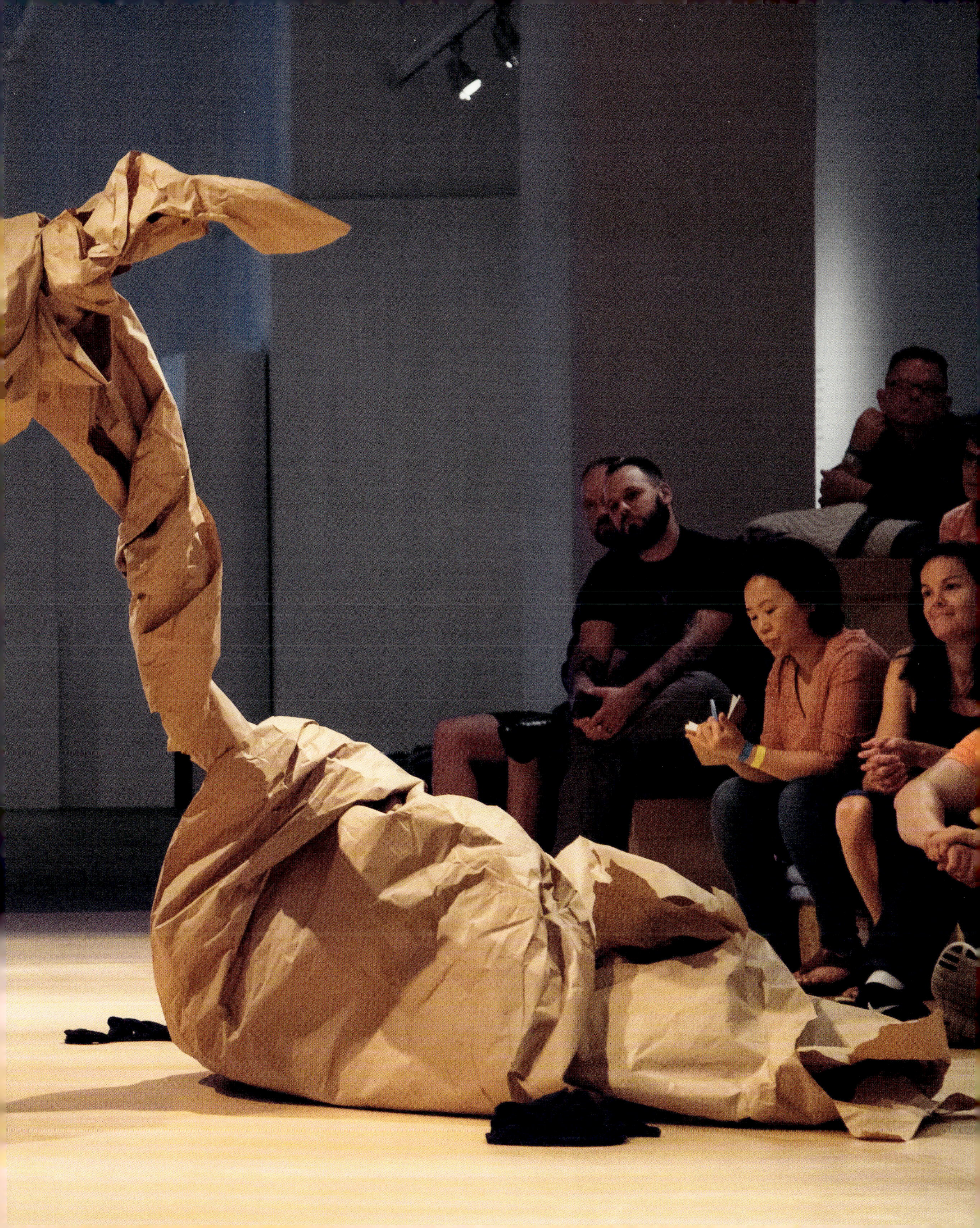

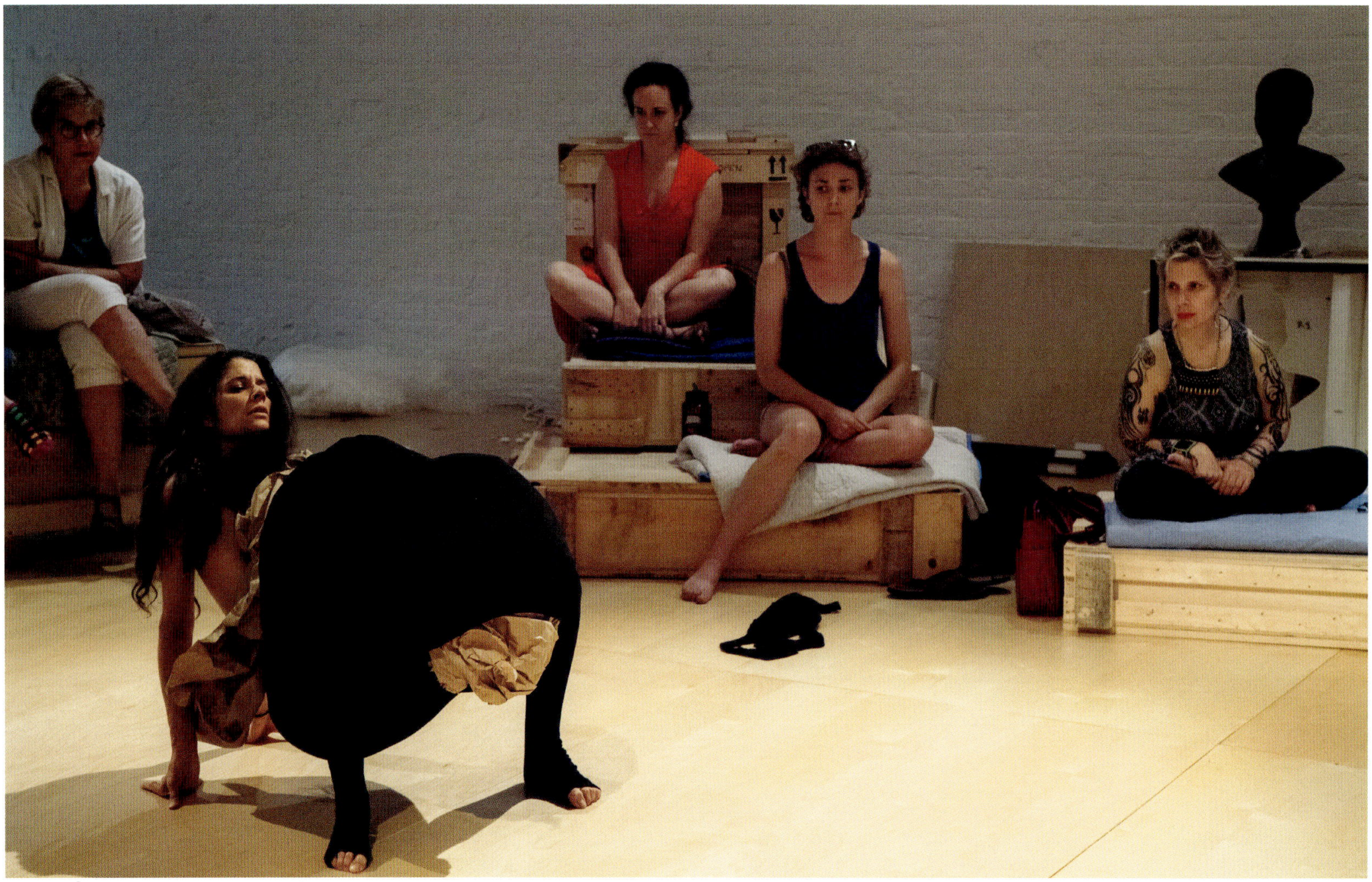

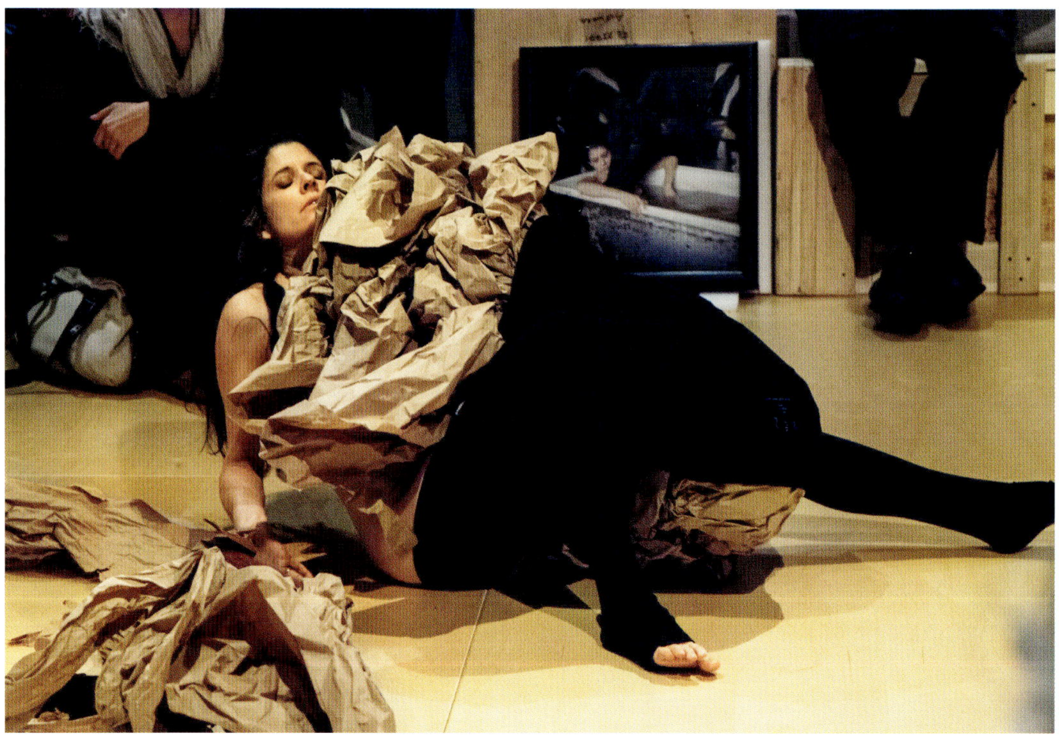

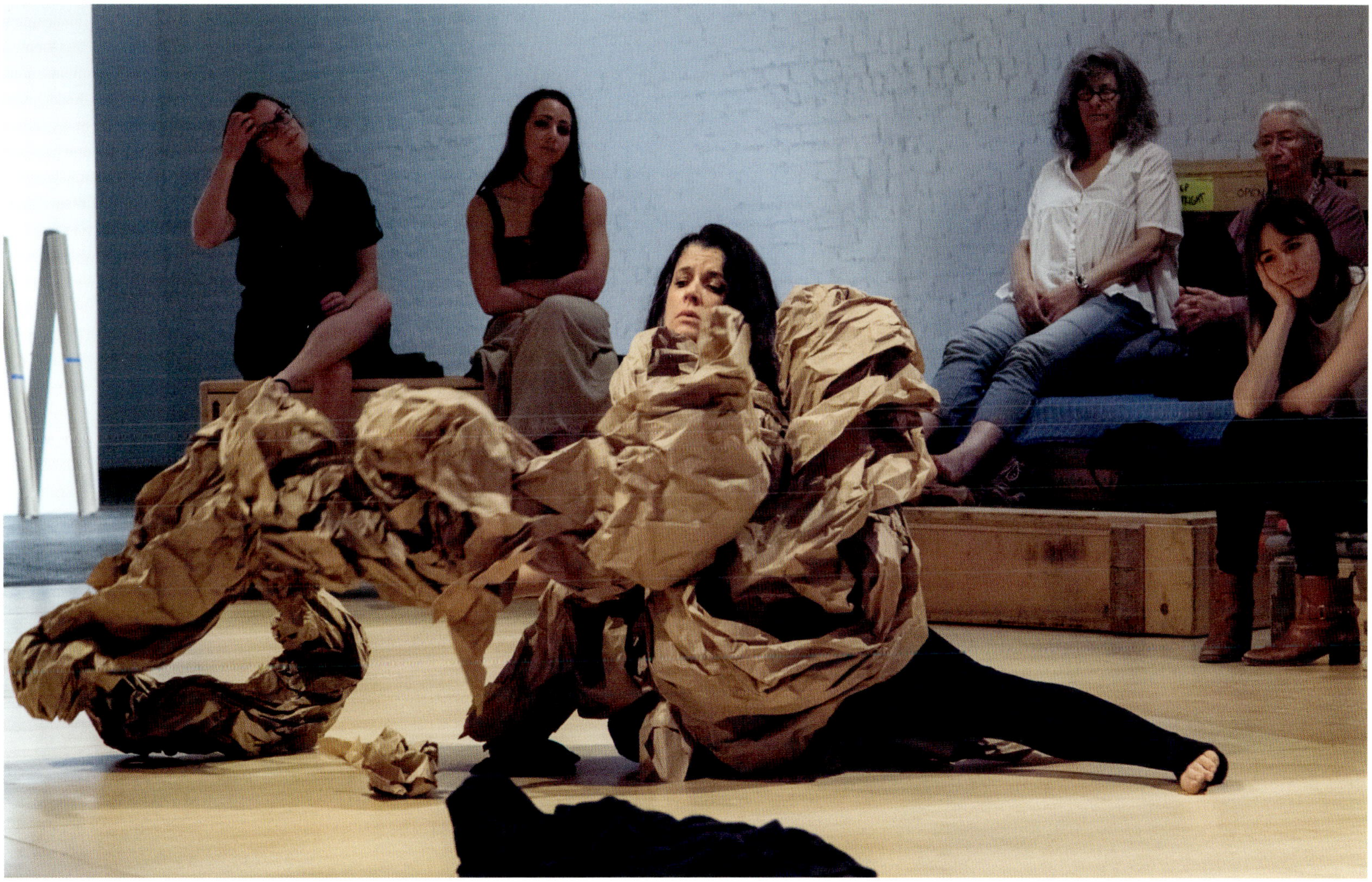

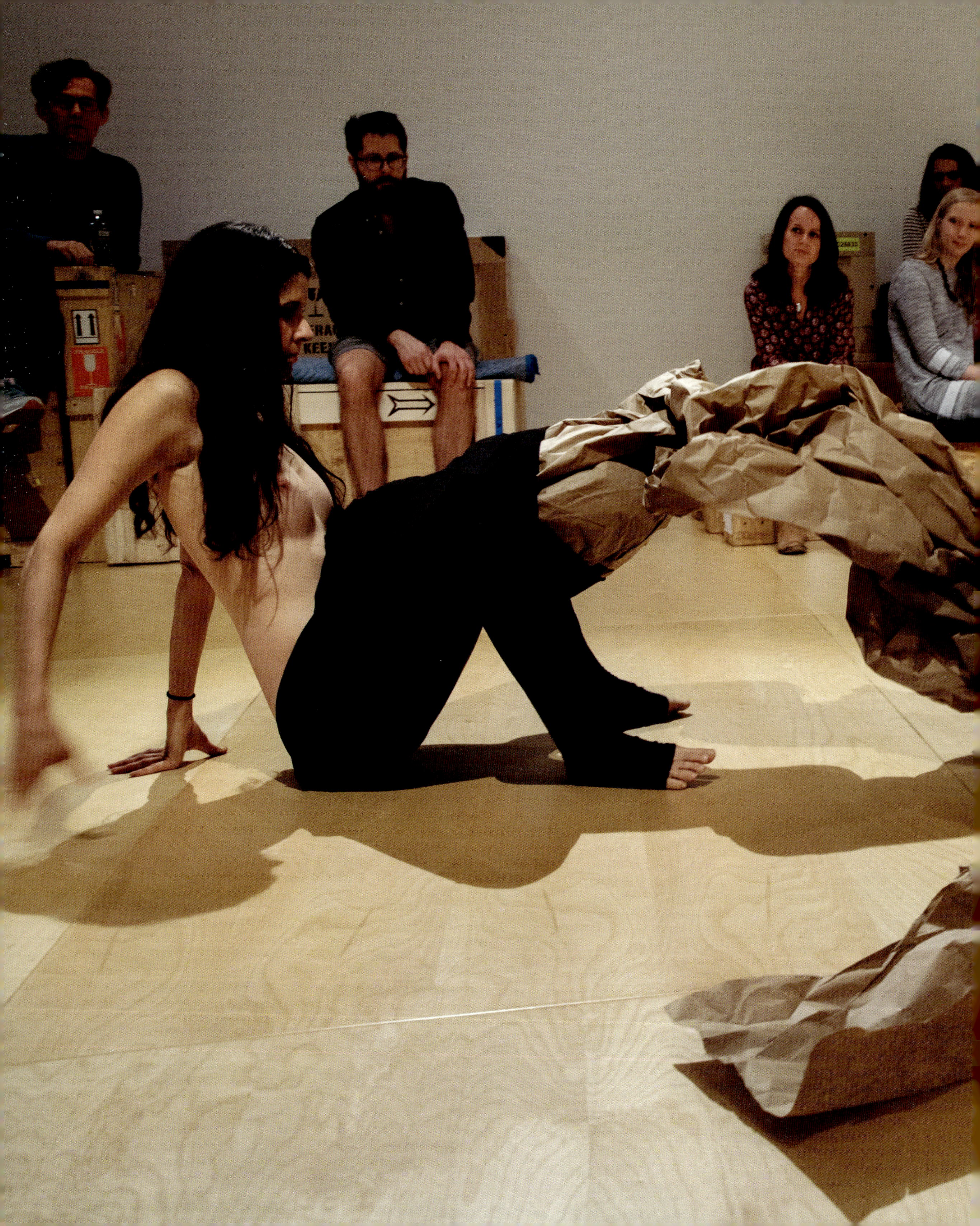

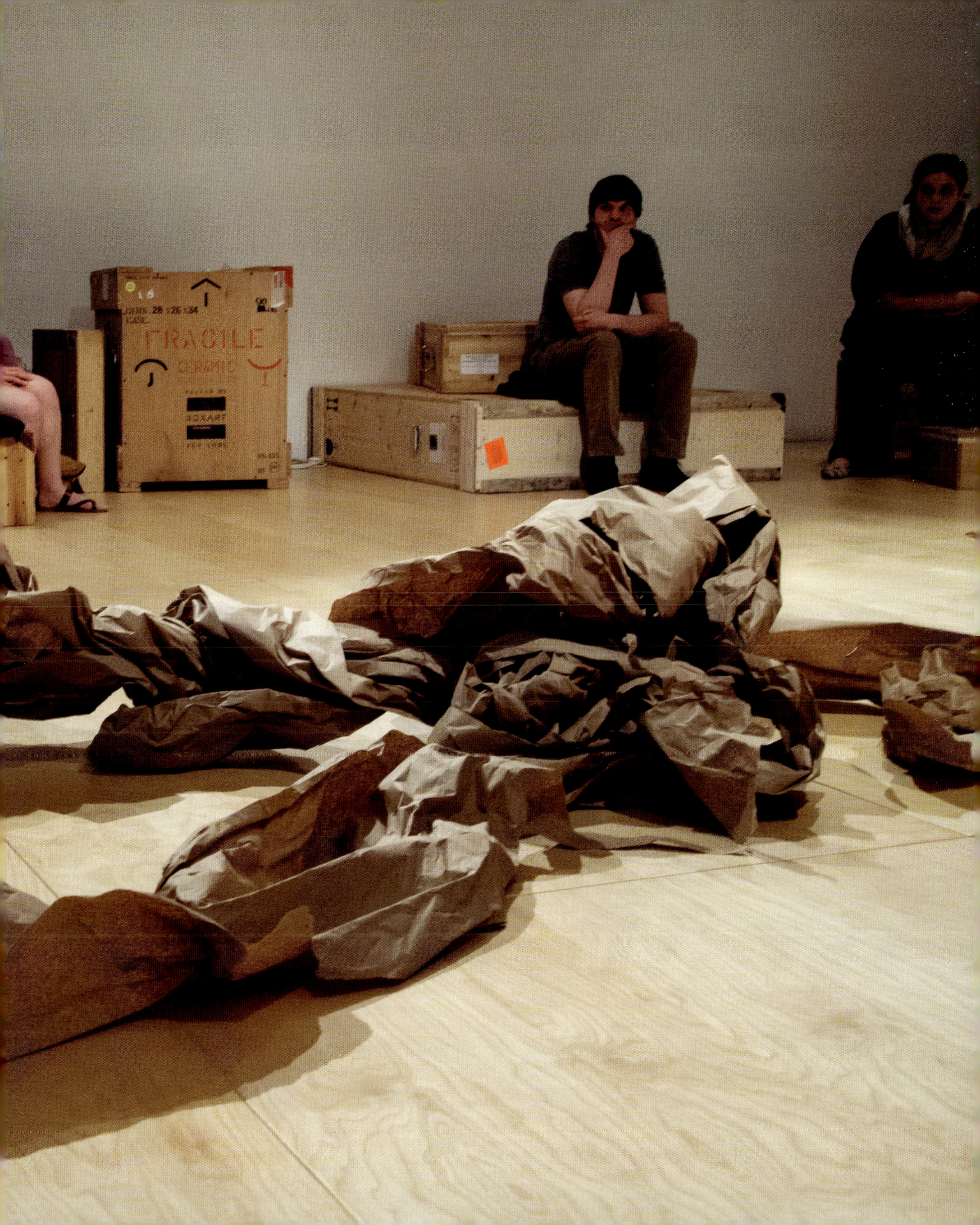
FRAGILE
CERAMIC

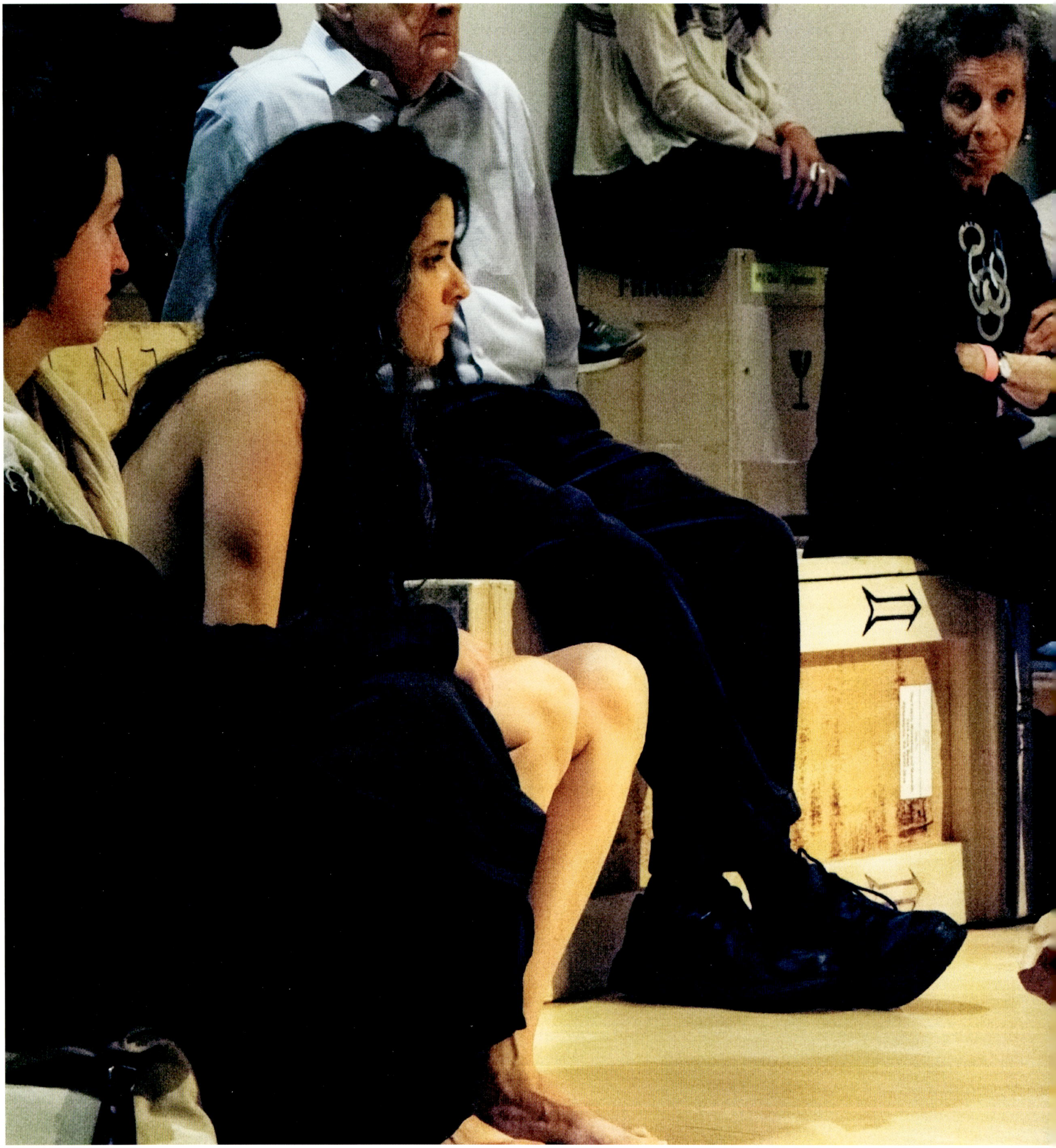

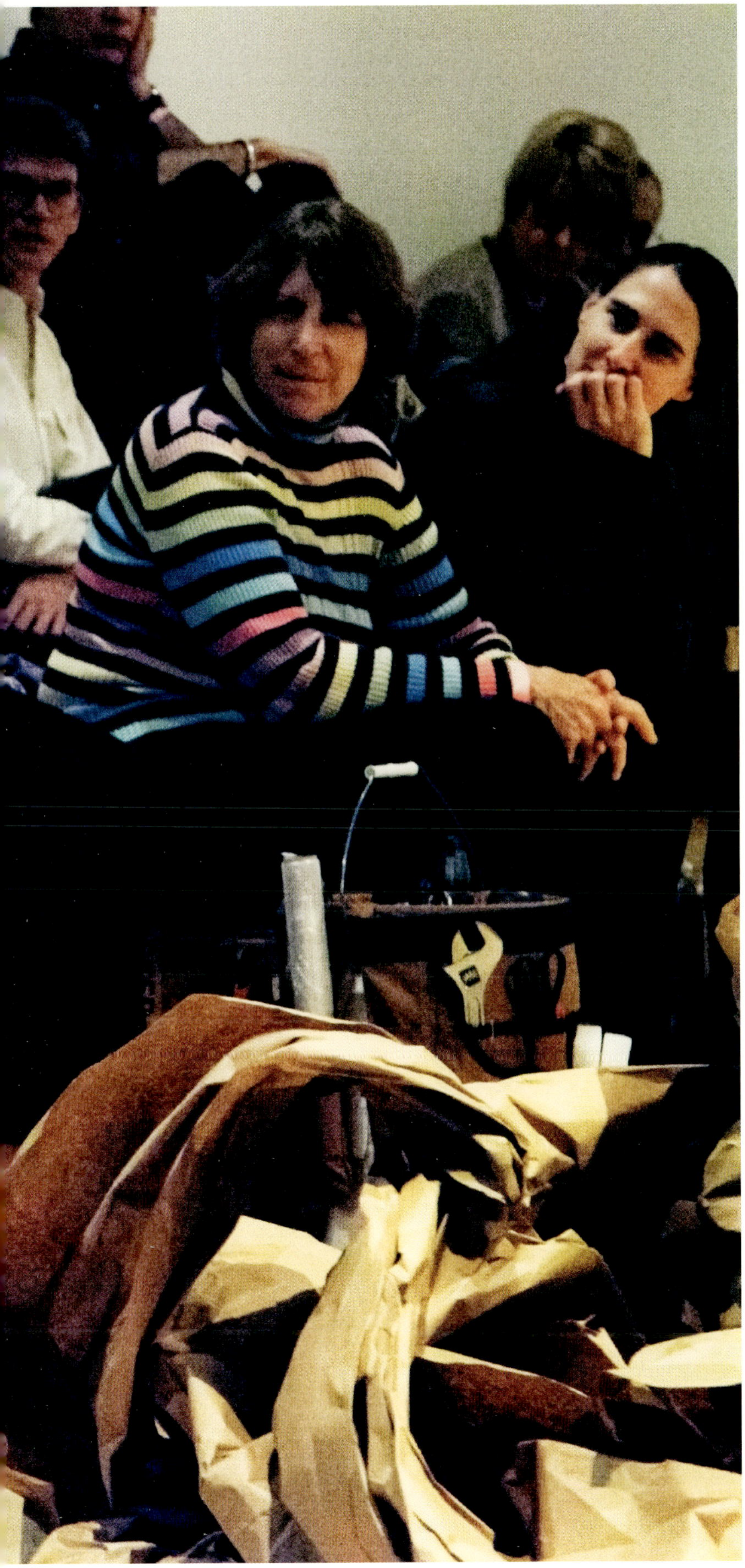

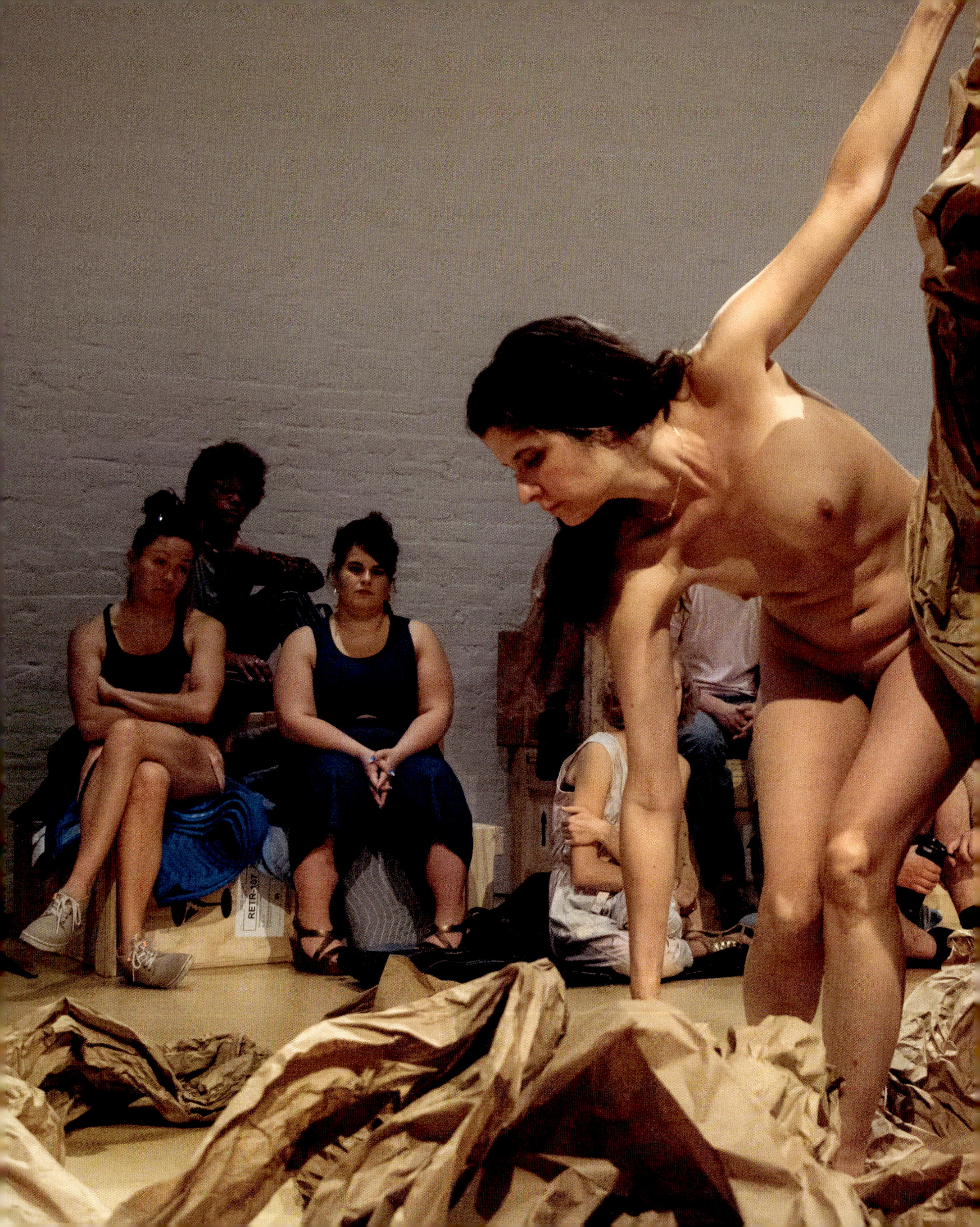
RETR-107

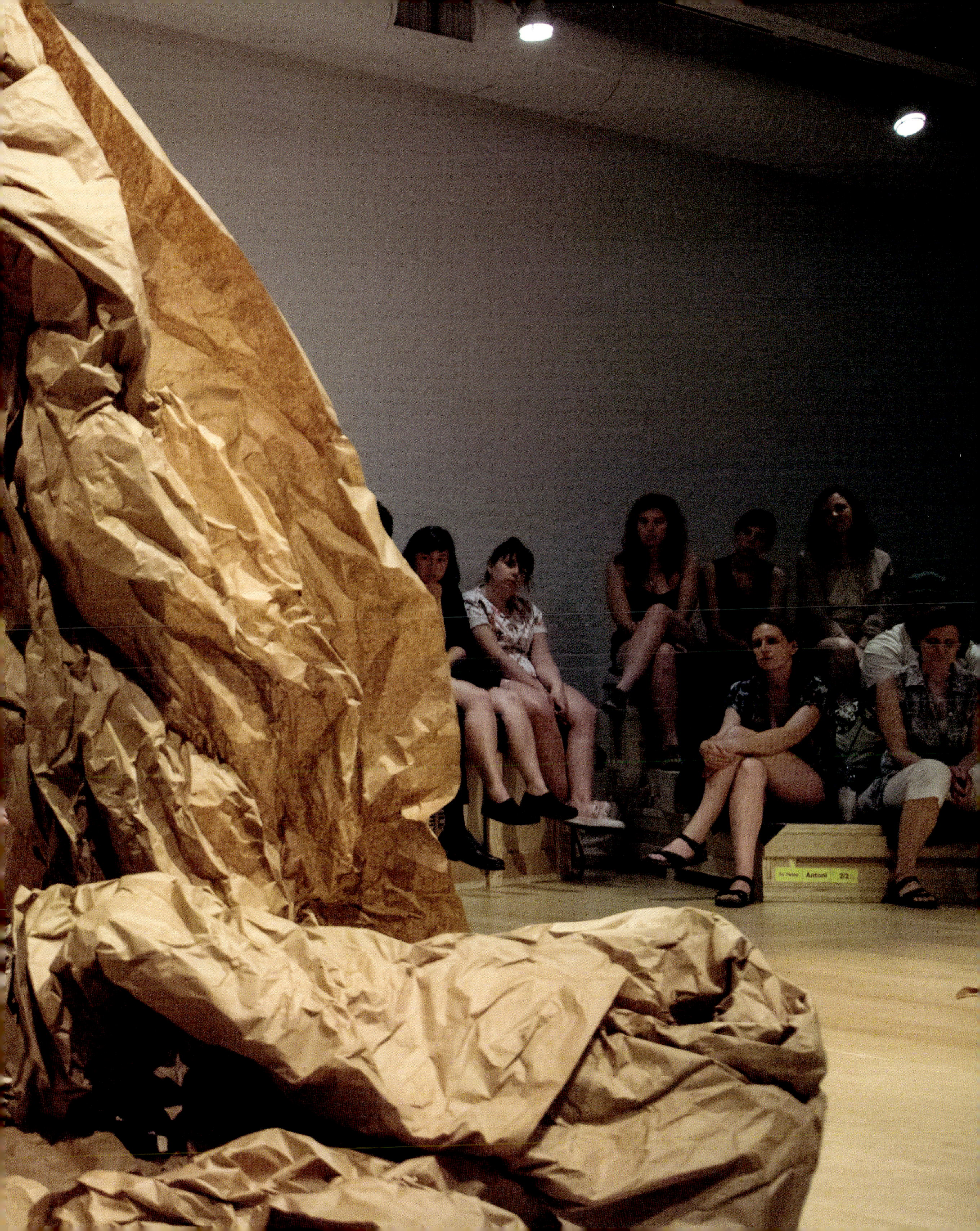
Antoni
2/2

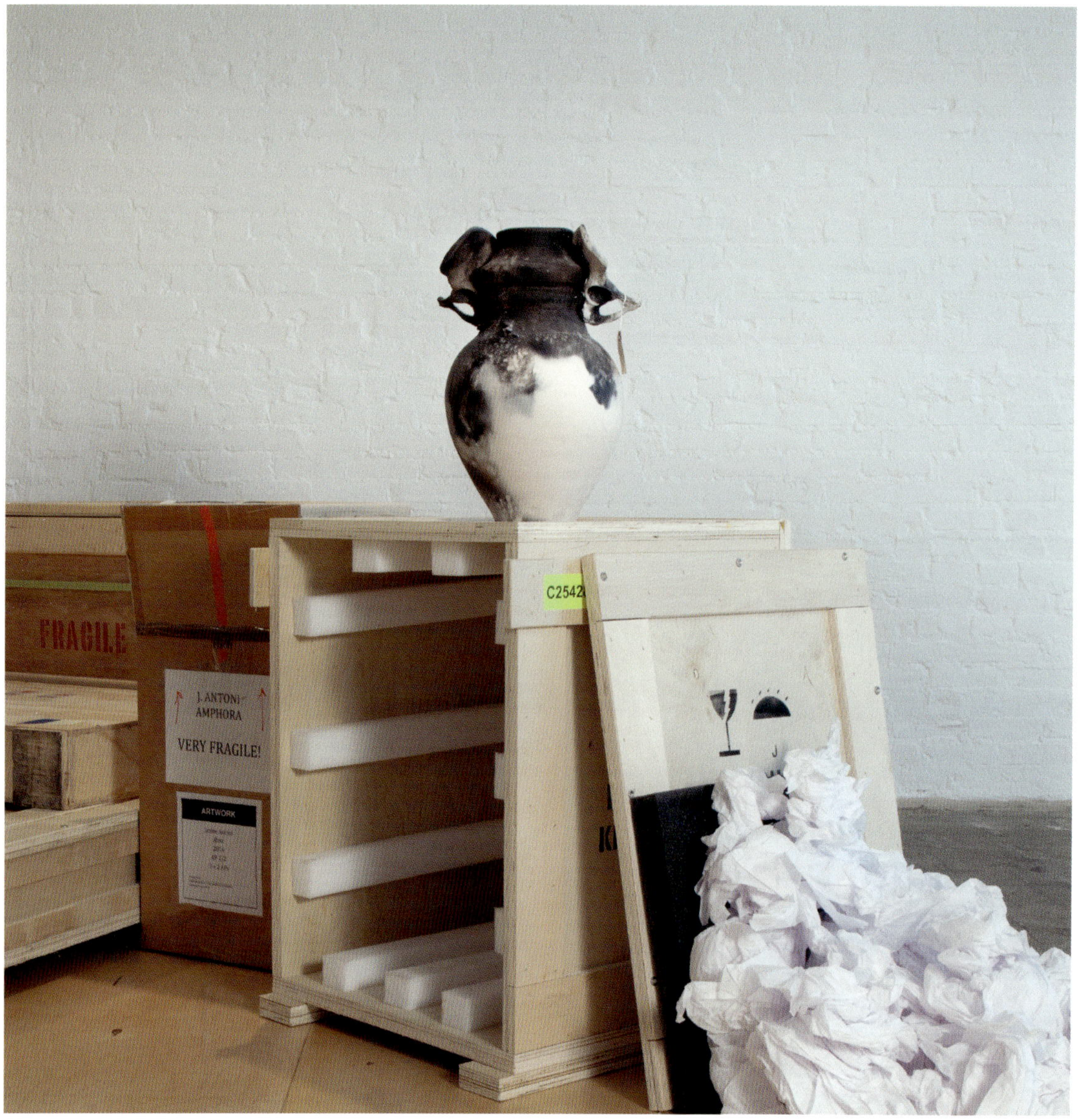
FRAGILE
J. ANTONI AMPHORA
VERY FRAGILE!
ARTWORK
C2542

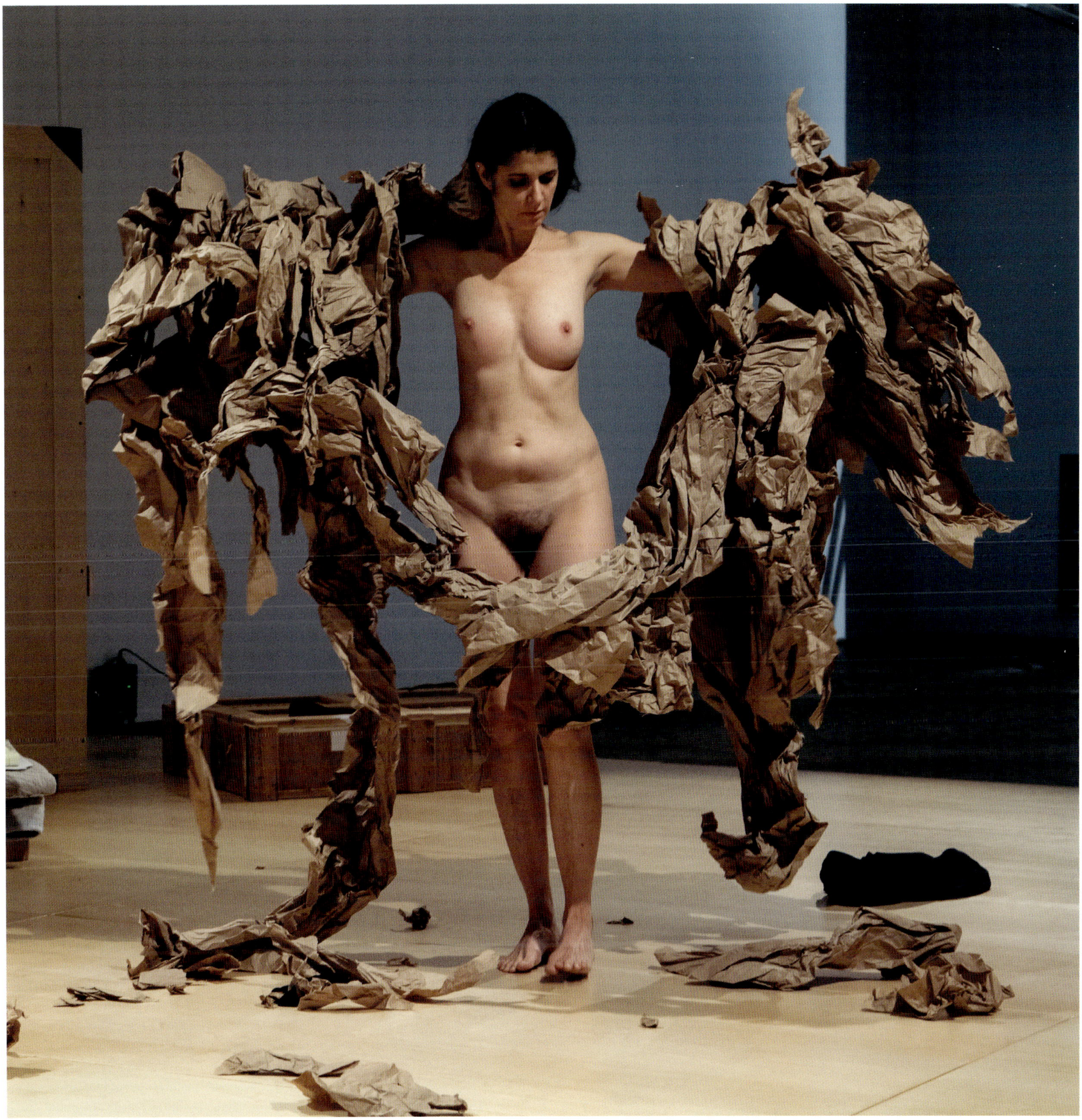

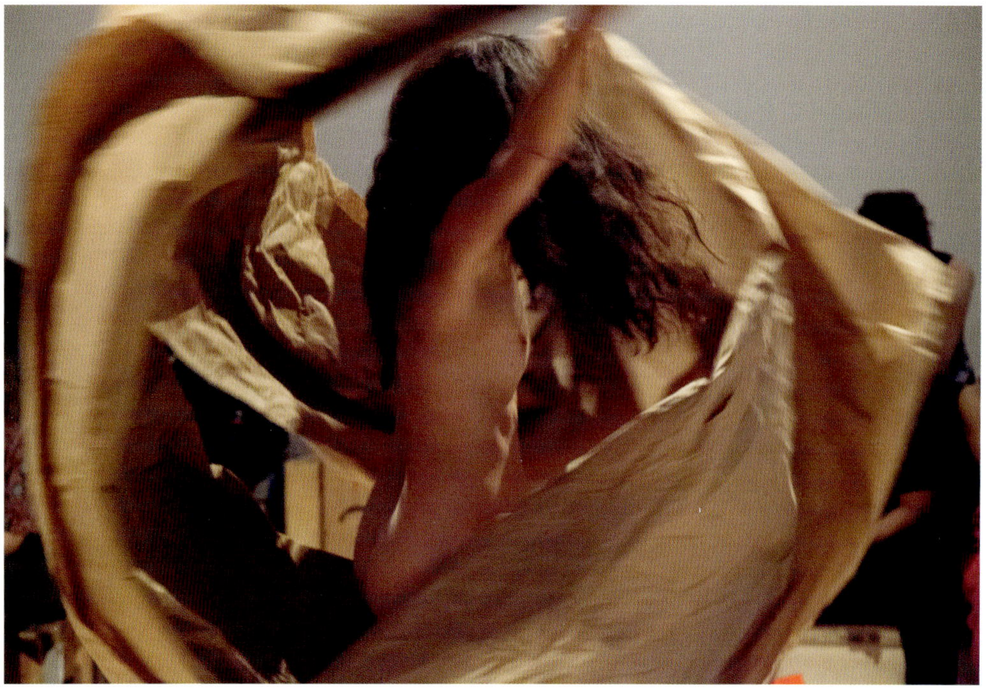

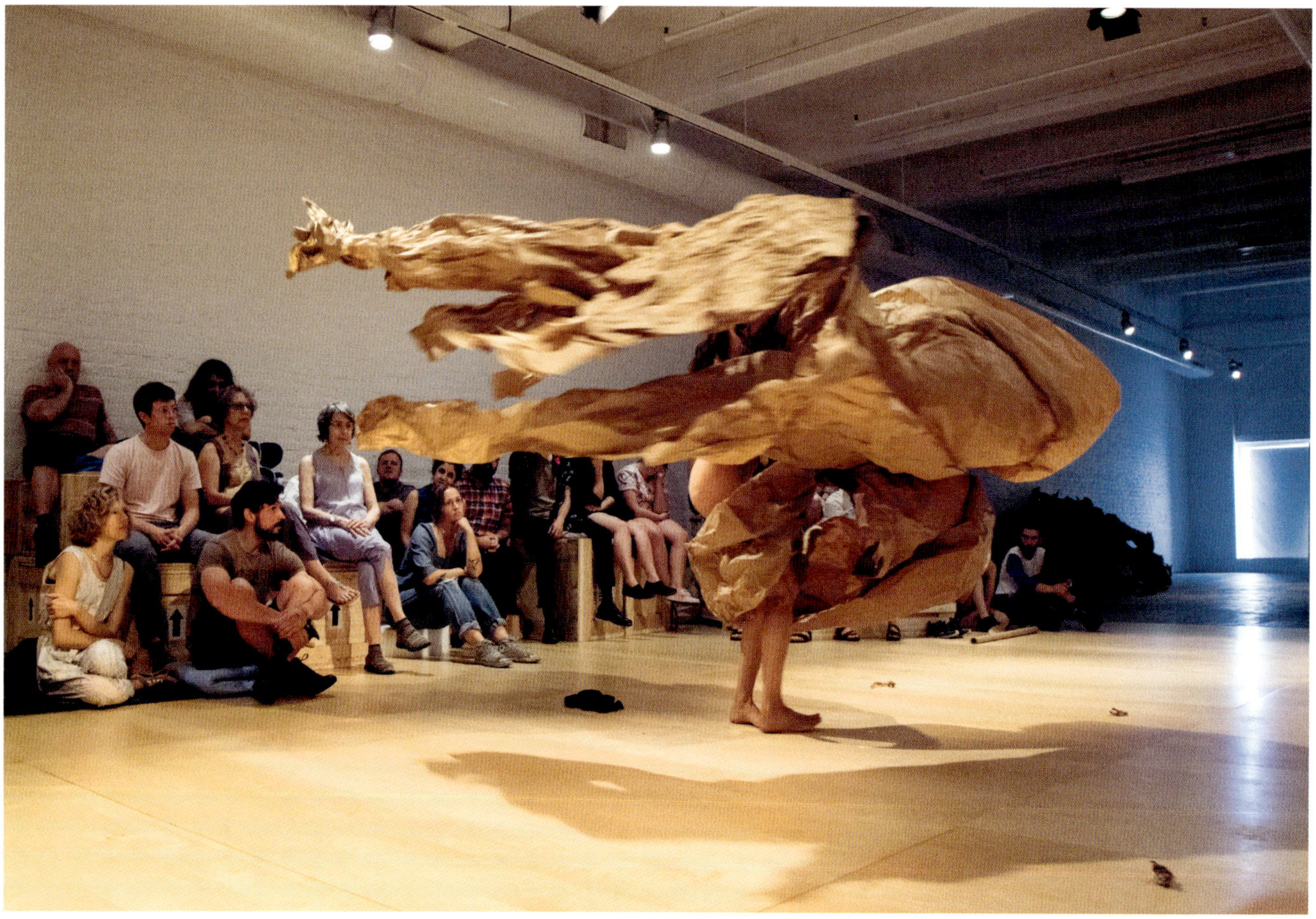

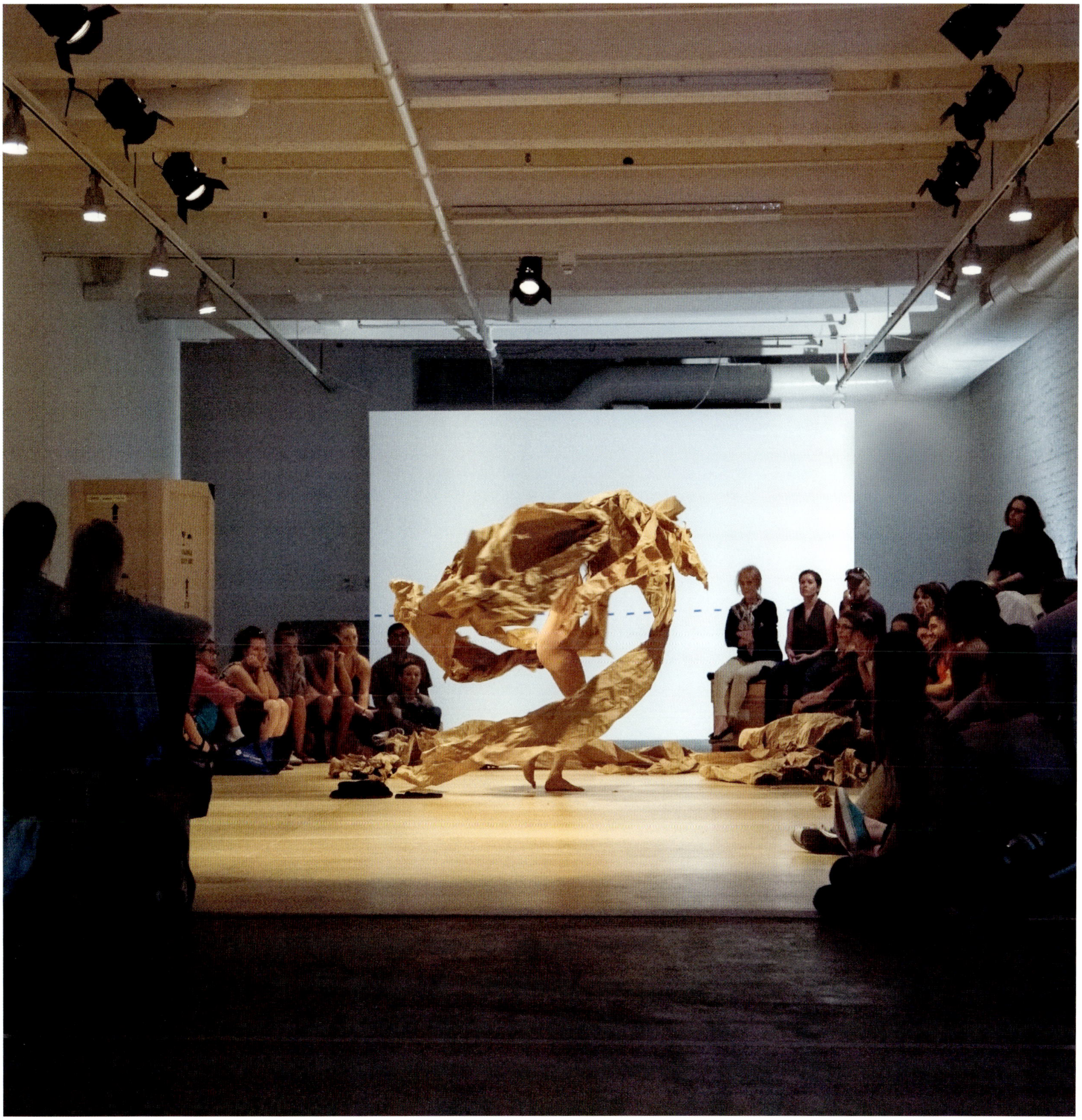

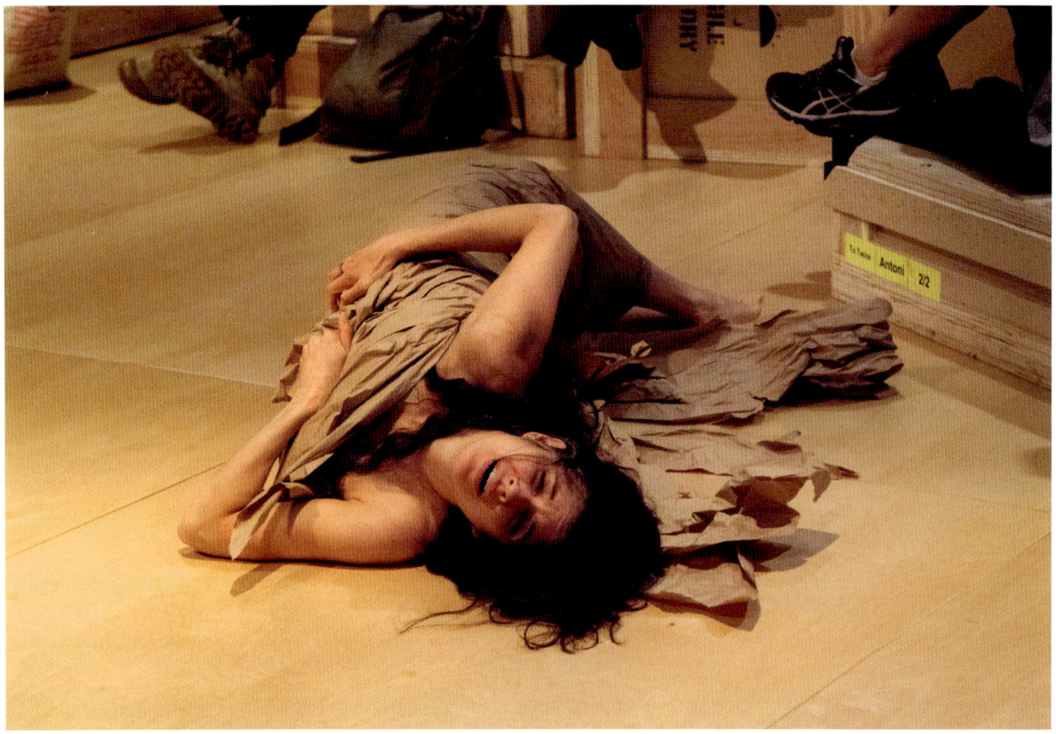
Antoni
2/2

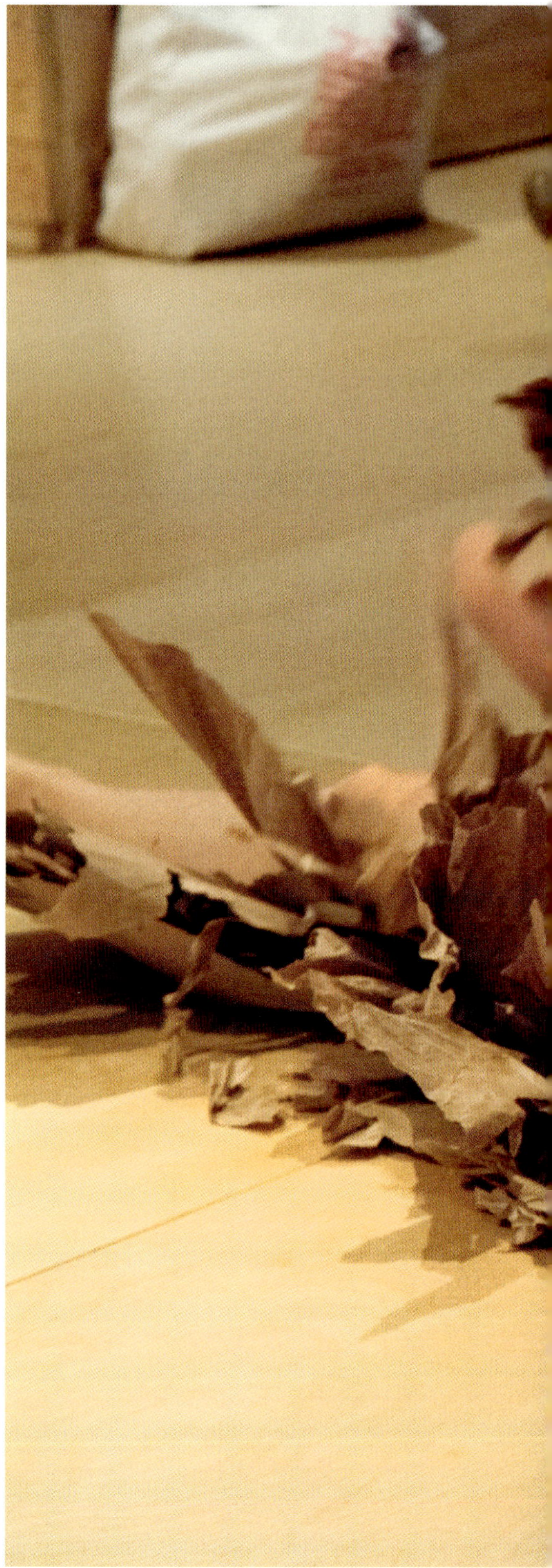

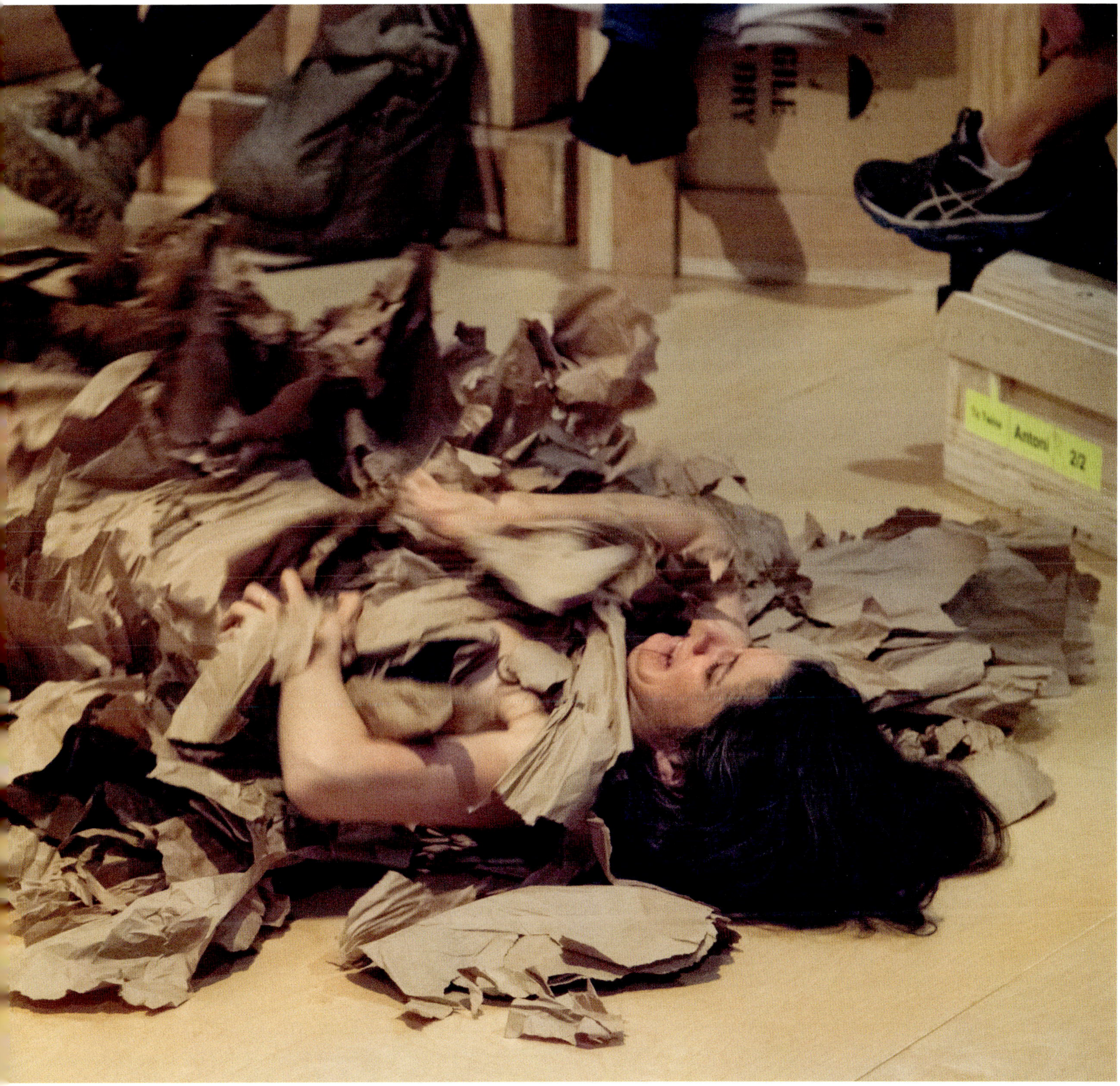
Antoni
2/2

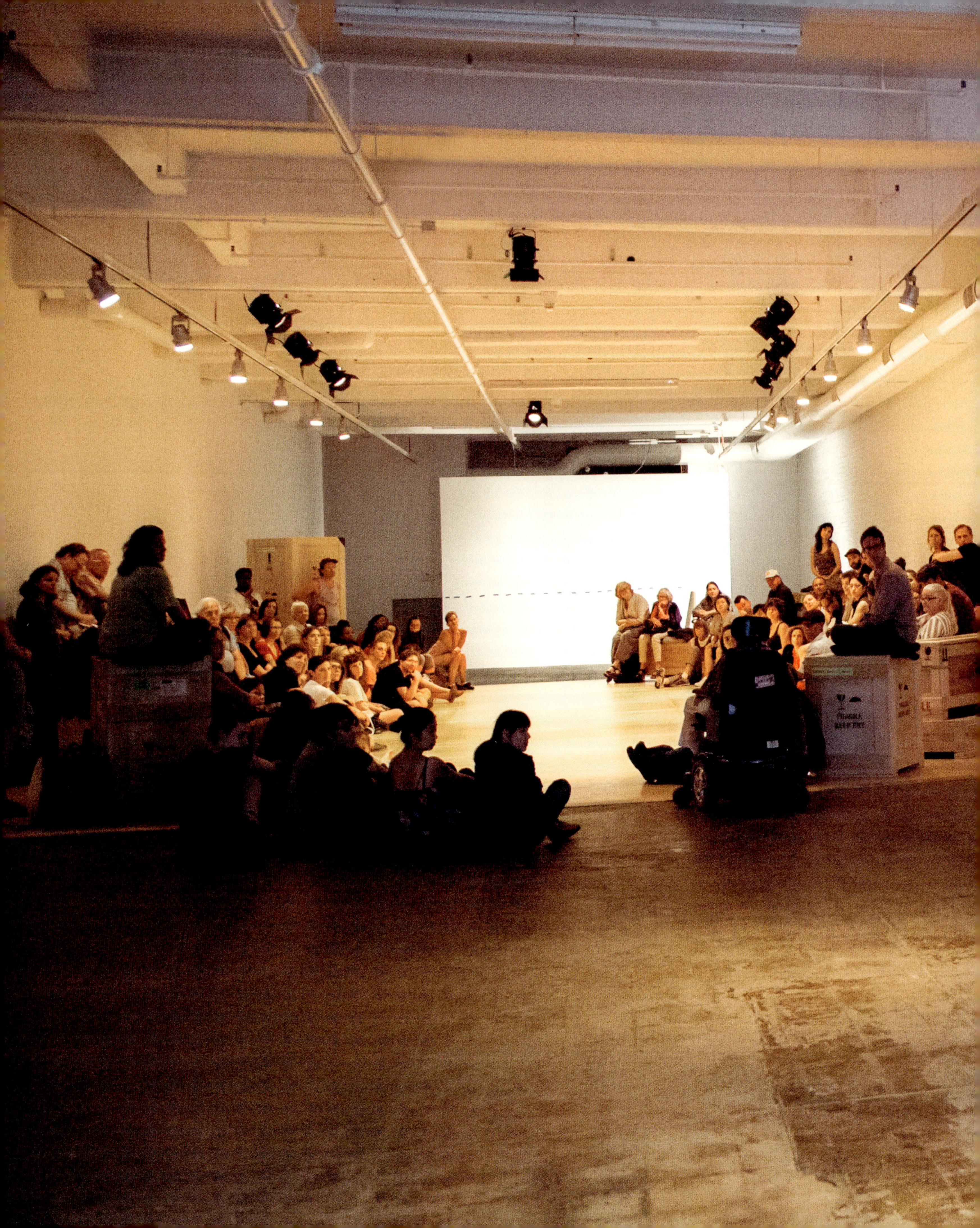

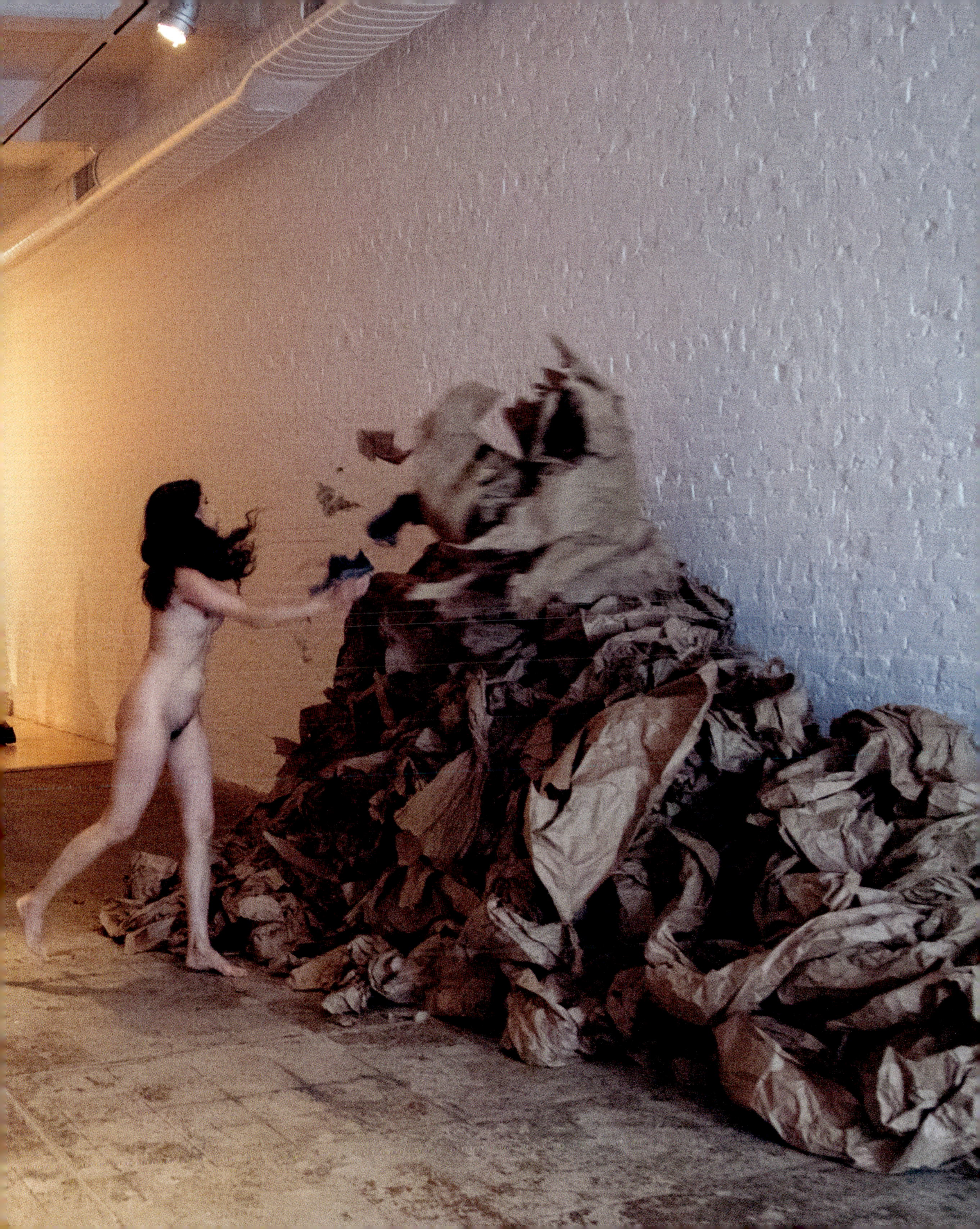

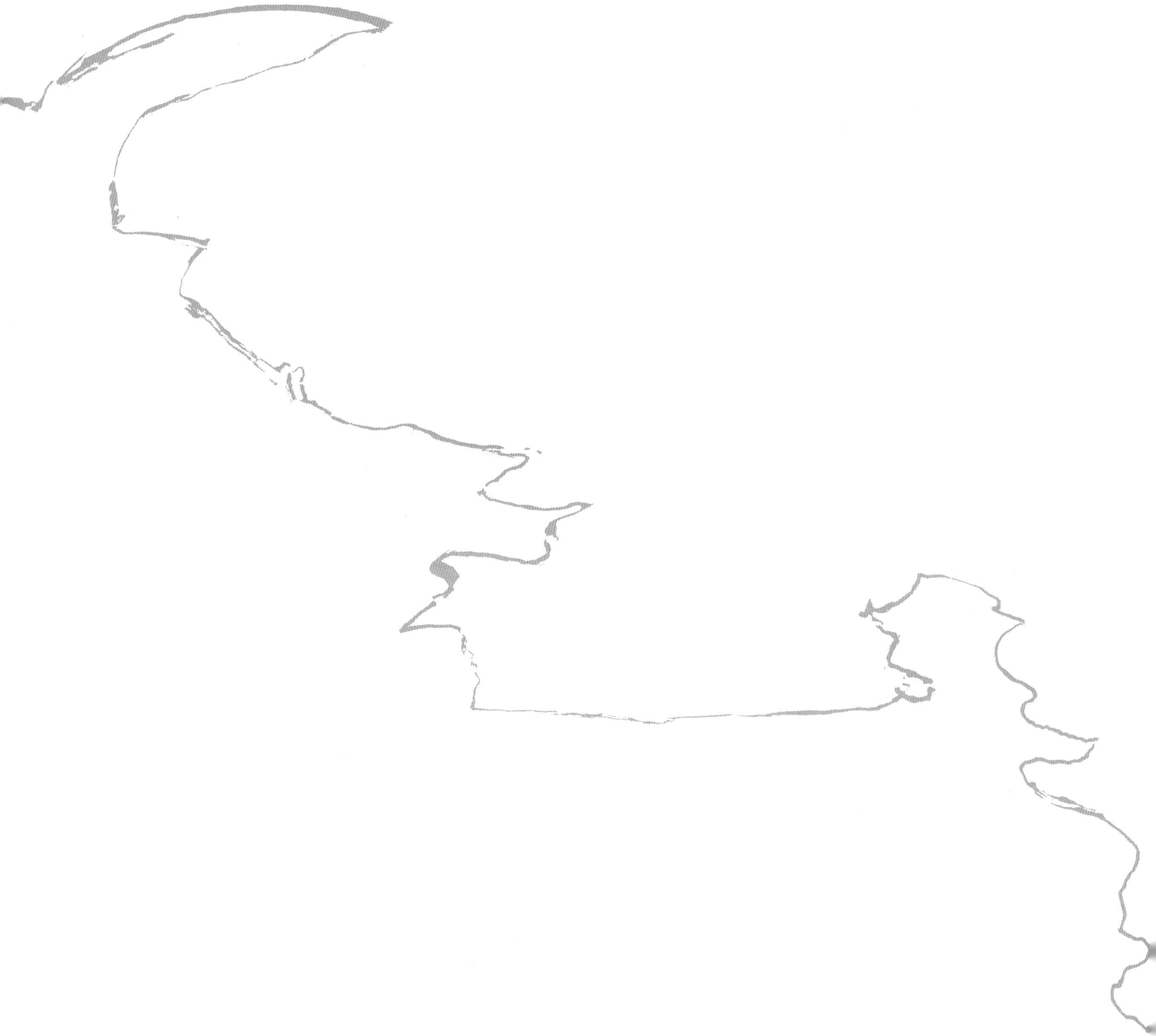

JANINE ANTONI
INGESTING THE WISDOM BODY

Carol Becker

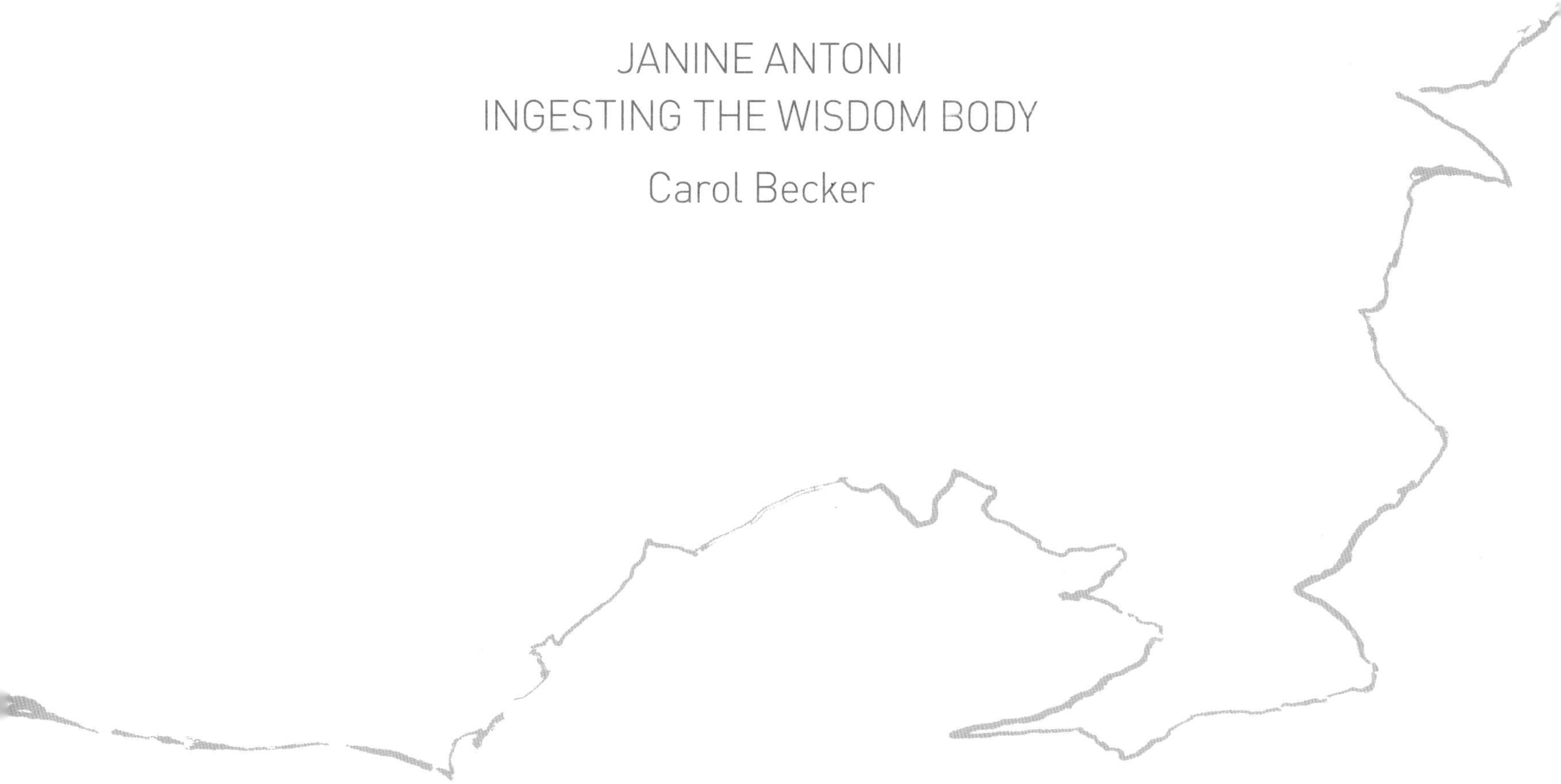

Artists often are chasing after something that sometimes is also chasing after them. At those moments when "the creation stands between the observer and the artist's creativity," it might be best, as D. W. Winnicott suggests, to focus on "the creative impulse itself."[1] In September 2015, when Janine Antoni arrived at the conference "Afterlives: The Persistence of Performance" to present her work, she announced that she would be reading a short selection from "one of her favorite children's books," *The Velveteen Rabbit: Or How Toys Become Real*.[2] Because it is one of my favorites as well, I took special note. It is a story about deep affection, separation, abandonment, redemption and transformation. It is also a story about the time of life when children animate the world around them with ferocity, as they fixate on certain objects that teach them to love and care for something outside themselves.

Antoni positioned herself centrally among the assembled group of artists, writers, and thinkers. She lifted up the book, moving it in a semicircular motion from left to right, so all could see the images, with the familiar gesture of inclusion employed when reading to a group of children. She read from the chapter "The Skin Horse Tells His Story." It begins with a dialogue between a Velveteen Rabbit, a recent addition to the nursery, and a worn stuffed horse whose hair has been "loved off" and whose tail has been pulled out to "string beads." The rabbit, curious about his ontological condition, asks the most senior member of the nursery a question that he has been pondering for some time:

> "What is REAL?" asked the Rabbit ...
> "Real isn't how you are made," said the Skin Horse. "It's a thing that happens to you. When a child loves you for a long, long time, not just to play with, but REALLY loves you, then you become Real."
> "Does it hurt?" asked the Rabbit.
> "Sometimes," said the Skin Horse, for he was always truthful.
> "When you are Real you don't mind being hurt."[3]

Antoni's performative reading brilliantly set the stage for a journey through her early work, much of which has focused on the making of objects — on their transformation from the physical to the metaphysical — and on the impossible primordial human longing to return to an earlier state of consciousness and dependence.

Such concerns and their manifestations in form bring to mind D. W. Winnicott's seminal text *Playing and Reality*. Winnicott observes that children often adopt a "transitional object" — a creative solution to the originary anxiety of dependence and separation.[4] In the earliest stages of development, children often create their own transitional object. It is not usually an articulated "toy" as representational as a velveteen rabbit, for example, but rather a unique condition that infants find around them and imagine into being — comforting textures such as a fuzzy bit of flannel blanket kneaded into a ball, a cord of rubber binding along the edge of a pillow, a frayed spot on the crib's sheet. The found object is something that appeals to the child sensorially and that he or she experiences as an extension of the self, even before the child is aware of the self. As the object gains familiarity, it acquires the magical property of assuaging anxiety. Thus the child is able to sleep and play without worry, having found a creative solution to a challenging, developmental need to experience safety when apart from the mother (or the primary caregiver) and even when completely alone.

As a result, the object garners the child's total devotion. To misplace, lose, or in any way alter it before the child is ready to permit such a transition — even by washing it and changing its texture or scent — can set off the child's sense of loss and an hysterical response. He or she invests deeply in this relationship with the object and, in so doing, makes it into something "real." The child's invention represents an act of independence through creativity at a time of almost complete dependence.

The adoption of stuffed animals, dolls, and toys comes later, as the child begins to negotiate between the objectively real and the imagined. At that time, a child may have many such loved or serially loved objects. Later in development, children mostly abandon these self-constructed intimacies for the expansiveness of the world. Yet, in practice, many people — and many artists (at least in their art making) — never do completely decathect from imaginary, animistic relationships to things. They move in and out of these multiple systems of reality and learn to play in the new symbolic or dream universes they create. In his research, Winnicott observed play and anxiety as polarities of the human experience. If one is anxious it is difficult to play; if one is playing, one is usually not anxious. But if one is able to play through the anxiety, then perhaps one has found a way to live beyond these dualities. Art making, often involving the animism of childhood, allows a relief from anxiety through focused abandon. One can be lost in work, as one can be lost in play.

Freud assumed, because the evolution of the individual mirrors that of the species and vice versa, that beliefs the species once held remain lodged in the unconscious long after the species has supposedly "evolved" beyond them. In Freud's analysis, the ability to access this unconscious world of imagery and symbols is never completely erased. Adults, able to cultivate dreams and the imaginary, often tap into this deep reservoir. Artists in particular play confidently in these interstitial spaces. They hope to entice the viewer to enter into such locations with them, to re-see these images, engage them, and perhaps also to move beyond them, or at least gain a greater understanding of how they might motivate, shape, actualize, or inhibit our actions — individually and collectively. An adult's capacity to play depends in part on his or her ability to suspend the conscious self long enough to engage these images and dreams of the individual and the "collective unconscious" which in Jung's understanding is the repository of those archetypal images, species memories, and associations that haunt myths, fairy tales and our collective dreams.[5] The capacity to vitalize inanimate objects is essential to creating metaphor, symbols, and art. Such imagery can represent the immaterial, and the immaterial can manifest in the material. The wine and the wafer can, for believers, "become" the body and blood of Christ, not just a stand-in for the idea, but rather, the thing itself — an agreed-upon "transubstantiation" of the ephemeral.

Artists such as Janine Antoni consciously choose to evoke this spiritual and psychological dimension that, in some, manifests before the ability to differentiate the real from the imagined. The work of such artists can compel us with its beauty or performativity. It can also strike a deep cord, tapping into a moment in the individual and collective psyche that catapults viewers far back into an early childhood memory of complete dependence that some would rather avoid. With wit and determination, Antoni approaches these collective obsessions that focus on objects and their transubstantiation through projection and animism, attempting to deep-dive into the unconscious and reemerge from the process, back into the world. Rarely have artists revealed their internal process so deliberately or allowed us to be so close to their actual intention. Because the work is both overtly about this subject matter and also carefully, dramatically, and at times humorously executed, we are disarmed and seduced into safely journeying with her into this primal, precarious, and intimate terrain.

In the Beginning

> An interviewer asked Antoni: "Does your art help you cope with your separation anxiety?"
> "My art is all about separation anxiety. I'm obviously working on that issue," Antoni responded.[6]

In her early photographic staging of *Momme* (1995), Antoni mischievously plays with the post-Freudian assumption prevalent in Western and other archetypal systems of thought that there is a collective desire to return to the womb — "the original home," "the uterine paradise," and "the nocturnal bliss of sleep in the unconscious."[7] In Antoni's image the artist's own mother gazes dreamily out a living room window while Antoni hides under her skirt. She rests her head on her mother's lap, creating a bulge so that her mother appears pregnant. One of her long legs sticks out from the garment joining those of her mother resting on the floor. Her mother, complicit in this provocative prank, appears resolved and calm, as in some Renaissance paintings depicting the biblical Annunciation. But Mary's gaze in such paintings can also, at times, convey shock, fear, or incredulity; most often it is filled with patient resignation and humility. The Child is expected. Mary will be the mother. God himself is the Father. All is as it should be. This atmosphere of resolve appears again in Antoni's depiction.

Never one to deliberately mystify her sources, Antoni discussed this provocative image in a 2001 interview with the Aldrich Foundation.[8] She referenced the famous Leonardo da Vinci drawing, *Madonna and Child with St. Anne*. In the foreground of one of Da Vinci's many versions of this image, the Christ Child plays with a small lamb (in another version of the drawing, Da Vinci places John the Baptist as a child in place of the lamb). Mary sits on the

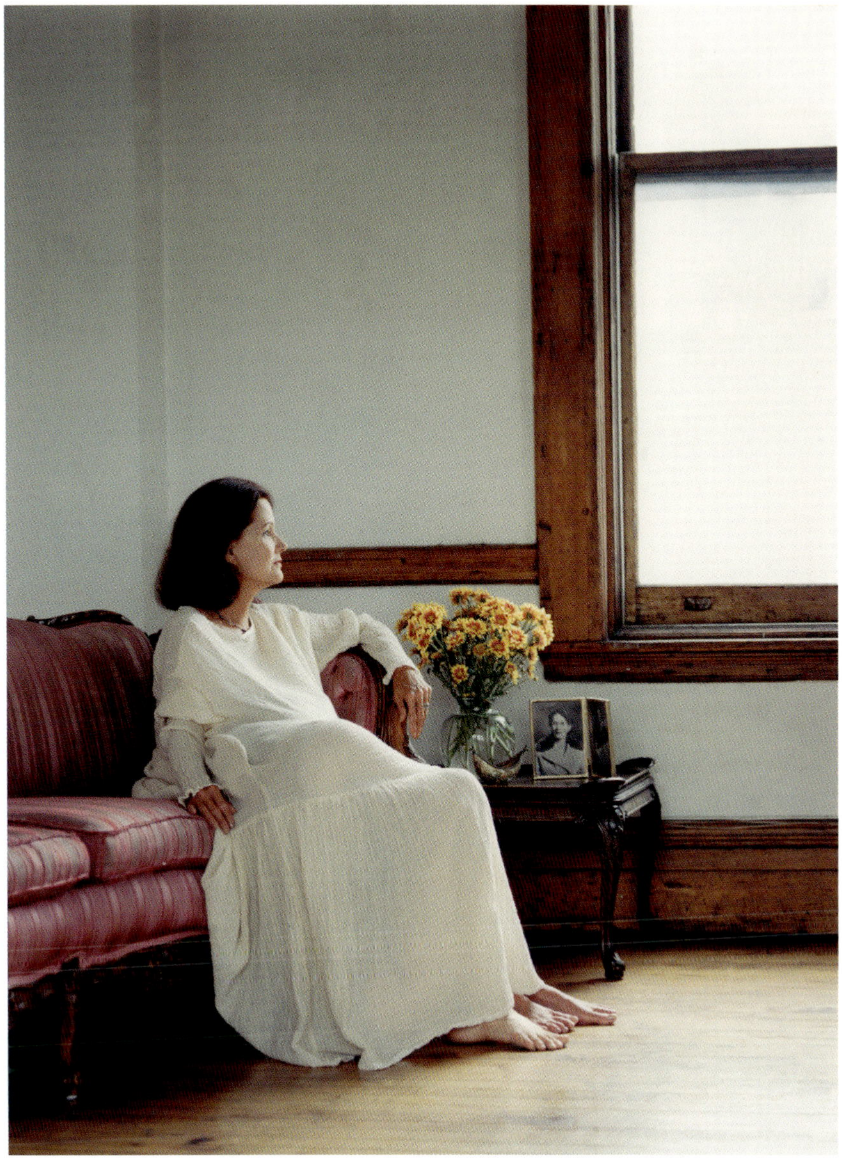

Janine Antoni, *Momme*, 1995. © Janine Antoni. Courtesy of the artist and Luhring Augustine, New York.

lap of her mother, St. Anne, and watches the child. Both women admire the cherubic toddler, who looks up at Mary as she gazes at him. St. Anne looks lovingly towards her daughter and also across to the child. Mary is depicted as large and fleshy, Anne as much more slight (and almost as young as Mary). St. Anne, the most renowned mother in Christian iconography, nevertheless seems comfortable holding the weight of her daughter.

Here too we are reminded that, "the woman's motherliness resides not only in the womb, but also in the seated woman's broad expanse of thigh, her lap on which the newborn child sits enthroned."[9] Da Vinci's image triangulates the gaze of the figures as if to say: "I, the mother of the Mother, see you, Mary, my daughter. I, the Mother of Christ, see you, my child, the Son of God. You are known to me and to my mother. You are safe. My loving gaze and hers each hold you in consciousness and make you 'real.'"

Da Vinci appears to understand fully that the mother's gaze has deep psychological importance to the well-being of the child and the species. Without it, and without the connectivity it represents, the possibility for the child's comfort, play, and creativity is rendered impossible or is certainly diminished. A child deprived of this affirmation will forever seek that which was withheld, the simple reassurance of entering life with the full sense of one's own being affirmed and intact. A child who has received the completely enveloping look, as has the Christ Child in Da Vinci's depiction, can play in front of his mother and her mother, confident of his security and potential independence in the world. This transmission of ontological certainty to the child must occur early on, through the focus of the biological mother or of the person or persons occupying this essential role.

Of this particular attentiveness, psychoanalyst Josh Cohen writes:

> In rocking, stroking, touching and talking to her, a mother gradually and imperceptibly confers the security of a shape on the dizzying obscurity of her baby's world. The more this physical and emotional attentiveness is lacking, the more unintegration is liable to shade into *disintegration*, into a traumatic sense of the absence of any support for her very being, felt as a fall into a bottomless void.[10]

When Winnicott writes of the "good enough mother," he is referring to just this sense that, if successful, the "mother," or the person in the role of mother, allows the baby to feel that his or her actions are controlled completely by desire (i.e., that there is no separation between the mother's breast and the child). The first primal and essential illusion is that the breast is not outside the self but is, in fact, of the self. The "good enough mother" is one who negotiates this terrain well, but she must also be able to anticipate the rupture of this sense of oneness and the resultant "disillusionment," the acceptance of reality, when the breast is taken away during the weaning process.

Winnicott assumes that the "task" of "reality acceptance" is an ongoing process that humans negotiate throughout their entire lives, while they attempt to relate inner and outer reality.[11] There are several locations that can serve as "intermediate" spaces helping people to cope with this integration. Art can be one of these areas where illusion, disillusion, and reality converge, potentially creating a safe space within which to re-experience, or even to willingly get lost in, the imaginary restaging of this personal but collective original trauma. In *Momme,* Antoni seems to be announcing: "I am trying to go back inside. I really am, but look how long my legs have grown, how impossible and absurd is my attempt." Because she assumes we share this desire, if only at an unconscious level, the artist can confidently speak to that collective longing for "the mystical union in which there is no loneliness."[12]

In 2001 Antoni created an exhibition called *The Girl Made of Butter.* The eponymous title is taken from a folk tale about a girl made of butter who can only remain alive if her mother is constantly vigilant in dousing her daughter's butter skin with cold water to protect it from the "heat" of the male gaze. When her mother leaves the room (or withdraws her love and attentiveness) to prepare food for the suitors, the girl is left alone to deflect their desire. Unable to do so and not confident enough to hold onto the solidity, shape, and boundaries of her own form, she slowly melts.[13] Antoni's exhibition focused on the transition from complete dependence on the breast to the substitution of cow's milk and latex nipples, marking the moment when the child must begin to become autonomous, to develop (or not)

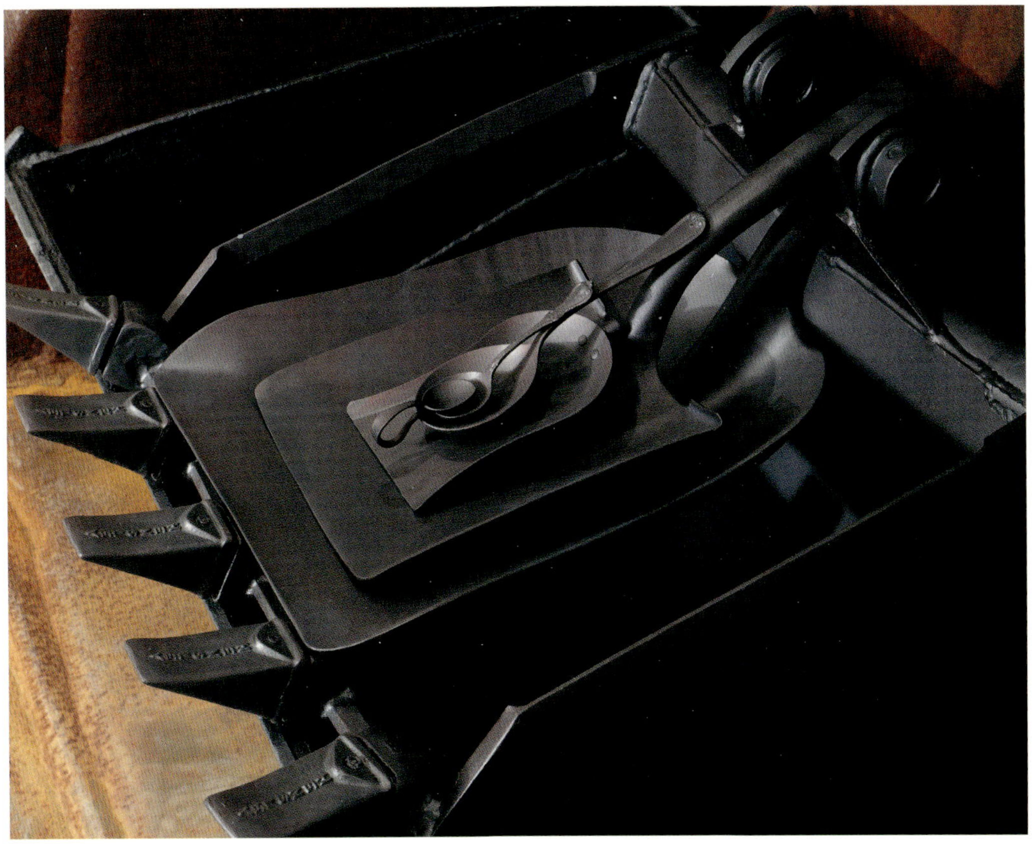

Janine Antoni, *Cradle*, 1999. © Janine Antoni. Courtesy of the artist and Luhring Augustine, New York.

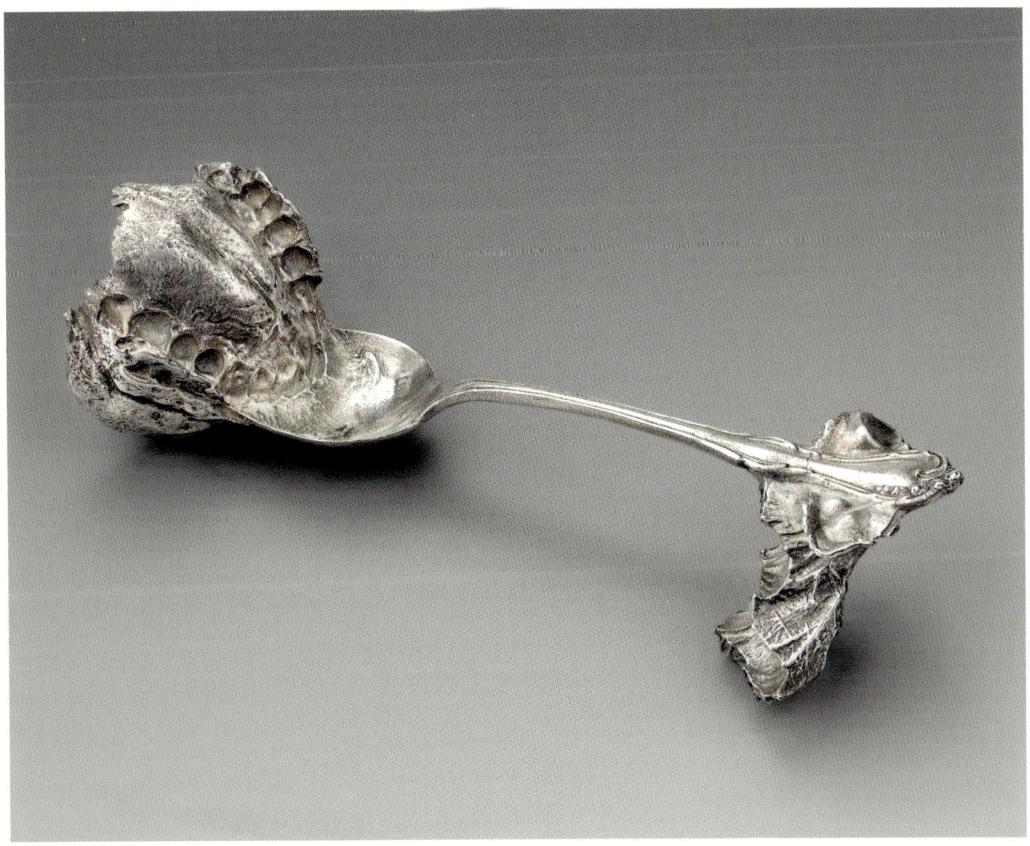

Janine Antoni, *Umbilical*, 2000. © Janine Antoni. Courtesy of the artist and Luhring Augustine, New York.

the ability to survive on the food of the world alone. Reflecting on this moment of transition, Antoni created an "empty loop spoon" as part of the piece entitled *Cradle*. This utensil, she explains, "is designed for the baby to begin feeding itself," marking another significant moment of "separation."[14]

In this and other early works, Antoni explicitly immersed herself in the needs, desires and expectations of the child's body or the body of the adult attempting to reconcile the vulnerability of the child within. Grounded in sculptural representations of this quite literal loneliness of spirit, the artist often appeared to be seeking a mystical union in what poet William Blake might call the "mundane shell" of matter — the earthly, physical, cognitive plane that often separates itself, and therefore us, from the poetic, symbolic, or spiritual dimension. By extending her physical body beyond its assumed adult boundaries, Antoni seems to want to return herself and her audience to the deep psychic spaces of an idealized or remembered connectivity out of which emptiness, need, longing, and memory inevitably arise.

In *Momme* and other early embodied works, Antoni focused on the body's relationship to itself and to society in extreme, poignant, and, again, often humorous ways, extending the sculptural to the performative as she famously: mops the floor in big, bold swirls with her hair soaked in black dye metaphorically named after the Clairol hair dye that served as paint (*Loving Care*); gnaws at enormous blocks of chocolate and lard, leaving her teeth marks on these massive blocks (*Gnaw*); is lowered into a bathtub of lard, displacing and then extracting her weight into a large cube (*Eureka*); licks representational chocolate busts of her head and neck until the facial features disappear; bathes with soap sculptures of herself which she molds as they dissolve *(Lick and Lather);* touches the eyeball of her husband with her tongue (*Mortar and Pestle*). All of this was achieved while playing with classical references again, as in the piece *Coddle*, a photographic work, displayed in an oval Victorian frame, in which the artist, with her long dark hair loose around her face, strikes a traditional Madonna and Child pose, adoringly and irreverently cradling her own leg in her lap as if it were the Baby Jesus.

There is often a sense of dematerialization — a diminishing of the physical object with her mouth or her body, as with the chocolate, soap and lard pieces — and the churning out of metaphor, as laborious physical acts assume a more ephemeral meaning. In *Gnaw*, the removed chocolate was cast into heart-shaped packaging for chocolate candy; the lard was mixed with beeswax to make lipstick. Yet no matter how gravity-bound the resultant objects or gestures may appear, the process of interacting with them demands an act of transformation, not just on the material plane but on the spiritual plane as well. One is forced, for example, to ask what do these giant, edible, minimalist cubes represent? Are they blocks in consciousness that need to be worn away? What does it mean to ingest parts of one's own image or to "coddle" one's own leg? Is the child finding fulfillment in her own body? Are the actions motivated by a healthy narcissism gone awry? Or is the work a play on all of this? If there is an unconscious rebus, pun, or allusion to note here, it takes a moment to announce itself. And sometimes we simply need to be told: Why would you lick your husband's eyeball? "To know the taste of his vision."[15]

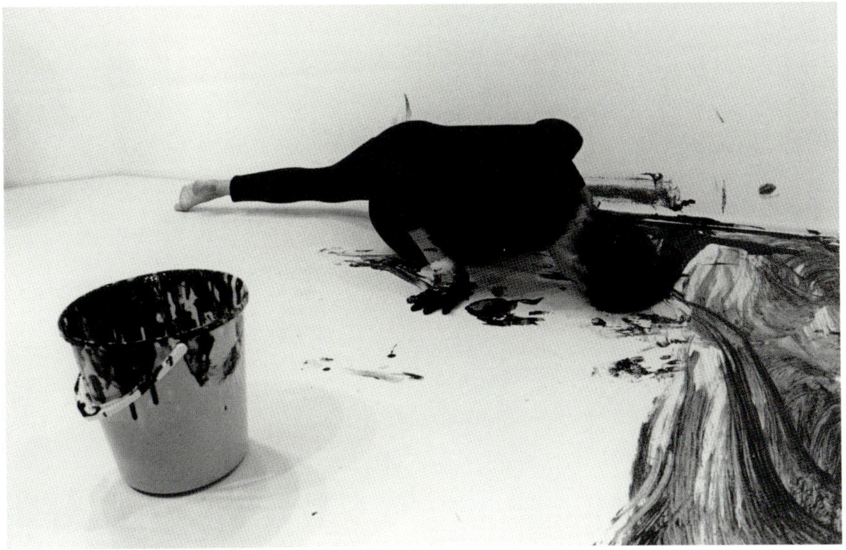

Janine Antoni, *Loving Care*, 1993. Photo: Prudence Cumming Associates at Anthony d'Offay Gallery, London, 1993. © Janine Antoni. Courtesy of the artist and Luhring Augustine, New York.

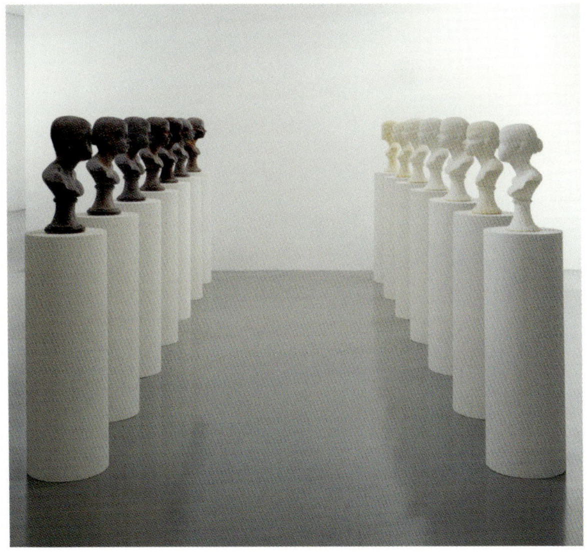

Janine Antoni, *Lick and Lather* (installation view), 1993. Photo: Lee Stalsworth, Hirshhorn Museum and Sculpture Garden, Washington, D.C., 1999. © Janine Antoni. Courtesy of the artist and Luhring Augustine, New York.

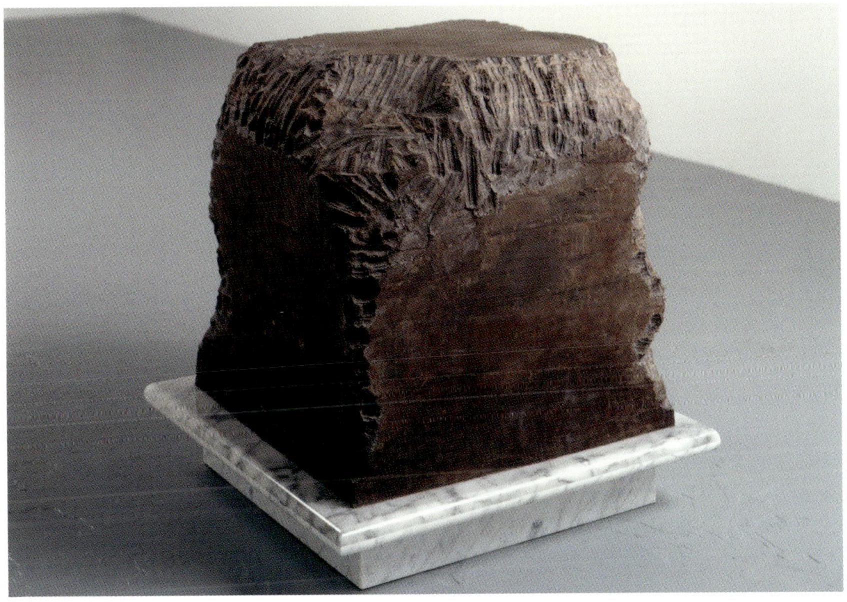

Janine Antoni, *Gnaw* (detail), 1992. © Janine Antoni. Courtesy of the artist and Luhring Augustine, New York.

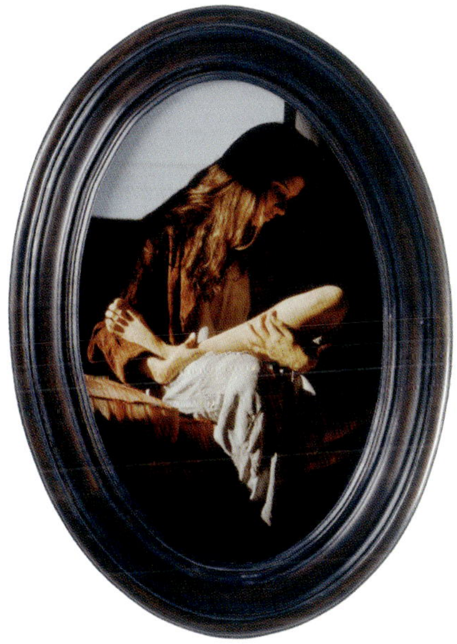

Janine Antoni, *Coddle*, 1998. © Janine Antoni. Courtesy of the artist and Luhring Augustine, New York.

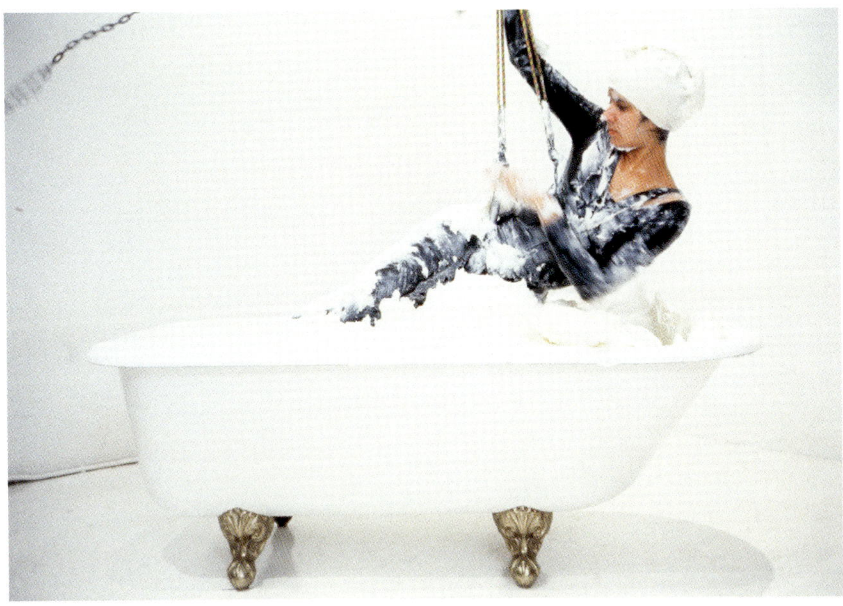

Janine Antoni making *Eureka*, 1993. Photo: Scott Cohen. © Janine Antoni Courtesy of the artist and Luhring Augustine, New York.

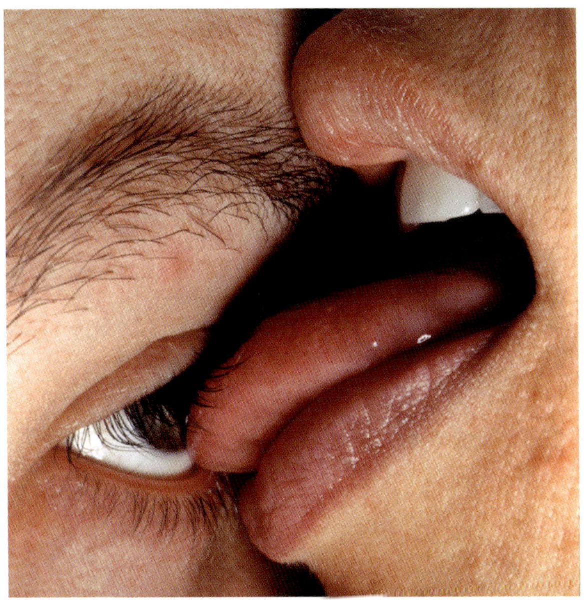

Janine Antoni, *Mortar and Pestle*, 1999. © Janine Antoni. Courtesy of the artist and Luhring Augustine, New York.

While awaiting the recognition of meaning in these works, the viewer is successfully disoriented, and/or physically engaged enough to react, and, perhaps, to give oneself over to whatever might arise. The element of surprise in art making that jostles us out of the day-to-day experience, often touches on these hidden moments of revelation or dream remembrances, revealing how we stitch the world together for ourselves, one encounter and memory at a time. Winnicott refers to this quotation from Milner, who studied the relationship between play and "symbol-formation":

> Moments when the original poet in each of us created the outside world for us, by finding the familiar in the unfamiliar, are perhaps forgotten by most people; or else they are guarded in some secret place of memory because they were too much like visitations of the gods to be mixed with everyday thinking.[16]

For her 2015 Luhring Augustine show *From the Vow Made,* Antoni returned to non-cognitive body memory. *Honey Baby* — a collaboration between Antoni and Stephen Petronio, with videographer Kirsten Johnson, and composer Tom Laurie — recreated yet another representation of the prenatal period. A naked, male dancer (Nick Sciscione) floated weightlessly in viscous liquid (50 pounds of honey), which was a stand-in for amniotic fluid, as Antoni readily admits. Sciscione, a perfectly-formed adult dancer (surely not an undifferentiated fetus), dreamily and uncannily churned around in an interior space which resembled a turbine, a tunnel entrance, a passageway, or a somewhat rigid womb. He did not appear to feel trapped, distressed, or eager to exit the space or to enter the world. Rather, he seemed to be relishing his condition, content to defy gravity in the globular fluid, enveloped in the swooshing sound of a reverberating heartbeat. Within this cylindrical space, he also appeared caught in a dreamlike state, as if in the repetitive cycle of birth and rebirth — Samsara — the rack of illusion that harnesses and seduces most humans, as Buddhists believe, so that they are mesmerized and unable to escape.

This large video projection at first appeared in contrast with the rest of the exhibition in form and content. It seemed perhaps more overtly connected to the themes of the early work and to the artist's absorption with returning to a place of origin. But in fact this strange womb-like image also mirrored the collective impact of the other sculptures in the exhibition that allude to the evolution and disintegration of the body and the ways in which singular limbs are constructed to make a whole, both in reality and in the imaginary. Luminous, uniform body parts, cast in polyurethane resin and sanded to resemble sea glass, create equally unexpected juxtapositions while allowing light to shine through: a bony skeleton leg crosses another thick with flesh and muscle; a head sits atop a rib cage, listening; a coccyx fits in the palm of a hand. All parts are lusciously white and not visibly specific to any particular body, although those representative of flesh and bones were cast from Antoni's body. Rather, they are meant to reference the *milagros* found in Catholic churches (called *tamata* in Greek Orthodox churches) — amulets that are often hung from the ceilings of such churches or on statues of saints as meditations or as grateful offerings when prayers have been answered. These amulets call attention to a specific ailment or condition and function as miniature body parts in need of healing. They remind us that spirit can work through physical objects to fix that which is broken. Antoni playfully reimagines these objects, relocating their identities in relation to each other, so that the inside of the body meets its outside, and is literally "grafted" to its environment.[17]

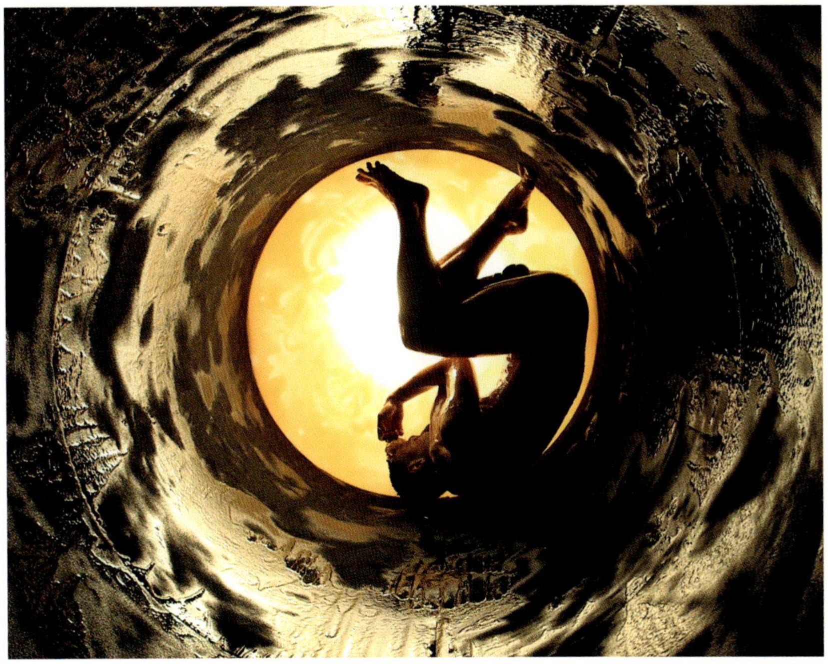

Janine Antoni and Stephen Petronio, *Honey Baby* (video still), 2013. © Janine Antoni and Stephen Petronio. Courtesy of the artists and Luhring Augustine, New York.

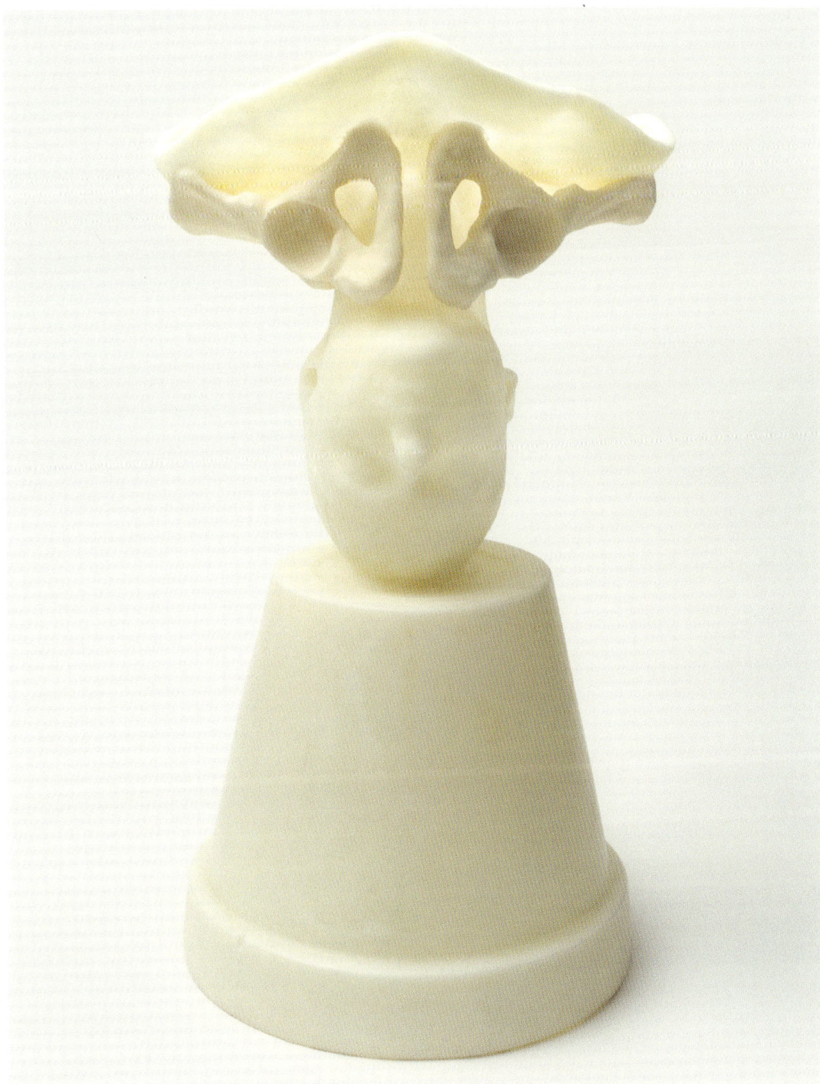

Janine Antoni, *to channel*, 2015. © Janine Antoni. Courtesy of the artist and Luhring Augustine, New York.

In *From the Vow Made*, the body turns in and around itself, perhaps attempting to know itself as it never truly can. A cast female pelvis shows the moment of "crowning," the dramatic and decisive event when a baby's head reaches the top of the mother's pelvis and is "crowned" by her pelvic bones. The mother welcomes the child into the world as a sovereign, sporting a crown. He or she then will be "enthroned" when seated on her lap to be fed. Here the body seems stripped down to its most basic forms, so that we might be led to ask: "How does the body actually evolve? How does it come to be organized with such functionality? How can we be so agile when the structures that hold us in place appear so fragile, albeit gracefully designed? Without this upright structure, we would crawl on the ground like amphibians. And yet as much as this reference to the body reminds us of life, it also signals death, when the flesh that has wrapped the bones in place disintegrates and the structural relationships holding us together come undone. From the skeleton we are formed and to the skeleton we will return. These are the revered bones, the relics, the sacred locations where meaning is forged as spirit and matter converge.

Antoni has always sought to connect deeply with the "invisible social body, the audience" so that together they might experience all parts of the self — physical, psychic, and spiritual — simultaneously.[18] This evolving process of embodying has become even more urgent and unique now that the species appears to want to exit the body, to live virtually, to project its image out into the world for recognition continuously, while aspiring to rid itself of the messiness of physical decay and death. As this desire to escape the bounds of the physical body has become a ubiquitous cultural phenomenon, Antoni appears to have made an even greater commitment to the knowledge that resides in a body, waiting to be read.

Her extraordinary and relatively recent relationship (2012) with artist, dancer, choreographer and visionary Anna Halprin has aided Antoni in this process. In their collaboration, Halprin can be understood as the embodiment of a powerful artist-mother for the powerful artist-child, a mentor who can free the creative self and the performing self from the weight of the karmic past and from the child's individual familial memory. The relationship of teacher-student and artist-artist can best be understood through the Buddhist term "transmission," a psychic and spiritual exchange across space, time, and age that can occur when the wisdom body (the highest state of consciousness) of a seeker meets the wisdom body of a true teacher and is able to absorb the teacher's knowledge into his or her own consciousness. As Robert Thurman has written, "Such a being, whatever his or her form, is the focal node of a field in which other beings find maximal opportunities for their own evolutionary advancement."[19] The mentor, willing to share his or her knowledge, is the key element that makes the teachings "practicable" for the seeker. He or she can appear in multiple forms and "in whatever way tames whomsoever."[20]

Winnicott might say that such figures create a "holding environment," a safe, timeless place, such as that of the mother holding the child in physical space, or the psychoanalyst holding the psyche of the analysand in mental space, so that the unconscious self (which comprehends the world in symbols and dreams) and the wisdom self (which is perfectly intuitive and has lived hidden in deep consciousness for some time) can encounter a true teacher.[21] In the meeting between Halprin and Antoni, Halprin offered Antoni the gift of transmitting her own, uniquely evolved artistic practice; the dances, movements, choreographic events, strategies, and methodologies developed over decades while collaborating with many other trained dancers and novice groups in private and public spheres. In retrospect, it seems inevitable that they would encounter each other; the wonder is that it took so long.

In 2008, Antoni, a quintessential and strong performer, began to dance more seriously, and soon dance was occupying a greater portion of her creative life. She put Marley dance flooring in her studio in 2009 and invited choreographers to create new work in her own art-making space. Dance became a way to venture beyond the object. "As I move I receive visions of potential artworks," says Antoni. "It is very curious, as though my ideas are lodged in my body, and, through movement, they come out."[22] Antoni attended a workshop with Halprin at Esalen in 2011. But too shy to say who she was or what she needed, she waited. A year later, Antoni wrote to Halprin to tell her how much the workshop had meant to her creative life. Halprin quickly responded that she was familiar with Antoni's work and wondered why Antoni hadn't introduced herself during the workshop session. Halprin asked her to visit the next time she was in San Francisco. Antoni soon left for California.

The Journey

> The advanced levels of the Buddha's teachings emphasize the union of two interrelated features that intertwine with every experience of mind. These are penetrating insight … and skillful means.[23]

Buddhist philosophy offers important insight into the complexity of how knowledge is passed along, how lineage is created, how one apprentices one's consciousness to that of another, and how one moves from psychic dependence to independence through the proximity of another person. This process of transmission is particularly significant when talking about artists whose influence on each other can be multilayered and profound, offering permission to venture into previously inaccessible form and content. As a seeker moves independently through the world, he or she relies on intuitive perception to make the best choices in every situation and to do so with the skills acquired through the teacher's rigorous training. Both attributes are surely invaluable to an artist. But such knowledge is not passively acquired. Buddhist teachings often state that it is not enough to sit by the "fire" of the teacher's wisdom to feel the warmth; the student must also be *set on fire and become the fire itself.* In order to receive wisdom, to burn away the misconceptions of the past — the illusions that hold back consciousness — to transmit tradition and encourage a wiser consciousness to emerge, the flame must leap from one to another. Heat is essential to the process of transmitting knowledge, just as it is to the "brooding" that a hen might offer a chick.

Anna Halprin, a ninety-seven-year-old artist — vital, physically attuned, lucid, engaged, experimental — is profoundly rooted in place. As an artist-teacher, she has found a force larger than herself within which to gain solace, rejuvenate balance, be healed, inspire, and be inspired. That force is nature, the original and originary home, the source of all organic things. Halprin healed herself of an illness through movement and through her relationship to the natural world. She also found sustenance in nature during the radical transformations taking place in California in the 1960s. From her immersion in nature through dance, Halprin has learned its inherent rituals and extracted a great strength and authority. She is not only powerful enough to function as a creative, spiritual mother to a unique artist such as Janine Antoni, but she is also confident enough in her own development to encourage Antoni to perform the completion of the self. The artist, no longer fixated on the image of the biological or psychological mother or held back by her own dependence, reticence, or fear, is now able to leap into her vast potentiality. Halprin notes, "As life experience deepens, personal art expression expands, and as art expression expands, life experience deepens."[24]

Halprin is a legend whose personal history and that of California are inextricably interwoven. Having moved with her husband — the revered landscape architect and environmentalist Lawrence Halprin — from the East Coast to the West Coast in the 1950s, she emerged as a great innovator, essential to the evolution of modern dance. In the 1960s and 1970s, she was swept up in the exuberance of California and the revolutionary currents of thought and action there, mostly generated by protest against the Vietnam War. Organized, massive acts of resistance became a global force essential to ending that war. It was impossible not to feel the changes occurring or be influenced by the radical rethinking of all forms that was emerging in the United States in academia, in government, and in the arts. Because California was inventing itself and its future anew, it became pivotal to this struggle. At the same time, California was also a locus of activity for civil rights, Black Power, and the Chicano, Native American, gay rights, women's, and ecology movements. Old forms and constructs were challenged daily as exemplified by the women's movement's core proposition that "the personal is political." Artists, architects, academics, and activists caught in this energy wanted to throw off historical constraints and invent new relationships between the self and the world and between art and its audience. The New York art scene, with its traditional categories of art making, dance, and success, could appear limited and restrictive in comparison to the scene in California, which was wide open in comparison.

Halprin found that the most meaningful art came through a process of "discovery."[25] Attuned to "the ritualistic beginnings of art as a sharpened expression of life," Halprin opened up a new sense of the potential importance of movement, for herself and for generations to come.[26] She collaborated with, taught, and influenced many young dancers, who, over time, changed the shape of postmodern dance: Yvonne Rainer, Trisha Brown, Simone Forti, Meredith Monk, Robert Morris and many others. These artists came to study with her and to dance on the famous dance deck, which Lawrence Halprin brilliantly had designed for his wife. Halprin's desire to bring artists into the public sphere, to have them take a leading role in addressing and healing the traumas of society, to move away from the notion of spectators to that of witnesses and participants, is very close to what we now call "social practice." Such a philosophy came out of a deep belief that art — and movement in particular — could liberate people to express and therefore to dissolve those blocks holding them back and thus, in aggregate, preventing society from moving forward. Over the years her practice collided and coincided with the inspirational work of such dynamic figures as Fritz Perls, the new landscape architects (for whom Lawrence Halprin was a central figure), and artists such as John Cage, Merce Cunningham, and Alan Kaprow, whose radical approaches to creation and performance are still in practice today. Artists of the future, Halprin imagined, might no longer be solitary heroic figures but rather "guides" who worked to "evoke the art within us all."[27]

Into this enormous endeavor decades under way entered Antoni, who had become immersed in 5Rhythms (founded by the late Gabrielle Roth) and in somatic therapy and Continuum Dance Meditation (founded by Emilie Conrad). Antoni was determined to find a new way to create through authentic movement, something more akin to Joseph Beuys's notion of "social sculpture," a concept that art could subvert society and explode the repressive structures that held the individual in a state of suffocation. But for art to achieve such a utopian efficacy, Beuys believed it had to occur performatively and in public. When Antoni and Halprin met, the flames leapt from one wisdom body to the other. Halprin quickly made the conditions for learning available. She put Antoni on the dance deck — the site of so many historic creative encounters — and told her to try Halprin's "Paper Dance" segment from the legendary *Parades and Changes* performance, which, from 1965 to 1967 had rocked the North American and European dance and art worlds with its exuberant energy, freedom of form, and matter-of-fact nudity.

> Emptiness like space is the ultimate nature of all phenomena,
> which allows everything to occur.[28]

Halprin placed a roll of brown paper in front of Antoni and suggested that she might want to take off her clothes (as others had in the past). Antoni said that when she started to move and saw the paper forming a pile, it "reminded me of a baby, so I immediately picked it up." She began to wrestle, dive, fuse with, and imitate the paper — inventing new forms as she lunged ahead. Always the sculptor, Antoni morphed one shape into another, fearlessly — first rolling in it until it formed a layered carapace, both noisy and awkward, then slithering out from under it like a snake shedding its skin. As she shredded, ripped, tore, flayed and animated the paper, shapes emerged: a big coat with a wrap-around hood, a bouffant cotillion dress, the *Winged Nike* herself, a meditation pillow upon which she immediately sat, earrings that she hung around her ears, and enormous flowers that she gathered in front of her like a bouquet. When she pushed the paper down her bra and underpants, a bloated chrysalis emerged. Stuffing it in her nose, ears, mouth, and belly button, the paper closed off all orifices, silencing the senses that connect us to the physical world (and distract us from the inner world). Finally, she rocked an armful as if it were a baby, caring for her creation, birthing herself. And so the initiation went: Halprin witnessing the process, Antoni inventing new shapes intuitively, without artifice, allowing the paper to direct her, grounding the performing body, creating art moment by moment, no longer thinking the form into being, rather enacting the making spontaneously, allowing the improvisation to orchestrate her movement, freeing herself to act.

Emerging two hours later, having felt only the "wind and the floor" as Halprin had advised, Antoni obviously had performed something so monumental in Halprin's eyes that Halprin immediately called the Berkeley Art Museum (which had opened with *Parades and Changes* in 1970 and had reopened with a restaging of the piece in 2012). Halprin insisted that she and Antoni come right over so that Antoni could perform it all once again for curator Dana Beard and others. Antoni had taken up the process of the piece so organically that the results startled them both.

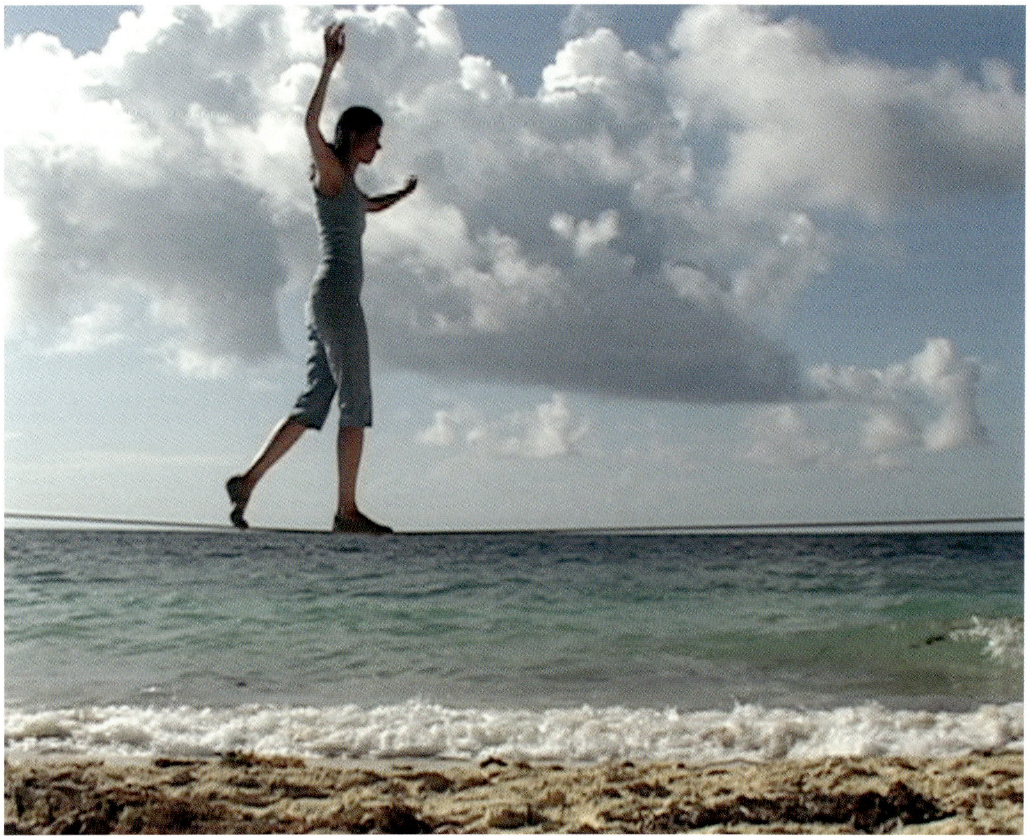

Janine Antoni, *Touch* (video still), 2002. © Janine Antoni. Courtesy of the artist and Luhring Augustine, New York.

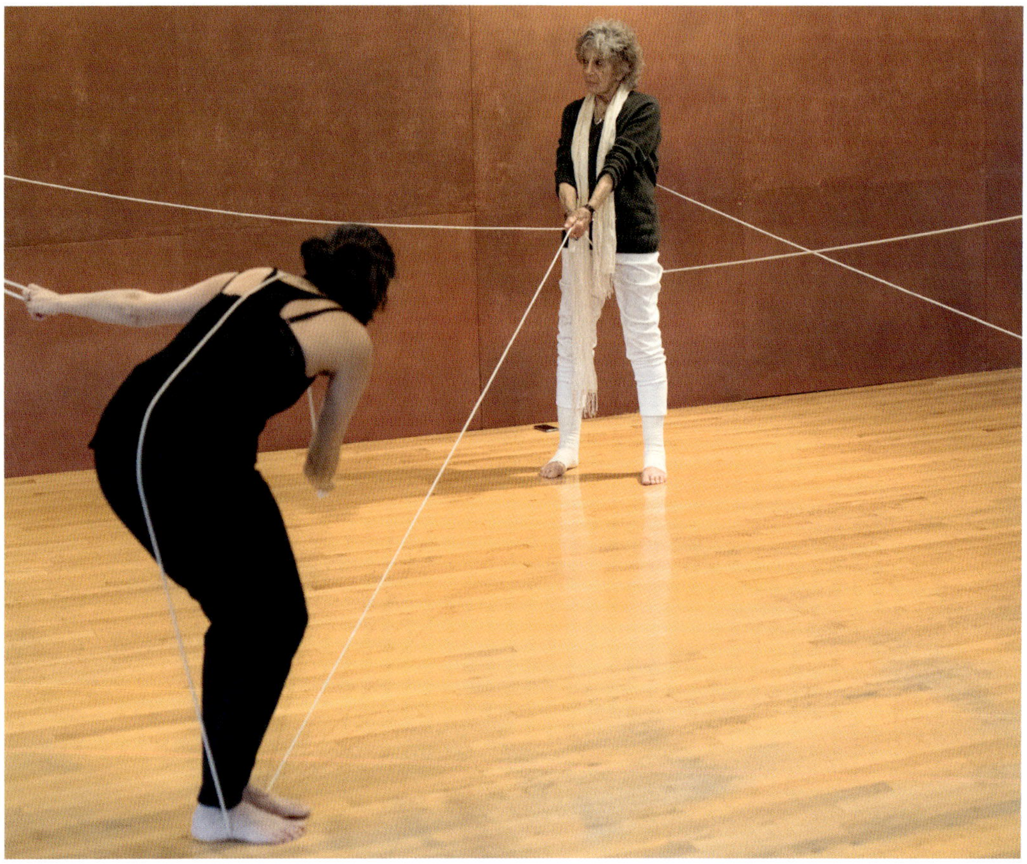

Janine Antoni (left) and Anna Halprin (right) rehearsing *Rope Dance*, 2015. Photo: © Hugo Glendinning, 2015. Courtesy of the artists.

Because of this unique relationship, Antoni's creative life has transformed. At least for now, she is no longer just a solo artist developing her craft from one iteration to the next. She has been "collaborating" both with Anna Halprin and also with dancer and choreographer Stephen Petronio. The influence of Halprin on Antoni's work is omnipresent. In spring 2015, the Rhode Island School of Design (RISD) was about to inaugurate Rosanne Somerson as its new president and asked Antoni if she would "share greetings" at the inauguration alongside other well-known RISD alumni. The college wanted these artists to help welcome a leader chosen to heal the institution after a tumultuous period in its history. Antoni is a graduate of the college, and it is there that she met fellow artist, Paul Ramirez Jonas, whom she later married and with whom she has a daughter, Indra. Their creative partnership has provided ballast for Antoni's life and productivity. Historically connected to the institution on many levels, Antoni was an obvious choice of artist to ask for an original and meaningful acknowledgment of this important transition.

For this event, Antoni invented a simple, yet resonant, gesture. Each person present would clasp the hand of the person next to him or her to create a connection between everyone there, from the back of the tented auditorium to the front. This chain would reach all the way to the stage where Antoni and the president stood, sending collective energy and affirmation to the hand of the new leader. With 1,000 people in attendance, the piece, which was obvious enough in concept, was nonetheless complex to execute. Antoni made a "score," not unlike those that Anna and Lawrence Halprin had developed for similarly interactive, collective performances — diagrams that at first might appear abstract but which are actually efficient mappings of the movements and sequences involved in each piece, allowing it to be reproduced. By working in this public way, Antoni moved her practice out of the studio and the gallery, off the legendary dance deck, and into the collective, bringing this large group together, touching her audience directly, helping them to touch each other as witnesses in the moment, practices that from the beginning have been essential to Antoni and to Halprin as well. Whereas in the past, the concept of reaching out to the viewer was embedded in the content of Antoni's sculptural and performative work and its potential to reverberate within the interior lives of her audience, now these aspirations have become more immediate, direct, communal, inclusive, and physical.

The Gaze Returned

> The body has deep wisdom within it — memories, ancient knowledge, and personal and collective experiences beyond anything we can imagine with our collective minds.[29]

On one of the visits that Antoni and Petronio made to Halprin's home and studio, Halprin offered these two extraordinary performers a "rope dance" as a way of bringing them and their unique training and practices together in collaboration. They were each to walk blindfolded toward the other, staying on the rope as much as possible. Their assigned goal was to reach each other at an unspecified point. In 2003, Antoni, who has a tightrope in her studio, made a video in which she balanced on a rope that appeared stretched across the horizon of the Caribbean, creating the illusion that she was walking on water. Petronio, a renowned choreographer with a reputation as a virtuosic dancer, did not yet have this particular expertise when they first came together, but of course, movement, the body, precision, and grace are tools he had honed over decades. The two did finally encounter each other, awkwardly at first and almost by chance, enacting another metaphor for the initial clumsiness and complexity of collaboration.

Halprin created a movement exercise, a "score" that mirrored the meeting of these two artists. The quality of their encounter would be recognized by touch, a connection not of the mind, but of the body and spirit. *Rope Dance* posed metaphysical and physical challenges appropriate to the nuances of their collaboration: Could they come together? Could they reach each other? How would their skills balance each other's? How long might that take? How complex would the process become? How engaging? Finding each other in a third, unknown space literalized the concept of collaboration. Blindfolded, unable to turn to the outside world for affirmation or direction, they were forced to "look inside" or fail badly.

One might think of this exercise as a koan in motion, literalizing a question or a problem designed by a master to create doubt or to unsettle the student's perception of reality and to measure the quality of his or her progress on the path to "perfect omniscience."[30] The koan is chosen with the particular person or persons directly in mind. The "answer" to the question posed is never a conscious, reasoned response. It must be spontaneous and come directly from the intuitive or wisdom body of the seeker, without calculation. The answer can be a gesture, an action, or a non-action. And if it occurs in language, it simply might be one word — and shouted out into a vacuum at that. Only when a student's response meets the unspecified and unarticulated criteria of the master can a student move on to the next question and to the next level of spiritual development.

In *Ally*, a video projection as large as the gallery wall itself documents Halprin's face as she sits almost silently watching *Rope Dance* performed by Antoni and Petronio before her. As audience to her solitary response, all we see are Halprin's expressions in reaction to the performers' movements, yet we are riveted. Her approving gaze is completely focused on what is happening before her. Her expressive witnessing becomes the entire subject of the film. As Halprin sits on the sidelines watching, we hear only the wind in the trees and her occasional gasp when, we assume, the performers have taken an unusual or unexpected turn. The camera is focused solely on her beautiful face, recording every nuanced response. She is rapt, with her attention completely present and on the performance, an ideal observer, her face the perfect mirror reflecting their collaborative endeavor. What is most astounding is how enthralled she appears to be.

Those attending the opening of *Ally* and subsequent performances were also invited to take part in a rope dance exercise. Petronio called out the instructions as the audience, now participants, became entangled in the formations they and others were creating in response to Petronio's directions. As they dipped and dived around each other, taking up the slack of the rope, or letting it languish, the exercise turned the experience of observation into one of action that then became social sculpture. Participants began to understand the freedom of play the rope allowed and to imagine, in their own bodies, what Antoni and Petronio might have been experiencing and what Halprin might have been responding to in the expressions captured by the camera.

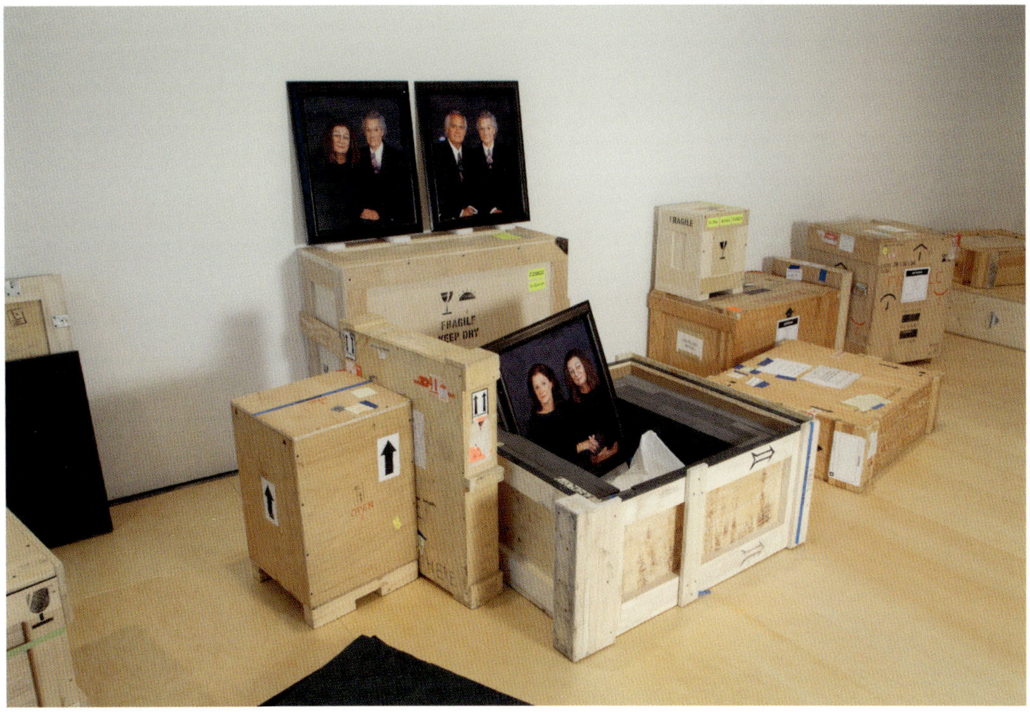

Janine Antoni in collaboration with Anna Halprin, *Paper Dance* (detail of installation including *Mom and Dad*, 1994), 2016.
Photo: Carlos Avendaño, 2016. © Janine Antoni. Courtesy of the artists and FWM.

Psychically and spiritually Antoni and Halprin are fulfilling their own destinies. Halprin, like *Prajnaparamita* in Buddhist thought, provides the space of the Great Mother, "a guide and consort who activates profound awareness."[31] She has created an open, inviting site of "unlimited potential" that "permits everything to occur." Among the many female aspects that comprise this idea of the Great Mother, who has many male aspects as well, is that of the "spontaneously dancing Dakini, an inspiring and unpredictably playful flow of changes," evocative of the movement of energy in space.[32] On the opening day of *Ally*, there appeared to be two overt sources of inspiration, breathing life into Antoni and her performance of "Paper Dance." The first was her own sculpture: many of Antoni's works, produced throughout her lifetime, had been shipped to the gallery, but the work was hidden from the audience, who used the closed crates as benches during the performance. But for each performance (there were twenty-two), Antoni selected one work to uncrate, reveal, and feature. After the performance, that sculpture would remain on view until she performed again, when Antoni would return that piece to its crate and select another. The choice and significance of which piece or pieces were chosen, especially for the opening event, was not lost on the audience. Antoni uncrated the early and iconic photographic triptych *Mom and Dad*, in which her mother and father, appearing in formal photographic portrait mode, morph into each other through the use of makeup, wigs, and costumes. This photographic maneuver, in which her parents were co-conspirators, showed Antoni trying to break down all distinctions between these mythic figures, perhaps to find her own identity in the fusion of the two, which her actual being represents.

The second presence in the space was a small film projection of the "Paper Dance" segment of *Parades and Changes* that Halprin and others performed in Stockholm in 1965. In the background, recordings of Petula Clark singing "Downtown" alternated with Beach Boy Brian Wilson singing "Warmth of the Sun," quietly filling the space like a memory. The avant-garde composer Morton Subotnik had arranged the sound score for that original performance. His intent was that the radio would be turned on at a specific moment during the piece, and whatever song was playing would become the soundtrack for that day, or so it would appear. Hearing the music of that performance at this historical moment inevitably took some of the audience right back to California in the 1960s. These two additions to Antoni's performance resonated as the most essential and originary "sources" of this particular moment: the triptych of Antoni's biological parents, whom she had successfully morphed into each other through the illusion of art, and the original version of the "Paper Dance" segment she was about to recreate and transform. But this was not a fashionable art world reenactment of an historic, archival event performed fifty-one years ago; rather it was a re-embodying of the essence and meaning of that event to the performer(s) who took part in it. It was also Antoni's homage to Halprin as the guide and teacher who had helped her reach this moment so that she could freely, exuberantly, and brilliantly enact this "Paper Dance" without reservation or guile, thus adding her imprint to the historical meaning and resonance of this piece and to the legend of Halprin, whose influence and spirit filled the room.

Halprin has seen the child, and the child has observed herself being seen. The artist-mother has transmitted knowledge to the artist-daughter who has basked in the reflection of the gaze, ingested the wisdom offered, and taken what she has learned out into the world as practice. Extraordinarily, these two artists have affixed their wisdom bodies to each other across categorization, generation, space, and time.

For Antoni, always engaged in reimagining herself and her practice, this profound connection to *Prajnaparamita* and the concept of "going across to the other side," which it represents, marks yet another monumental and transformative plateau in the pursuit of the "real."[33] As the Skin Horse explains to the Velveteen Rabbit:

> "Real isn't how you are made ... It's a thing that happens to you ..."
> "Does it happen all at once, like being wound up," he asked, "or bit by bit?"
> "It doesn't happen all at once," said the Skin Horse. "You become.
> It takes a long time."[34]

Notes

1. D. W. Winnicott, *Playing and Reality* (London: Tavistock, 1971), 69.

2. Adrian Heathfield and André Lepecki, in collaboration with the Museum of Modern Art, Columbia University School of the Arts, and the French Institute Alliance Francaise, "Afterlives: The Persistence of Performance" (Crossing the Line Festival, Museum of Modern Art, New York, NY, September 25–27, 2015).

3. Margery Williams, *The Velveteen Rabbit: Or How Toys Become Real* (New York: Doubleday, 1922), 5–6.

4. Winnicott, *Playing and Reality*, 6.

5. C. G. Jung, *The Spirit in Man, Art, and Literature*, trans. R. F. C. Hull, Bollingen Series XV (Princeton: Princeton University Press, 1966), 80.

6. Julie L. Belcove, "Artist Janine Antoni Takes on Childbirth and the Female Body in Two New Shows," *New York Magazine*, February 27, 2015, http://nymag.com/thecut/2015/02/veteran-feminist-artist-takes-on-childbirth.html.

7. Erich Neumann, *The Great Mother: An Analysis of the Archetype*, trans. Ralph Manheim (Princeton: Princeton University Press, 1955), 68.

8. Janine Antoni, *The Girl Made of Butter* (Ridgefield, CT: Aldrich Museum of Contemporary Art, 2001), 3. Published in conjunction with the 1999 Larry Aldrich Foundation Award Exhibition, January 21–May 20, 2001.

9. Neumann, *The Great Mother*, 98.

10. Josh Cohen, *The Private Life: Why We Remain in the Dark* (London: Granta, 2013), 118.

11. Winnicott, *Playing and Reality*, 2.

12. Neumann, *The Great Mother*, 67.

13. Antoni, *The Girl Made of Butter*, 3.

14. Janine Antoni, interview by Megan Luke, 1999, publication insert, *The Girl Made of Butter* (Ridgefield, CT: Aldrich Museum of Contemporary Art, 2001).

15. Janine Antoni et al, *Janine Antoni* (Kusnacht, Switzerland: Ink Tree Editions; Ostfildern-Ruit, Germany: Hatje Cantz Publishers, 2000), 98.

16. Winnicott, *Playing and Reality*, 39.

17. Joshua Reiman, "My Body is Your Vehicle: A Conversation with Janine Antoni," *Sculpture* 34, no. 4 (2015), 28.

18. Janice Ross, introduction to *Moving Toward Life: Five Decades of Transformational Dance* by Anna Halprin, ed. Rachel Kaplan (Middletown, CT: Wesleyan University Press, 1995), 72.

19. Robert A. F. Thurman, *Essential Tibetan Buddhism* (San Francisco: Harper San Francisco, 1995), 22.

20. Ibid.

21. The term "holding environment" is fundamental to most of D. W. Winnicott's work. It appears in "The Theory of the Parent-Infant Relationship," *International Journal of Psycho-Analysis* 41 (1960): 585–595.

22. Reiman, "My Body is Your Vehicle," 24.

23. Karolina Pospisilova, "The Female Wisdom: The Female Aspect in Buddhism," Estetyka i Krytyka 3, no. 22 (2011): 187, http://estetykaikrytyka.pl/art/22/eik_22_14.pdf.

24. Janice Ross, *Anna Halprin: Experience as Dance* (Berkeley: University of California Press, 2007), 318.

25. Anna Halprin, *Moving Toward Life: Five Decades of Transformational Dance* (Middletown, CT: Wesleyan University Press, 1995), 74.

26. Ibid., 101.

27. Ibid., 131.

28. Pospisilova, "The Female Wisdom," 187.

29. Halprin, *Moving Toward Life*, 207.

30. Thurman, *Essential Tibetan Buddhism*, 9.

31. *Prajnaparamita* is often depicted as an embodiment of the Buddha's teaching. She is a feminine principle, which conjoins the practitioner with reality. "*Prajna* means wisdom, … it is said to be transcendent *(paramita)*, which is the second part of her name. *Paramita* literally means, 'gone across to the other side' … it is often translated as 'gone to the other shore'" (Pospisilova, "The Female Wisdom," 186 and 191).

32. Ibid.

33. Ibid., 186.

34. Williams, *The Velveteen Rabbit*, 6.

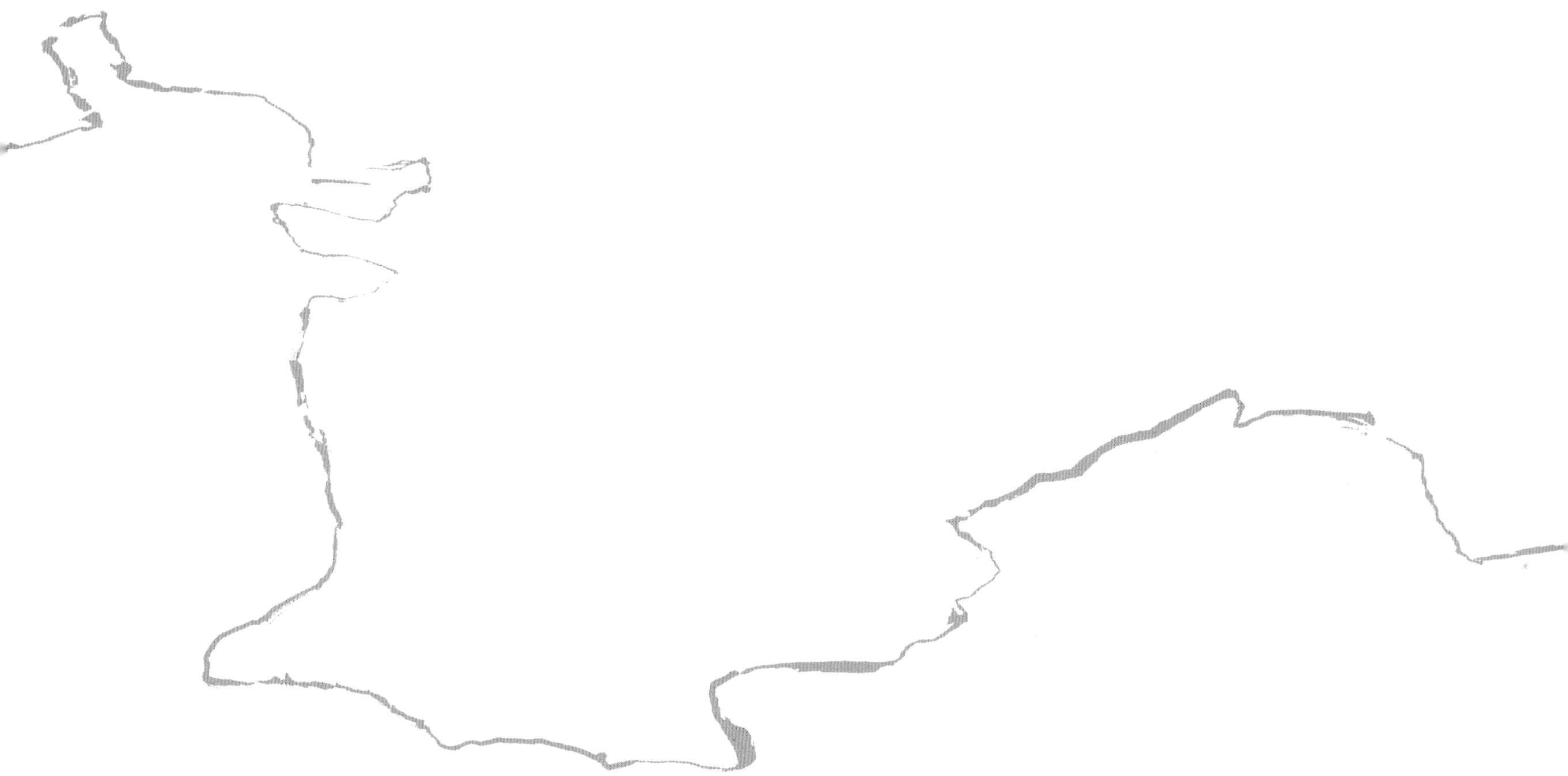

SWALLOW

Janine Antoni, Stephen Petronio

The installation bears the stories, relics and traces of a singular act by Janine Antoni and Stephen Petronio in November 2015. A delicate material, specially woven at The Fabric Workshop and Museum, was used in a visceral ritual of communion. Ten people were witnesses to the event; visitors to the exhibition could listen to their individual testimonies on conjoined chairs. A sculptural reliquary containing the original cloth was placed opposite a single photograph of the act, printed on wool, in the process of being consumed by colonies of moths.

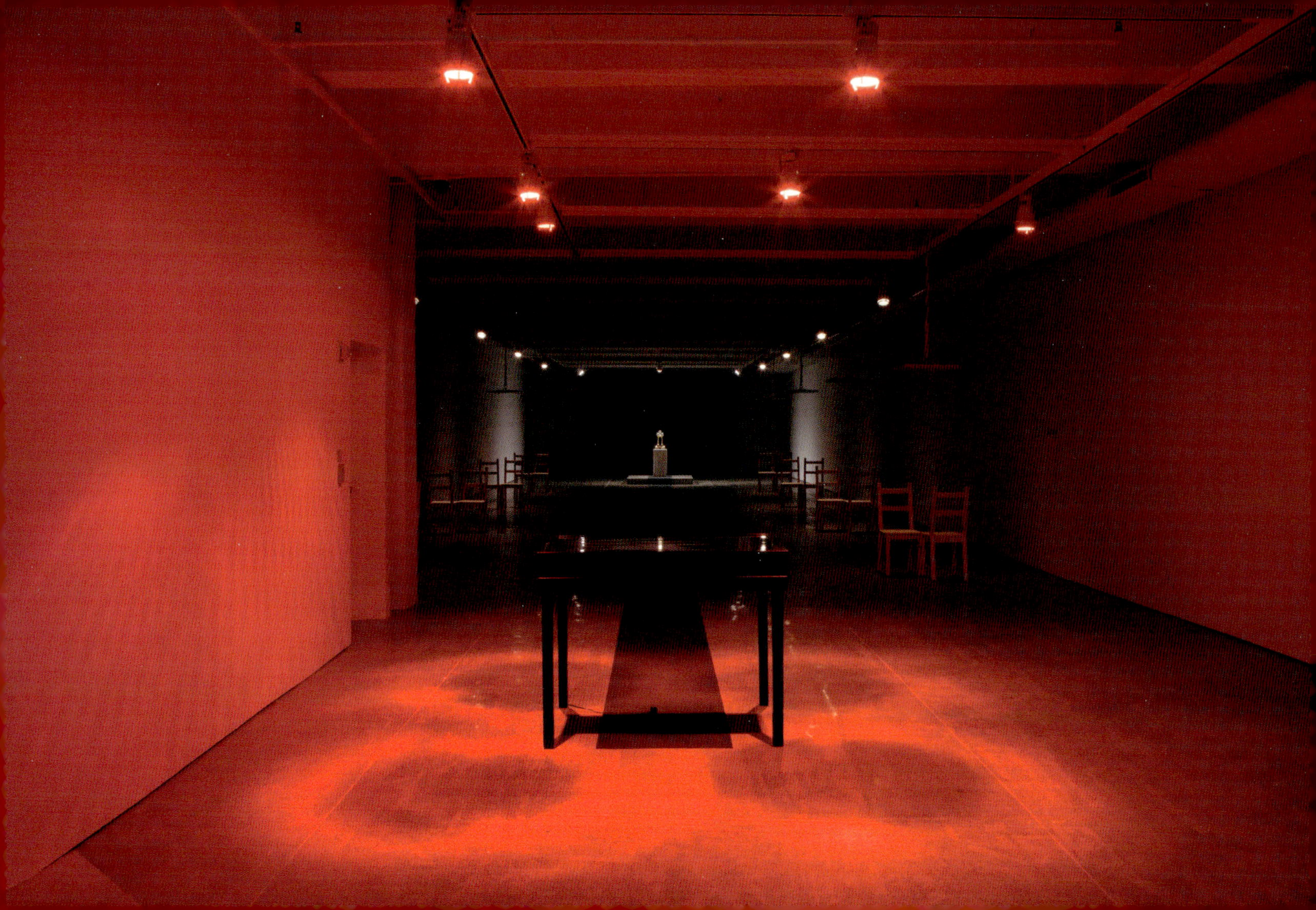

… Three pans of water. Several pans of water. They seem to be multiplying in my mind. Two glasses of water. A roll of gauze. Two small stools that reminded me of tribal chieftain stools …   She asks him if the water is too hot. He says, "No, it feels good." So they unravel the gauze — they pour water into the basins. And they wet the gauze and they take the gauze out and they fold it …   And then of course the shock is that they begin feeding it into their own mouths, either end of the same strip of gauze, each individual is feeding it into his or her own mouth …   An unscripted moment in the middle of it is Janine drops the glass of water and it breaks and the water spills on the floor …   It's impossible at this point now, as we see the gauze disappearing — well not impossible, impossible for me — not to think of magicians and sword swallowers on one hand and the two dogs and the pasta, the spaghetti. What's the name of the Disney movie and the dogs? Don't recall. Which makes me think there's a romantic element to this. At first, I thought it was just visceral because every now and then each of them gags and you can see the tension of trying to hold this thing down, to keep from from chucking it up. But they continue swallowing the gauze until their noses meet. This seemed to be the point at which the experiment was over which struck me as romantic, touching, endearing, and made me rethink the point, the purpose of swallowing the gauze being some other form of intercourse frankly. That they were sharing this material and then, a metaphysical level of intercourse where it is oral, it is communicated,

The Poet

it is shared, it is understood, it is physical. It was resonating on a number of levels. So after the noses meet, then they start backing away from one another and the gauze is pulled out from the depths of their bowels so to speak. (laughter) …   The staging of it goes beyond any immediate expression of desire. In fact it precludes any expression of desire — or rather, incorporates and normalizes a desire — in the ritual performed in a way that all the expression is happening on a symbolic level. My interest is in looking at this gauze as a surrogate for language. As a stand in for the thing that is the unspoken, which is shared and is mutually understood: it is mutually intelligible …   So it's anticipated that this thing is going into my gut and so not only are Janine and Stephen and the participants made to confront the bodily-ness of this interaction but we, the audience, we know that as this thing is coming up what we're seeing is — there was a spot. I guess it's my morbid fascination. I'm looking to see what residue is there, what trace of them is on this gauze as it comes up and there was a spot, I don't know who it came from and I just wondered what moment of tension, what moment of stress caused that spot …   The end of it was a kind of resolution and (laughter) — now I'm self conscious about my analogies — there's a coital resolution, there's a post-ness afterwards, that something has been accomplished, they've both prevailed, they have both made an effort to do something together and have achieved the goal, whatever their goal was, I don't know, but the goal of the ritual was completed and the only harm that came was the broken glass but no harm came to either of them and they seemed satisfied with — my response is one of relief, I suppose. Just mere seconds into putting the gauze in their mouths I realized this thing is gonna go until the thing is gone. But I kept anticipating, wondering what else …   there was heightened tension around …   what else might this ritual entail? …   If I think about eating, about the idea of consumption: so the consumption between Janine and Stephen seemed directed at one another and the gauze was a means of arriving at that consumption, which is not in the sense of sharing a meal. Well, I mean   and it is. Yeah, the shared meal (laughter) …   being the prelude to the further consumption of one another. My sense is I'm projecting meaning onto whatever it is that I'm seeing and I say that as an attempt to do justice to the thing I'm describing, so that I don't presume that what I'm describing is actually what is.

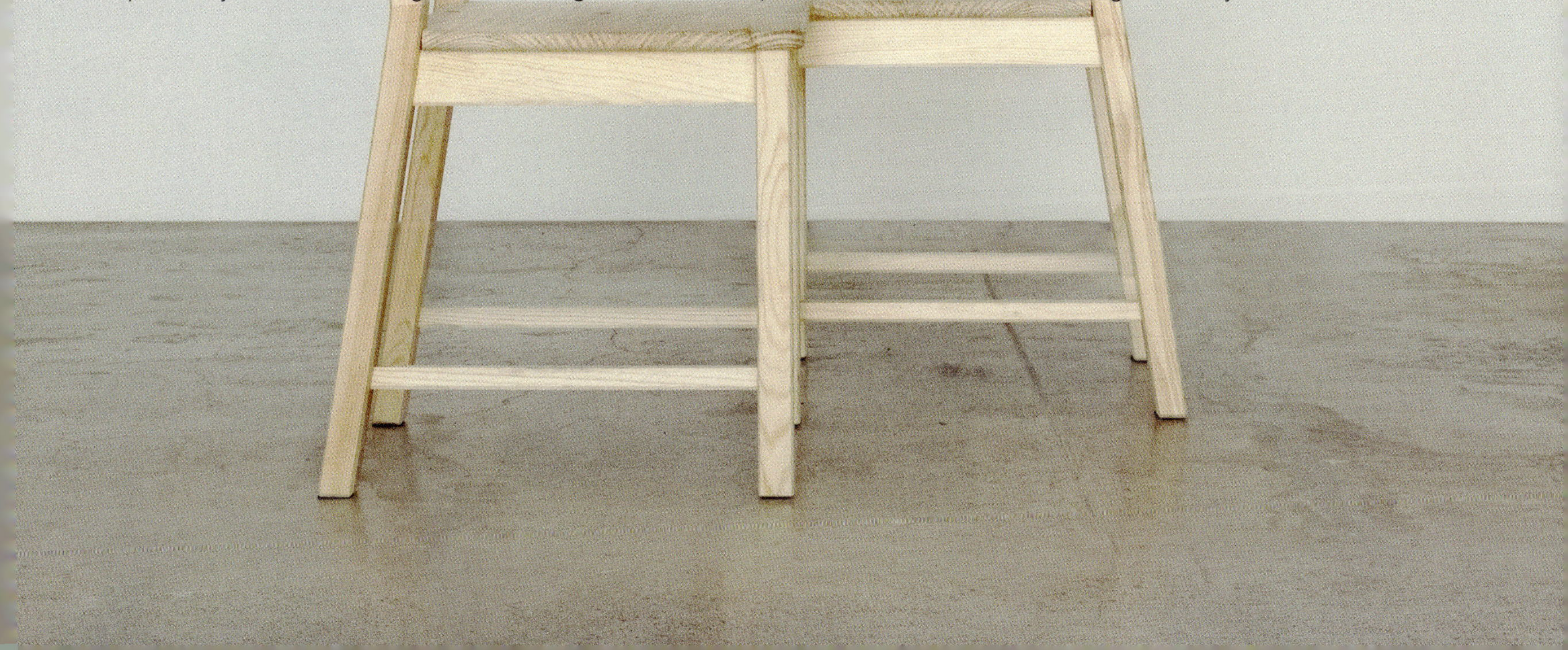

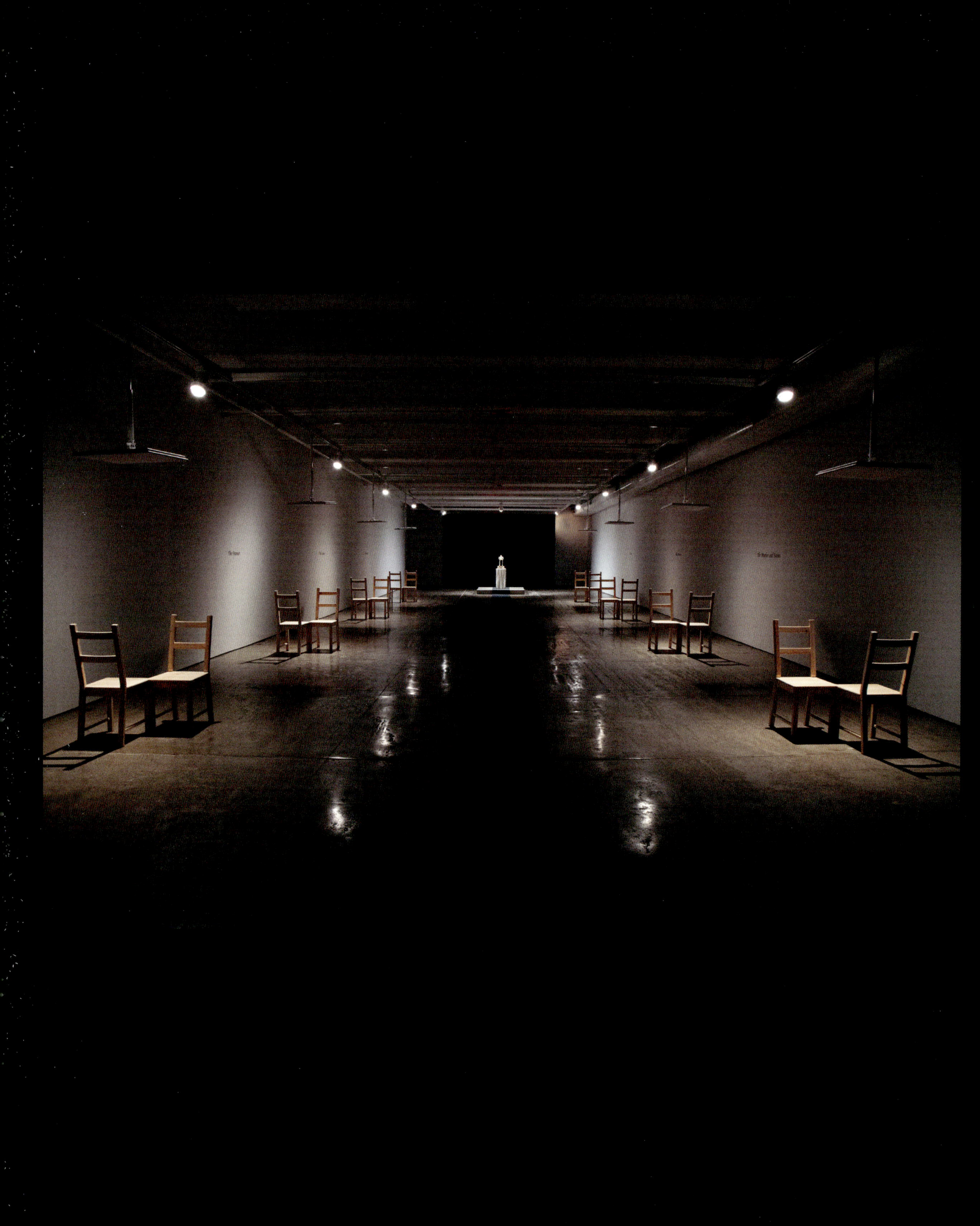

I felt like he calmed her in the swallowing of the cloth. I thought she was having a hard time and then he raised his hand, and at one point for her, I think, to look up because I thought, almost like he was trying to help her in doing it. I don't know too much about rituals. That's what I thought it was, two people coming together. I felt it from the outside looking in. To be honest with you I thought about — somebody looking from another building with binoculars looking in. It felt like you weren't there — I don't feel that they thought that anybody was around them. I felt like they felt like they were alone, even though we were there. I thought it got more intense toward the end. I felt they almost needed each other more … or maybe that she needed him more, I think, to concentrate on. I would say that … I would look at it almost like they did the feat together. They did it together and now they're going to move on after that together. I was expecting them to do something else. I didn't know what, but I thought when the cloth came out and they were done, I didn't feel they were separated then. I felt that they were together more. And that's why I thought there was going to be something else after that … I thought it was very impressive to stay calm — at some point you could tell they could get panicked, but they didn't. That's where I felt they calmed each other. I saw Stephen rub his — go like this on his chest (laughter) moving it around, there's a knot or something. That's why I call it very impressive. They had to concentrate so

The Mole

intensely. I think that's where they helped each other. I think if I was trying to do that by myself, I don't think I … I don't know if it's some kind of ritual from the past or, I would guess that would be — I didn't find it offensive at all. I just found it different. And I've never heard of it, anything like that, I've never seen anything like that, but offensive, not at all. That's why I just — I liked how they looked at each other. I don't know. I liked that part of it. I'm a Sandhog: I build the tunnels. Yeah the TBMs, the tunnel boring machines. That's what we are — they call us urban miners. All the subway tunnels we're doing in New York, we're down three, four hundred feet. And I come from a family of — that's how my family came over from Ireland. They were all miners in Pennsylvania. My great-great grandfather, when he came he was a coal miner. He worked on a gang and then he became management. And then the gangs he worked with were trying to organize, become a union and he was bucking them, he was kind of pushing them off, fighting them. And he came home from work one day, came out, had a beer, lit a cigarette up and somebody came by and just killed him. One of the guys from the union, for him blowing him off, so … What is his purpose, what is their purpose for doing it? What does it do for them? Does it make them feel coming together, I don't know, is it something, a ritual that is from somewhere else or did they come up with it? … Honestly I'd probably tell them, "Listen, I went to this thing, it was weird." But this is what they — I would say I don't know— or I'm not around too many creative people in my life so I don't know exactly how I would explain it.

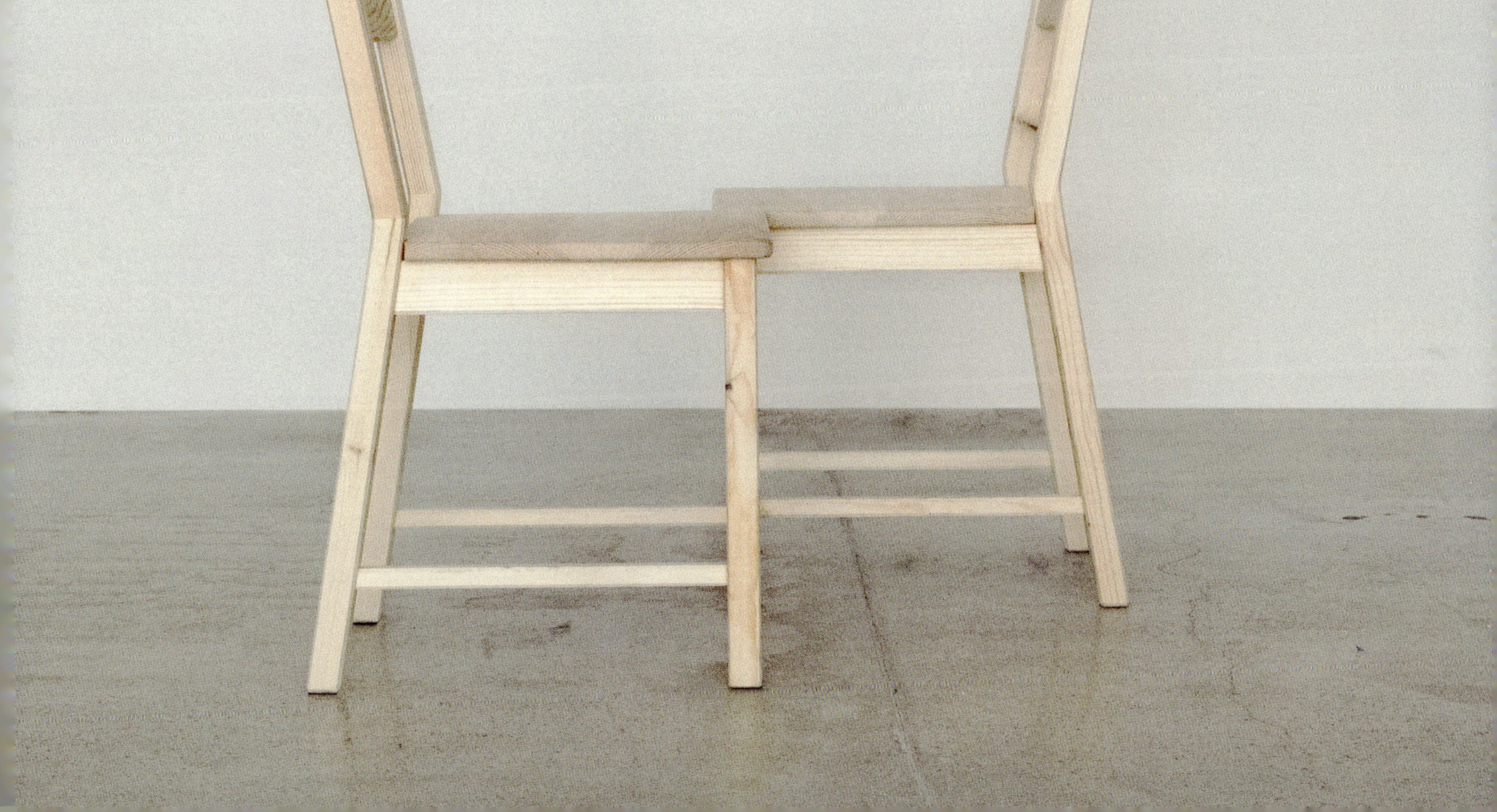

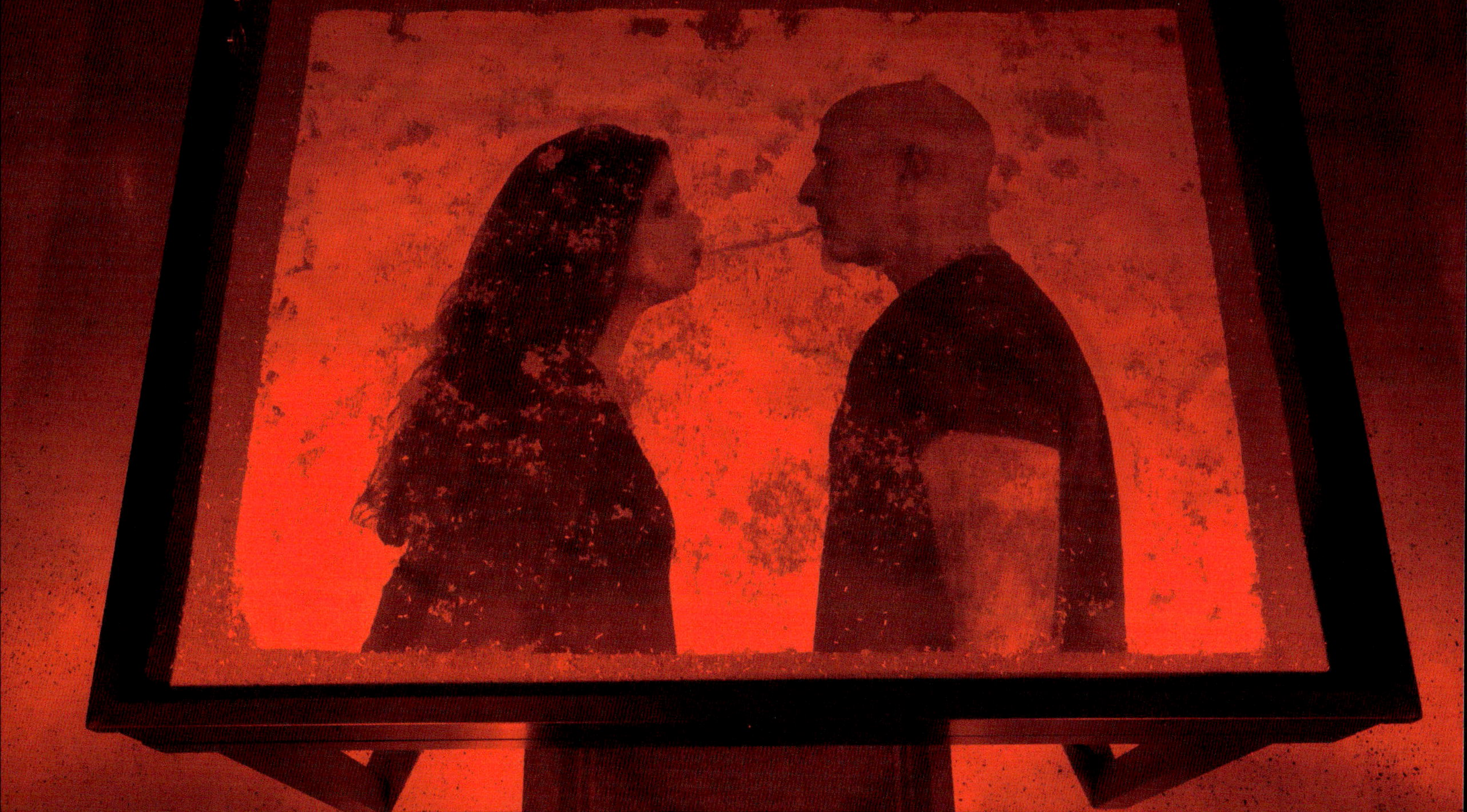

… They were unrolling it, so slowly, slowly, it was like a U shape and slowly, slowly as they swallowed it, it became almost like a tight rope. That was sort of interesting to watch, that fabric go from this loose — because you didn't know how long it was really, and then suddenly they inhaled it, they swallowed it and it got tight and they got closer, closer, closer, boom, they hit their noses. They both swallowed it lip to lip I guess. And then slowly it came out of their mouths and they regurgitated it, I guess you could say … Someone recently asked me, "Do you get to see the performances beforehand so you know what's coming?" And I said, "That's a luxury." Usually I don't. Usually I just show up and I just photograph it and it keeps me on my toes and makes me very sensitive to all the action, rhythm, tempo that I'm seeing. Like I said, I would take the camera away and look at the whole piece and I might zoom in closer to parts of it that I think would be interesting, but it might not be what the entire piece is about because you can't really say all that in one photograph. It was like a physical thing for me. Watching it became a physical thing like, "Oh God, that's coming out of his mouth, coming out of their stomach, coming out of their esophagus." So, it was a physical sensation which I would feel, I would remember that physical sensation. And I really would remember taking the picture. I would remember the physical sensation of the moment when they were excreting it out of their mouths. They were definitely connected and they would stare into each other's

The Framer

eyes. That was kind of beautiful, the connection was really beautiful, then physically with the fabric — the physical manifestation of the connection was there with this fabric, that they came together … When it was coming out of his mouth, especially more Stephen than Janine — I can think of my son gagging when they had to put braces on and they had a serious gagging issue and it was gross. So I was thinking a little bit about that. But this was not — certainly wasn't gross or anything. I was thinking how you have to really — they were opening up their gullet to let the fabric in, the swallowing. They did it very gracefully, really. It was very graceful and beautiful. It was a dance performance in a way but it wasn't disgusting. It wasn't physically repugnant or anything like that, it was beautiful really. It was definitely ceremonial, a ceremonial connection in a performance … I guess Janine dropped a glass that she was trying to drink from. She dropped the glass and it broke, so that was a little bit startling because they had such deep concentration to swallow the fabric, but they didn't lose their concentration. I think everybody got a little startled, but they seemed to be concerned about the broken glass because she reached out and pulled it away from the middle of the room and then at another point he reached out and pulled it away from the room. So that was interesting because this unexpected moment happened — unexpected, spontaneous — you can't account for what might happen … happened! They didn't expect that and they dealt with it and they didn't break their concentration it wasn't like somebody pulled back, I guess that could've happened.

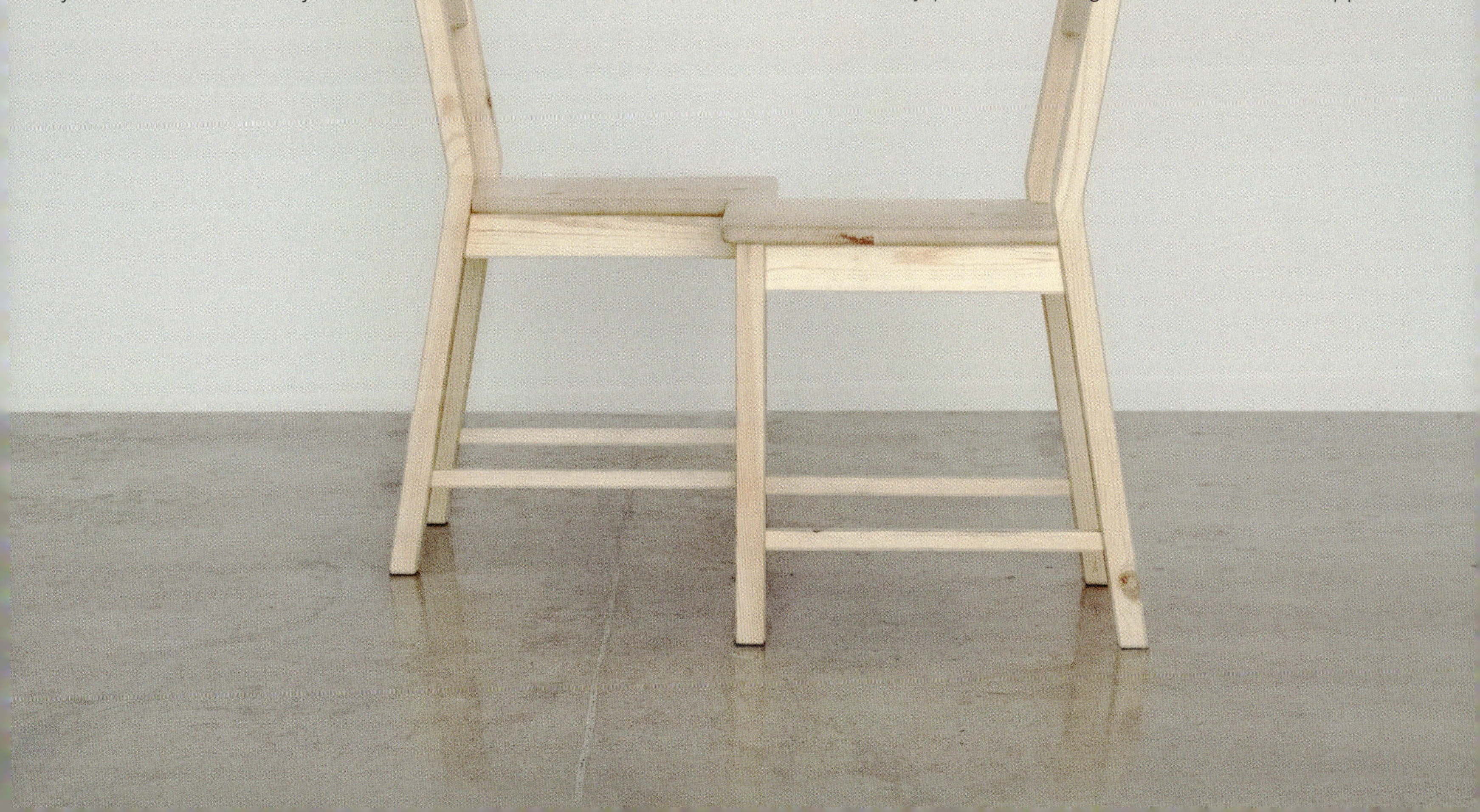

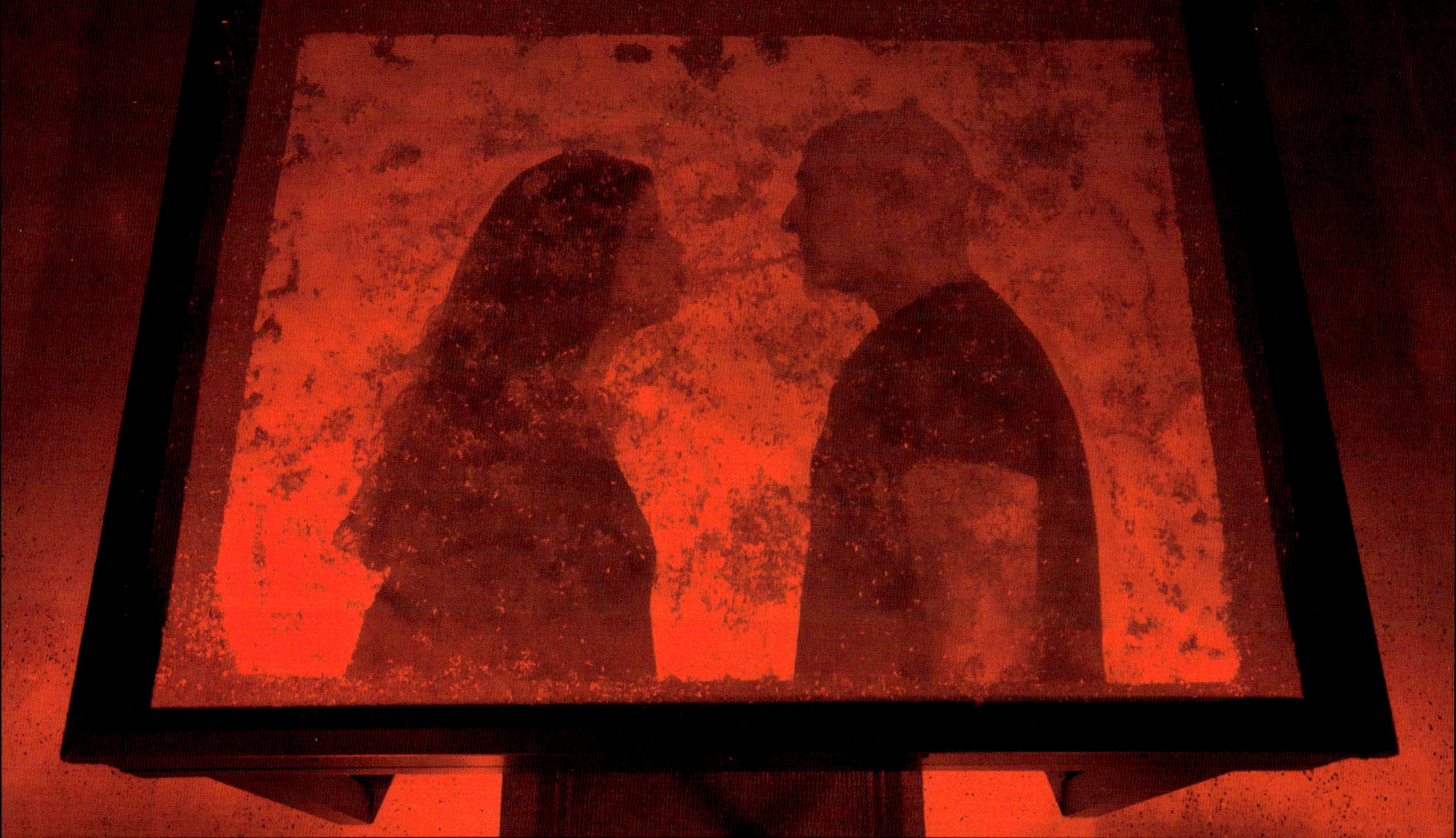

… The initial thought was excitement. I felt excitement that this mundane thing that I do everyday has been elevated in art form — the subject of an art form. Swallowing, who would've thunk that swallowing can be art. But I think that a mundane thing, something that's very common, has become something exceptional — something that's artistic. Something that's a primal thing becomes a unique thing. That's exciting … In a way it's also amazing to see them do it. It's an amazing feat to swallow something if it's just a sip of coffee or tea or a piece of cheese. It requires the action of fifty muscles working in a coordinated fashion happening in a few seconds. To be able to swallow a five-foot piece of cloth each continuously is an accomplishment in itself. I'm amazed from a physiological standpoint, how they were able to do that. At the same time, feeling proud, like a proud dad with their child performing on stage saying, "Hey," (laughter) … "there she is, getting the spotlight." … There's that layperson feeling: "Wow, this is a strange performance, a one of a kind performance going on." There's the clinician in me, also looking at the tongue, how they're moving the piece of cloth to the back of the mouth, how frequently they're swallowing, now I see the larynx elevating as they're swallowing the cloth. "Oh, he burped there and probably swallowed too much air," things like that. That's the combination of being the layperson and being the clinician … Looking at this — something we do so frequently, something very subconscious. We swallow two thousand times a day and we don't

The Mender

even think about it. And so something there, which is subconscious, is being brought to the forefront of your awareness … I think during the performance, even the kids — you can feel this sense of calm in the room and you can feel the connection between the two performers. It's almost like you're privy to a really intimate moment, between these two people you are watching from the outside. So I got that kind of emotional response … From seeing it over and over — thousands of patients over the years — you can see these commonalities, common threads that go through these different patients, but I think what keeps it exciting for me is that there's that singularity, there's still that individuality, that uniqueness. So it's not seven muscles or fifty muscles that I do in my sleep. Each person is different and brings in different perspectives to the table when you work with them, making work exciting … I think on a physical level, swallowing a piece of cloth and then taking it out does physically cleanse you in some way, but again, if you look at it as a ritual, you're not only cleaning your physical self but maybe also cleansing your spirit as you are pulling this piece of cloth out of you. It's almost like you're releasing or you're pulling out the negative energies, in addition to the physical things that are being cleansed from your body. Different levels of cleansing … They had some control during the performance: pacing back slowly controls what's coming out. But I think having that willingness for it to come out, not even holding back, tightening your muscles to keep that material in, is part of the release to let it go … The same way we feed the young to nurture them, to show our affection, to show our love, we feed the elderly or sick family members that we have. In a way, eating food or liquid can be symbolic, a powerful symbol of control. If someone is held prisoner and not given food or liquid it's a punishment, or someone who wants to protest and go on a hunger strike. On a very a basic level, the main reason we eat or swallow something is to nurture the body. But in this piece the eating part is not for the purpose of nurturing the body to get nutrition or to eat each other. But I think maybe it's nurturing the soul? … So, that physical connection …

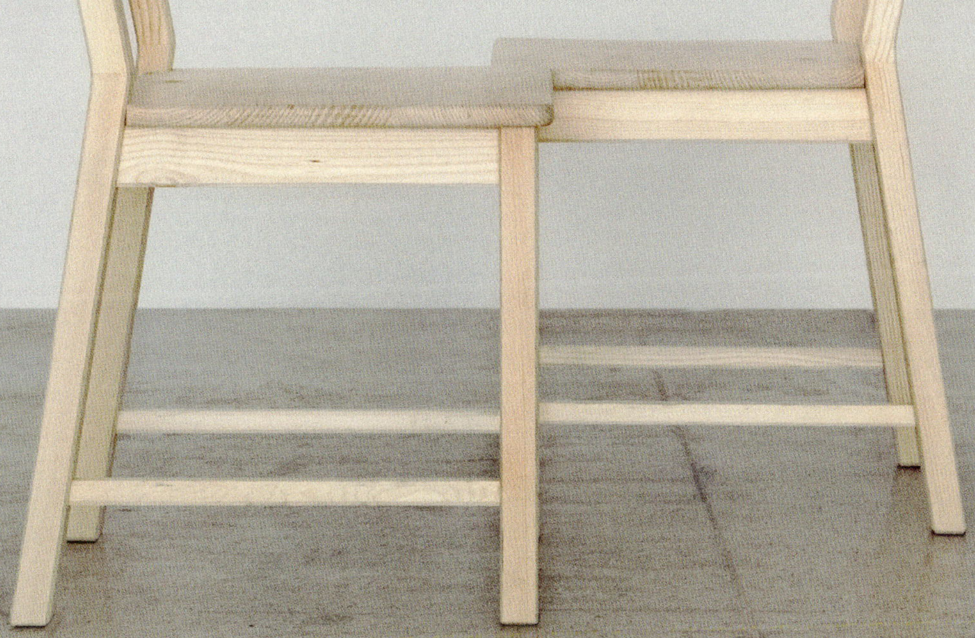

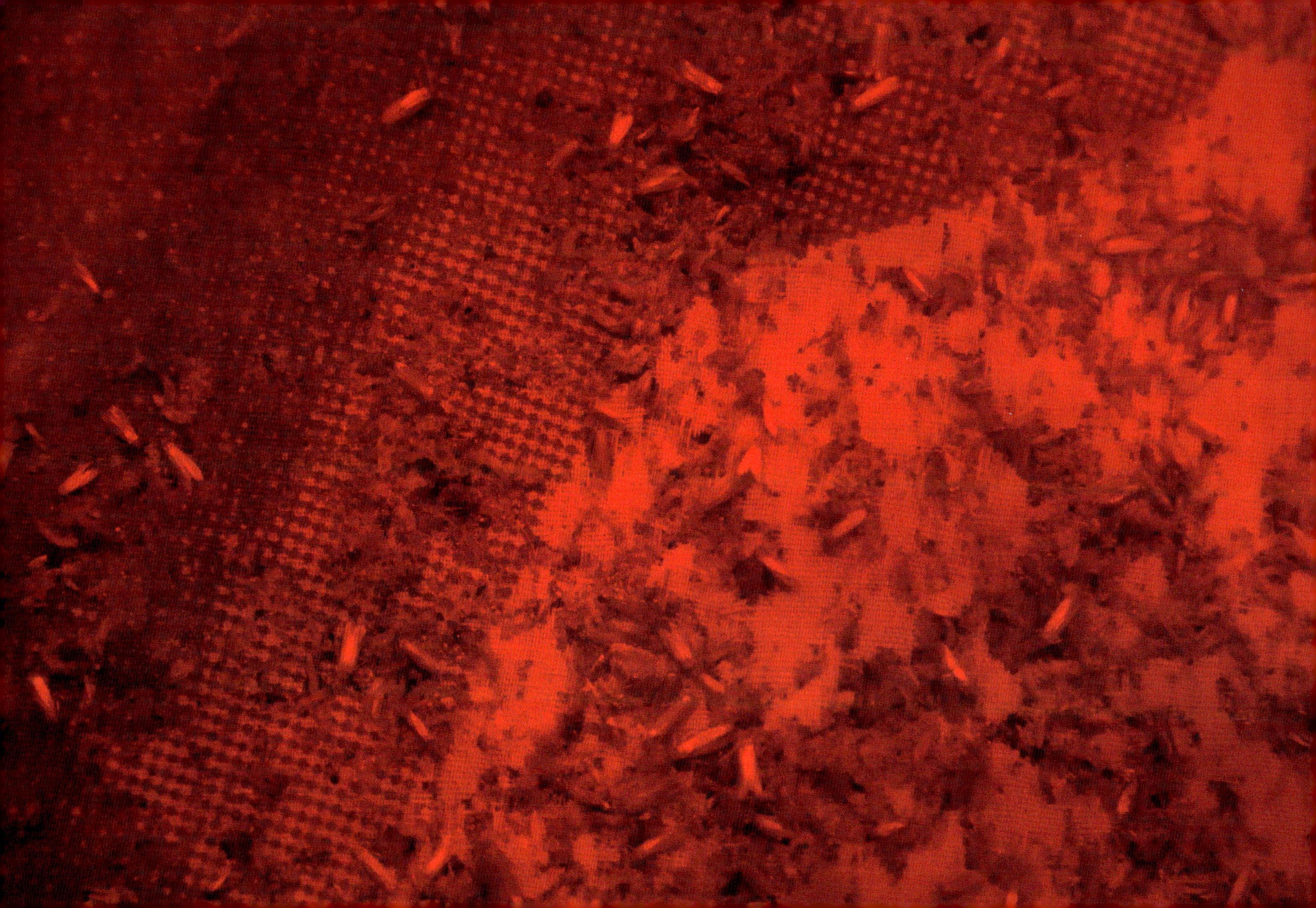

… There was an Ace bandage on the ground and I noticed that they put some sugar, or Epsom salt, or salt into each bowl — each of them had a bowl in front. And I was taken by the silence and then the noise of spoons stirring up the salt or sugar or whatever it was. And then I watched them begin — with what appeared to be an Ace bandage at first but obviously was not an Ace bandage — prepare for what was going to be some kind of ritual which, I had an idea of, because I knew the name of the piece was Swallow. Then they proceeded to open it up and prepare in a very formal way. And then collaboratively started to swallow it. And there seemed to be a tension between competition on one hand and collaboration on the other hand. And it became apparent after just a short period of time that they were going to have to consume this entire roll and that they would each have to do their part. She was drinking water, or she was drinking liquid, I don't know what, out of a cup over a period of six or eight minutes, or maybe a little longer than that. They quietly were able to bring in the entire roll starting at each end until there was just a little bit left in the middle. And then they removed it. And I frankly don't remember if they used their hands to remove it, I think they did. And they slowly removed it and then put it into an empty clear glass bowl, holding each end up in the air and then slowly, each person put their part of the roll from the end into the bowl and then put the bowl in another bowl, or put another bowl on top of that bowl and took the bowls out … And then when they were swallowing — if you've ever seen a

The Defender

snake eat a rodent, how much trouble and how hard it is for that snake to be able to consume — and he was struggling, as was Janine, struggling to get that substance down and it reminded me of a snake, a predator moving very slowly, very deliberately, very carefully, and then consuming the prey … The only time there seemed to be anything that would get close to the description of violence was when the man struggled to be able to keep the wrap down and started to almost regurgitate it and I was feeling like it was me that was about to upchuck or let it go … When they first started, I was dying to know what was going to happen. And frankly my initial — I had a very unusual childhood and one of the things that I first thought about when I saw the water and then the substance go in was, I had a lot of young friends and when they misbehaved their mothers would whip them and soak their legs in Epsom salt and put Ace bandages around it and that brought me back to when, if I would get in trouble with them and they would get whipped they'd come to school all mad sometimes and have Ace bandages on and they would describe how they got whipped and had to sit in the bathtub with Epsom salt. So that brought me back to that memory. I was dying to see — because then I forgot about the title of the piece — I was dying to see where this was going to go. So rather than affirmation, it was more anticipation to see what was going to happen. And the Epsom salt's about soothing and about disguising, really, because I think that a lot of times the mothers would do that so that the marks would disappear … I've been trained to work with memory. Not so much trained — it's been important to me as a criminal defense lawyer — to understand memory and how memory gets influenced. And if you're able to articulate that in examining witnesses, you can have other people understand an outside influence on memory and thereby paint a picture of somebody either being accurate or inaccurate or calling into question people's ability to recall and remember and articulate what they saw. So maybe that's why I'm able to do that or why that's important to me … So anybody who gets up on a witness stand and takes an oath, the first question you want to ask yourself in your preparation is, where does this person stand vis-à-vis the case, or more importantly, the person who is sitting next to me: my client. So here, I thought about the relationship between the two participants and what role each was going to play: was it going to be a race? Or were they going to cheer each other on? He put his hand up as though, "Look up and you can do this." And he put his left hand out high in the air, I don't know whether that was planned or not, and so I was looking at the way in which they were observing each other and it seemed as though what they were doing was, with their eyes and non-verbal communication, supporting each other and cheering each other on.

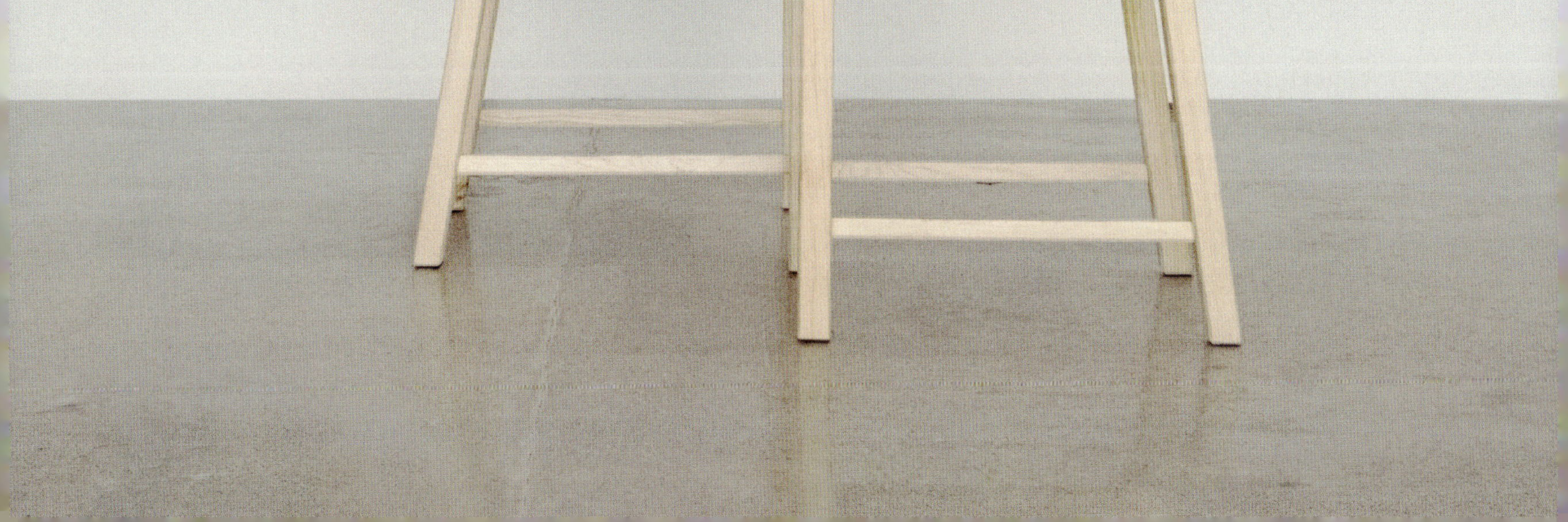

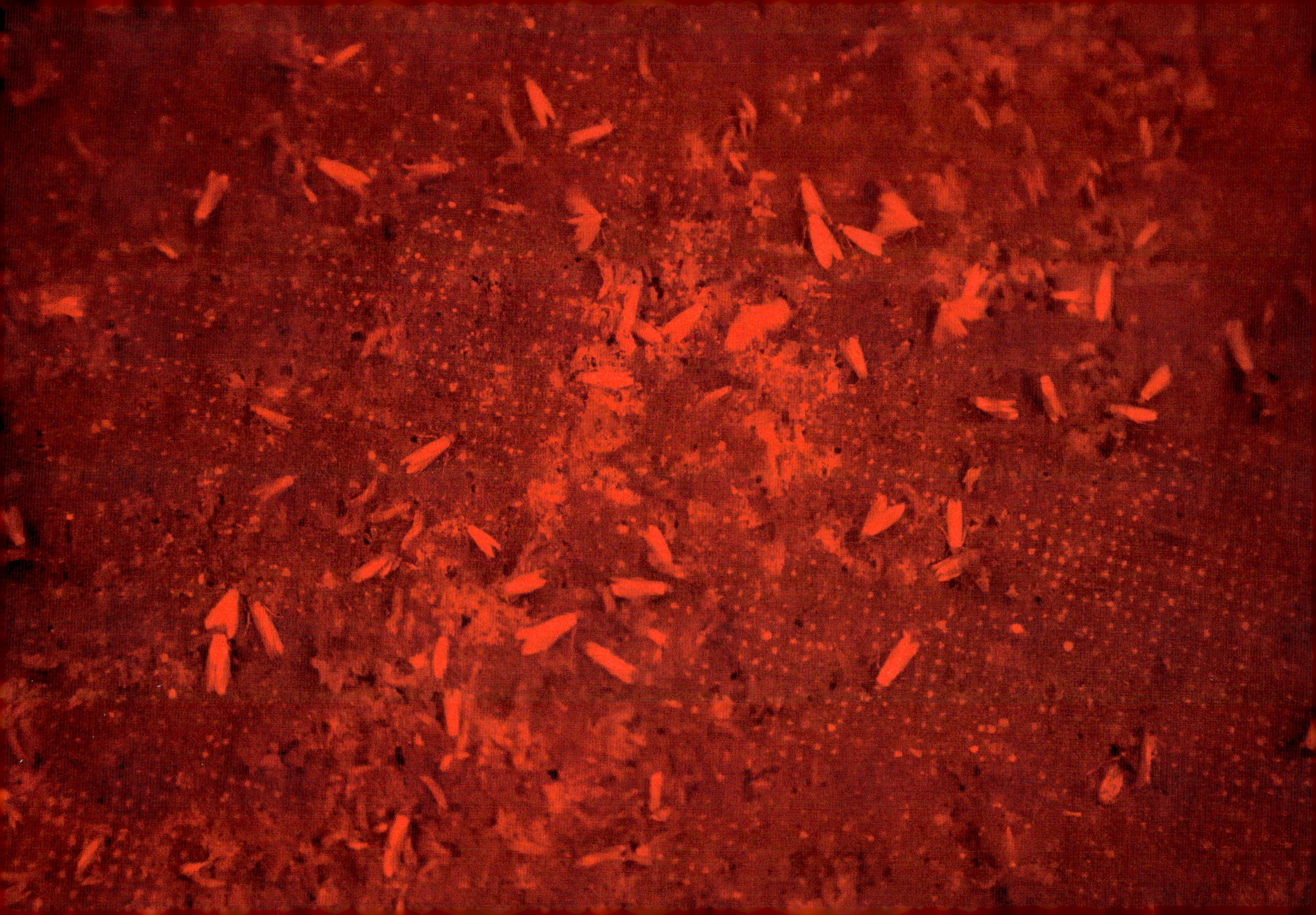

… So I thought that he really opened his throat locally, which I thought I could see. I can't see inside, but I thought I could see a very clear pathway for the cloth to go down. And he was connected through his torso, so I would put it head to tail and he was connected from his sitz bones down into the chair and with his feet down into the floor. He really had his whole body globally connected and locally connected to receive the cloth. I thought Janine struggled with that a lot more. That at one point she didn't — one foot was up and one foot was down so she didn't even have full contact with the floor for herself. She was kind of tilted forward so she was hyperextended in her back and I didn't feel like she ever really opened her throat physically. Obviously she did, she did it. But I think she struggled more than Stephen did because of the body — well, I don't know why really. I'm kind of making — I really don't know why … I felt it. Reading it, I was looking at it on a body level more, especially the swallowing. The parting, though, I got more emotionally involved with and I found … how can I explain this? I found … the parting almost more precarious than the — there was work going into the advancing. And that was somehow more controlled. But then the parting was scarier. Because it felt like there was a lot less control. I think emotionally, there was separation to it and that has sometimes sadness to it and I'm not sure if I was feeling sad or feeling scared. Maybe I was feeling both … I didn't like the cloth at the end. It was something that was — it became almost —

The Healer

the beginning was very beautiful and ritualistic to me and the end got a little bit gross and medical and the bowls that they were using — I think they were the tinny kind of medical white bowls and at the end they really looked like it. At beginning they didn't particularly read like that. They read more Eastern and at the end they read Western. Ucky Western. Like at the end of an operation, cleaning up at the end of an operation … It was almost gut wrenching when it came out. And then there's an image of Stephen's throat almost elongating that I think I'll remember … And there was — they were coming at it from, it was almost like Stephen was like, "I know how to do this, I can do this." And Janine was, "I'm gonna do this anyway." So there was beauty in that for sure … And that might be what I will remember the most actually: the difference and the value of both sides. That the image is just a moment in time and doesn't show the process. In a way, it's not of value, because it was the process that mattered. I can really hold both at the same time … In a bodywork system that I do called Zero Balancing there's a concept of interface: clearly knowing where I begin and end and where they begin and end. I don't feel like I merged with them, so I don't feel like I was having the experience, I feel I was watching them have the experience. And that might be because I train myself to do that — I don't want to pick up what my patients are feeling. I want to be with them and know what they're feeling but I don't want to feel their pain. If I want to be there for you, I need to be clear in myself and well in myself and then I can be there for you to help you, but I don't want to absorb your problems as then I don't think I can help you because I'm now having a problem … When I am — I do feel that when I'm working on somebody one of the ways a person does heal is by going into an altered state where their belief systems and their injuries are less tightly held and where you can override the injury and also that — in terms of having an image of yourself — can change the image of yourself. And I think I, as a person working on that person, can also go into an altered state and also have an experience of expansion where healing can take place. And I feel that in art the audience, the viewer, can have an expansive experience where they're changed, as well as the performers having some kind of expansive experience where they're changed. And I do think that's almost the definition of art, where you're touched at a level of your spirit where it can be a transformative process. I don't really know — I know how I'm feeling right now, but I don't know how I'll feel tomorrow or in a year, whether this is something that's gonna stay with me or not. So this also is just a snapshot.

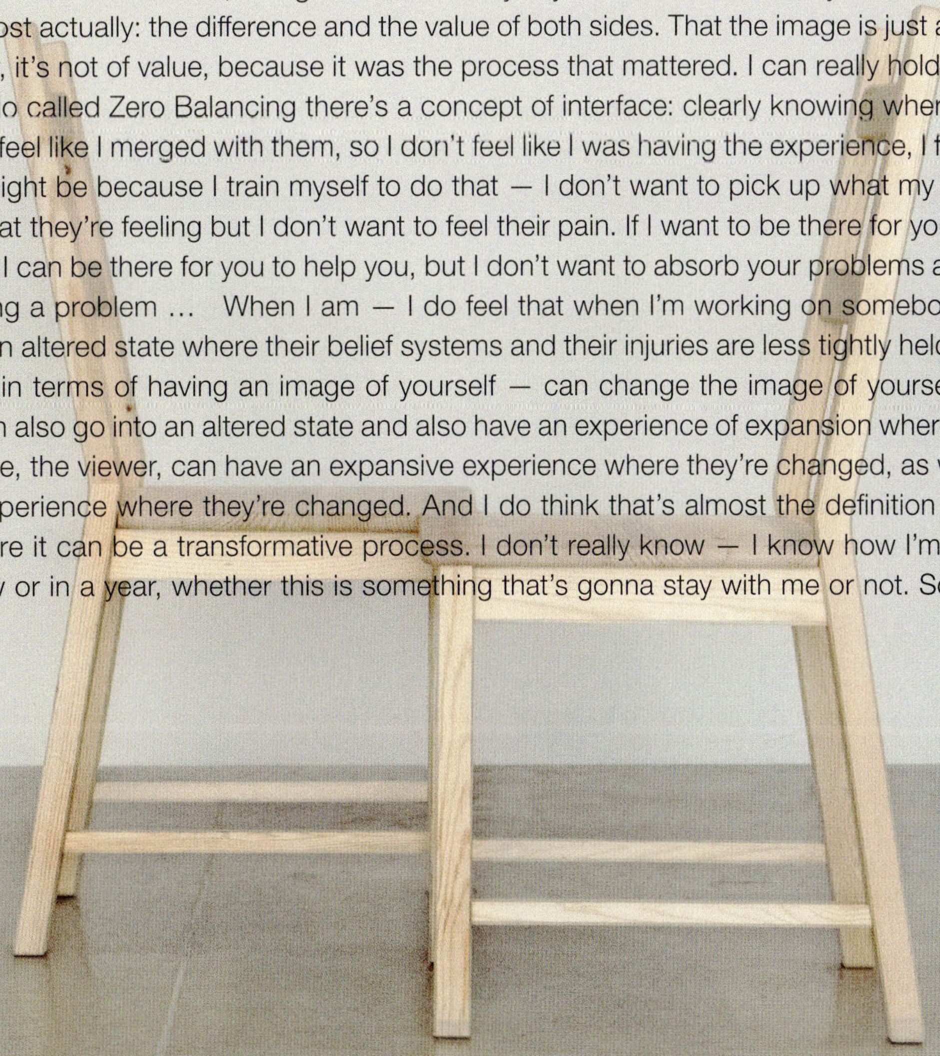

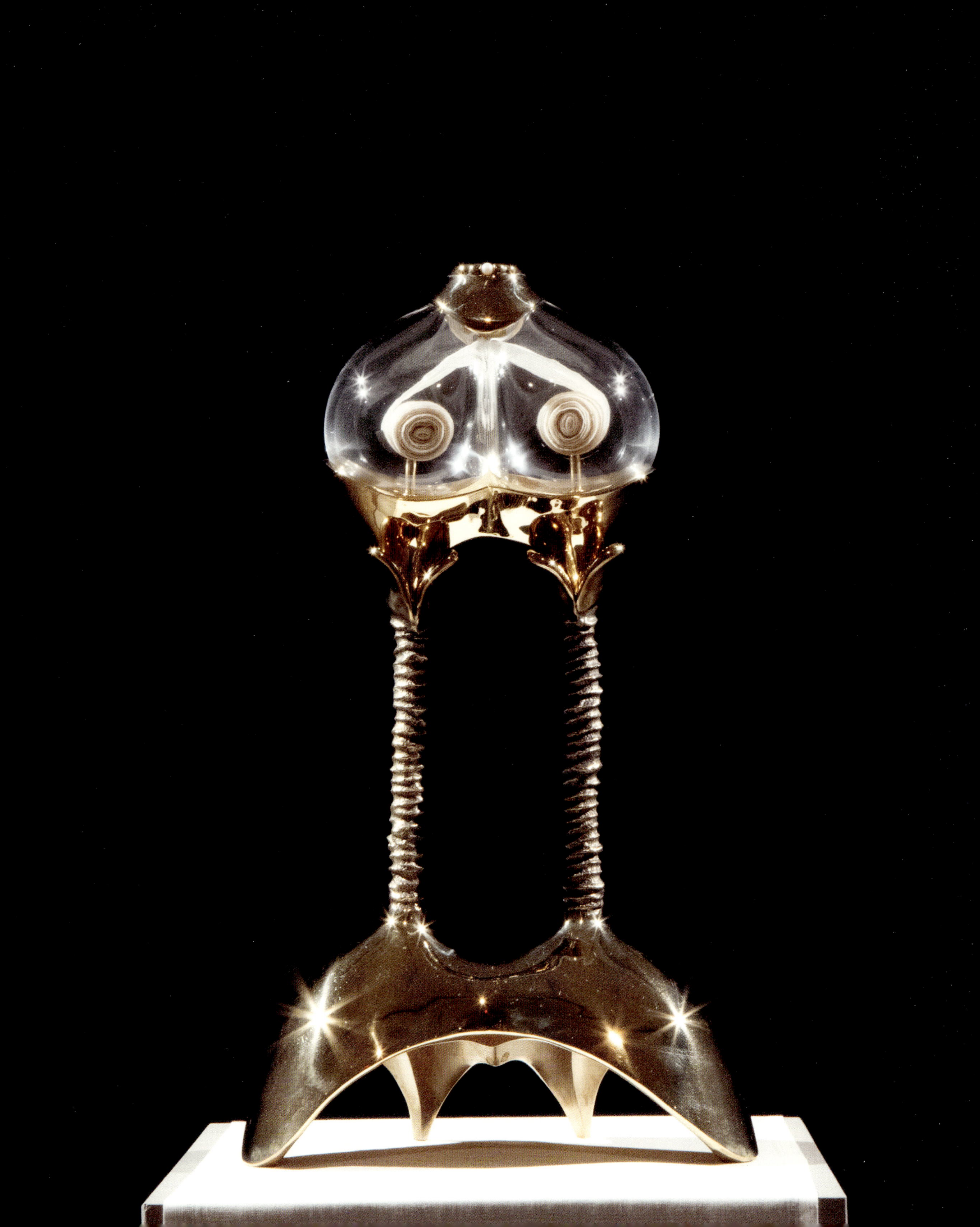

… Boy: Put in water. Mother: And then what? Boy: Put in sugar. Mother: They put sugar in and then what did they do? Boy: Swallowed the string. Mother: And where did the string go? Boy: To their tummy. Mother: And was it one string or two strings? Boy: One string. Mother: So the one string went where? Boy: In their tummy. Mother: And were they really close when they swallowed everything? And then what happened? When they were really close what did they start to do after that? Girl: Pull it out. Mother: What was the man doing when the string was coming back up you guys? Girl: Taking it out. Mother: He was taking the string out? Girl: With his hand. Boy: But it was her hands. Girl: No, just one string. Boy: They just had one glass. Girl: No, had two glasses. Boy: No, one. Girl: Three glasses. Boy: Because the glass breaks I was surprised. Mother: Who dropped the glass you guys? Boy: A girl … Mother: The thing that moved me right away with the children was that they seemed to know they were watching something important and that they were watching a ritual. And they were holding their own bodies with a purpose. And then I felt it shift. I felt them realizing it was going to take some time, and then it felt like they needed comfort. So I think he climbed into my lap first — is that right? I can't remember now — and was really there and needing me while watching it and he completely leaned into my body. And then at a certain point, she came up and then I thought, oh I'm going to have to share my body and will they fight over it? Because sometimes that's what happens, they're not getting enough of my body and then they start squirming

The Mother and Twins

around and pushing each other off my legs … In watching them it felt distant to them and in some space that made no sense to them even though they knew they were supposed to watch it. And it was only when he began burping that I think they both sat up and that made sense to them. That was something a body would do in response to what was happening. And I have to say I was completely floored that he said he was angry about it … I often feel divided when I know that they have strong emotional needs because they might want to sit on my lap but I have to share my lap. And so what I'll do is I spread my legs open and they each sit on one leg. The other day she said, "Mama needs four legs." … Mother: You felt angry while you were watching them? Boy: Yeah. Mother: Why? Boy: Because I don't want that lady and that man to swallow the string so I'll be angry. Mother: Why didn't you want them to swallow the string? Boy: Because I think they'll get sick so I don't want the man and the lady to swallow the string. Mother: You thought they were going to get sick? Boy: Yeah, so that's why I be angry. Mother: But it made you angry because you didn't want them to do something that might hurt them? Boy: Yeah. Mother: What did you feel when you were watching it? Girl: Silly. Mother: You felt silly? You know what you guys? It surprised me, there was a moment that it made me feel really sad. Boy: Why? … Mother: When I said what I did, it was really interesting to me that they both turned around and wanted to know why I had been sad. I felt it more … that he was angry at them for doing it to themselves. And that it made him feel like he couldn't understand the world, why someone would do something that might be hurtful to themselves. And he wanted them to stop. And why were they forcing themselves? Because that was clear: that they were forcing themselves to do something that was difficult to do and uncomfortable and unnatural … I feel like there's a way in which we become complicit by watching. So that in the watching them and the not stopping them we are all a part of the same body that is continuing to do the harm … They didn't come close enough together for me and they didn't hold that moment long enough for me. I really felt the whole piece was going to be in that moment when their bodies had to touch each other and be united by this thing that was inside of both of them. So it felt like it faltered at the most intimate moment. That it retreated from intimacy as quickly as possible. So I was disappointed. I wanted the intimacy to become unbearable. Probably the most dangerous, the most fragile, and the moment if you held on too long someone could just throw up the whole thing right there. I wasn't thinking any of this consciously at the time at all but I just felt sadness and whatever is deeply inside of yourself, you may or may not ever get to show it … Yeah, having your guts be one with another's guts. Really, the most visceral — I feel you get to do that through sex. That sex actually, you go into this zone where your guts are connected and you are inside out with someone, you're inside of each others' bodies in some way. But I think with this, because it's so connected to words, I always think of sex as abstraction, it's so inarticulate and it's so physical and visceral. But this is connected to words and breathing and control maybe. There's a gag reflex, right, whereas in sex once you're in you're in. And so — it just seemed like the impossibility of words to connect to each other's guts … And I tell you, I lived forty-six years before I knew that feeling too. I was a woman in the world for forty-six years before I imagined and felt what it was to have two people living and growing inside of me. And they're moving around and trying to make space for themselves. So that thing of them negotiating for space is something that started on the inside and begins on the outside of my body so that they're negotiating for the space around my body and their proximity to me and their relationship to each other. So they'll often sleep with their heads against each other's heads or I'll come in and one of his legs will be tossed over her body. But there'll usually be some point of physical contact if they're sleeping next to each other. Which feels like what they've always known: some place where their two bodies meet each other. And then with me, their bodies have met with my body. I'm really interested in the ways that I'm transformed by knowing these children … They remember things that matter to them. So I think they will remember this. But I think it will still be a question mark. They will remember something that made no sense to them.

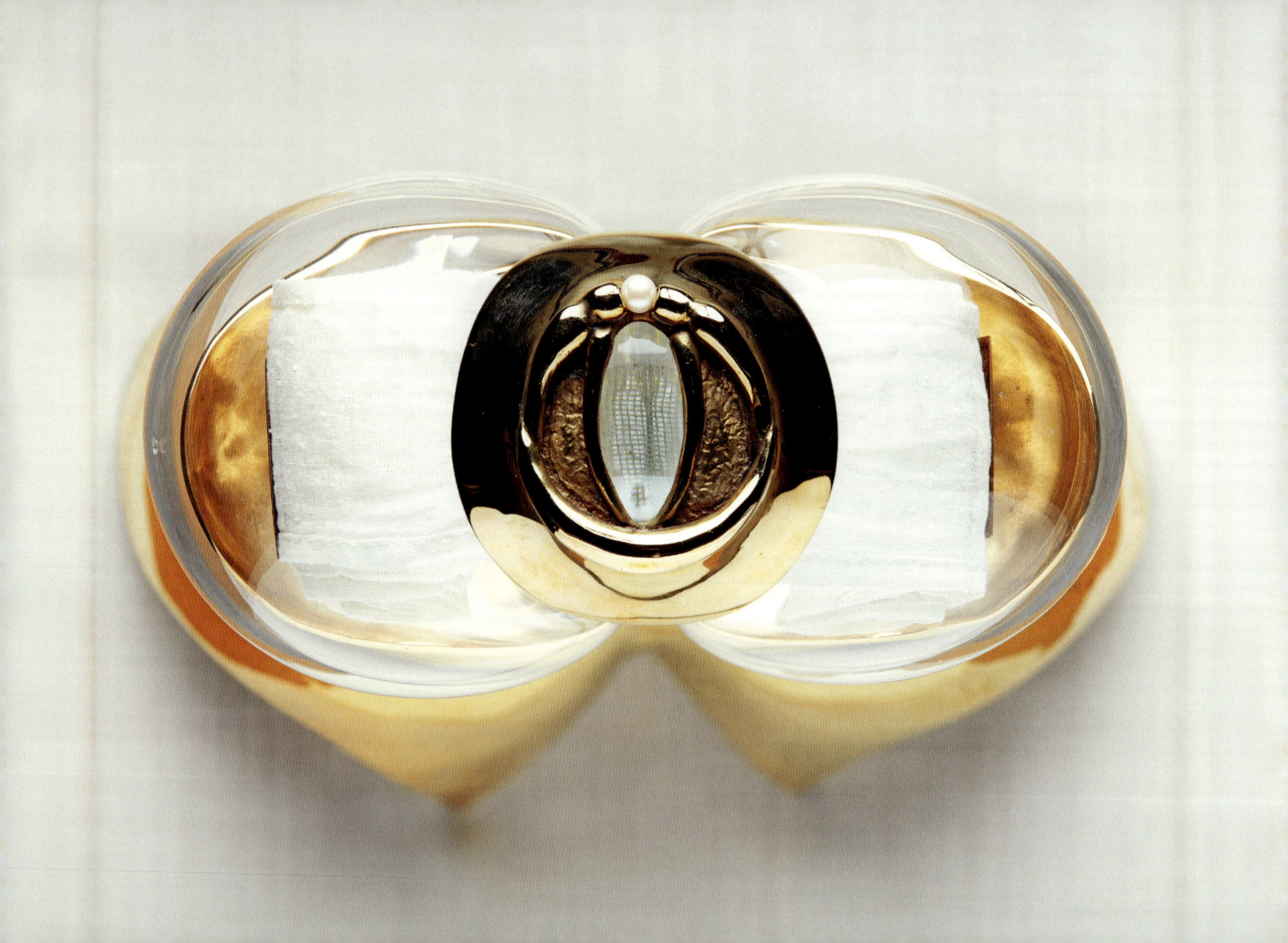

My very first thought when it began was — there were some buckets and some basins, Janine was pouring water from a kettle into these basins — does this look more medicinal or culinary? Or is it like a pair of lovers preparing for some sort of ritual in which maybe they're going to bathe each other's feet? … My first psychological thought, since that's the background from which I come, is the idea of a man and a woman facing each other at a little distance to begin swallowing this long fabric rope. And introjection — psychologically — means swallowing whole. It's taking in another person, like a child taking in a parent through imitation, identification. But to introject … comes to mean taking in without chewing, just swallowing. And here were the two of them doing it mutually, which psychologically is what a pair of lovers who've become infatuated with each other would tend to do: to swallow the other person whole, usually through a process of idealization and feeling almost like you have become the other. So mutual swallowing, you could say, is the beginning of some process of infatuation. As they took in more and more of the rope, it brought them closer and closer together. So here we have the process of infatuation turning into intimacy. Of course it happens with adults all the time, particularly in falling in love, which is a pretty quick process. This form of introjecting, swallowing with such difficulty and so much labor, it's a little more like the real hard work of intimacy rather than the quickie take on infatuation … I guess we may have seen something like a miniaturized high-speed ritual version of marriage and

The Listener

divorce … We can spend even some years getting together, then we come together and sometimes the unraveling and coming apart can be pretty quick but very painful … The sort of carefulness and difficulty and movement of coming together in which two first person singulars — two Is — are becoming a We. And to become a We, the I that you experience yourself as being, is radically changed. You've taken in a good deal of this other person and you've put a good deal of yourself over in them. And so the We is a mixture of selves and the coming apart may be rapid. But often when a relationship breaks down — one that has been intimate and has so much investment of self in it — you feel like a big part of yourself is going with the loss of the other person. The process of grieving that loss is really a process of ultimately healing, if you see it through all the way, of recovering the self you had invested in this other person. Reeling it back into you. But then we're only a We. They struggled, each of them taking in, to get to a point where there was no more rope between them, and then they were as if merged. And then they quickly disgorged it, rather painfully nevertheless. They got out of it quickly and there they were … The umbilical cord seems a very relevant image of a situation where you're so thoroughly connected to another being: you are fed and your blood circulated by this other being that you're deeply connected to. So, in a state that a school of psychotherapy that I'm very much learned in called Gestalt therapy calls "confluence." Confluence is a kind of connection in which there's really no psychological boundary of difference … It's a little like having sex and then immediately heading for the airport or checking out of the hotel room without any contemplative post experience. Creating a work of art, having a sexual experience, are among the most intense things that we do and certainly they call naturally for some post experience of reflection, of exploration, of seeing how this has affected you, where it might take you … I might think of it in terms of a broader spectrum of possibilities of relationship. I think the struggle to get together, not quite perhaps as viscerally difficult as swallowing the fabric rope, but the difficulty of moving into real closeness with another person is always a bit fraught and uneasy. Actuality, and the fact that there's all this biology going on — orifices, swallowing, gastrointestinal, not so far removed from the biology of sex — tends to point things in that direction. But I think that whole question of affiliation, of connection, of friendship, isn't really so determined by psychosexual filaments and tendencies as certainly the psychoanalysts tend to think. And culturally we're still pretty much of that mind. I think it has much more to do with the fact that of all the species, we have the most prolonged dependence on adult caretakers and that connection is one that haunts us all our lives. So many of us live in haunted houses with ghosts in the attic rattling the chains of our old dependencies. They are bringing some intriguing ideas to me. It's a nice give and take because the way they're working together inspires a lot of thought about the nature of relationship: what's involved in trying to create a We? And I really would like to broaden that beyond sexuality. The whole business of what happens to the self, one's sense of self when you enter into a We of all kinds and there are many, many forms of it. I think we are by far the most relational of all living creatures …

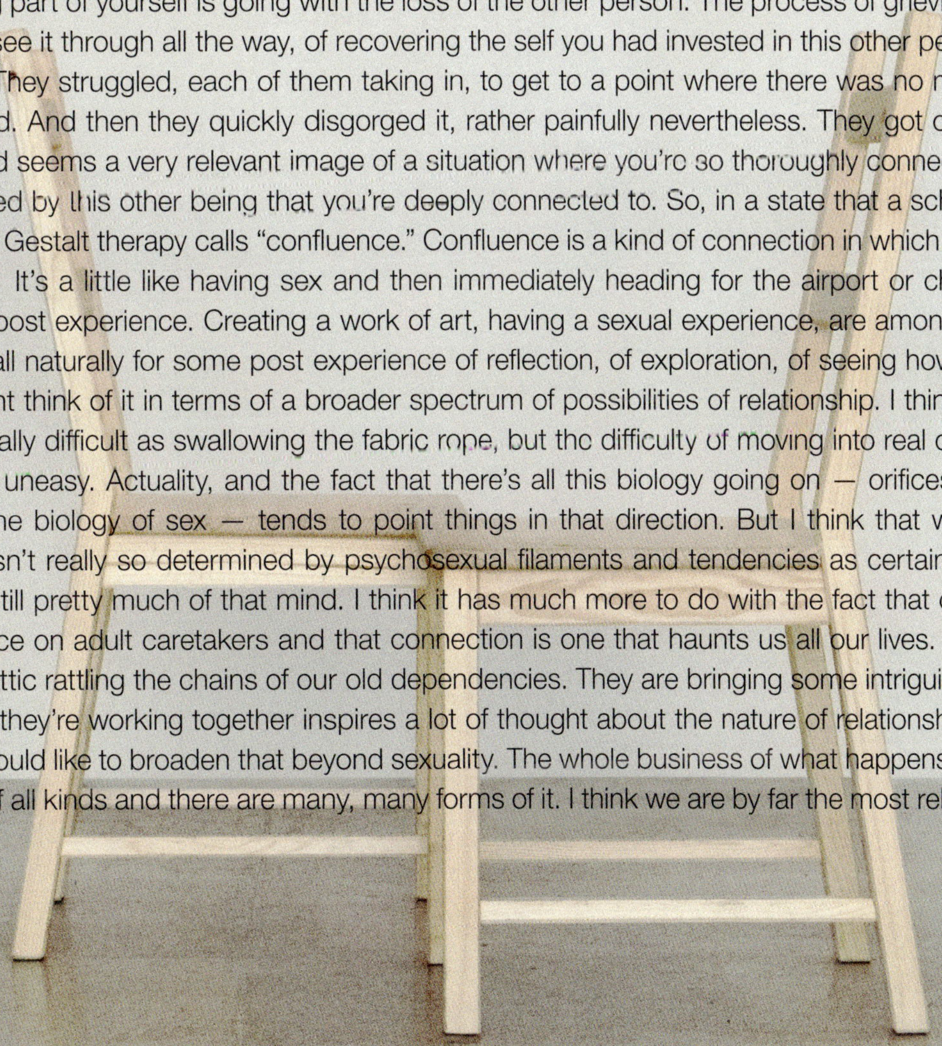

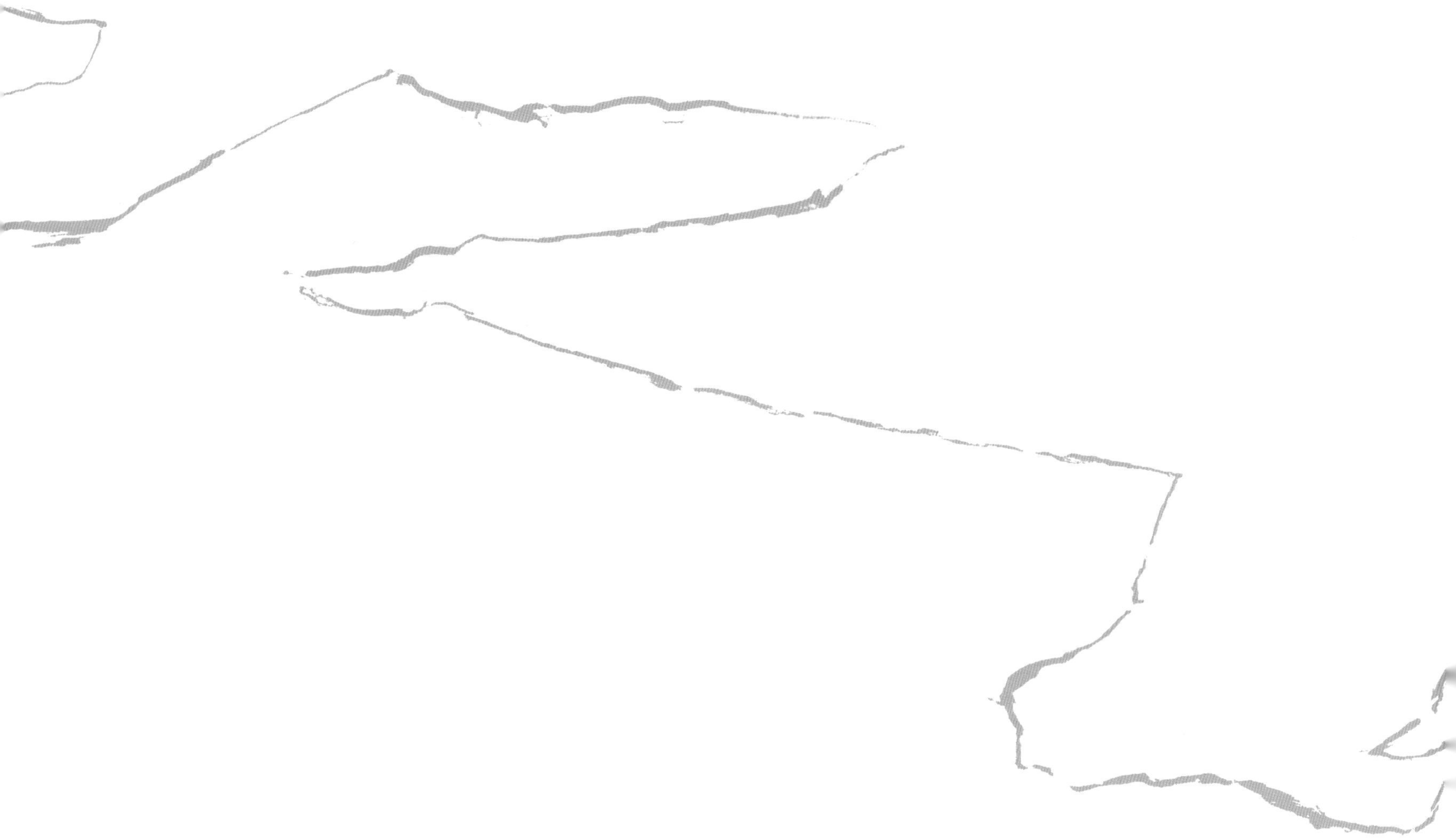

GOD SAVE PETRONIO!
IN THE PARADISE OF FIRST GRACE

Richard Move

If he alone is to receive the Precious Blood, there should be
enough wine for him to consume the contents reverently in one draught.
The Liturgy of the Eucharist[1]

This is my body with flesh and bones and blood
that take me out into the world for better or worse.
Stephen Petronio[2]

Typicon (An Introduction)

Stephen Petronio's body and body of work, either apart from, or with that of his allies, Janine Antoni and Anna Halprin, is a choreography of baroque beatitudes inextricably linking dance, religion, sexuality and iconography. The juvenile Stephen stands with his heart and mouth open wide to receive the Holy Eucharist and to drink the Precious Blood at Holy Family Church in Nutley, New Jersey. In adulthood, he continues to seek enlightenment and salvation through a heightened state of kinetic corporeality.

While his prolific body of work created in over thirty years for the Stephen Petronio Dance Company vibrates with this velocity of belief, it is with *Ally* that Petronio's lifelong, faithful quest to achieve life everlasting may finally be realized. This is the paradise of first grace for Petronio the dancer, the believer, and the acolyte. The obedient worship of idols and icons, gods and goddesses of dance, music, fashion, the sanctity of sex and all things punk, are the genesis of his creations and fuel the fire of his addiction to motion. Petronio's dance and Petronio himself become supremely and substantively present in the corporealities of his flesh, bones and blood, drawing us as witnesses into his form of perfect worship. The divine mystery becomes apparent in the shared human network of Petronio's collaborators, and the resultant transformative powers of the bodily craft of dance making. Through dance, he comes to know something of what remains to most an incomprehensible mystery.

Petronio's signature masterpiece *MiddleSexGorge* (1990), his honorific *Bloodlines* project (2015) with its faithful enactments including Trisha Brown's *Glacial Decoy* (1979), and *Ally*'s enactment of Anna Halprin's *The Courtesan and the Crone* (1999), culminate with the transcendent blessing of *Swallow*. With *Swallow*, Petronio is ultimately transported to life everlasting by another seemingly unlikely ally, Tineola Biselliella, or the webbing clothes moth. The Christian themes of his historic artistic adventure embody and personify resurrection, eternity and glory.

Petronio is the second son of a second generation Italian-American "blue collar hero."[3] Bred and informed by Roman Catholicism and all things Italian-American, Petronio's first idol was Thomas Petronio, his truck-driver father. As an inexperienced student at Hampshire College, a confluence of postmodern dance teachers forever changed the course of his life and he became the "bastard child of Steve Paxton and Trisha Brown," his "surrogate parents in dance," who instilled in him "a deep love of pure physics in motion."[4] While the primary and most influential deity of Petronio's pantheon of dance icons is Trisha Brown, it is first Paxton, a "postmodern Hermes, a winged messenger," who introduced the eighteen-year old Petronio to contact improvisation, and delivered him "tumbling into dance."[5] Paxton was a leader amongst the maverick, postmodern experimentalists of the 1960s Judson Dance Theater. Paxton opened the door and Petronio walked into a life.

Paxton prepared Petronio for another postmodern renegade, Trisha Brown, the "mercurial force who agreed to let a mortal boy into her inner circle of sophisticated female calligraphy."[6] These visionary emissaries of postmodernism were Petronio's "early gods of motion ... open with their gifts ..."[7] Petronio's body "soft and young and caught between its inheritance and desire for this life" received their gifts and his fate was sealed.[8] At the age of twenty-three, and shortly after he moved permanently to New York City in 1978, he became the first male dancer in the Trisha Brown Dance Company, where he remained for seven years from 1979–86, carrying out the duties assigned to him by his elder icon, and reveling in the "delights of abstraction and purity of form."[9]

Petronio had only been dancing for four years before penetrating the sacred female circle of Trisha Brown's company. He considered himself "a rank beginner with a very lucky body" who was shocked at Brown's invitation to join her group where he absolutely knew he was home.[10] The "blocky, unformed, hairy, sweaty, Italian boy from New Jersey" found himself in flight with "the sylphs of the 21st century" with no other men, thus redefining masculinity and the male dancer.[11]

With a wholehearted commitment to the experiential process and elemental incandescence of Brown, Petronio entered the, "interior space made visible in time and place ... filled with passion, volume and peculiar curves."[12] Blissfully, Petronio was enveloped in the aerodynamics of Brown's polyrhythmic vocabulary, negotiating its teeming range of movement possibilities with all cylinders afire. Her body and body of work, and his within it, created a new paradigm, "spinning and moving in a gyroscopic kinesphere that's at once organic and virtuosic."[13] Despite being created for the proscenium stage, Brown's choreographies are neither presentational nor frontal. Her focused gaze travels in fully concentric orbits, moving much more quickly than that of her predecessors or peers. Brown was like a new religion for the impressionable and malleable Petronio. He became an extension of her, able to negotiate the multidirectional geography of her sensuous, sumptuous, perception-altering choreography in a "shifting spherical world in which all information was equal."[14] After seven years, Petronio was both Brown's progeny and a rebellious "bastard child" who set out to develop his own equally compelling and unique body of work.[15]

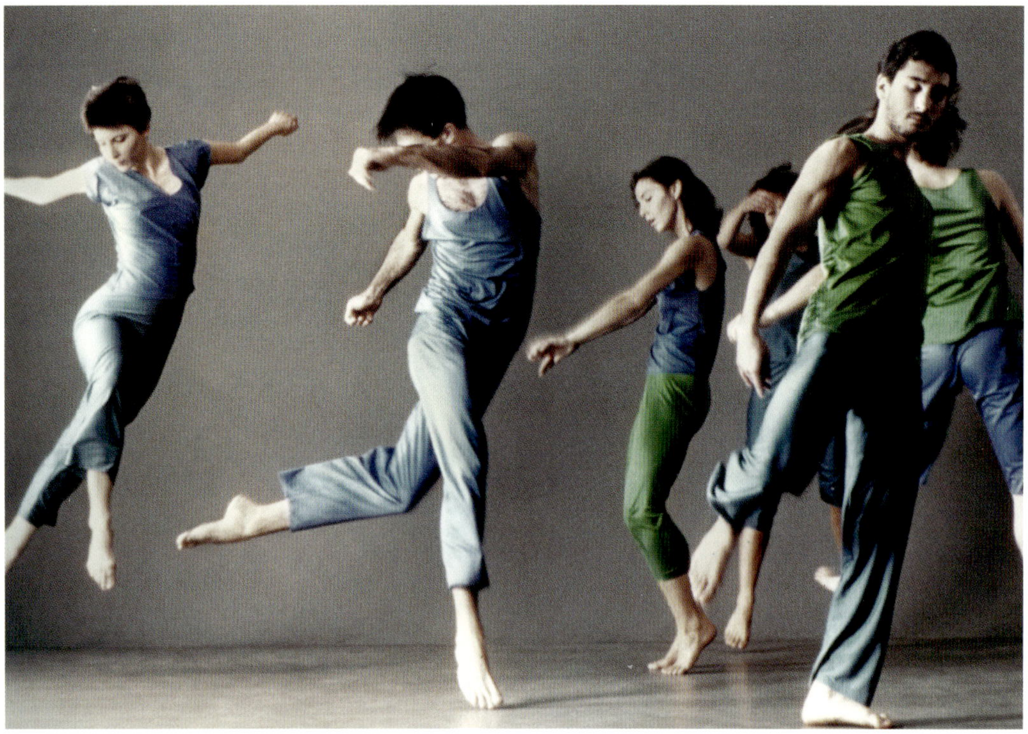

Trisha Brown Dance Company, *Son of Gone Fishin'*, 1989. Dancers (left to right): Eva Karczag, Stephen Petronio, Vicky Stick, Lisa Krauss, Randy Warshaw, Diane Madden. Photo © Lois Greenfield.

Punk Icon

Petronio, a boy raised in a heteronormative Roman Catholic household, emerges in the 1980s as a quintessential punk. A punk with a rebellious stance against a life he could not live and a future he could not have. A queer Catholic boy, Petronio had to become someone his parents and family could not imagine. Upon his arrival in New York City, Petronio rode the crest of the countercultural zeitgeist, surfing the currents of fashion, art, music, and queer culture flourishing downtown in the late 1970s and 1980s. His love of fashion and particularly, his love of the high priestess of punk couture, Vivienne Westwood, provided the rebel's uniform, outfitting him for his allegiance to the dance floor and the social practice of nightlife.

Petronio, like many a creative misfit, both finds and makes a home for himself in the queer utopias of loft performances, live music and gay dance club venues. He embraces and is embraced by the demimonde. He fashions his own identity and sets out to create a life as a cultural arbiter with the platform of an insolent dance-artist springing himself upon a surprised but ready public of other radical misfits and art rebels. He is a gifted provocateur and malcontent whose works, appearance and worldview reject the mainstream. He happily abandons hope of following the strict rules and regulations of his upbringing, straight society and the conventions of modern dance. However, the refrain "No Future," from the Sex Pistols 1977 "God Save the Queen," an anthem of the punk rock movement, does not apply to Petronio. The facticity of his flesh, blood and bones generate their own form of radical productivity and futurity. Petronio, along with other like-minded artists, defines the queer and post-punk aesthetics of downtown New York City. His future could not be contained by the narrow scope of his disciplined childhood. Instead, Petronio reconfigured that discipline and applied that rigor to shape his work, define his aesthetic and claim power over his flesh. He happily rediscovered and relived a childhood as an adult pervert, free of

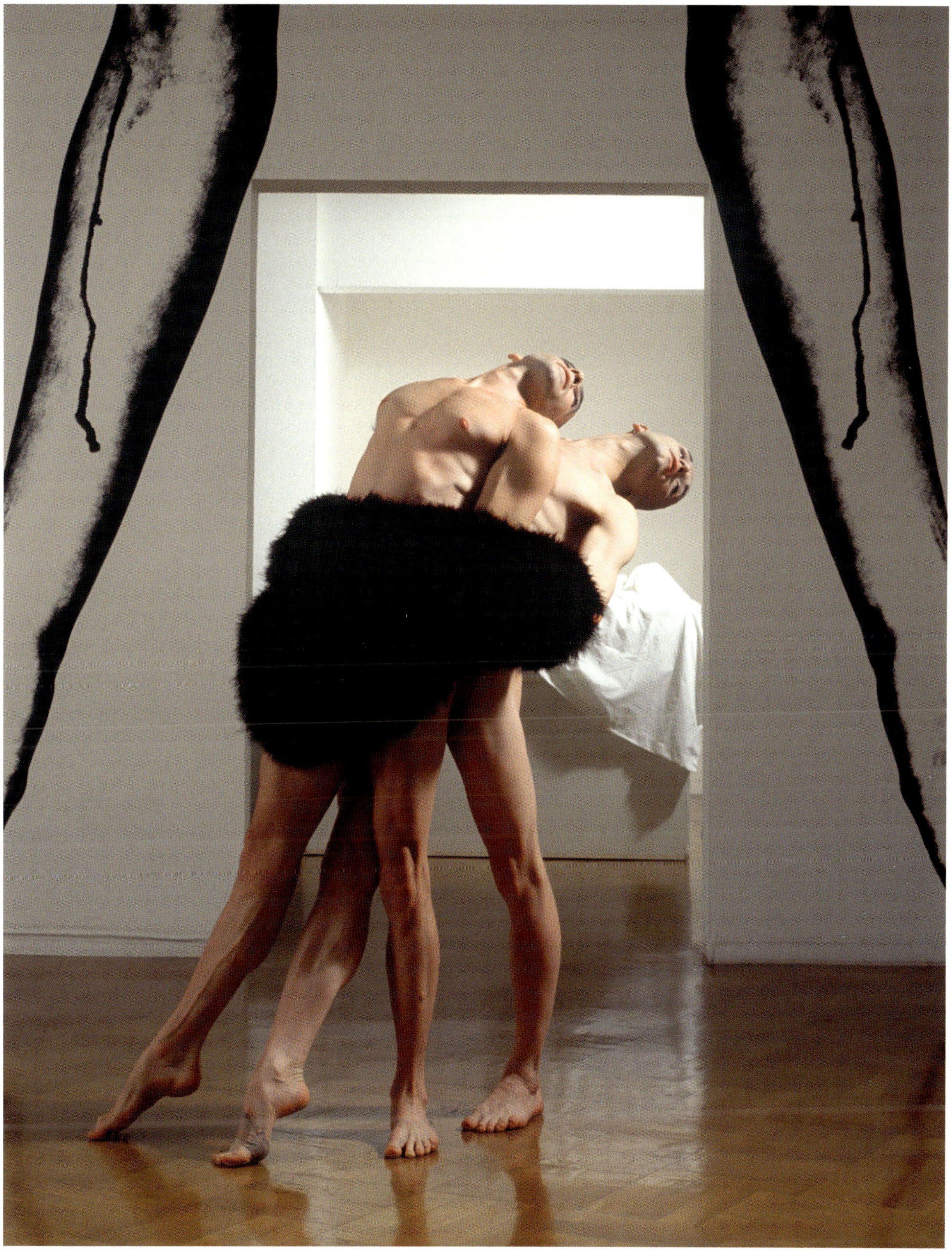

Michael Clark Company, *Heterospective*, 1989. Dancers (left to right): Stephen Petronio, Michael Clark. Photo © Chris Nash.

the hetero temporalities of propagation and generational succession. His dance is a subaltern and resistant mode of political engagement: a conflation of the obscene and sentimental, the unrestrained and the uncontrollable. His knowledge is a carnal consciousness of the body that seeks shelter in the vast openness and expanse of choreographic creativity. Perhaps Petronio's greatest achievement as choreographer lies in his ability to channel the punk sensibilities of wild abandonment and situate them within a highly formalized and structurally refined aesthetic sensibility.

Sex is Gorge

In the late 1980s, at the height of the AIDS epidemic and threatened with extinction, Petronio found his "essential body" and the basis of his iconoclastic vocabulary.[16] In 1988, he joined ACT UP, a radical group of political activists that interjected their bodies into social spaces with acts of civil disobedience and demonstrations that effectively drew attention to the government's refusal to recognize and respond to the AIDS crisis. During the course of ACT UP's activities, Petronio was forced to challenge his own Catholicism by interrupting masses at New York's St. Patrick's Cathedral, where anti-gay propaganda propagated by the Church was espoused by its representative, Cardinal O' Connor. This was the era of a full-on assault on gay men as carriers of the disease whose behavior was blamed for the epidemic. It was also an era that mobilized queer artists to produce work that became its own form of social protest. Far-right politicians such as Jesse Helms openly condemned both the sex and art practices of homosexuals in an ongoing, aggressive assault against queer bodies.

In the fall of 1988, Petronio was repeatedly arrested in New York City. With ACT UP, Petronio emphasized that he "began to feel very urgent about leaking my life into the work during a very sexual period in terms of what was happening in the streets of New York and in my life."[17] In the crossfire of contagion, bodily fluids, a blood-borne virus and the moral panic of a Rapture-like plague, Petronio interjected his body into the political theater of his own choreographic work with the same volition as he did the protests of ACT UP. Faced with his own mortality, and that of his peers, Petronio was forced to reconsider his aesthetic motivations and asked himself, "How could I possibly do anything honest if it wasn't related to the thing that I was doing?" He continued, "So I set myself a challenge to try and be as honest as I could in the work and try and put some of the immediacy of giving up control and grasping control of my sexuality, of my body, of my partner's body and to have that be the fabric of the dance."[18]

With the rigor of Catholic obedience, Petronio forged his vocabulary by "taking your tailbone and your pubic bone and dragging it through the floor and swinging your arm like a machete if someone's in your way. That's the type of infusion and those are the physicalizations."[19] He crafts the sensual, sexual and most uninhibited aspects of his nature into a language of movement that pushes the pelvis forcefully forward into the face of the audience, with his head and hips carving arcs, while his legs and arms slash through the space.

On January 16, 1990, his masterwork, *MiddleSexGorge* premiered in New York at the Joyce Theater, the same date the United States entered the first Gulf War. Onstage in the heart of New York City's Chelsea neighborhood, just north of Greenwich Village and at the epicenter of the AIDS crisis, while friends, peers, colleagues and great artists lay dead or dying, Petronio unleashed a meta-kinetic assault in response to the world around him that unfurled with lightning speed before the audience's eyes. Resistant fists, aggressive twists of

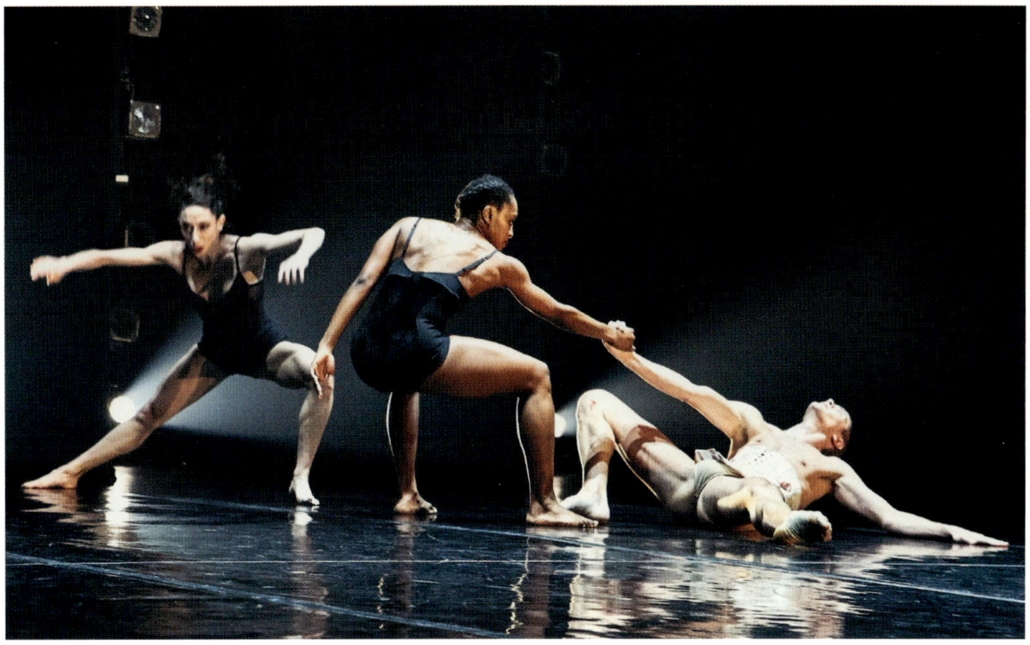

Stephen Petronio Company, *MiddleSexGorge*, 2016 [1990]. Dancers (left to right): Jaqlin Medlock, Davalois Fearon, Joshua Tuason. Photo © Robert Altman, 2016.

the torso, karate-like slices and chops of the arms and legs, warrior-like stances of the upper body, alternating changes of direction, levels, facings, women partnering women and men partnering men, constituted the defiant character of *MiddleSexGorge*.

The fetishistic costumes of flowered shorts, tops, pants and corsets by H. Petal objectified the men and placed the women in more functional dancewear. It is the men who wear restraining corsets above exposed buttocks in chap-like tights. The rhythmic induction of *MiddleSexGorge* and Petronio's love of all things punk, post-punk, alternative and electronic are exemplified by the soundtrack, Wire's "Ambitious," from the English group's *Ideal Copy* album of 1988. Fittingly, the phrase "ideal copy," repeated throughout, is a reference to DNA. It is the most appropriate anthem for its "hotness," and its refrain, "When it's hot, I feel ambitious," is the perfect soundtrack for Petronio's unbridled and determined success in forging his artistic identity and triumphing over social conservatism. The lyrical refrain of "Are you hot?" is answered with an exclamatory and defiant YES. Especially with the pairing, at its premiere, of Petronio with his then lover, the virtuoso Michael Clarke, placing Petronio's sexuality "in the public domain full tilt."[20] The choreographer and his dancers are "hot on the heels of an angel," each other, and the worlds of dance and art. The "hotness" of bombastic, virtuosic technicality exhibited within a formalist structure, became a defining feature of *MiddleSexGorge* and Petronio's choreography, while it captured the zeitgeist of the politics of sexuality, fashion and music.

The deviant sexuality of *MiddleSexGorge* is a living, life-affirming triumph over the hegemonic apparatus, both at the time of its premiere and today. Its transgressive ethos is as striking now as at the time of its creation. Petronio returns to it with company revivals every several years to relocate his creative center and to ensure his dancers understand and experience the urgency of what he deems his "essential body" within the context of this signature work.[21]

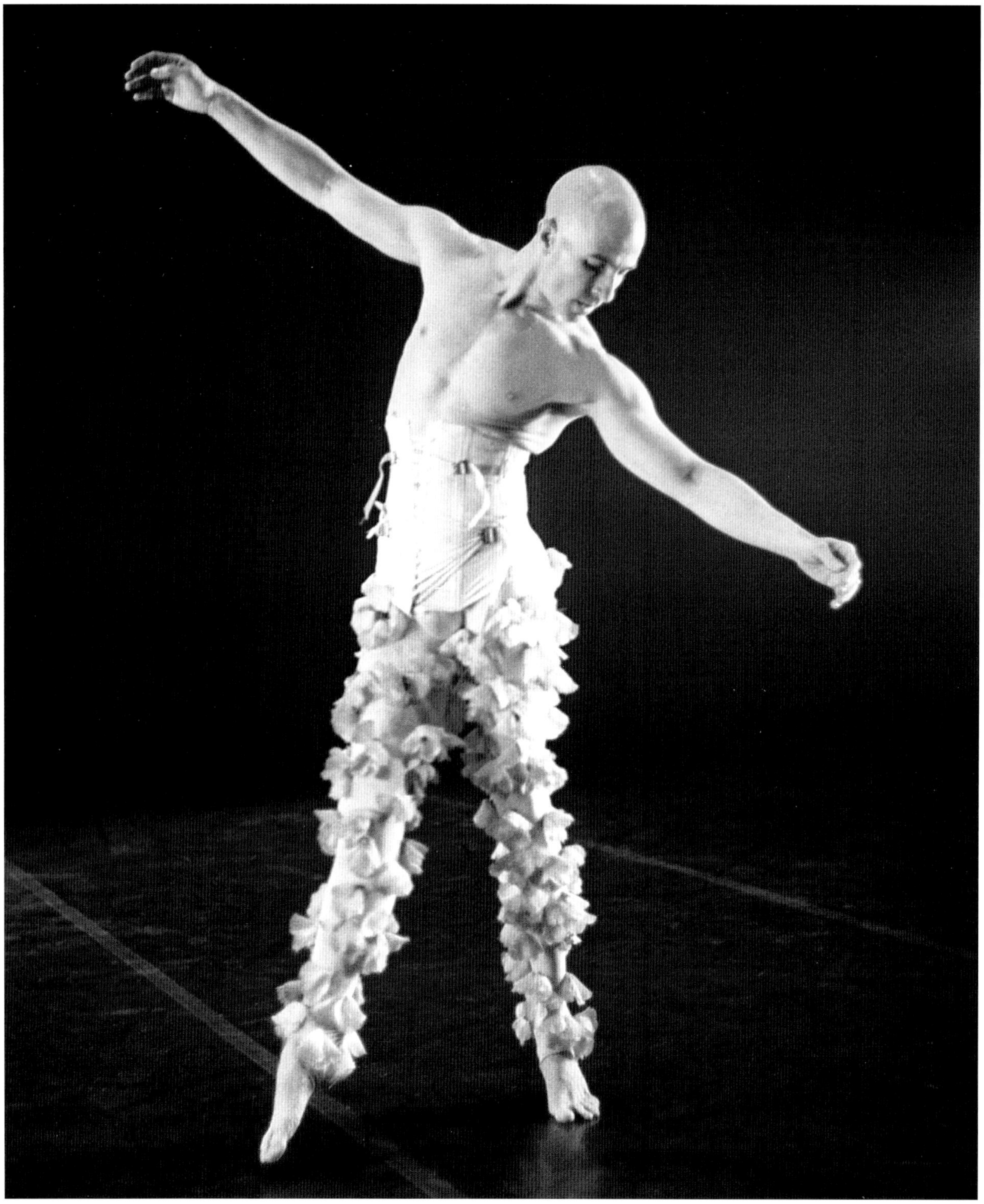

Stephen Petronio Company, *MiddleSexGorge*, 1990. Dancer: Stephen Petronio. Photo: © Tom Brazil, 1991.

Bloodletting

Acts of remembering and reconstructing his own repertoire with its bridges from the past to the present and toward the future of eternal return are taken further with *Bloodlines*, Petronio's multi-year project, which presents Petronio's choreography alongside that of the most influential artistic predecessors central to his own creativity. There is an imperative necessity to the project, as the dance world witnesses the passing of its pioneers like Merce Cunningham, whose legacy remains in question, and Brown, who became incapacitated and unable to work around the time of the 30th anniversary of Petronio's company, causing Petronio to ask, "What do I want for myself?"[22] This question is crucial both to his own legacy and to the preservation of the art form. In answering with *Bloodlines*, Petronio is the archon, the custodian of his own archive, and also a living archive of contemporary dance history.

Bloodlines embraces Petronio's icons. The project began with the work of Cunningham, whom Petronio recognizes as "the father of it all" and continued with Petronio's mentor Brown, follows with *Ally*'s Anna Halprin, and will include Steve Paxton.[23] With Petronio's past, present and future works on the same programs, *Bloodlines* is a vital archive of twentieth and twenty-first century dance. It houses the lineage of modernism and the influence of Cunningham and his partner John Cage that birthed the postmodernists, including Paxton and Brown. Appropriately, the first iteration of *Bloodlines* in 2015 was the iconoclastic and iconic union of dance and visual art, Cunningham's 1968 *RainForest*. The aesthetic lineage was made clear with the inseparable, yet independent collaborative contributors to the work, visual artist Andy Warhol and electronic composer David Tudor. By placing Petronio's company in this modernist masterpiece, the Petronio aesthetic comes into sharp focus: from the extraordinary, virtuosic technicality of the company's dancers, to the integration of a collaboration with a visual artist. When seen next to Petronio's own works, the formal, Abstract Expressionist *RainForest*, both affirms and confirms Petronio's place in this dance making lineage.

Like habitués of a cross species rainforest, Petronio's dancers bring the same clarity, purpose and technical precision to the demanding work as they do to the repertoire of the Stephen Petronio Dance Company. They attack the singular vocabulary of Cunningham with an animal-like angularity, alertness and primal attention to detail. Petronio's dancers expertly navigate this ever-surprising terrain and its evocative, jarring soundscape reminiscent of an Amazonian jungle, but never in a literal sense, as the piece retains Cunningham's entirely unique sense of abstraction. The setting is exemplary of Cunningham and Cage's use of chance procedures. Warhol's silver helium balloons are as unpredictable as nature itself and, with their own choreographic patterns, may be at any time and any place a continual surprise to the dancers and audience alike. The pillow-like balloons drift and float in their own dance of chance. They can glide offstage, into a lighting instrument and, on occasion, into the audience. They may veer directly into the path of the dancers whose swift kicks of the leg or gestures of the arm may send a balloon on a fast trajectory through space as the dancers find themselves partnering with the objects as they would with other dancers.

RainForest is the ideal inaugural choice for *Bloodlines* for a choreographer whose "goal has often been to disorient the dancer to the point of reflexive unconscious response, to bring out the unconscious reaction to a situation."[24] A choreographer who finds that, "there is nothing sexier in my mind than watching these highly skilled and sophisticated bodies disoriented and solving problems from an intuitive place. It brings out the animal in them. Intelligent animals.

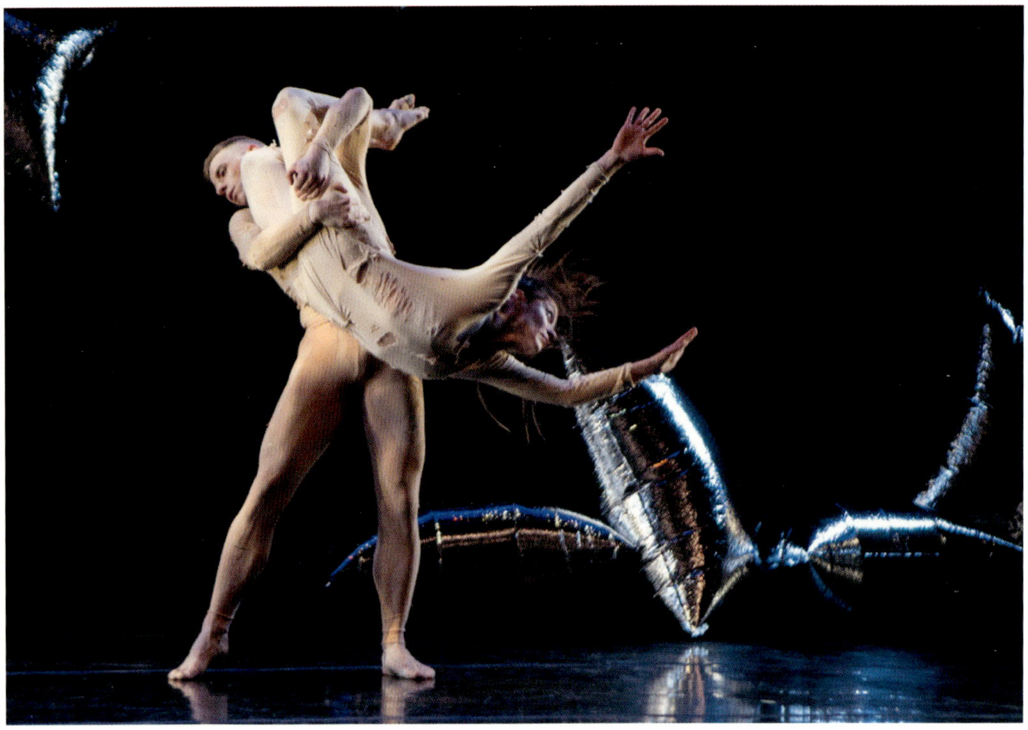

Merce Cunningham, *RainForest*, 2015 [1968], performed by Stephen Petronio Company.
Dancers (left to right): Nicholas Sciscione, Melissa Toogood. Photo: Yi-Chun Wu.

That creates a drama like no other."[25] The aesthetic affinities and drama of *Bloodlines*, paired with a signature work like that of *MiddleSexGorge*, reveal the absence of Petronio himself as dancer. He nonetheless undergoes a kind of encryption through transmission, with the character and action of Petronio palpably felt in the presence of his company's dancers. He is viscerally present through the bodies of his own dancers taking on the modernist bodies of Cunningham's dancers.

The encrypted presence of Petronio is as visceral in the second installment of *Bloodlines*, Trisha Brown's *Glacial Decoy*: a sylph-like feminist gift from Petronio to the women in his company, and a work made by Brown at the peak of her powers. Petronio's inclusion of *Glacial Decoy* is a return for him, his company and *Bloodlines* to the sacred feminine "gyroscopic kinespheres," and orbs from which Petronio emerged, fully formed, as a dancer. *Glacial Decoy* was also made in collaboration with a visual artist: Robert Rauschenberg. Significantly, it was the last work Brown choreographed in silence and her final all-female work, before Petronio was taken in by the "den mother of feminist wolves."[26] *Glacial Decoy* premiered on March 15, 2016 on the same program with *MiddleSexGorge*.

Bloodlines and *Ally* merge with the inclusion of Halprin's *The Courtesan and the Crone*. Halprin created this four-minute work in 1999 at the age of seventy-nine. Petronio's cross gender interpretation of the dance includes an installation of the work's costume, props and setting for the *Ally* exhibition that remains in situ when Petronio is not performing the piece. Petronio's installation of these elements and his performance simultaneously encompass Halprin's intentions while also producing a work which is different and new, transforming the dance and reanimating its objects.

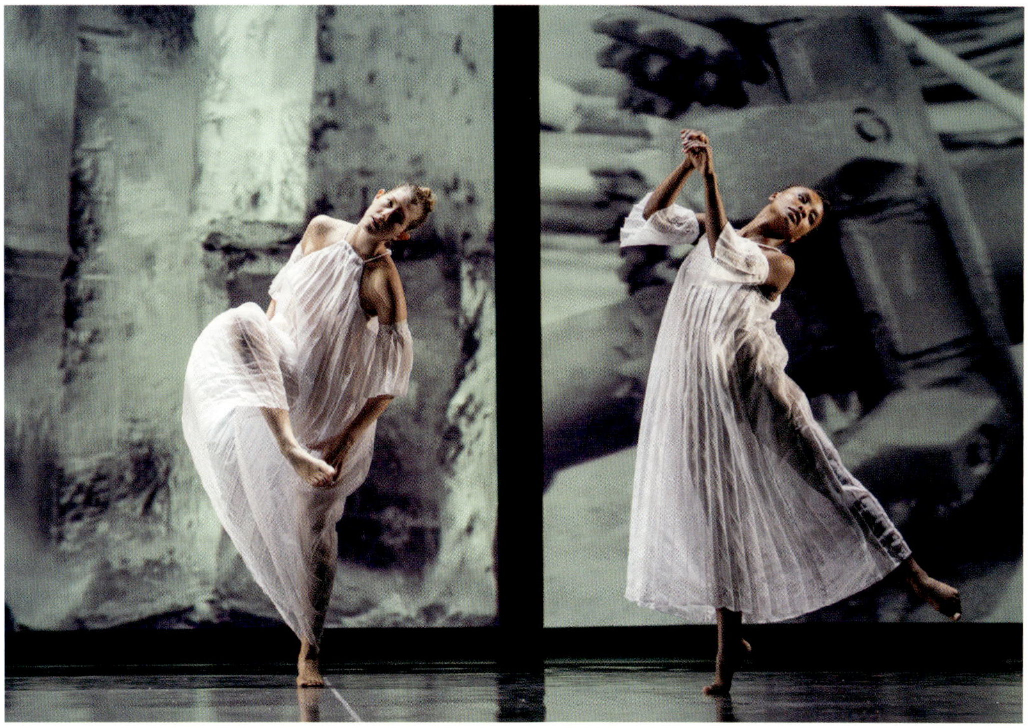

Stephen Petronio Company, *Bloodlines: Trisha Brown's Glacial Decoy*, 2015 [1979].
Dancers (left to right): Emily Stone, Davalois Fearon. Photo © Ctibor Bachratý.

Courtesans and Crones

A red velvet opera curtain is raised as if it is on the stage of a marionette theater, self-consciously revealing both its diminutive size and the artifice of the theater, while concealing nothing as it is situated within an otherwise large and empty room. Enter Petronio as the courtesan who places, or rather drops, her high heels with a thud. The music of Alessandro Marcello is cued to begin. S/he knowingly seduces, commands and commandeers her amorous courtiers and paramours with a delicate, yet direct bidding of ornate flutterings and inviting gestures with the arms, hands and fingers. This courtesan dons a courtly Venetian carnival mask, golden cloak and white gloves. The focal placements of the masked face and head are as flirtatious and intentionally seductive as the rest of the upper body. With a flourish and lurid lift of the robe, s/he reveals a bit of leg to her amorous witnesses. In Petronio's rendition the viewer sees a hint of his flaccid penis constrained by black stockings. This lurid and transgressive differentiation from the original further sexualizes Petronio's courtesan, whose wiles, and whose courtier's desires, will not be denied and cannot be resisted. The fetishistic striptease continues. What seems most suited for an intimate, private setting becomes entirely public. The seduction continues with the ornate removal of the lady man's long, white gloves and the comparatively unceremonious, yet similarly sexualized drop to the floor of the embroidered golden cloak.

The ageless and timeless beauty of the mask is then removed for the big reveal. The courtesan's youthful sexuality, once in full bloom, is no longer. The act is met with a silent, gaping mouth scream of the aged crone. It is a cry of bitter realization on the part of the crone that mimics the cry of horror of her would-be suitors as well. It is a mournful moan that amplifies both the crone's and the viewer's pity and revulsion.

The installation elements created by Petronio to frame *The Courtesan and the Crone* are tightly choreographed and detailed with the "weight of the robe in counterbalance with the weight of the curtain rig, and then tied off to the architecture of the space … the theatrical device of the curtain, the signifier for the stage, the locale for the theatrical, is in counterbalance with the costume that both conceals the body and creates identity."[27] Petronio delicately positions the cloak on a weighted pulley, and once hooked, hoists the garment so that it dangles above the floor. Each action of this sequence is choreographed musically, like all of Petronio's gestures as the courtesan and crone. Once left to hang, the knotted rope used to hoist the pulley eerily resembles a hangman's noose, swinging above what would be the head of the courtesan, had she been hung herself. Her accoutrements remain like a gallows. The crone then exits to the back of the space and disappears with a sense of shameful embarrassment. The long, dejected walk is brought into sharp focus by a spotlight that accentuates her lonely departure. In the otherwise stark room, the courtesan's costuming, the only remaining image, is also carefully lit, leaving a lingering memory of a glowing and ghostly affect.

The courtesan and crone's dance of seduction is set to a Baroque concerto by Alessandro Marcello: a divinely inspired choice by Halprin which, together with the costume, perfectly situates her courtesan and her crone in the setting of the Carnival of Venice. The Venetian carnival mask itself is much more than a costume and much more than a mask. The veneer of the *maschera volto* (face) tells the story of the courtesan and the crone. The *volto* or *larva* (ghost) is the most iconic mask of carnival. It is stark white, decorated like a gilded lily, worn most traditionally with a tricorn hat and a cloak, just as Halprin intended here. Unlike its sister masks, the *volto* obscures and covers the whole face, enveloping the chin, back to the ears, and up into the forehead which sprouts the tricorn. It also differs in that it displays the sensual facial features of the eyes, nose and lips, with the mouth completely closed.

The carnival mask is not merely a signifier or representation. It is the courtesan and the crone herself. As it was permissible in the time of Marcello for Venetians to spend the greater part of the year in disguise, it's quite possible the aging crone could have lived and worked fluidly in the guise of her *volto larva*. Seventeenth-century Venetians expected and longed for this sort of secrecy and the indiscretion afforded by the *maschera*. Like much of Italian culture itself, the pagan and the Roman Catholic fuse in an artistic, ritualistic creation of spectacular pageantry. The Carnivale di Venezia ends with the Christian celebration of Lent, forty days before Easter and the day before Ash Wednesday, when, unmasked, ashes adorn the forehead of the face in the shape of the crucifix. Ash Wednesday to Easter Sunday six weeks later, however, is a time of penance, atonement and above all, denying oneself the luxuries of carnal pleasure. This is understood as a period of spiritual discipline and daily, devotional rituals to bring oneself closer to God, including the performance of the Stations of the Cross.

This highly theatrical meditation on aging and sexuality translates effortlessly across generations and genders. It is most poignant when performed by these choreographers whose perceived prime as dancers parallels that of societal presumptions around sexual prime, most generally considered to be synonymous with youth. That Petronio is a gay male adds to this poignancy with the weight of gay culture's emphasis on a youthful, virile masculinity informing his every gestural utterance. The queer portrayal of Halprin's character is perversely traversed by Petronio, who both embodies Halprin's intent and imbues it with a theatrical dimension not present in the original.

Fama Eterna

The experience upon entering the second floor of The Fabric Workshop and Museum is similar to that of entering a holy cathedral. Upon crossing the threshold of *Swallow*, the visitor is enveloped in divine mysteries of light and color, the sound of whispering voices, and discrete zones for viewing, listening, contemplation and worship. Visitors become parishioners upon entering. Dimly lit, as if with candlelight, a long carpeted pathway leads the visitor-parishioner on a pilgrimage to the altar. A shaft of light from high above shines brilliantly upon a shrine of gilded opulence where a strikingly Baroque monstrance is placed. This reliquary invites the visitor to view what it displays: a remnant of coiled fabric. Directly opposite and across the sacral space, visitors encounter a glass vitrine. It is an ossuary containing another fabric relic. Pews along the connecting pathway take the form of contemporary chairs, wrought in pine with the stark simplicity and functionality of a Shaker design. The radiant monstrance houses the remains of the *Swallow* performance that united Petronio and Antoni. It is the 10-foot strip of cloth that the two obediently endured swallowing in an act derived from an Indian yogic cleansing ritual called Vastra Dhauti. Their interiors are externalized on cloth; the interior spaces of the stomach, the esophagus and their very beings. The ritual's remnant is forever enshrined.

Despite its erect stance, the monstrance embodies the sacral feminine, with spherical orbs of concentric circles radiating like the kinespheres of dancing bodies within dancing bodies. If this monstrance is to be referred to with a pronoun it is decidedly a *she*, in keeping with the matriarchal, life giving god(dess) force that permeates the whole of *Ally*. The breast-like base is a horizontal rhizome that produces two vertical spinal cords with detailed vertebrae blossoming like stems sprouting immaculately from its aureoles. The fabric is neatly coiled on both sides, suspended within the blown glass: breast-shaped globes that echo the voluptuously rotund shape of the base. Like eyes, the suspended coils on either side gaze back at the faithful witness gazing at her. A portal atop, designed for viewing the relic, is in the rousingly sexual and sensuous shape of a vulva, complete with a pearl for a clitoris. Magnification allows for the adoration of the artifact of these present-day saints. This feminized monstrance defies the Holy Roman Catholic patriarchy. She is fertile and poised to reproduce and birth more iconic reliquaries. Although Antoni and Petronio are connected via Halprin, within the collaborative and simpatico artistic, aesthetic and spiritual concerns of *Ally* as a whole, it is *Swallow* that symbolically and literally unites the two artists. *Swallow* is the consummation of their collaboration, a complete and porous merging of their blood, body and souls. It is an unprecedented performative act of faith. An act so intimate there are only ten witnesses.

The visitors hear the recorded testimonies of the individual witnesses recounting their interpretations of the ritual's ingestion and excretion of the cleansing cloth via audio speakers suspended from the ceiling above the pairs of chairs. The sonic character of the installation situates the witnesses in a sound environment that envelops the parishioners when seated. The chairs are placed formally and equidistantly so that the parishioners may be seated facing each other, either away from the altar or toward the vitrine. Their placement encourages communication and connection. This is a placement conducive to contemplation of the act, its relics in the reliquaries, and the psycho-geography of the sacral space. The tone is that of the hushed confessional in a Catholic church and of communal prayer. As the setting indicates, spectator-parishioners are participants with the witnesses, as they are able to hear them bearing testimony to the once private performance made public within the hallowed sanctuary of the holy church of *Swallow*.

Swallow is a life-affirming, spiritual union. The cloth, as Eucharist, transforms the oral act of Holy Communion. With *Swallow*, Petronio realizes his need to "connect on some deeply spiritual level."[28] He transcends his own body, "the only tool" and has found the means to "reach into the humanity and soul of a partner."[29] The act of *Swallow*, and the display of its material artifact housed in the monstrance, brings Petronio closer to the *fama eterna*, eternal renown or salvation he so devoutly seeks in his work in dance and through the elements of *Ally*. Iconography takes vital, material form that is alive with an aura produced by the display and its setting. However it is the vitrine, the final resting place of the only other documentation of the event, a single photograph which, through the life cycle of its inhabitant webbing clothes moths, allows life ever lasting to finally be achieved. This fabric devouring moth, the antagonist of the museum and workshop whose very purpose is the creation and preservation of material, of materiality, enters the sacred space and is welcomed as it facilitates salvation. Unlike the Holy Roman Catholic Church's vast archive of effects, the authenticity of the contents of the monstrance and the vitrine is not in debate. The photographic evidence encased in the glass vitrine is the only photograph taken of the act. The photograph is printed on cloth with pigment and infused with Petronio and Antoni's saliva.

The fate of the photographic artifact is neither static nor concrete, unlike that of the fabric artifact displayed in the monstrance. The vitrine houses the photograph with Antoni on the left and Petronio on the right, swallowing the fabric that conjoins them like an umbilical chord. This vitrine is more aptly named an ossuary: a final resting place for remains used where burial space is scarce. For *Ally*, the ossuary is the last processional step toward immortality with the addition of the Tineola Biselliella, the webbing clothes moth. The ossuary both teems with life and serves as a mass grave for a colony of approximately 6,500 moths throughout the duration of the exhibit. The photograph is animated and imbued with physical life by these winged allies in all stages of life and death, beginning with eggs that hatch between four and ten days into white caterpillars, which immediately feed until the pupal stage is reached. The caterpillars then spin cocoons and develop into adults. The adult moths emerge and their only goal is to reproduce. The entire life cycle, under the most favorable conditions which have been created in the vitrine, is under one month. The caterpillars, in their larval form, feed primarily on the cloth remnant. The saliva is of particular interest to the caterpillars, which steadily destroy and devour the image.

In contemplating the complex choreographies of the ossuary, the rapturous fascination with life and death is redesigned, allowing parishioners to rethink death. The finite becomes infinite via trans-species transmission. A human act and an image of its labor are eaten by creatures and become new life with insistent and simultaneous degeneration and regeneration. What appears at first to be the destructive decomposition and decay of the shroud-like photograph may instead be met with a peaceful acceptance that the living accompanies the dying. The world of the moth colony as domiciled and woven into the photograph, allows for a universal overcoming of the fear of death. The photographic cenotaph embodies its own sort of choreographic concern aligned with Petronio the formalist, whose recent interest in "more illusive forms, forms that hide, disappear and fall apart before the eye" is borne in another kind of dance: a danse macabre.[30]

The moths transform the ossuary into its own highly choreographed and formal kinesphere. In constant motion with each stage of life, the moths ingest the photograph with its residue of saliva, mate, die, decompose, and replenish the colony with a frenzied and hyperkinetic urgency. The *fama eterna* commenced the moment the first 100 adults, 20 pupae, 1,500 larvae and 1,000 eggs were placed in the vitrine at the opening of the exhibition. In no uncertain terms, upon the closing of the exhibition on July 31, 2016, the ingested remains of *Swallow*'s subjects will have undergone a cross-species metamorphosis. Upon their release, these winged messengers will continue to transport the DNA of Petronio and Antoni to places unknown and toward eternity.

The swallowers' material remains live on in perpetuity via Tineola Biselliella, made materially immortal through time and space. A divine state of life everlasting is achieved ... At last, God saves Petronio!

Notes

1. "The Liturgy of the Eucharist." *CNA-Catholic News Agency*, www.catholicnewsagency.com/resources/liturgy/holy-mass/the-liturgy-of-the-eucharist/. Source: Roman Catholic Diocese of Galloway, Scotland. Accessed 25 June 2017
2. Stephen Petronio, *Confessions of a Motion Addict*, (CreateSpace Independent Publishing Platform, 2014), 183.
3. Ibid., 12.
4. Ibid., 119.
5. Ibid.
6. Ibid.
7. Ibid.
8. Ibid., 183.
9. Ibid., 119.
10. Stephen Petronio, conversation with the author, NeueHouse, Madison Square, New York, March 21, 2016.
11. Ibid.
12. Stephen Petronio, *Confessions of a Motion Addict*, 66.
13. Ibid., 94.
14. Ibid., 69.
15. Ibid., 119.
16. Stephen Petronio, conversation with the author, NeueHouse, Madison Square, New York, March 21, 2016.
17. Ibid.
18. Ibid.
19. Ibid.
20. Stephen Petronio, *Confessions of a Motion Addict*, 157.
21. Ibid.
22. Stephen Petronio, conversation with the author, March 21, 2016. Brown subsequently passed away on March 18, 2017.
23. Ibid.
24. Stephen Petronio, *Confessions of a Motion Addict*, 192.
25. Ibid., 192-3.
26. Stephen Petronio, conversation with the author, NeueHouse, Madison Square, New York, March 21, 2016.
27. Stephen Petronio, email correspondence with the author, June 10, 2016.
28. Stephen Petronio, *Confessions of a Motion Addict*, 225.
29. Ibid.
30. Ibid., 223.

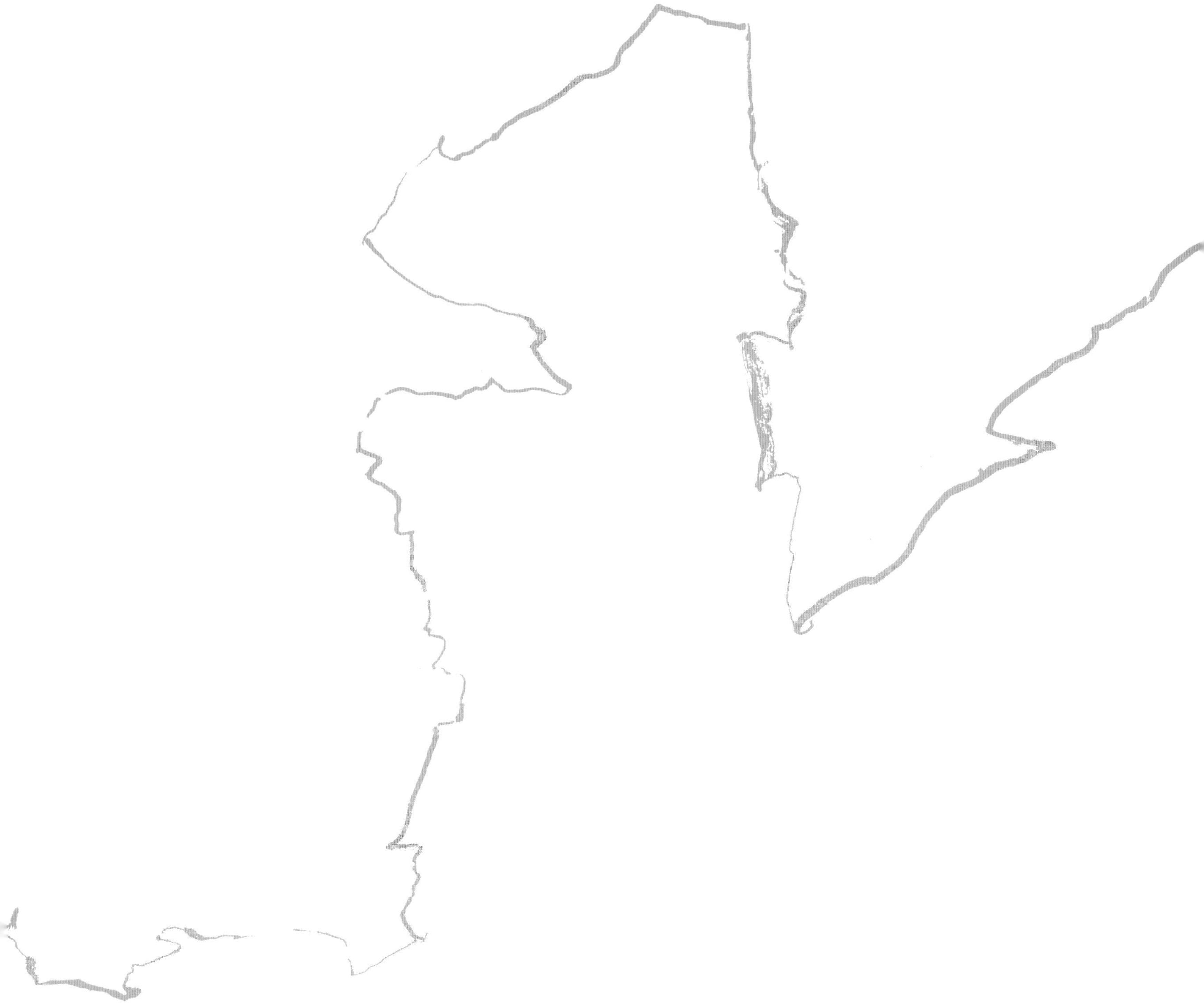

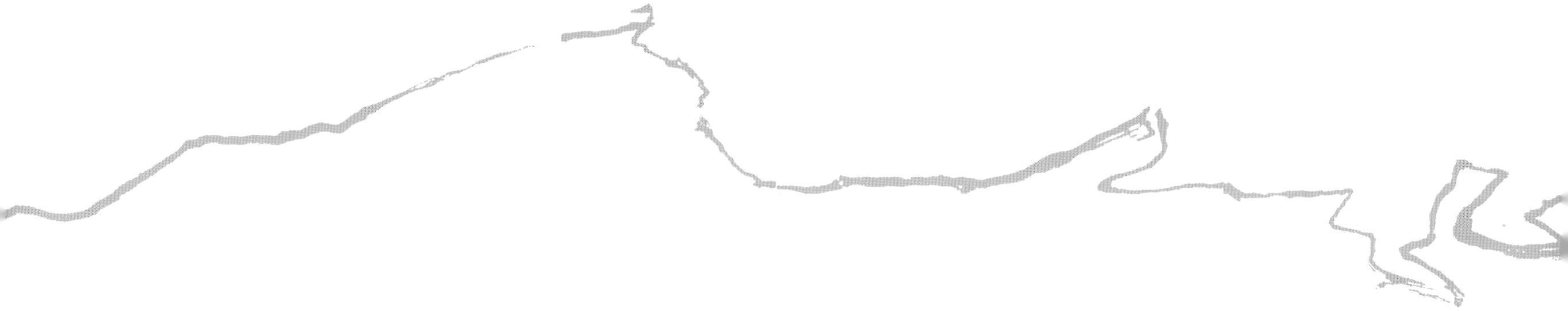

ROPE DANCE

Anna Halprin, Janine Antoni, Stephen Petronio

Anna Halprin created a performance with Janine Antoni and Stephen Petronio at her Mountain Home Studio in Kentfield, California in September 2014. Ropes formed the connective material between the artists' bodies in motion. In the gallery, the dance was given presence through a thirty-minute film of Halprin's face witnessing the performance, and the sounds of Antoni and Petronio's enactment on Halprin's dance deck. On specific occasions Antoni and Petronio would invite visitors to the exhibition to re-explore the materials and potentials of the performance in a participatory event.

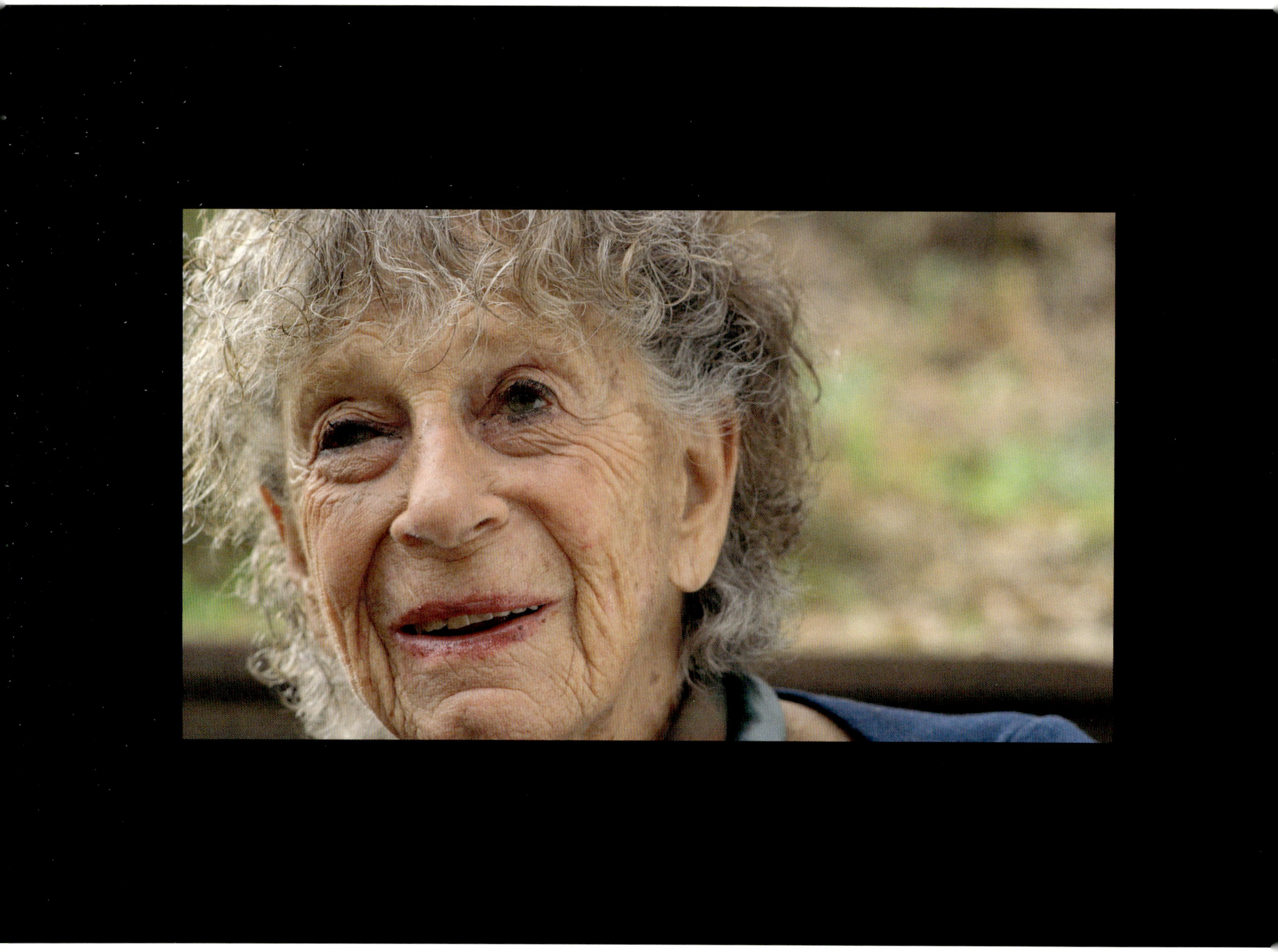

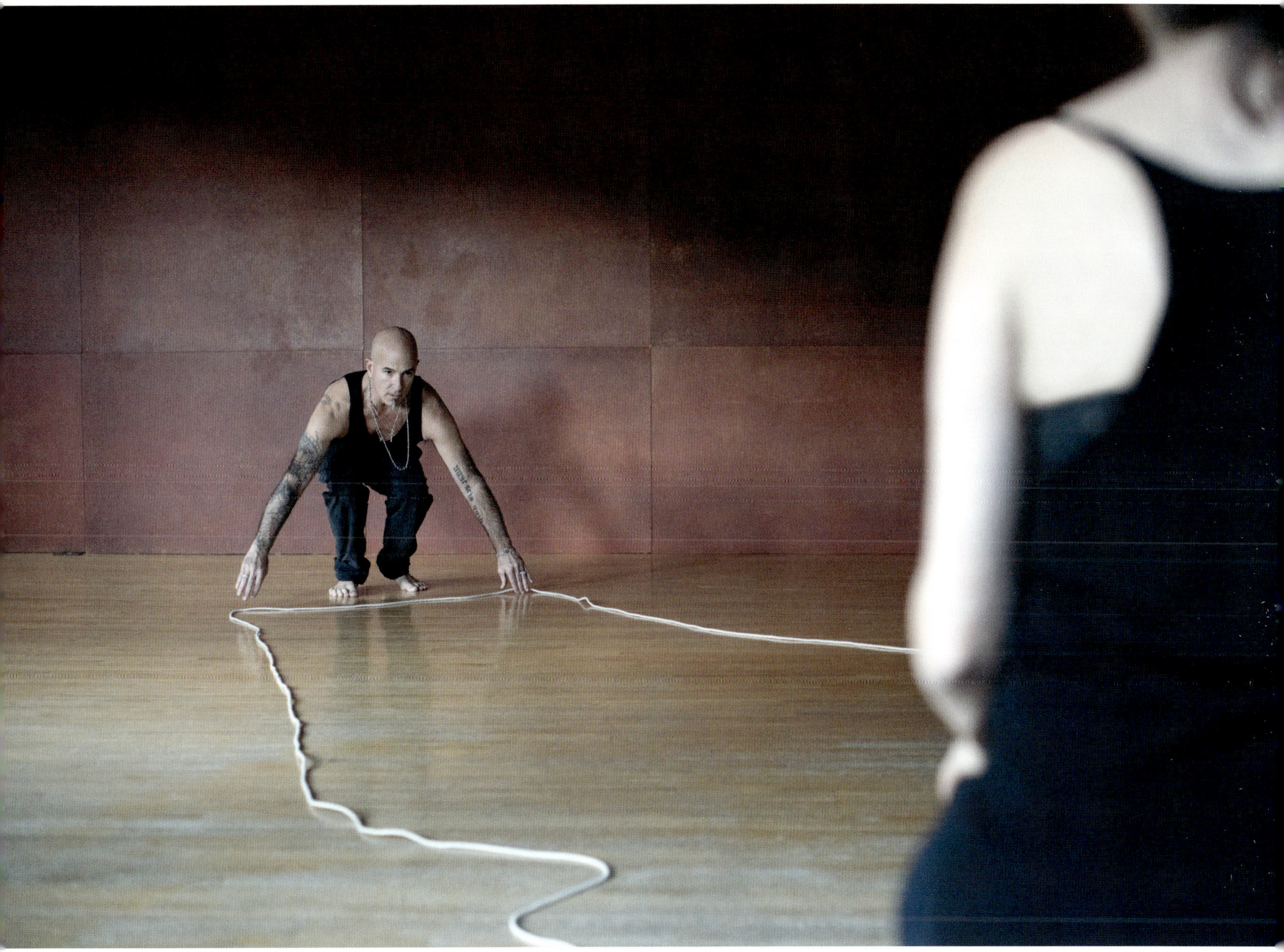

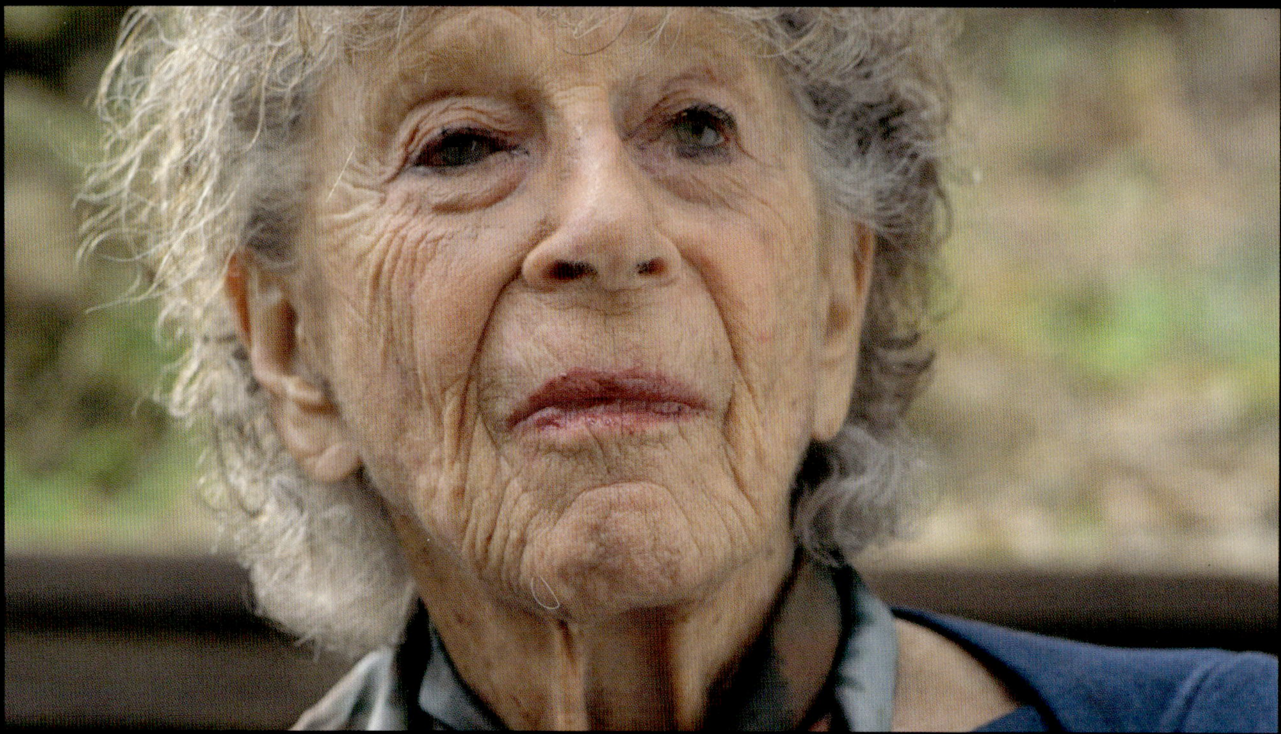

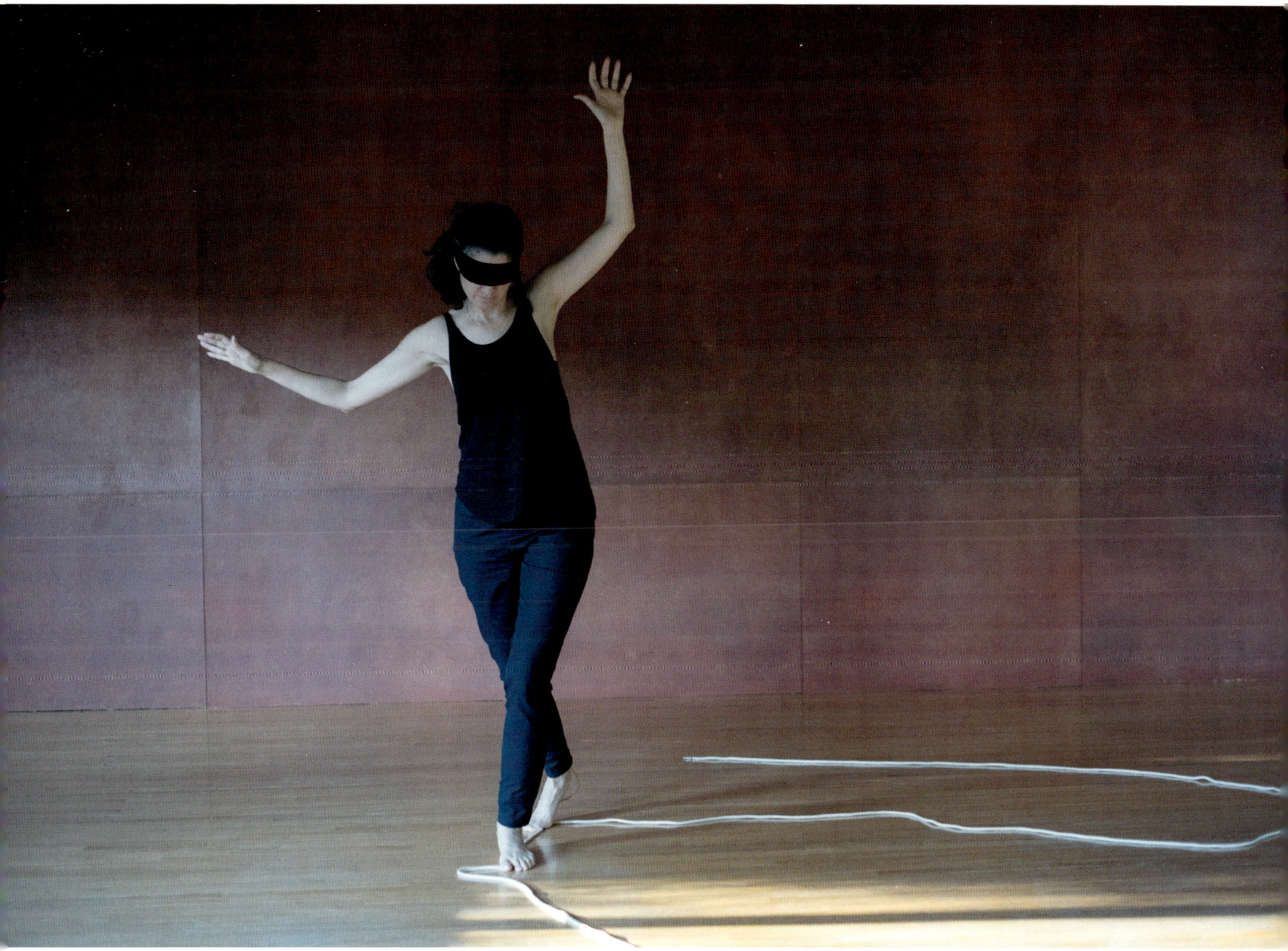

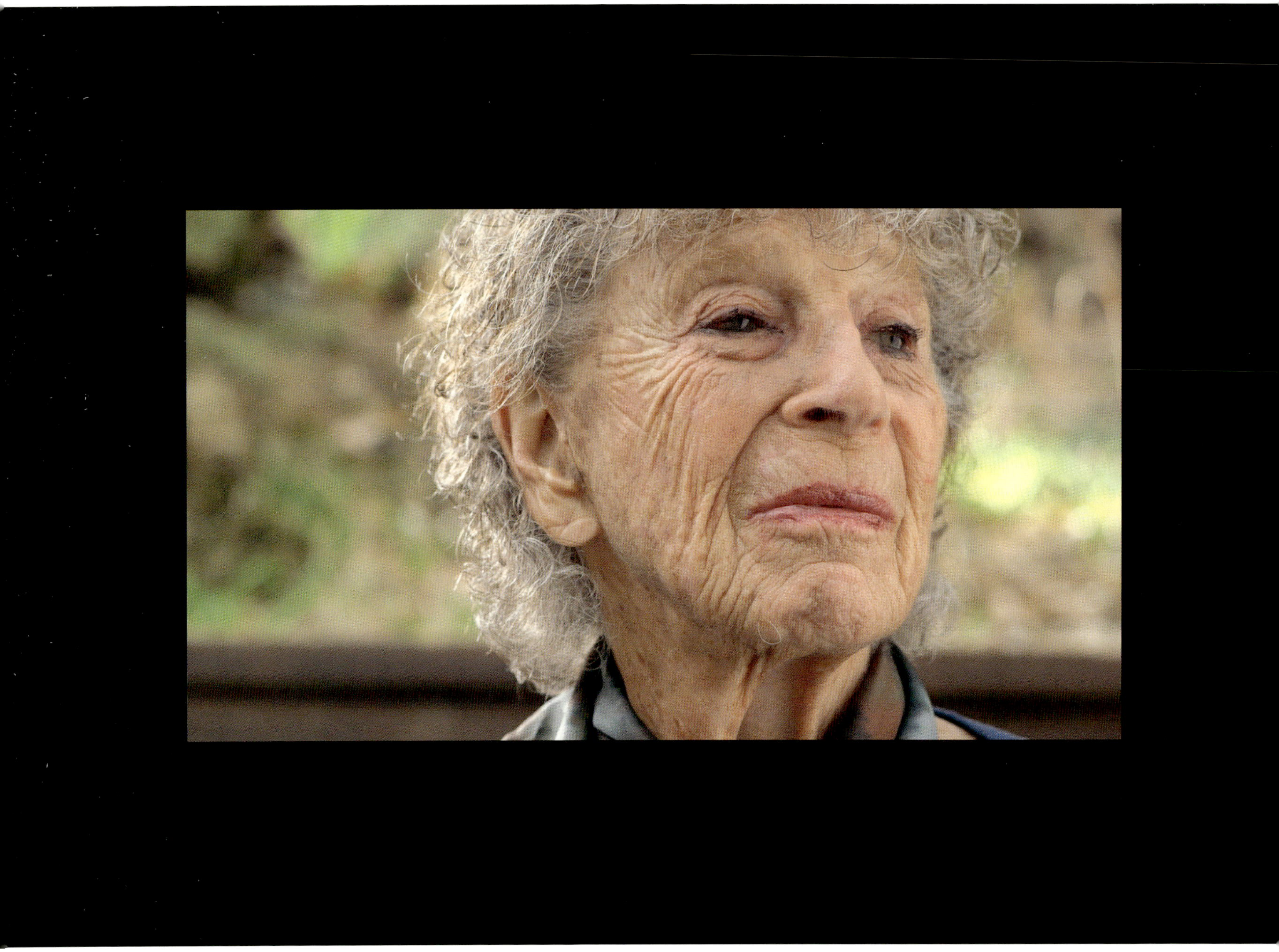

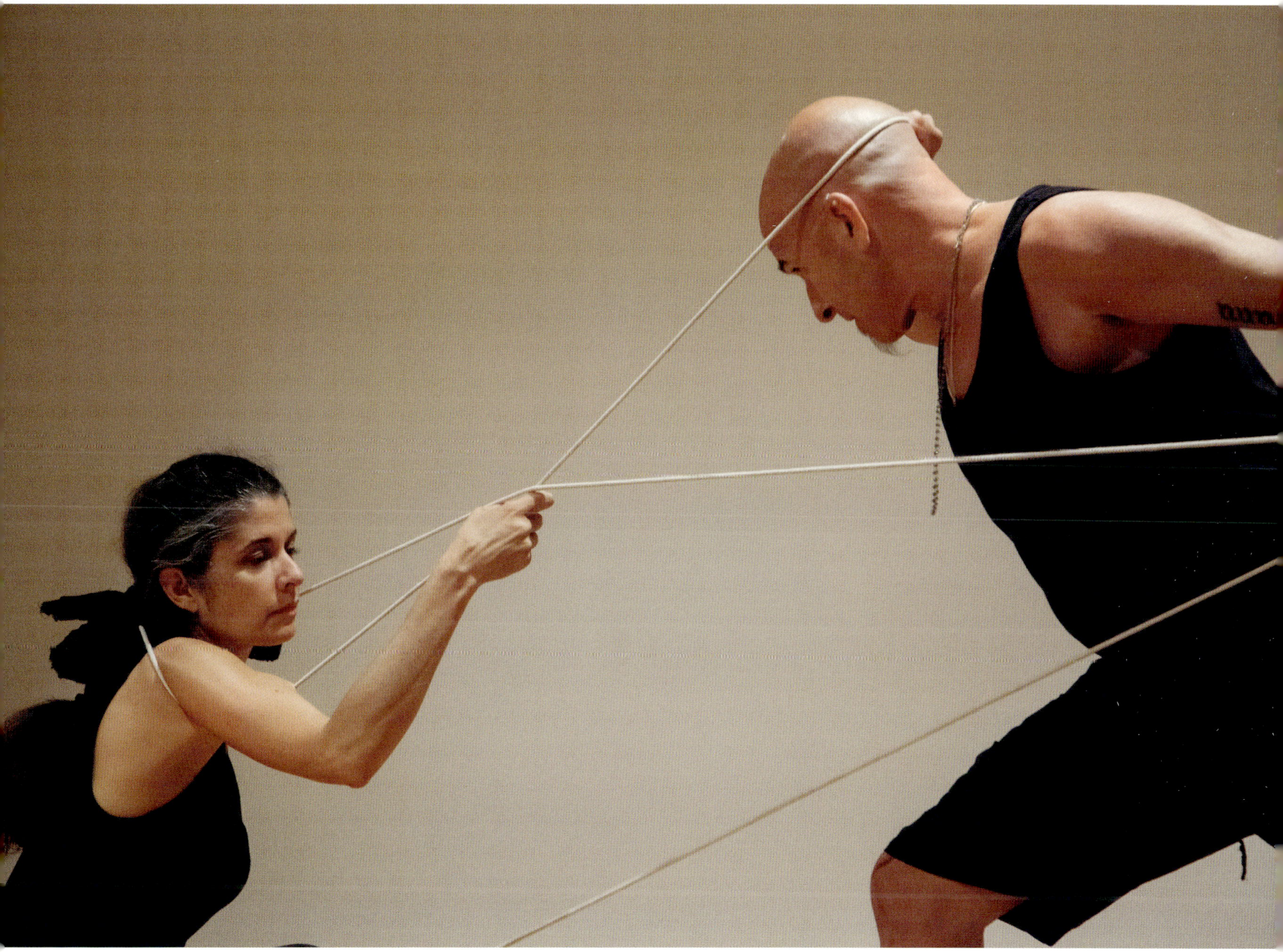

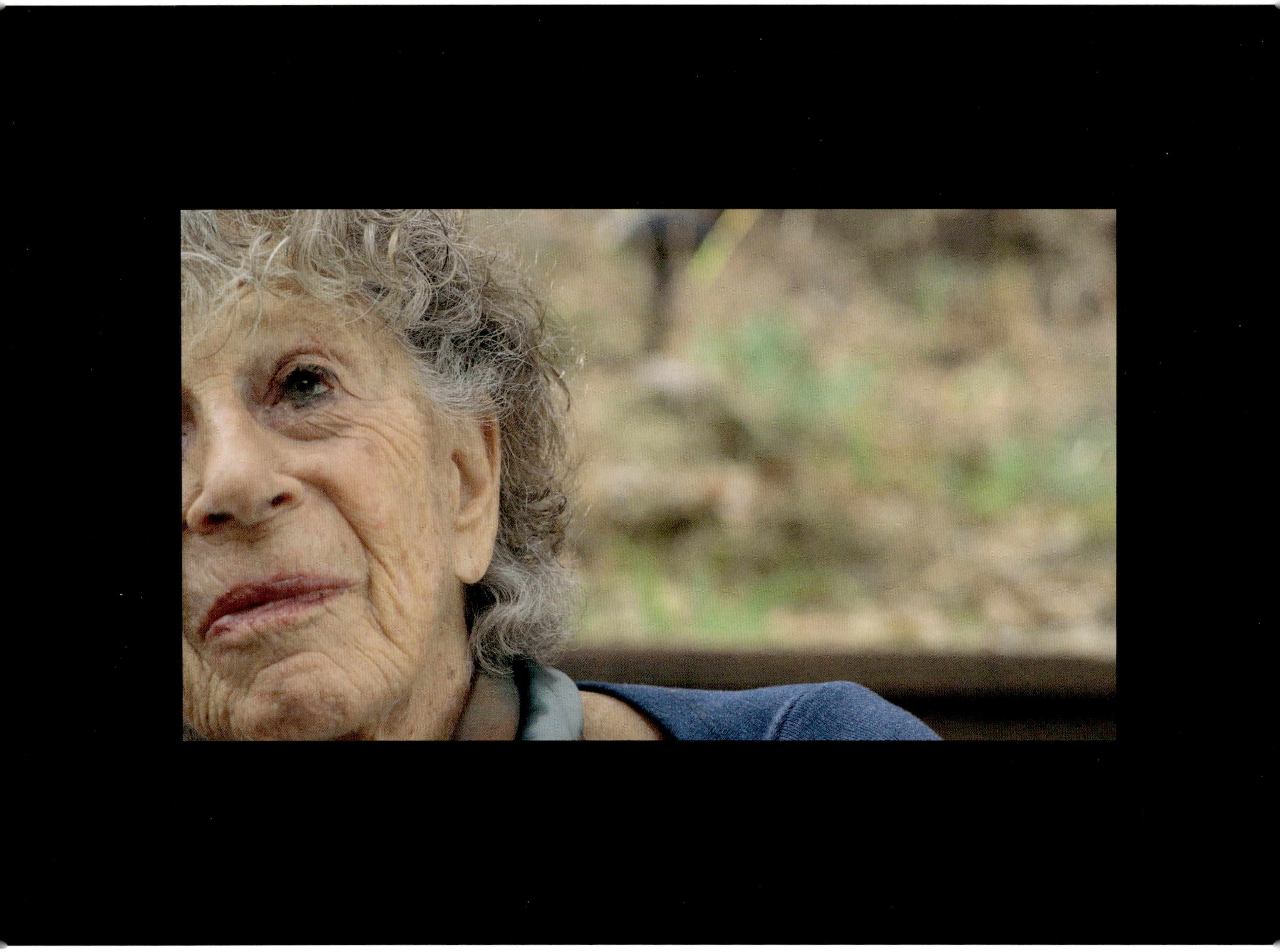

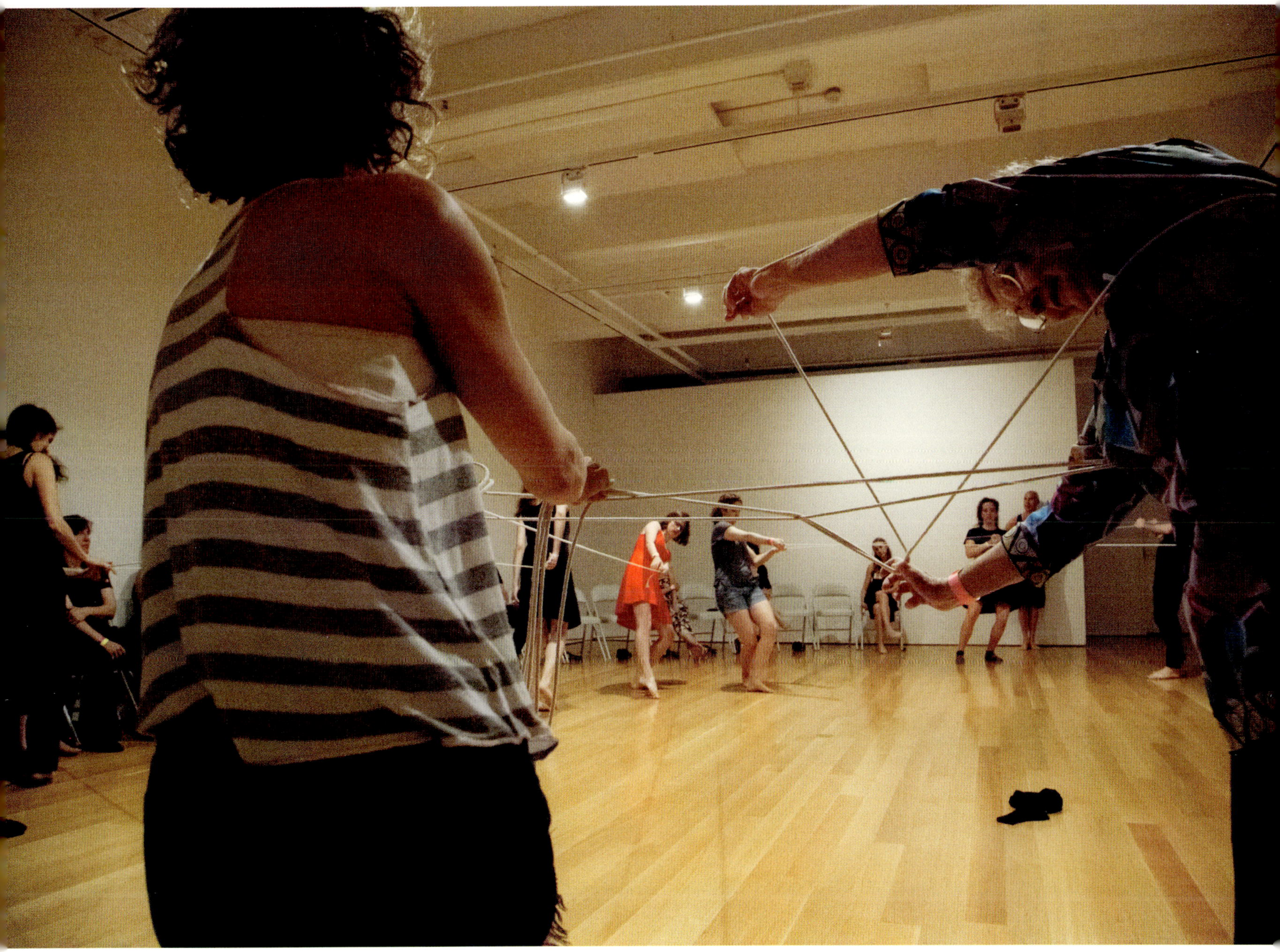

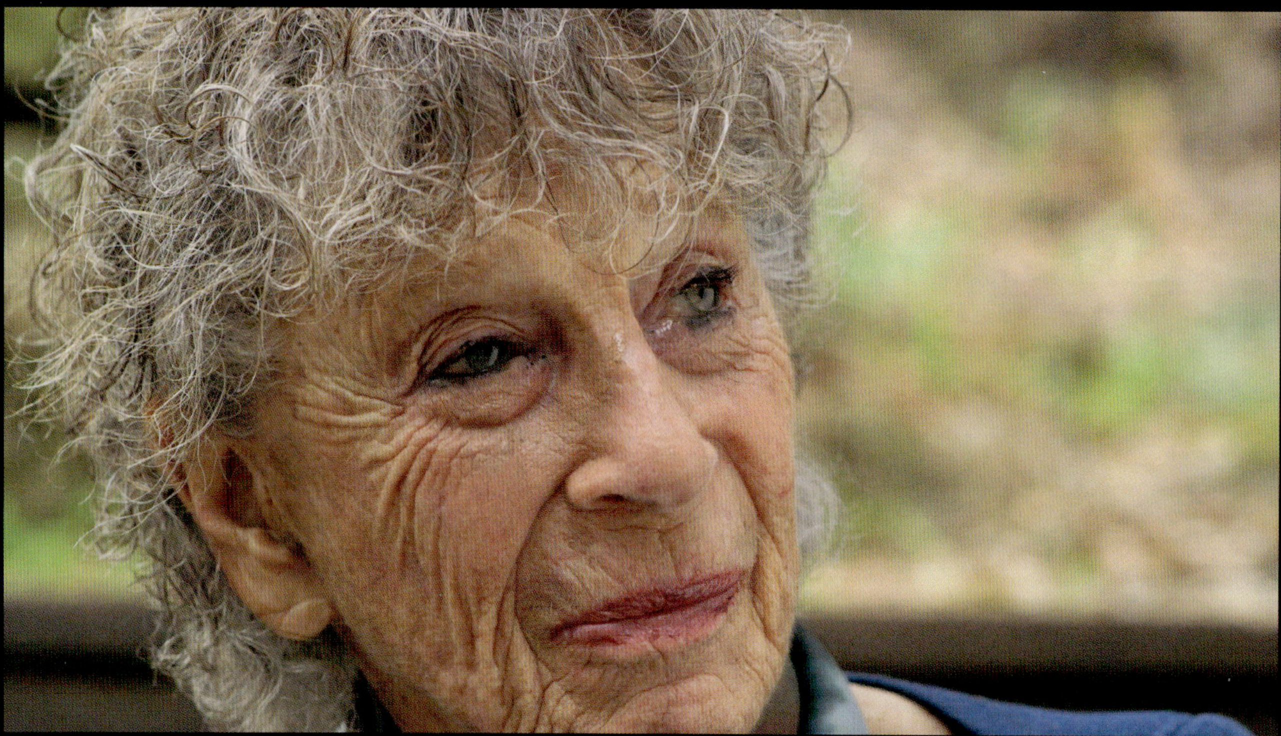

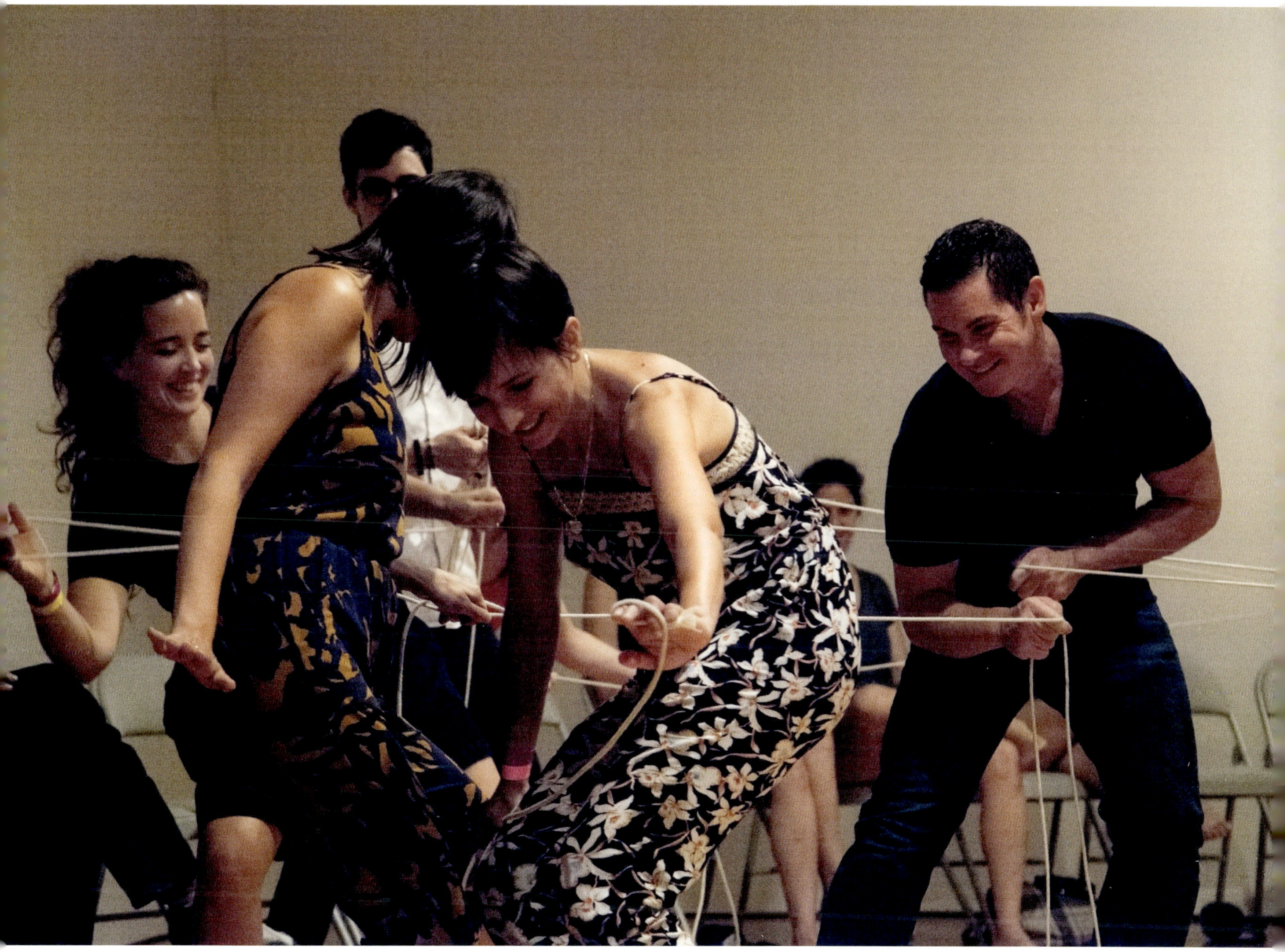

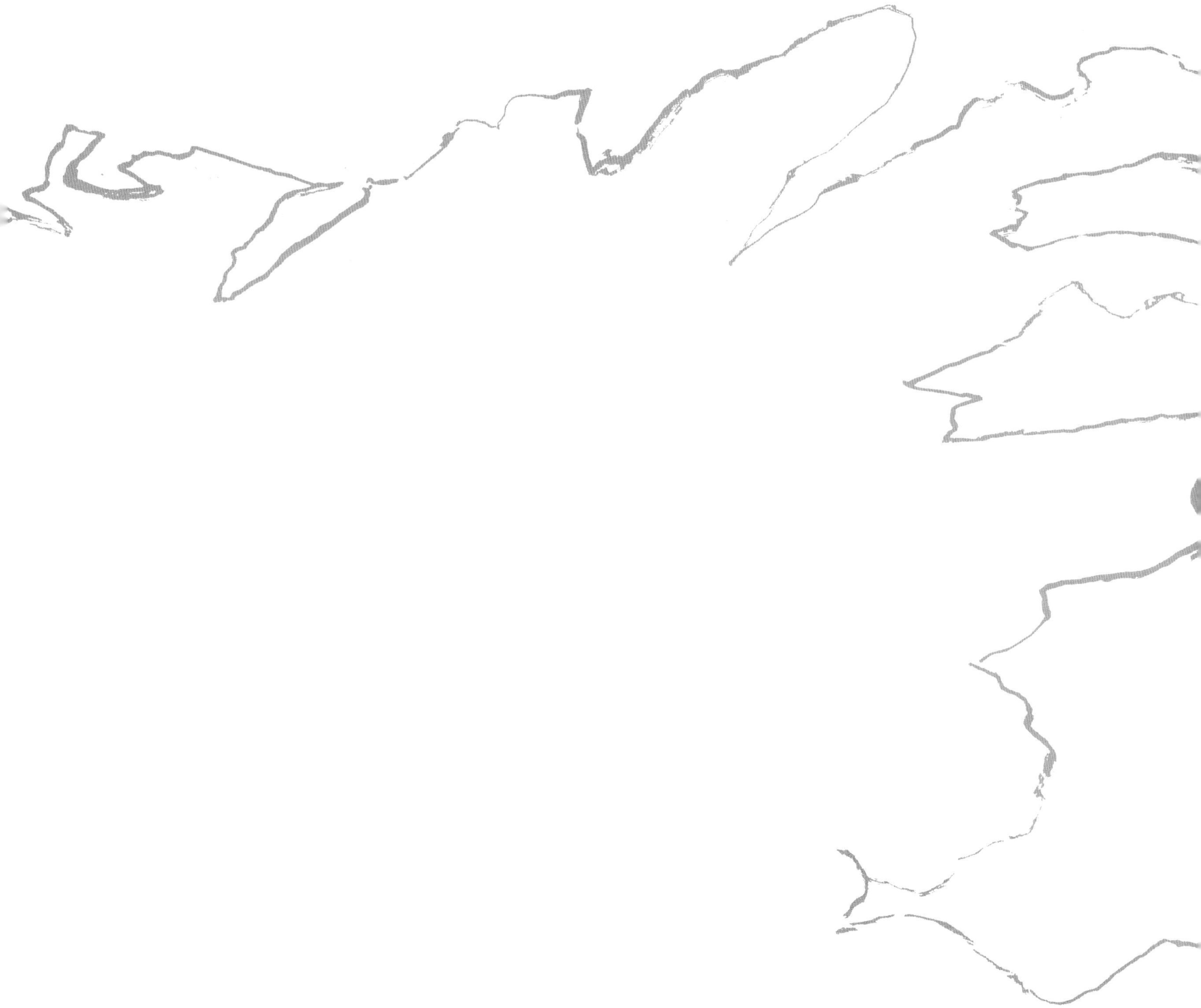

REVOLVING TOGETHER LIKE STARS
THE ART OF ANNA HALPRIN

Jacquelynn Baas

Can you feel now how we are changing places?
My king, my king, what is heavy turns to spirit.
If we just keep hold of each other,
you grasping the young one and I the old,
We could revolve together like stars.

Rainer Maria Rilke, "David Sings before Saul,"
from *The Book of Images*[1]

The Hindu tantric goddess Chamunda Devi embodies the timeless metaphor of the Earth as mother. Chamunda is a "terrific" aspect of Devi, the Hindu Divine Mother — "Chamunda" combines the names of two monsters killed by her. She haunts cremation grounds. In Basohli, India, near the border with China, Chamunda manifests herself in her temple in the form of a natural rock far older than humankind, older even than the mountains and river where her temple is situated. The nature of ritual and myth associated with this weathered stone in her mountain temple informs the art of Anna Halprin (b. 1920).[2] Stone forms the mountain on which Halprin's world-famous dance deck extends, surrounded by redwoods, madrones, and fragrant coastal live oaks. The wind-whipped bluffs of The Sea Ranch are formed of weathered stone, looming above broad beaches where participants in Halprin's workshops perform for themselves and with each other. The sand beneath their bare feet is stone ground fine by the action of wind, water, and moving earth. These natural elements inform and become a part of their movements. "Our bodies are composed of the same elements as the earth," Halprin says.

> Rather than imitate the outward forms of nature or use nature as a backdrop, I identify with its basic processes. … Although this work is generated primarily by a kinesthetic connection, it also includes the feelings, associations, personal and communal images, and life scripts that are part of our human nature. In that way, the interface between our human ways and the ways of nature are integrated.[3]

Another stone Chamunda, originally from Odisha (formerly Orissa), now resides in the British Museum. Carved in ninth-century India, this Chamunda is an energetic dancer. Her emaciated body and necklace of skulls suggest a dance of death to most westerners. Those able to integrate the reality of Chamunda, however, know that hers is simultaneously a dance of life. Chamunda's dance affirms "life's other half" — Rilke's characterization of death, and the "essential meaning and theme" of his work: "To discover the unity of dread and bliss, these two faces of the same divinity."[4] To discover the unity of dread and bliss within the processes of nature, including those of the human mind and body, has been the lifelong task of Anna Halprin.

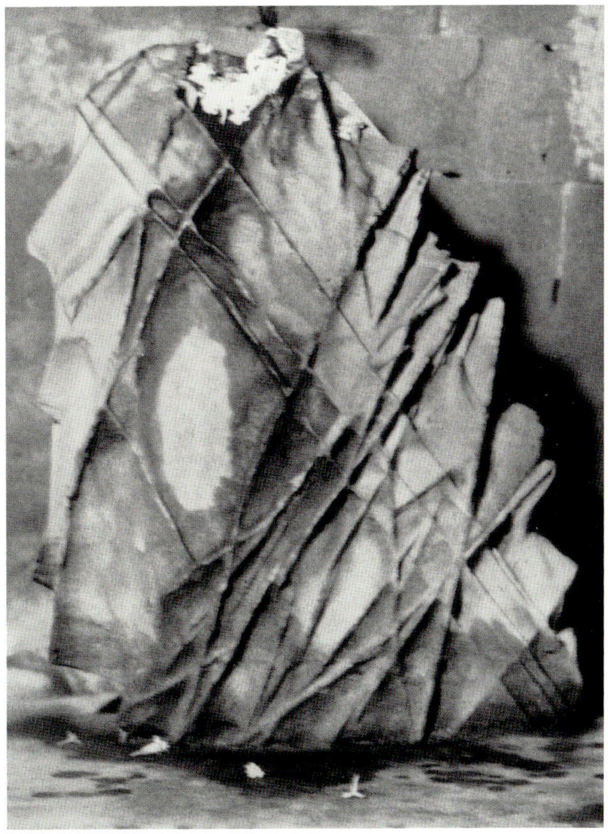

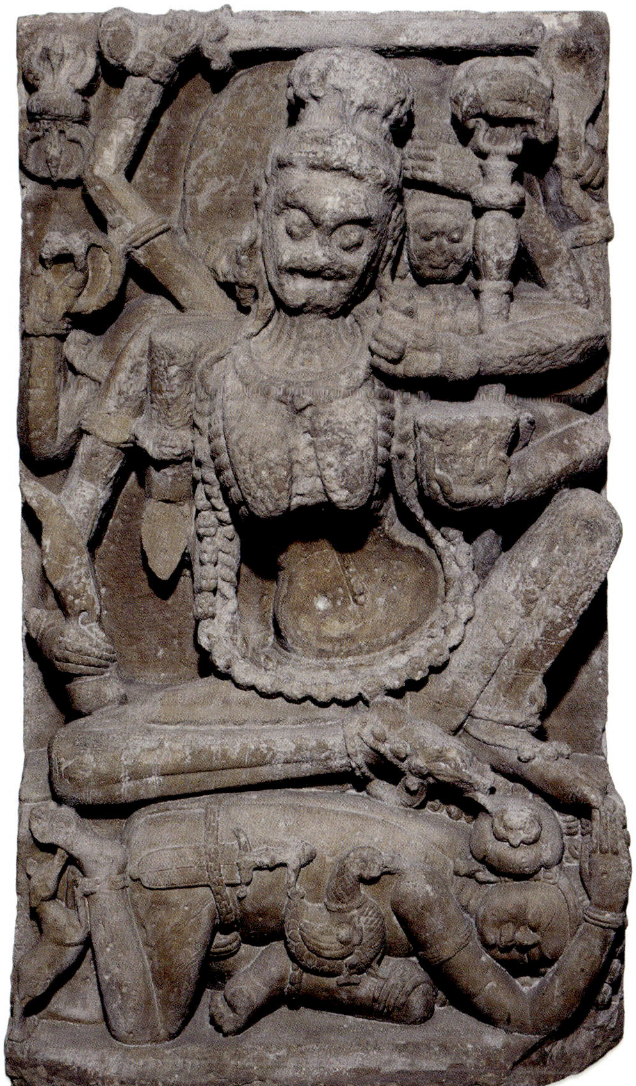

Top: Devi Chamunda. Stone, Chamunda temple, Basohli, Jammu-Kashmir, c.16th century. Photo: Archaeological Survey of India. From Ajit Mookerjee, *Tantra Art, Its Philosophy and Physics* (New Delhi: Ravi Kumar, 1966).

Bottom: Chamunda. Carved sandstone, 94 x 72.4 x 29.2 cm. India, Odisha (formerly Orissa), 9th century. © The Trustees of the British Museum.

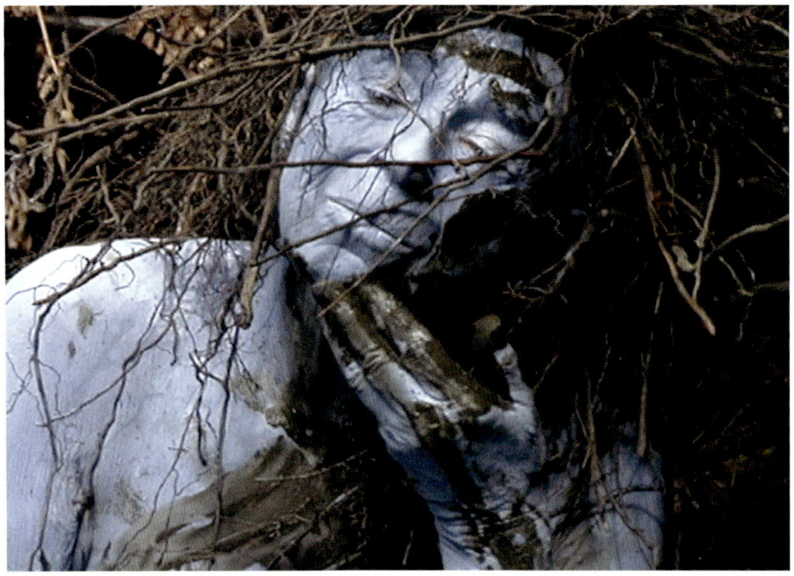

Video still of Anna Halprin from *Returning Home*, 2003, directed by Andy Abrahams Wilson.

Halprin's artistic medium is movement. Her instrument is the body, with its rhythms of breath and pulsing blood. "Dance is the breath made visible," Halprin says. Dancers "have to breathe in the planet — breathe in the trees that emanate into the air."

> There are absolutely no boundaries. … The other element, the pulse, is universal too. Everything exists in time, which is pulse. That tree has a pulse. It has a time when it is born, and it has a time when it dies. … Pulse is measurement of time and space.[5]

Understood in the context of time and space, even the ancient stone Chamunda, the creation of both slow and cataclysmic movements over time, has a pulse.

∞

Over her long career, Halprin has been at the forefront of two interrelated trends in twentieth-century art: the identification of art with life, and the identification of the "object" of art with the process of experiencing it. As the philosopher John Dewey asserted in his widely read *Art as Experience*: "A work of art … is actually, not just potentially, a work of art only when it lives in some individualized experience."[6] The role of the artist in Halprin's terms is that of "a guide who works to evoke the artist in us all."[7] Paying attention — to the world, to ourselves, to each other — is the cornerstone of her method. The extraordinary combination of physical and intellectual energy that is Anna Halprin is the result not only of her own innate abilities, but also of the environment in which she grew up. At the age of four she watched, enchanted, as her Hassidic Jewish grandfather prayed "by singing, jumping up and down, and flinging his arms in the air. … To this day," the now ninety-seven-year-old Halprin recalls, "I still have vivid memories of his religious ecstatic dancing."[8] Halprin has retained her connection with her Jewish identity, traveling to Israel and, most recently, conducting workshops and leading peace walks in Jerusalem. Halprin defines "ritual" as "purpose beyond one's self."[9] Her work has been most strongly influenced by Native American ritual and myth, but the joy and interconnectedness implicit in Judaism's seasonal celebrations, along with its tradition of social conscience and commitment to community, marked her for life.

By the time Halprin began elementary school, her family had moved from the village of Wilmette, north of Chicago, to nearby Winnetka, home to the famous Winnetka Plan: a progressive, experience-based curriculum in the public schools informed by the theories of Dewey, linking pedagogy with individual development and social reform. In *Democracy and Education* Dewey wrote:

> To "learn from experience" is to make a backward and forward connection between what we do to things and what we enjoy or suffer from things in consequence. Under such conditions, doing becomes a trying; an experiment with the world to find out what it is like; the undergoing becomes instruction — discovery of the connection of things.

In traditional education, Dewey pointed out,

> the intimate union of activity and undergoing its consequences which leads to recognition of meaning is broken; instead we have two fragments: mere bodily action on one side, and meaning directly grasped by "spiritual" activity on the other.[10]

Things were different in Winnetka, where Dewey's "progressive education" grounded in experience was put into practice. Progressive education emphasizes learning by doing, an integrated curriculum, individual and group problem solving, and social responsibility. Dance was offered from the time Halprin was in kindergarten, and by high school, dance was part of everything she did:

> I was placed in "slow" classes. According to their system, if you were a slow learner, you would do better with other slow learners. I was in all the slow classes. Now, they call it "motor learning"; I'm a motor learner, I learn through motor activities.[11]

As a motor learner, Halprin — who is also a natural teacher — excelled to such a degree that by the age of twelve she was leading classes in movement and improvisation for her friends and their mothers. Two years later, she performed with a student dance group at the 1934 Chicago World's Fair.[12]

Dewey's influence on Halprin's artistic career continued in college, where from 1938–42 she studied at the University of Wisconsin with the legendary dance teacher and theoretician Margaret H'Doubler. Originally a biologist, H'Doubler was recruited from serving as the women's basketball and baseball coach to founding the first dance major at a public university. Her pedagogy was based on thorough knowledge of the human body, its capabilities and potential. It was also based on Dewey's theory of art as experience. H'Doubler had studied with Dewey at Teachers College, Columbia University in 1916, the same year *Democracy and Education* was published. In *Art as Experience*, published almost two decades later, Dewey emphasized the importance of "recovering the continuity of esthetic experience with normal processes of living" — in other words, the connection between art and life. "If artistic and esthetic quality is implicit in every normal experience," Dewey asks, "how shall we explain how and why it so generally fails to become explicit?" Dewey's solution to the problem of making explicit the implicit aesthetic quality of everyday life was contained in the interaction of the body with its environment:

> Life grows when a temporary falling out is a transition to a more extensive balance of the energies of the organism with those of the conditions under which it lives. … The rhythm of loss of integration with environment and recovery of union not only persists in man but becomes conscious with him; its conditions are material out of which he forms purposes.[13]

For humans, in contrast with amoebae, evolution can be purposeful. The implications for dance as a fundamental art form were not lost on H'Doubler, or on her student.[14]

H'Doubler integrated everyday events into dance. Halprin would go further, and incorporate emotional as well as physical interactions. For Dewey, the emotional content of an event is key to its meaning:

> Emotion is the conscious sign of a break, actual or impending. The discord is the occasion that induces reflection. Desire for restoration of the union converts mere emotion into interest in objects as conditions of realization of harmony. With the realization, material of reflection is incorporated into objects as their meaning. Since the artist cares in a peculiar way for the phase of experience in which union is achieved he does not shun moments of resistance and tension. He rather cultivates them, not for their own sake but because of their potentialities, bringing to living consciousness an experience that is unified and total.[15]

As her work developed, Halprin would court occasions for physical and emotional tension, both between dancers, and with the environment, in order to achieve new levels of equilibrium. She sometimes did this by generating emotional tension among the performers, as in *Apartment 6* (1965): an unscripted drama among the three longtime principals of Halprin's San Francisco Dancers' Workshop. Often, however, her technique involved the unexpected — taking people by surprise, arousing their aggression: "I never realized we were stirring people so deeply," she said of an Italian performance of *Five-Legged Stool* (1962). The audience apparently felt they had been given "permission to misbehave." They threw things, but asked Halprin to return: "they'd never had such a gorgeous scandal."

> I now know why. It gets at their pre-conscious and kinesthetic responses. It's very sensory and primitive. The more we know about this power, the stronger we can be using it. The audience has a power too, and if they can be given an opportunity to use it, we could have an encounter that would really send sparks.[16]

Sparks can be enlightening. Art reminds us of something, something about ourselves. At the same time, art affects us by pulling us out of ourselves, connecting us with others and with the world. This interactive growth experience is why art is inherently pleasurable, or at least satisfying, even when its content may be puzzling or unpleasant. During the second half of the 1960s Halprin would bring the psychiatrist and Gestalt therapist Fritz Perls into her workshops to enhance her understanding of bodily feelings, emotions, and behavior. Perls, who had practiced Zen Buddhism, emphasized awareness in the present moment, interrelationship, and contact between the self, the environment, and the other.[17]

At the University of Wisconsin Halprin met her husband, the influential landscape architect Lawrence Halprin (1916–2009), who referred to his own melding of modernism, nature, and movement as "choreography."[18] Born in New York City and reared in Brooklyn, as a teen Larry Halprin spent three years on a kibbutz in the British Mandate of Palestine (now Israel). He attended Cornell University and then the University of Wisconsin, where he earned a Master of Science degree in horticulture. In autumn 1941, Larry enrolled in the Harvard Graduate School of Design, which combined architecture, urban planning, and landscape architecture. Anna joined him in Cambridge after graduating the following year.

German émigré Walter Gropius, founder of the experimental, multi-disciplinary Bauhaus, had joined the GSD faculty in 1937 as Chair of the Department of Architecture. He brought

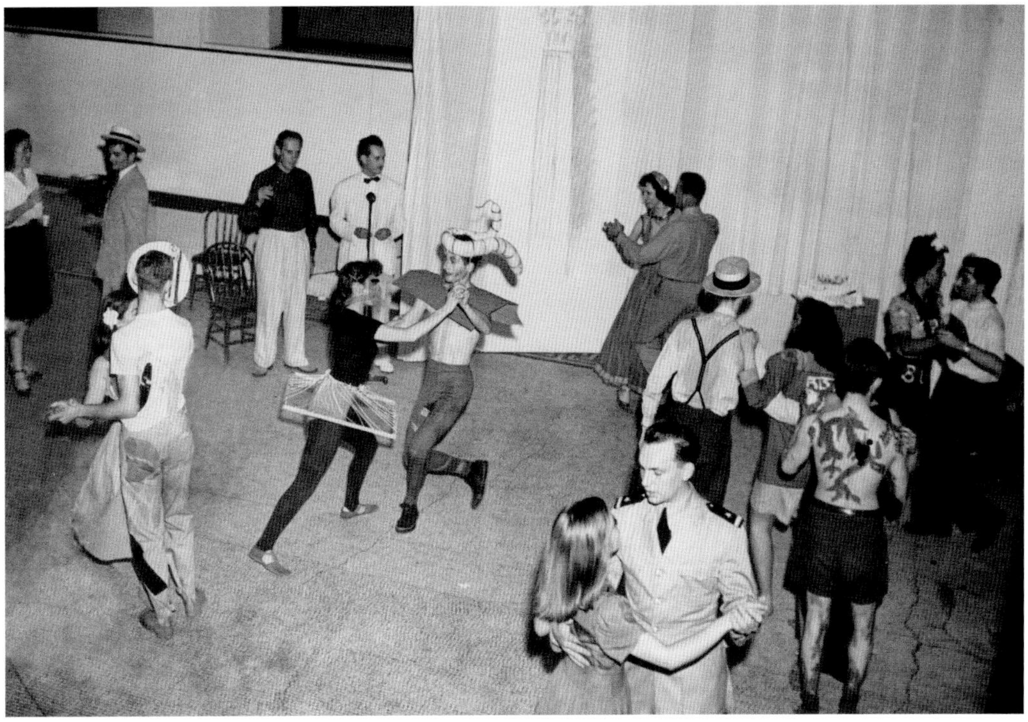

Anna Halprin dancing with Lawrence Halprin (center) at a costume ball for Walter Gropius's 60th birthday, Harvard University, 1943.

with him European artists, architects, and designers including Josef and Anni Albers, László Moholy-Nagy, Ludwig Mies van der Rohe, Marcel Breuer, and Herbert Bayer. Larry Halprin later told a reporter:

> There's a great deal of misinterpretation of what the Bauhaus was. Everyone thinks of it as big square buildings, but that isn't it at all. The idea was that groups of people — artists, theater people, painters, sculptors, costume designers — would all work on ideas that went beyond the capacity of any one of them.[19]

Anna Halprin was not personally involved with Bauhaus artists and designers to the extent that Larry was, but, she says, "I *was* influenced by their parties, which were like no other party you've ever been to in your life! They would do costume parties, and people would show up in costumes. They would do free dancing, and it was just wide open."[20]
In Cambridge, Halprin taught dance at a private high school and at a settlement house, worked on her own choreography, and performed for design faculty and students. She attended lectures, classes, and other events at GSD, absorbing the Bauhaus workshop approach to creativity. "I gave classes in movement to students who wanted to do that," she says. "Bauhaus architects and artists were so open to the other arts."

Asked to teach a summer workshop in New Hampshire, Halprin decided to give a course on space, which she had not studied at Wisconsin:

> I analyzed movement in space — sparse space, density space, planes in space, levels in space, open spaces, closed spaces. I did a whole analysis of space in movement, and taught that as a course one summer. That has affected me ever since. Most dancers think of themselves as objects in space, but I do not. … I developed a whole theory and approach around movement in space.[21]

Halprin instructed her students to go into the landscape and "bring back forms from nature they found exciting because of a design feeling. Bark, stone, twigs, foliage, fungi." At first, she asked the students to make drawings based on what they had brought back. Unsatisfied with the results, she shifted her approach and asked them to respond to their objects from nature in terms of movement: "One by one each person began to show through movement different ways of feeling space. We discovered that it was live substance. That we could act upon it and that it in turn could act upon our movements."[22] After returning to Cambridge in fall 1943, Halprin began offering classes to architecture and design students. She instructed them to use furniture and other objects to build an environment, and then asked them to move within the environment they had constructed: "as architects, if you are building a house or a building, how is this going to affect the people living in it? How does this make them feel? … So I translated what I understood about space into movement for the architects and into a conscious use of space for the dancers. It felt like we were pioneering."[23]

In 1944 Larry Halprin received his B.L.A. from Harvard Graduate School of Design and went off to fight the war in the Pacific. Anna moved to New York City, where she took a modern dance class (which she did not find interesting). As a member of the Doris Humphrey/Charles Weidman Dance Company, she performed in *Sing Out Sweet Land* (1944–45), a Broadway musical revue of American songs and dances starring Burl Ives. On April 6, 1945, Larry's ship was hit by a kamikaze fighter plane. After a survivor's leave in San Francisco he was sent to Hawaii and then returned to San Francisco, where Anna joined him. She was happy to leave New York, writing a friend: "I'm not interested in acclaim — I'm only interested in creating out of the soil and the people a healthy fresh dance that is alive and vital."[24] Halprin saw California as a promised land that offered her an opportunity "to reassess and redefine dance in the same way that my husband Larry redefined landscape architecture." In California, she could develop "a new definition of dance that I was left alone, on my own, to explore and experiment with. I even did human dissection for a year, so I could understand how the body actually worked. I had to really start from scratch."[25]

Both Halprins worked in San Francisco, but they chose to live in Marin County in order to be close to nature and raise a family. Larry, who had joined the landscape architecture firm of modern garden designer Thomas Church, created a small garden for their house that incorporated "found" objects such as a fence and pre-existing plant materials. Designed to enhance daily life, the Halprin garden was published in the July 1947 issue of *Sunset* magazine. For Anna, the garden was the site of an unanticipated, career-shifting event:

> I was looking at sunlight on a tree for no reason at all, and without apparent preparation, I became intensely aware of a foghorn in the bay, a red berry at my side, and passing birds overhead. I saw each thing, first, as a separate element, and then as independent elements related in unpredictable ways.[26] … That was a turning point. That was one of those moments when you go "Ah-ha!" I was looking for a way to think about choreography in a different way. I was on the lookout, and I didn't have a clue until that happened.[27]

Halprin's Northern California satori opened her up to a new way of seeing, and to new ways of working with improvisation.

In 1952 the Halprin family, which now included two daughters, moved into a new home on the redwood and madrone-covered slopes of Mount Tamalpais. The following year Larry Halprin, working with theater designer Arch Lauterer, designed an outdoor wooden dance deck. Fifty feet below their house, log-bench amphitheater seating built into the hillside allows this large, open-air studio to serve as an outdoor theater. The dance deck made it possible for Anna to work in proximity to her children, and to perform with nature — to experience herself as part of nature:

> I had to start anew with new ideas of what is the nature within me and how did that nature and my nature interface. That's where I began to develop a new approach to movement.[28]

Halprin's new way of thinking about making dance would encompass four stages: physical, sensorial, emotional, and spiritual. Her earlier garden insight into the shifting interrelationships between things expanded into a more comprehensive understanding that she could apply to her art form:

> I was working out on the deck, and suddenly I began to become aware of how I was taking in and experiencing the *environment*. How do I look at it? How do I give it some form? And suddenly, I said, "Oh, that's so interesting!" Like [seeing] the stillness of the tree in relationship to the bird that just flew by … that's *form*. That's organizing the way you experience things. Form is not necessarily cause and effect, because there was no cause or effect, when I absorbed that bird moving. Perception is giving form to sensory experience. And that's where everyday movement comes in. … Different forms became part of the total experience.[29]

In the process of analyzing her relationship with nature, Halprin was able intuitively to separate sensation, or feeling, from perception.

Sensation and perception are different body-mind activities that are thought to have developed at different evolutionary stages. Because they occur simultaneously, we tend to experience them as the same thing, but they are not. Sensation, the immediate, emotional, active response to stimuli from sense organs and the brain, is *feeling* — the ongoing, moment-to-moment physical feeling of being alive. Perception, on the other hand, is the organizing of sensation into thought processes, mental apprehension, and knowledge that generates *recognition*.[30] Perception gives rise to art. In *Art as Experience*, Dewey had framed art activity as problem solving on the individual level. Informed by the interdisciplinary Bauhaus process, Halprin's workshop concept approached creativity as group problem solving by individuals who together generated work that none of them could have created alone. Halprin's new way of approaching dance-making also reflected her continuing disillusionment with the current state of modern dance, which she re-experienced first-hand in 1955 as a participant in a three-day American Dance Festival in New York. Her sense when she first left New York in 1947 — that "modern" dancers were too reliant on imitating a particular style — was reinforced. She had been taught by H'Doubler that dance should emerge from the mental and physical nature of the dancer. Through interdisciplinary workshops on her dance deck, Halprin set out to integrate what she had learned from H'Doubler with the movements, rhythms, and relationships she observed in nature.

∞

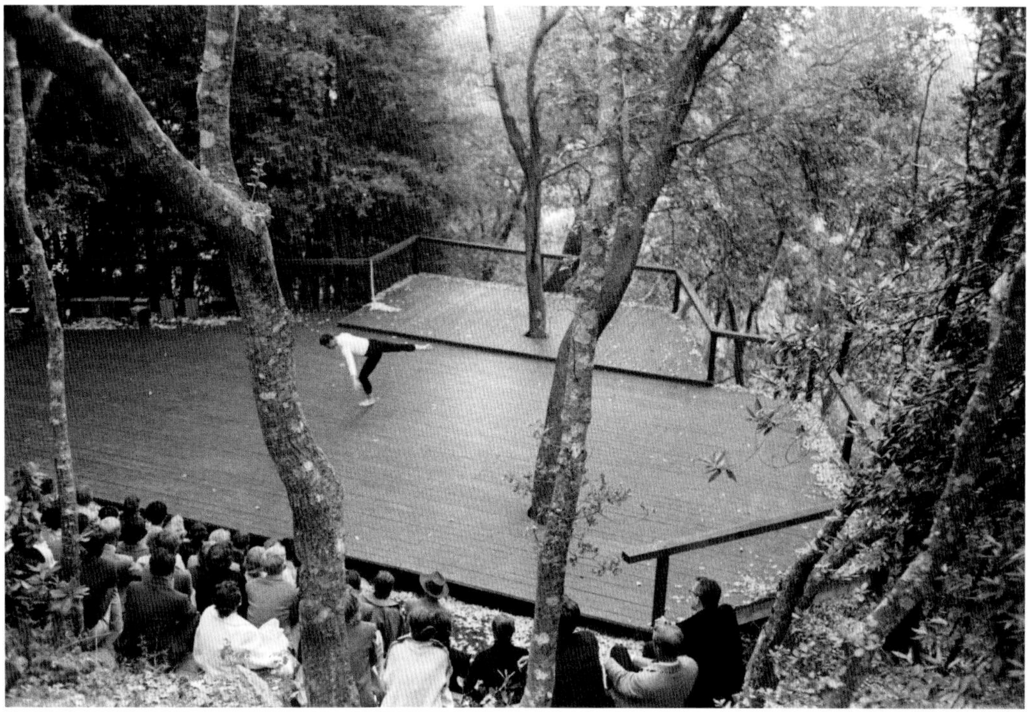

Merce Cunningham on the dance deck, Kentfield, California, 1955. Photo: Ernest Braun. Anna Halprin Papers, Elyse Eng Dance Collection, Museum of Performance + Design.

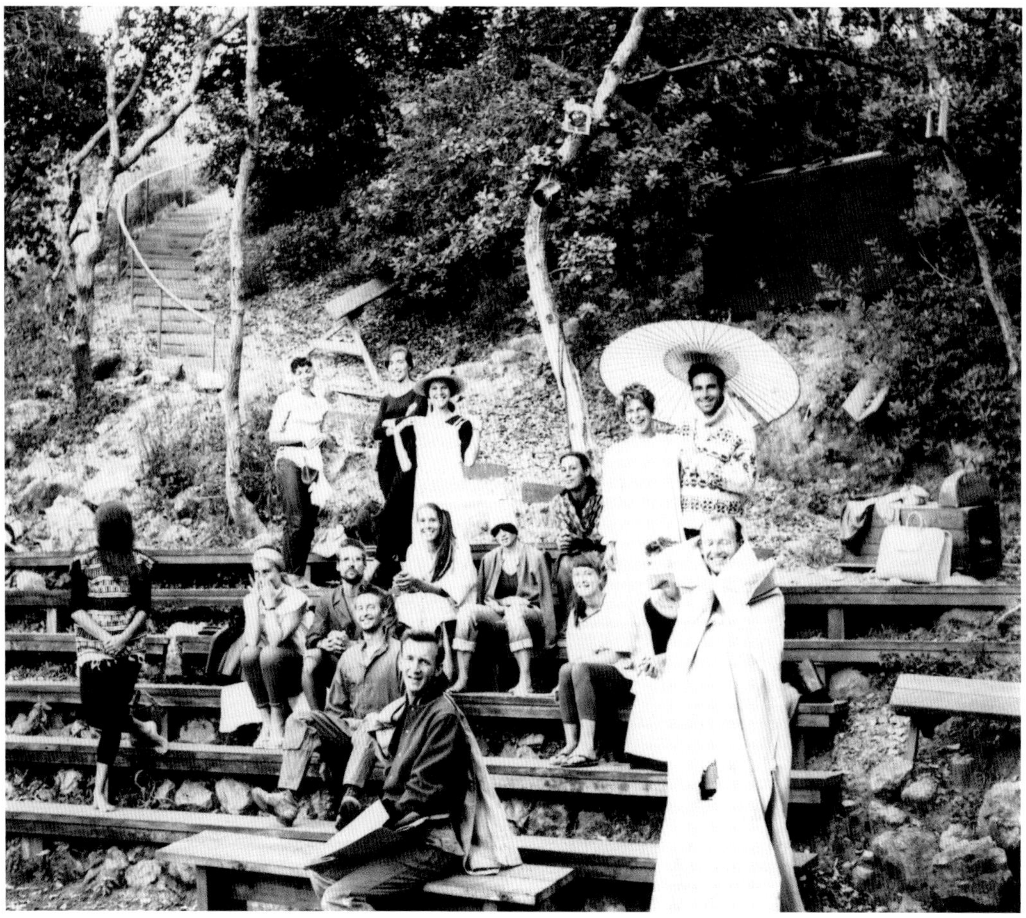

Summer Workshop on the dance deck, Kentfield, California, 1960. Participants: Sunni Bloland, Trisha Brown, June Ekman, Ruth Emerson, Simone Forti, Jerrie Glover, John Graham, Anna Halprin, A.A. Leath, Paul Pera, Yvonne Rainer, Shirlie Ririe, Lisa Strauss, Willis Ward. Photo: Lawrence Halprin. © Anna Halprin Papers, Elyse Eng Dance Collection, Museum of Performance + Design.

The dance deck became the site for Halprin's groundbreaking San Francisco Dancers' Workshop, which she established in 1955, and the Tamalpa Institute, co-founded with her daughter Daria Halprin in 1978. Despite its remote location in Kentfield, California, the San Francisco Dancers' Workshop has had immense ramifications in the world of art and performance, thanks to the quality of the people Halprin has attracted over the years. John Cage and Merce Cunningham spent time with her there. Among her students were Simone Forti, Yvonne Rainer, Trisha Brown, Meredith Monk, and Robert Morris, all of whom moved to New York and helped lead the explosion of performance and interdisciplinary art of the 1960s.

Halprin's students were among the co-founders of the influential Judson Dance Theater, an experimental composition workshop that began in 1962 at the Judson Memorial Church, a theologically and socially liberal Baptist church on Washington Square that was also home to the Judson Art Gallery and the Judson Poets' Theater. Led by musician Robert Dunn who had studied with John Cage, the Judson dance collective, like Halprin's earlier San Francisco Dancers' Workshop, was made up of visual artists, including Robert Morris, Robert Rauschenberg, and Carolee Schneemann; composers Herbert McDowell and Philip Corner; dancers Yvonne Rainer, Deborah Hay, Trisha Brown, Fred Herko, Steve Paxton, James Waring, David Gordon, Judith Dunn, Lucinda Childs, Meredith Monk, and others. Forti, Rainer, and Brown went on to become renowned choreographers and artistic directors. A painter at the time he was working with Halprin, Robert Morris emerged in New York as a sculptor, conceptual artist, and writer who contributed to both the Process Art and Land Art movements. Meredith Monk has become one of the most original performance artists of our time.

Halprin's own work from the late 1950s and 60s was often prophetic of developments to come. An example is her collaborative improvisation *Duet*, a 1958 performance with A. A. Leath that involved energetically moving while exchanging breath by "playing" opposite sides of the same harmonica. Halprin said later *Duet* could have been entitled *Kiss*.[31] It presaged the interactive performance art of Marina Abramović and Ulay in the 1970s, specifically *Breathing In, Breathing Out* (1977), in which Abramović and Ulay, microphones taped to their throats, their mouths connected in a "kiss," breathed the air from each other's lungs. *Duet* also resonates with *Ally*'s installation work *Swallow*, which is sourced from Janine Antoni and Stephen Petronio's yogic duet in 2015 in which Antoni and Petronio simultaneously swallowed two ends of a 10-foot strip of cloth until their mouths met.

Avant-garde musicians such as Pauline Oliveros, Terry Riley, and La Monte Young were also important to Halprin's workshop process. Riley and Young produced the sound scores for *Still Point* and *Visions*, performed in 1960, and Halprin selected Young's *Trio for Strings* (1958) to accompany her first long improvisational work, *Birds of America, or Gardens Without Walls*. In January 1960, John Cage had written Young, a graduate student at the University of California, Berkeley, suggesting that he get in touch with Halprin. Young played some of his music for her, including *Trio for Strings*. "She became interested in my work and my ideas," he wrote to a former teacher that April, "and invited me to become the musical director." He continued:

> I have been working with her for several months now and it has been a marvelous experience. … We improvise and Terry [Riley] and I make sounds even better than electronic sounds. Live sounds (no tapes, on the spot).[32]

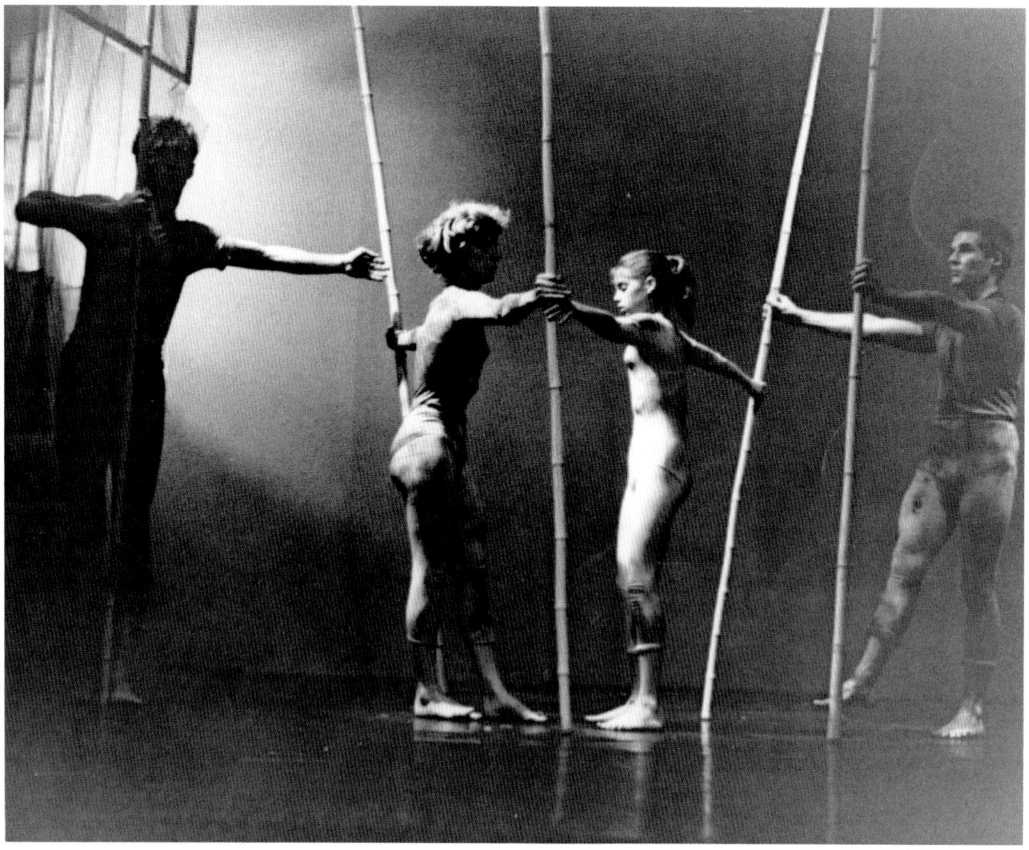

Anna Halprin, *Birds of America, or Gardens without walls*, 1961. Dancers (left to right): John Graham, Anna Halprin, Rana Halprin, A.A. Leath. © Anna Halprin Papers, Elyse Eng Dance Collection, Museum of Performance + Design.

Riley and Young created improvised sound accompaniments for the workshop participants without being able to see them responding to Halprin's "themes." Her goal for these juxtapositions was to make "new relationships, like in nature." I asked Halprin for an example of a theme. She replied: "move chairs around" — a more open-ended, improvisatory version of her 1943 instruction to architecture and design students to build an environment with furniture.[33]

La Monte Young moved to New York in the fall of 1960. He met George Maciunas and Jackson Mac Low at the New School and became a founding member of Fluxus, an international, intermedia, collaborative art enterprise organized by Maciunas in the early 1960s. It was probably Young who suggested that Halprin be invited to participate in Fluxus. As she put it:

> We used to send scores back and forth, but at the time we weren't calling them scores. ... I called them "events." On the East Coast, they were calling them "happenings" — people like Kaprow — but I didn't know about it, then. ... I remember setting up correspondence with Yoko Ono. She would send me events. One of them was a falling event, and I remember doing it in San Francisco, where every five minutes people would just let loose in the city — every five minutes fall, wherever you are.[34]

In an early prospectus for Fluxus Yearboxes, George Maciunas announced that Halprin would contribute to *Fluxus No. 1 U.S. Yearbox*, *Five Legged Stool (Dance Score & Photographs)* and, with her workshop, *Landscape Score for a 45 Minute Environment.*[35] *Landscape Score* was indeed published in 1964 in some versions of *Fluxus 1*, the contents of which could vary slightly. Halprin recalls:

> George Maciunas would write to me and ask me to send him what I was doing, and I said, "well, we do events, and we have a workshop." And so I would send him things. There is an event that Larry and I did, *Landscape Event*. You pull it out; it's a score of a city dance, all folded up. It was in a wooden box, and as you opened it there were all these different things. Our contribution that year was this folded thing.[36]

Fluxus 1 also included the score for La Monte Young's *Trio for Strings*, which had accompanied Halprin's *Birds of America*. La Monte Young wrote many of his seminal *Compositions 1960* — instructions to be performed or imagined in more-or-less open-ended ways — while working with Anna Halprin. He published ten of them in the proto-Fluxus publication, *An Anthology of Chance Operations*, in 1963.[37] That same year, Maciunas published *Composition #10 ("to Bob Morris")* as a small booklet entitled *LY 1961*. "Bob Morris" was painter Robert Morris, a fellow participant in Halprin's workshops. Each page of *LY 1961* repeats: "Composition 1961," followed by the number and date of a projected 1961 performance of *Composition #10*, with the instruction "Draw a straight line and follow it" on the next line.[38]

In September 1962 Fluxus artist Nam June Paik performed *Composition #10* at the first official Fluxus festival — the "Fluxus International Festival of Very New Music" presented at the Städtisches Museum in Wiesbaden, Germany. Paik, who called his performance *Zen for Head*, carried out Young's instruction to draw a straight line and follow it by unrolling a large scroll of paper onto the floor, dipping his hair into a bowl of sumi-e ink and, using his head as a brush, "drawing" a line down the paper. His body "followed" as a matter of course. Like Halprin, Paik's medium in this instance was his body as much as the ink and paper.

Janine Antoni is part of the lineage of visual and performing artists whose perspectives on art and life have been influenced by Anna Halprin. Antoni first participated in one of Halprin's workshops in July 2011. She conceived her FWM exhibition, *Ally* (2016), to incorporate interpretations of Halprin's works, returning to Northern California several times to refine her artistic concepts. With their shared interest in the body and in emotional reality, it was natural for Antoni to have made this personal connection in the course of her wide-ranging explorations of creativity. There has, in fact, been a kind of six degrees of separation between the two artists. Antoni's performance *Loving Care* (1993, not included in *Ally*), in which she "mopped" the floor with her hair after dipping it in dye, was created before Antoni met Halprin. Asked whether *Loving Care* had been informed by Nam June Paik's idiosyncratic performance of La Monte Young's *Composition #10*, Antoni responded:

> I didn't know *Zen for Head* when I made *Loving Care*, [which] was a … feminist response to the fact that Yves Klein had used nude women to make his art. So, in *Loving Care*, I would replace the paintbrush with my hair and imitate an everyday activity like mopping the floor. After I performed *Loving Care*, people told me about *Zen for Head*.

"A year after I took Anna's workshop," Antoni added, "I wrote her to tell her how it had a profound impact on my creative process. She responded by saying, 'Why didn't you introduce yourself at the workshop? I know your work *Loving Care*.'" Halprin invited her to come for lunch the next time she was in the Bay Area. "I traveled there specifically to have that lunch," Antoni says.[39] This sequence of events that originated with Anna Halprin and La Monte Young, only to come back to Halprin in the person of Janine Antoni, illustrates the complexity of artistic influence and the circuitous routes that forms can take within entangled personal histories. Antoni's exhibition *Ally* was both an acknowledgment and exploration of mysteriously intertwined artistic consciousness.

John Cage is generally given credit for the explosion of event scores around 1960. Cage's Experimental Composition classes at the New School were immensely influential, but Anna Halprin deserves more credit than she has received.[40] While La Monte Young's iconoclastic tendencies introduced a stronger improvisatory element into Halprin's public performances, Halprin's terse, multi-sensory "themes" provided an immediate, experiential prototype for Young's similarly experiential "compositions." For *Ally,* Antoni performed what is perhaps her most beautiful score: "Paper Dance," from *Parades and Changes* (1965). *Parades and Changes* has a complex structure whose performance is determined by choice, not chance, as was John Cage's practice. The elements include lighting, sound score, props, and choreography, all of which can be combined in a number of ways. "Paper Dance" had been performed many times, but never as a solo piece.

Halprin says that *Parades and Changes* "created a real revolution in dance when it was performed in New York. But it was also my demise, in a way. It was first performed in Europe, but I couldn't use nudity in this country."[41] *Parades and Changes* includes three slow episodes of dressing and undressing, followed by "Paper Dance," which begins with naked dancers unrolling large strips of brown paper onto the floor. The score reads:

> Make ten single sounds on the paper. Crumple the paper for sixty counts, then tear continuously, listening to your sounds. When you have had enough, collect as large a bundle of paper as you can, and exit.[42]

When I saw *Parades and Changes* performed at the Berkeley Art Museum and Pacific Film Archive in February 2013 (previously performed there in 1970), "Paper Dance" culminated in performers repeatedly coming together to toss large bunches of crumpled paper into the air. The experience of watching this ecstatic group ritual generated a sensation that transcended the aesthetic: "spiritual" would be a better word.

Janine Antoni performs her own *Paper Dance* as a solo piece with an emphasis on the senses, and on sculptural form. In one section she whirls, paper spiraling around her like the scarves of Loie Fuller, until she crashes dizzily to the ground. There are references not only to sculpture (including her own), but also to personal narrative. In an apparent reference to Halprin's *Visions* (1960), in which clumps of wadded fabric were stuffed into the dancers' leotards and tights, Antoni stuffs crumpled paper down the front of a stretchy top pulled onto her bottom. She pulls the paper out through the neck-opening and then cradles it in her arms — an overt reference to giving birth. Halprin says that Antoni has made an original contribution to the evolution of the work:

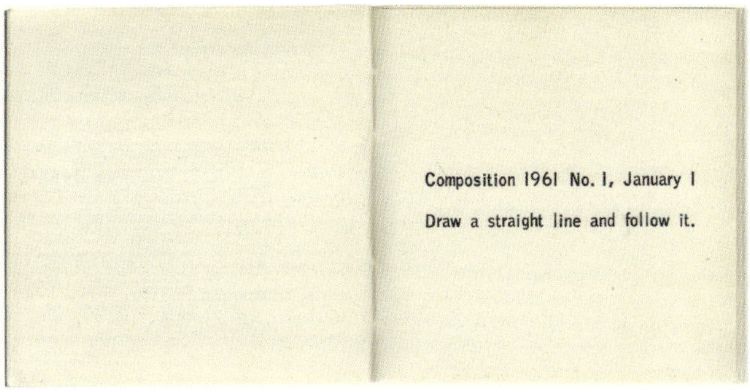

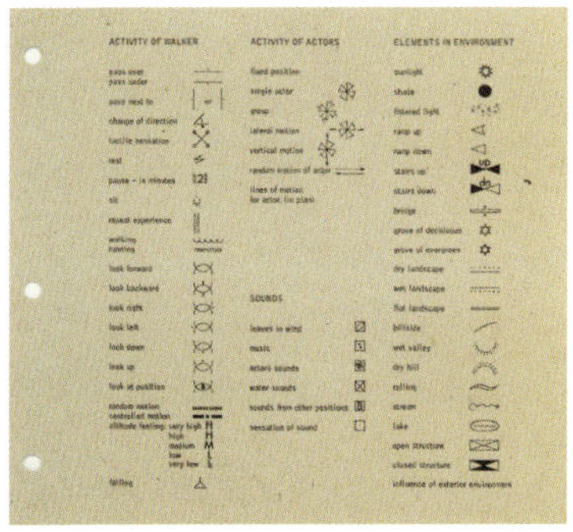

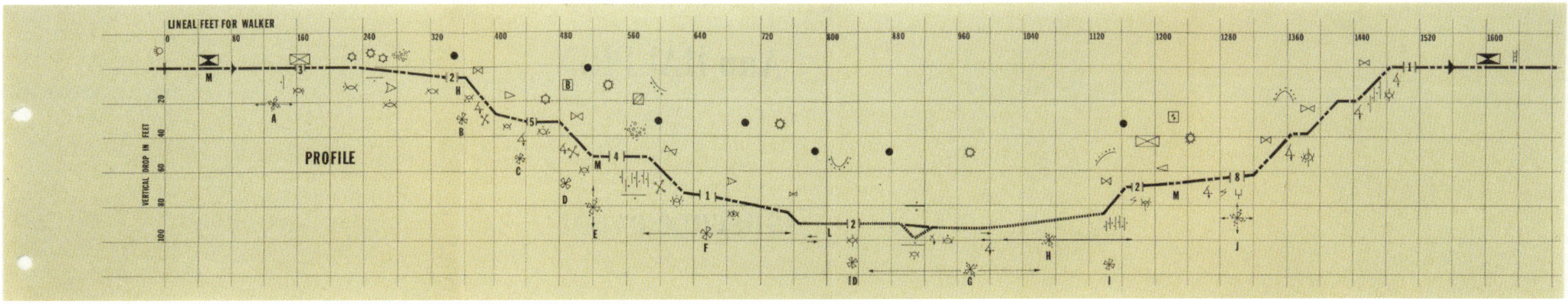

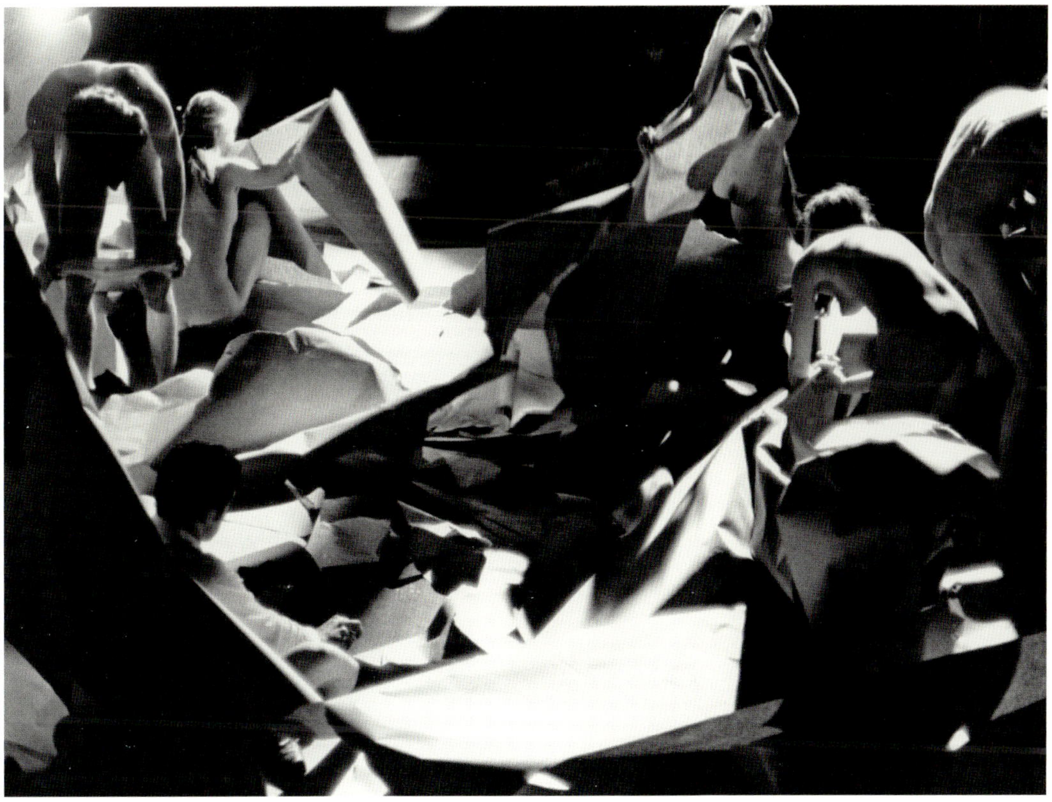

Top left: La Monte Young, *Compositions 1961* (Fluxus Edtions, 1963). Harvard Art Museums/Fogg Museum, Barbara and Peter Moore Fluxus Collection, Margaret Fisher Fund and gift of Barbara Moore/Bound & Unbound.

Top right and center: Anna Halprin, *Landscape Score for a 45 Minute Environment*, c. 1964, detail from Fluxus 1 (New York: Fluxus Editions, 1964). Photographed for the University of California, Berkeley Art Museum by Sibila Savage. © University of California, Berkeley Art Museum and Pacific Film Archive. Museum purchase: bequest of Phoebe Apperson Hearst, by exchange. 2012.26.

Bottom: Anna Halprin, *Parades and Changes*, c.1964–65. Photo: Nicholas Peckham. © Anna Halprin Papers, Elyse Eng Dance Collection, Museum of Performance + Design.

> Each time she does it, she finds unanticipated richness of material. Janine brings the sensibility of a sculptor who is both versatile and comfortable in movement. As much a dancer as a sculptor, she applies this freedom and sensitivity to her unique art form.[43]

∞

For Anna Halprin, the term “score” has a very specific meaning associated with the RSVP Cycles workshop planning system Larry Halprin developed in the late 1960s. The RSVP Cycles gave her a new way to approach dance making. This more inclusive workshop process was something Halprin had been “looking for” in the wake of *Parades and Changes*:

> Larry came up with the word “score,” and I immediately dropped “choreography” and starting using score. Now dancers are using it. I don’t know if they use it in New York, but in San Francisco that has become the term. … In order to utilize the RSVP cycle, you need to do it in a collective setting, and Larry had never done workshops before. That, he got from me.[44]

The initials RSVP stand for Resources, physical and human (including motivation and aims); Scores or instructions; Valuaction, meaning analysis and decision-making; and Performance — not just the end result, but the entire process, which is cyclical and builds on itself.[45] Anna has used this process as a “method” for generating creativity in others ever since.

During the late 1960s and early 70s the Halprins organized a series of cross-disciplinary “Experiments in Environment” workshops that brought together dancers, architects, environmental designers, artists, and others in an experiential process designed to foster group creativity through environmental awareness. The workshops took place over the course of several weeks in three distinct environments: the urban environment of San Francisco; the suburban environment of Kentfield; and the wildness of the Pacific Coast at The Sea Ranch (for which Larry had designed the master plan). Participants engaged in a series of multi-sensory activities based on loosely structured “open scores,” such as choreographed journeys diagramming everyday use and experience of urban plazas, blindfolded “awareness walks” through the landscape, and collective building projects using driftwood.[46] “Driftwood City”, was a later manifestation of Anna’s 1943 Cambridge classes for architecture and design students integrating the act of building with movement, the “connection between what you build and what you feel and experience.”[47] Among the participants in the 1968 Experiments in Environment was architect and artist Chip Lord, who would co-found the alternative architecture and media collective Ant Farm (1968–78).[48]

Anna Halprin was in the forefront of what today would be described as socially engaged art — art that aims to transform social, political, or ecological realities.[49] During a period of flaring racial tensions, she trained and then brought together black performers from the Watts neighborhood of Los Angeles with white performers from San Francisco in her *Ceremony of Us* (1968). The challenging situations Halprin created for her dancers were intended to “integrate emotional responses through an art process … I wanted the dancer to be a whole, socially aware person.”[50] She has also done workshops with HIV-positive and cancer patients (she herself is a cancer survivor), and created phenomenal group rocking-chair events with elderly people in civic center parks. Her annual community ritual on Mount Tamalpais, *Planetary Dance*, began in 1981 and continues to this day. It has been performed in thirty-six countries around the world.

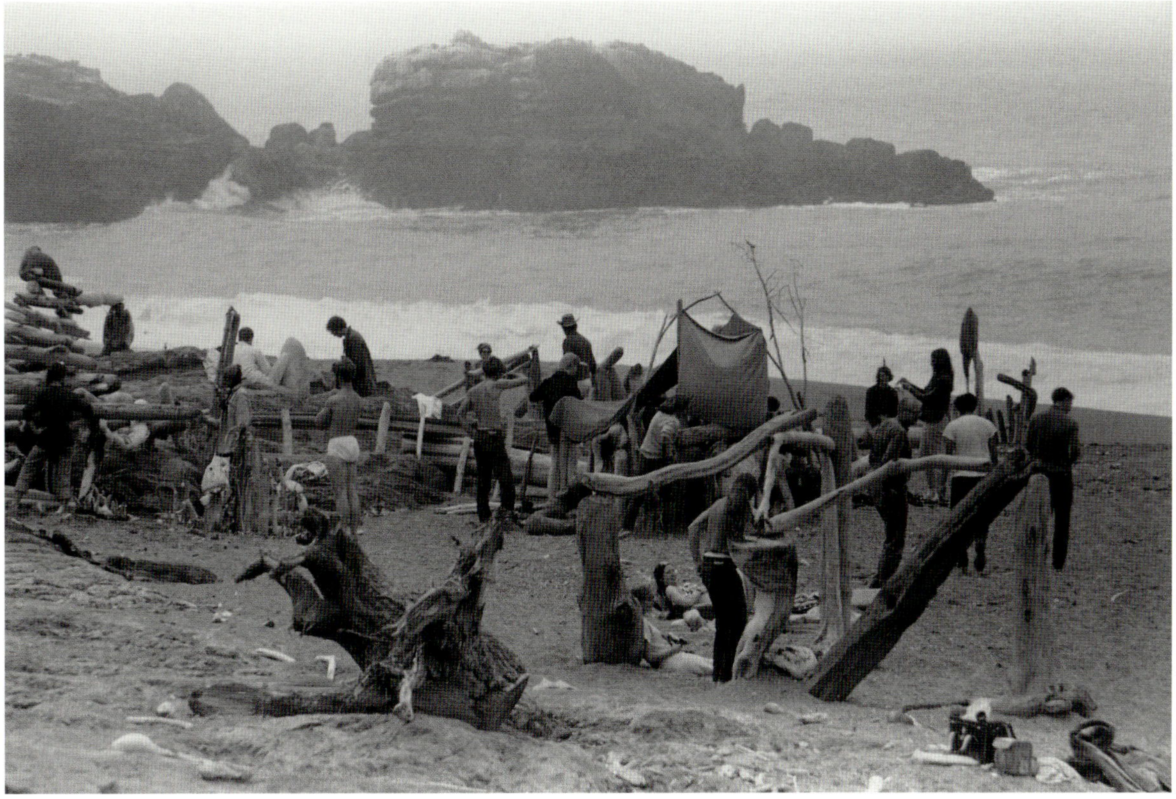

Experiments in Environment Workshop: Driftwood City, The Sea Ranch, California, 1966.
© Lawrence Halprin Collection, The Architectural Archives, University of Pennsylvania.

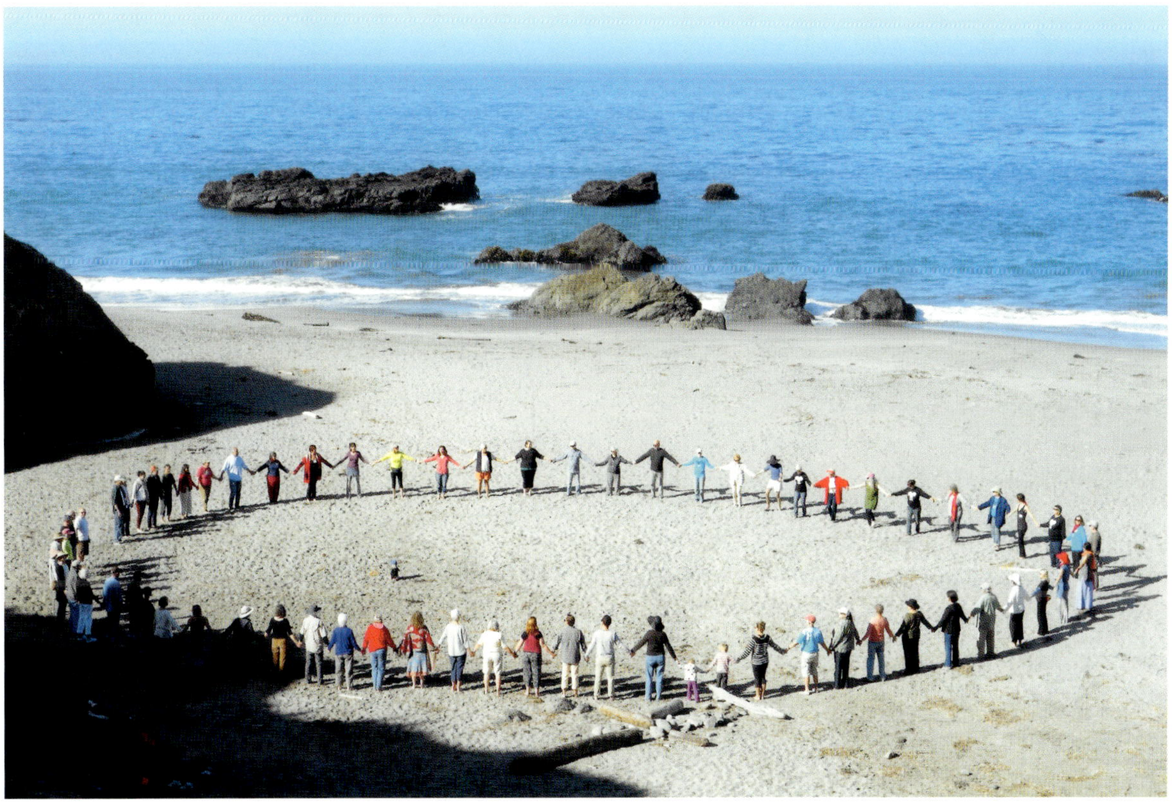

Anna Halprin conducting a *Score for Building Community* at The Sea Ranch, 2014. Photo: Jim Alinder.

As she has aged, Halprin continues to explore themes of change and our bodies' relationship with nature in performances that deploy the expressive power of her own naked body to powerful effect. She leads regular workshops in Performance Skills and Scoring, in which "new possibilities keep appearing." Halprin characterizes her current practice as "teaching":

> I teach all kinds of people, including seniors and children, not just dancers. Teaching, for me, is having a wonderful laboratory where I can develop ideas and experiment. I take very seriously whether what I'm experimenting with or exploring in my lab is useful to the people I'm working with, but it's also very important resource-gathering for me. I'm always finding something new that opens up new venues for me.[51]

The only thing that has changed, she says, is her subject matter, "which is more appropriate for my age and for my life experiences." Her advice for young artists today?

> As your life experience deepens, your art skills expand; as your art skills expand, your life experiences deepen. Build on that. Don't ever get discouraged. … If you look at your life as art, there is nothing in your life that can ever pull you down.

There is nothing, she emphasizes, "that can't be danced."[52] The dancer Anna Halprin is old now, but younger artists like Janine Antoni continue to draw energy from her intense creativity. Even in death, Anna Halprin expects to keep dancing. As Rilke wrote: "what is heavy turns to spirit. If we just keep hold of each other, you grasping the young one and I the old, we could revolve together like stars."

Notes

1. Joanna Macy and Anita Barrows, eds. and trans., *A Year With Rilke* (New York: Harper One, 2009), xi.

2. Regarding her name, Halprin writes: "I was Ann Halprin until 1972. … After my operation for cancer, I had an occasion to look at my birth certificate and noticed, to my surprise, that my name was Hannah Deborah, after my mother's mother. I was working with the multiracial company at the time, and reclaiming our heritage was a big part of our philosophy. … I changed my name from the Anglo-Saxon 'Ann' to the much more Jewish 'Anna'" (Anna Halprin, *Moving Toward Life: Five Decades of Transformational Dance* [Middletown, CT: Wesleyan University Press, 1995], 75).

3. Halprin, *Moving Toward Life*, 214–216.

4. Letter to Countess Margot Sizzo-Noris-Crouy, April 12, 1923. *A Year With Rilke*, 87–88.

5. From an interview with Jacquelynn Baas published in Mary Jane Jacob and Jacquelynn Baas, eds., *Chicago Makes Modern: How Creative Minds Changed Society* (University of Chicago Press, 2012), 239.

6. John Dewey, *Art as Experience* (New York: Minton, Balch, 1934), 108.

7. Janice Ross, "Introduction, Work in the Community," in Halprin, *Moving Toward Life*, 73.

8. Halprin, *Moving Toward Life*, 246.

9. Anna Halprin, written communication to author, April 10, 2016.

10. John Dewey, *Democracy and Education: An Introduction to the Philosophy of Education* (New York: The Free Press, 1997 [1916]), 140–141. For more on Halprin and the Winnetka Plan, see Janice Ross, *Anna Halprin: Experience as Dance* (Berkeley: University of California Press, 2007), 10–15.

11. Baas, *Chicago Makes Modern*, 242.

12. Ross, *Anna Halprin*, 17–18, 20.

13. Dewey, *Art as Experience*, 11–15.

14. See Margaret N. H'Doubler, *Dance: A Creative Art Experience* (New York: F. S. Crofts & Co., 1940).

15. Dewey, *Art as Experience*, 15.

16. From a 1965 interview with Yvonne Rainer, in Halprin, *Moving Toward Life*, 93.

17. For more on Perls, see Ross, *Anna Halprin*, 174ff.

18. See, for example, Lawrence Halprin, "The Choreography of Gardens," in *Impulse* 2 (1949).

19. Peggy Northrop, "Man In Space," *San Francisco Examiner Image Magazine*, August 3, 1986, 25.

20. Baas, *Chicago Makes Modern*, 243. Regarding Bauhaus parties, see Ute Ackermann, "Bauhaus Parties — Histrionics between Eccentric Dancing and Animal Drama," in *Bauhaus*, ed. Jeannine Fiedler (Köln: Könemann, 2006), 126–139.

21. Baas, *Chicago Makes Modern*, 243.

22. Anna Halprin notes from 1943, quoted Ross, *Anna Halprin*, 59.

23. Ross, *Anna Halprin*, 60–61.

24. Letter from April 1945, quoted Ross, *Anna Halprin*, 69.

25. Baas, *Chicago Makes Modern*, 240.

26. From a 1963 interview (Jack Anderson, "Manifold Implications," in *Dance Magazine* 37, no. 4 [April 1963], 46); quoted in Janice Ross, "Anna Halprin and the 1960s: Acting in the Gap between the Personal, the Public, and the Political," in *Reinventing Dance in the 1960s: Everything Was Possible*, ed. Sally Banes (Madison: University of Wisconsin Press, 2003), 29.

27. Baas, *Chicago Makes Modern*, 244.

28. Ross, *Anna Halprin*, 107. Halprin says she learned about movement by observing her own children's development (personal conversation with the author, April 10, 2016).

29. Baas, *Chicago Makes Modern*, 244.

30. See Nicholas Humphrey, *Seeing Red, A Study in Consciousness* (Cambridge: Harvard University Press, 2006).

31. Ross, *Anna Halprin*, 134.

32. Ross, *Anna Halprin*, 141–142. "Several months" suggests Young began working with Halprin in February 1960.

33. Anna Halprin, personal conversation with the author, April 10, 2016. This particular theme evokes La Monte Young's *Poem: for chairs, tables, benches, etc. (or other sound sources)*, composed in January 1960.

34. Baas, *Chicago Makes Modern*, 246. Young no doubt served as the go-between with Ono, who appointed him musical director of her New York loft concert series in December 1960.

35. Jon Hendricks, *Fluxus Codex* (New York: Abrams, 1988), 260.

36. Baas, *Chicago Makes Modern*, 246.

37. In the fall of 1960 the editor of the San Francisco publication *Beatitude* had asked Young and Mac Low to guest-edit an East Coast issue of *Beatitude East*. Young gathered material, and when *Beatitude East* folded, he asked Maciunas to design *An Anthology of Chance Operations*, for which Young served as editor and co-publisher, along with Mac Low.

38. For a more detailed account of *Compositions 1961*, see Jeremy Grimshaw, *Draw a Straight Line and Follow It: The Music and Mysticism of La Monte Young* (Oxford University Press, 2011), 82. See also Gerard Forde, "Plus or Minus 1961 — A Chronology 1959–1963" in, *± 1961: Founding the Expanded Arts* (Madrid: Museo Nacional Centro de Arte Reina Sofía, 2013), 256.

39. Email from April 6, 2016, which concludes: "For the record, it seems like, of all my work, *Loving Care* is the work that people from the dance world know about." Halprin says she had looked Antoni up, and *Loving Care* was the work that most impressed her (personal conversation with the author, April 9, 2016).

40. See Liz Kotz, *Words to Be Looked At: Language in 1960s Art* (Cambridge, MA: MIT Press, 2007), 61–98; Harmony Violet Wolfe's master's thesis, *Landscapes of Dance: The 1960 Summer Workshop of Anna Halprin* (University of California Riverside, 2012), 19–24 [http://escholarship.org/uc/item/9888f5p2#, accessed April 9, 2016]; and Grimshaw, *Draw a Straight Line*, 74–83.

41. Baas, *Chicago Makes Modern*, 244. According to Halprin, when the San Francisco Dancers' Workshop performed the work in New York in 1967, a warrant was issued and Halprin was warned not to perform there for a year.

42. Halprin, *Moving Toward Life*, 102. Halprin says the color of the paper mandated that the dancers be naked. For longer descriptions of the piece and its various performances, see Ross, *Anna Halprin*, 181–188, 191–198, and passim.

43. Anna Halprin, personal conversation with the author, April 10, 2016.

44. Baas, *Chicago Makes Modern*, 245.

45. See Lawrence Halprin and Jim Burns, *Taking Part: A Workshop Approach to Collective Creativity* (Cambridge, MA: MIT Press, 1974).

46. See http://grahamfoundation.org/public_exhibitions/5241-experiments-in-environment-the-halprin-workshops-1966-1971 (accessed April 7, 2016). See also Eva J. Friedberg, "Collective Movement: Anna and Lawrence Halprin's Joint Workshops" in, *West of Center: Art and the Counterculture Experiment in America, 1965–77*, eds. Elissa Auther and Adam Lerner (Minneapolis: University of Minnesota Press, 2011), 22–41.

47. Anna Halprin, personal conversation with the author, April 10, 2016.

48. See Constance M. Lewallen, Steve Seid, et al., *Ant Farm* (Berkeley: University of California Press, 2004).

49. Just three of many publications on the subject: Pablo Helguera, *Education for Socially Engaged Art* (New York: Jorge Pinto Books, 2011); *Living as Form: Socially Engaged Art from 1991–2011*, ed. Nato Thompson (Cambridge, MA: MIT Press, 2012); and Tom Finkelpearl, *What We Made: Conversations on Art and Social Cooperation* (Durham, NC: Duke University Press, 2013).

50. Ross, *Anna Halprin*, 267; Halprin's clarification, personal conversation with the author, April 10, 2016.

51. Baas, *Chicago Makes Modern*, 246. Halprin taught children for twenty-five years as part of a dance co-op, and was the first choreographer to use children in serious productions.

52. Baas, *Chicago Makes Modern*, 246, and personal conversation with the author, April 10, 2016.

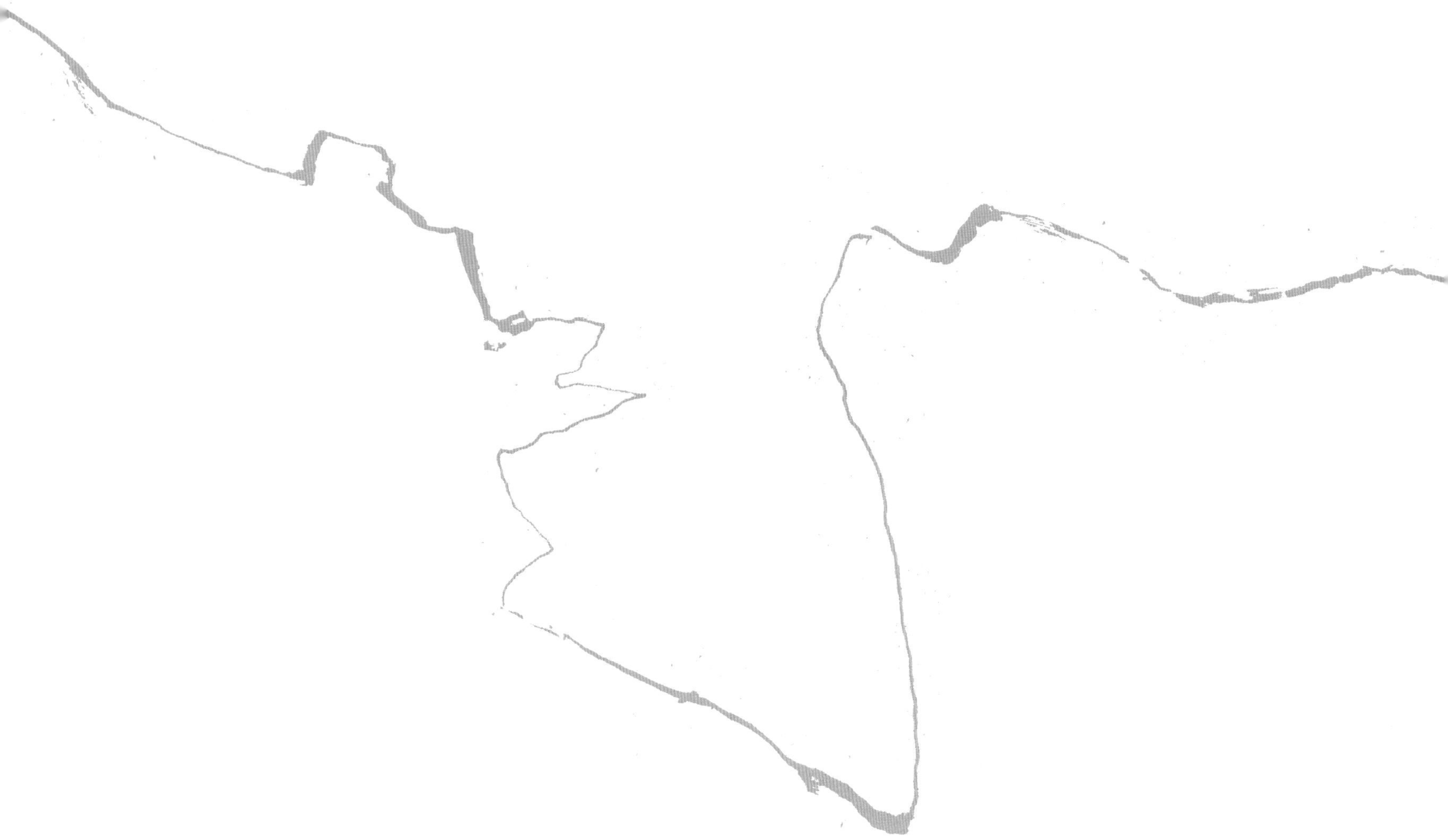

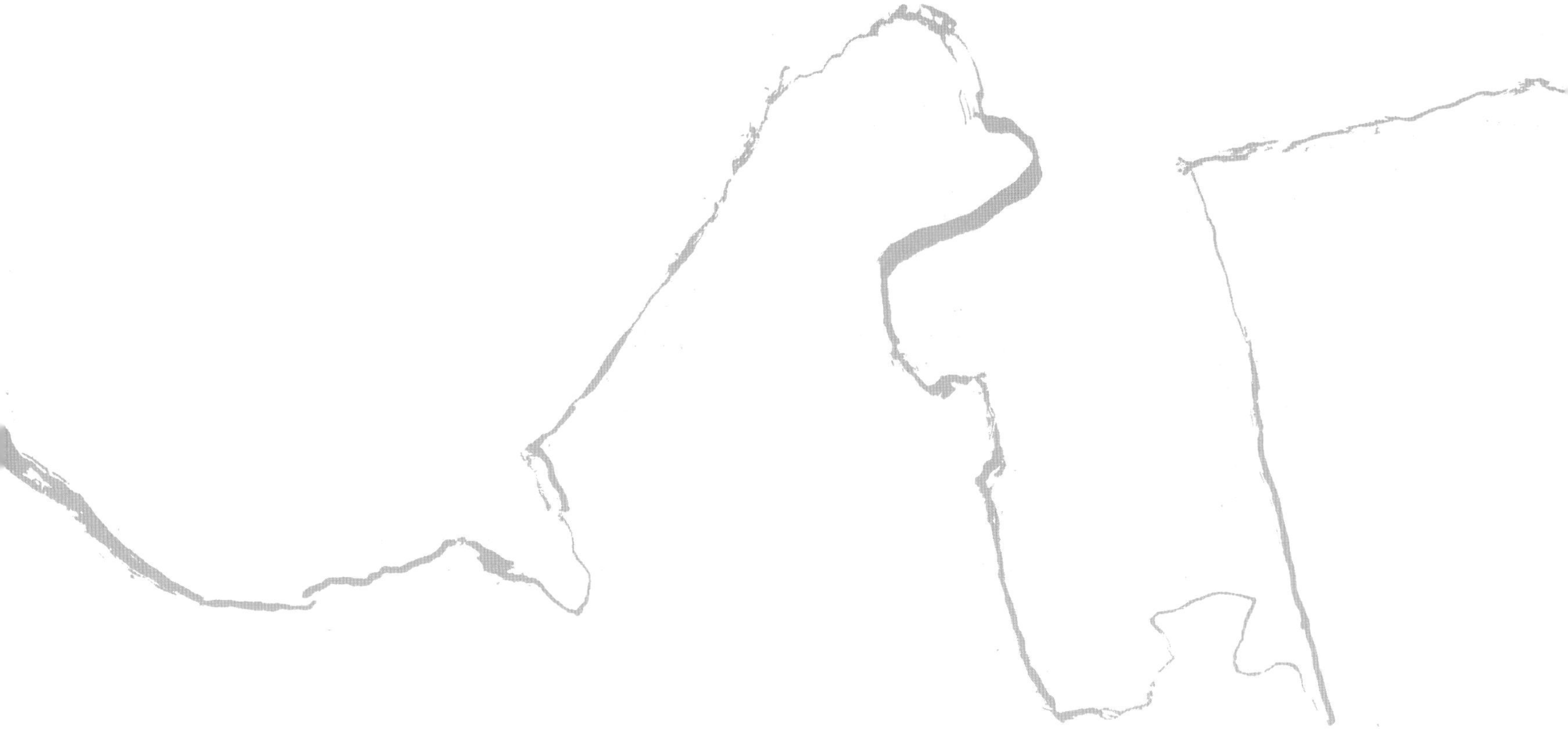

THE COURTESAN AND THE CRONE

Stephen Petronio, Anna Halprin

Anna Halprin conceived this short performance in 1999 when she was 79 years old. A courtesan dances and then removes a mask to reveal her aging face. Halprin invited Stephen Petronio to perform this work crossing gender and generations. A theatrical installation with pulleys, devised as part of Petronio's translation of the dance, held in balance the fabrics that sustain the illusion.

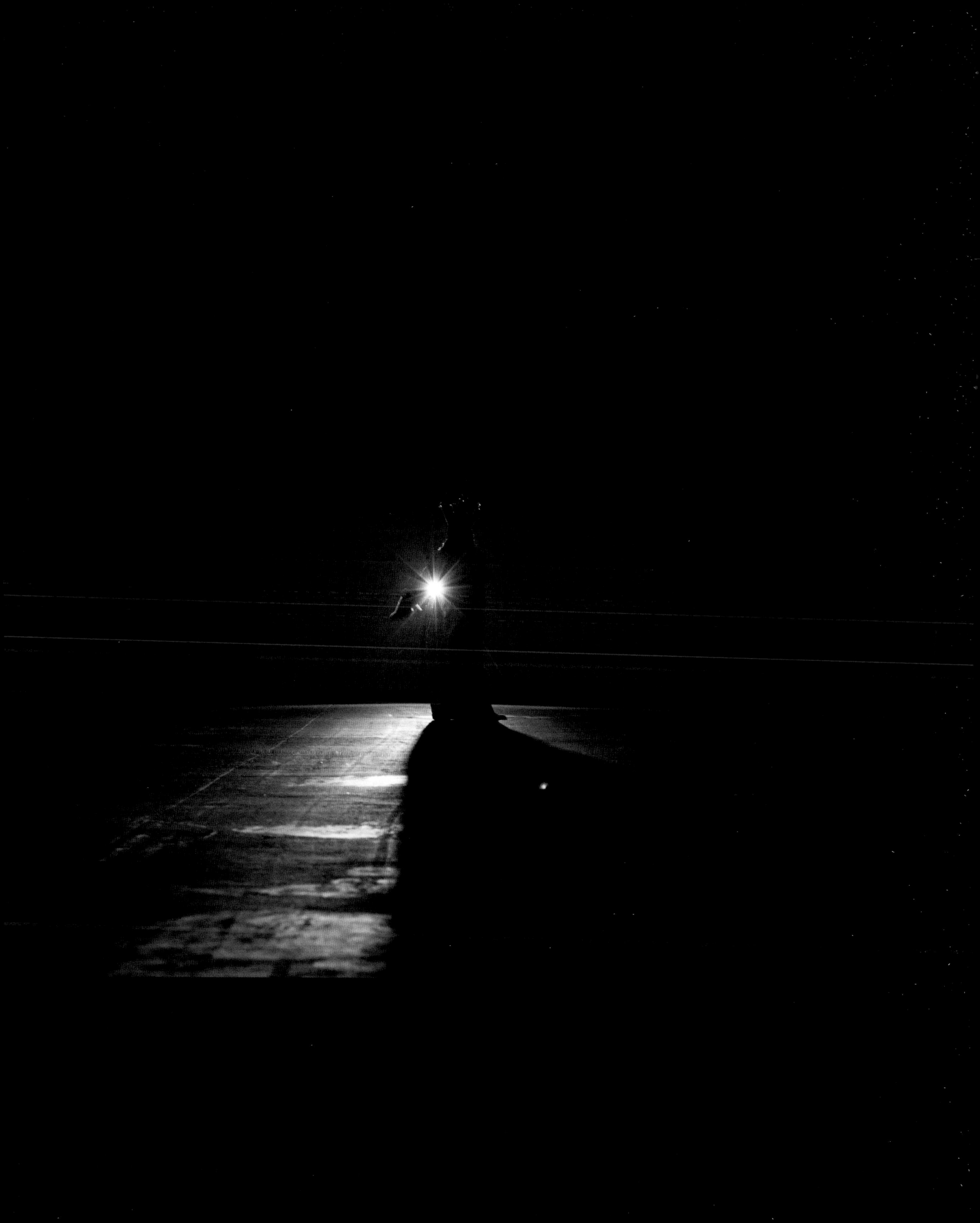

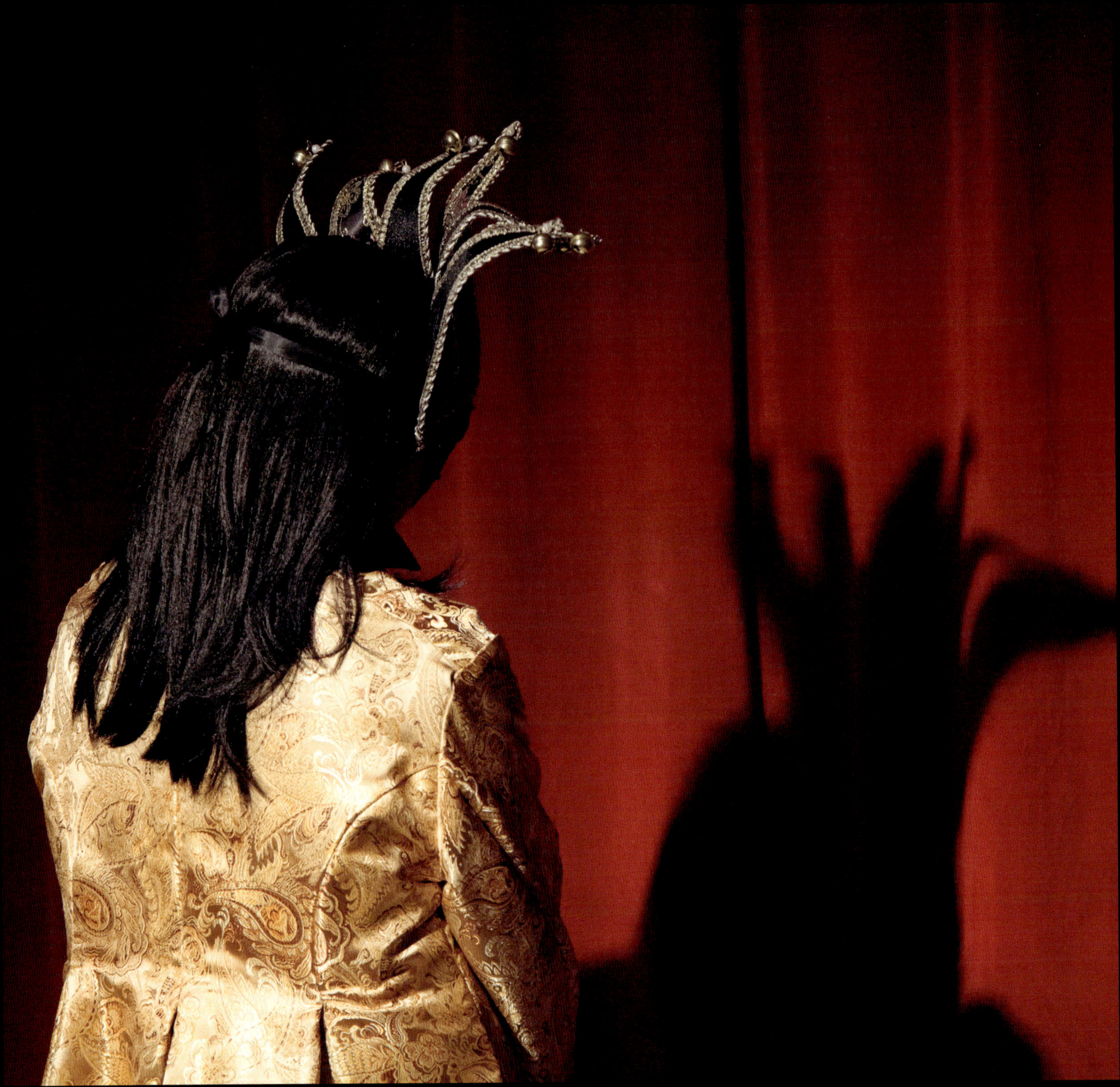

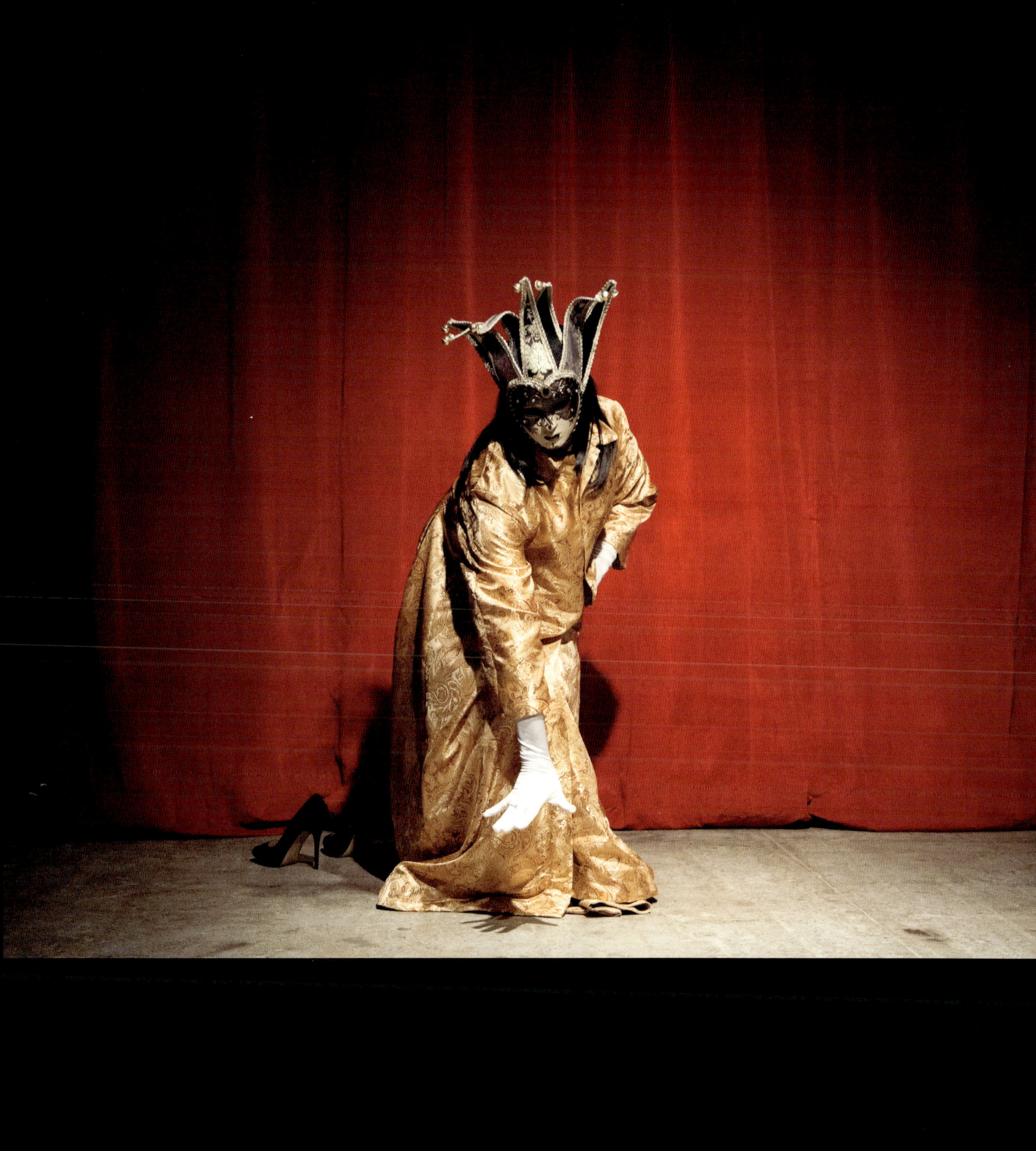

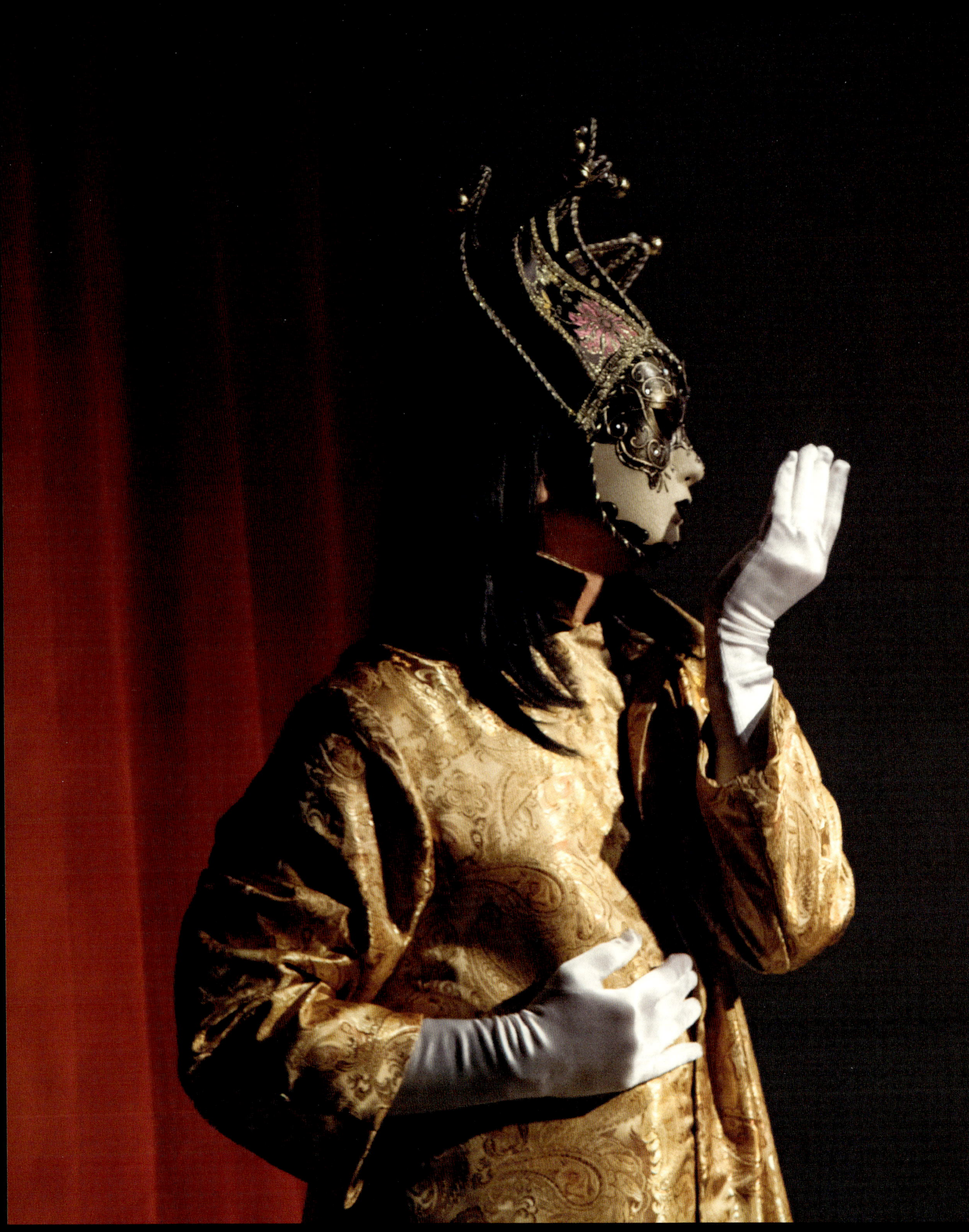

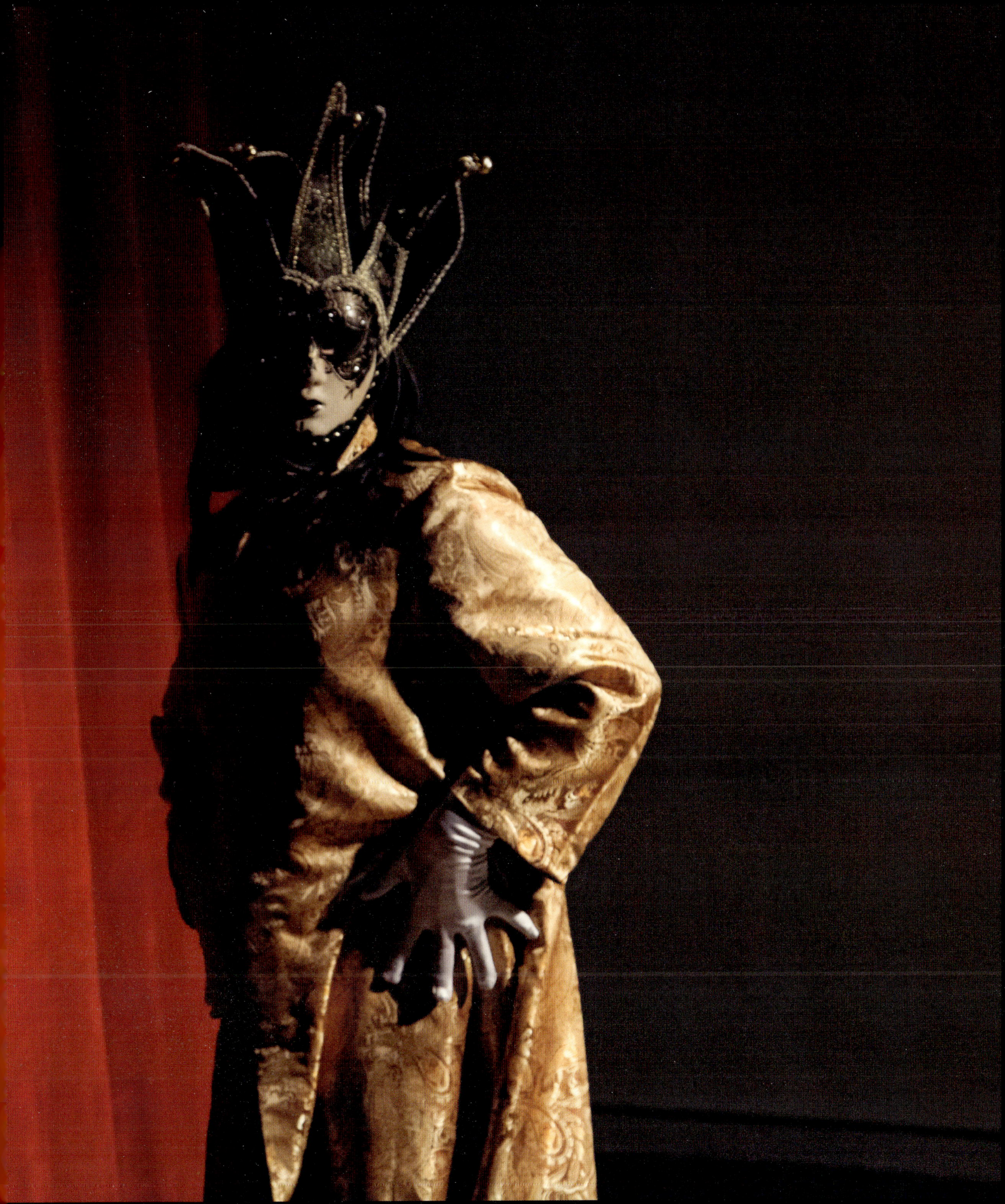

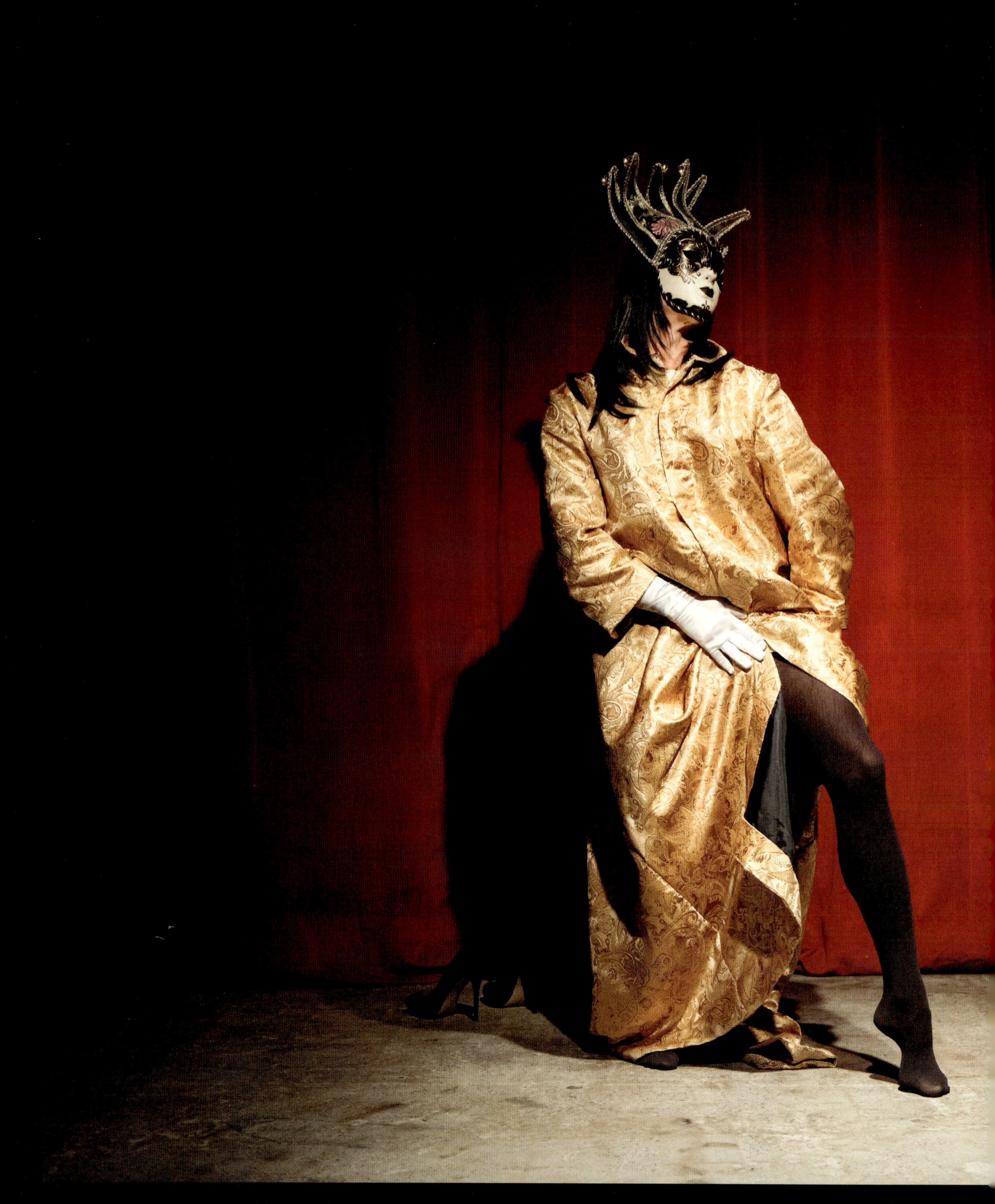

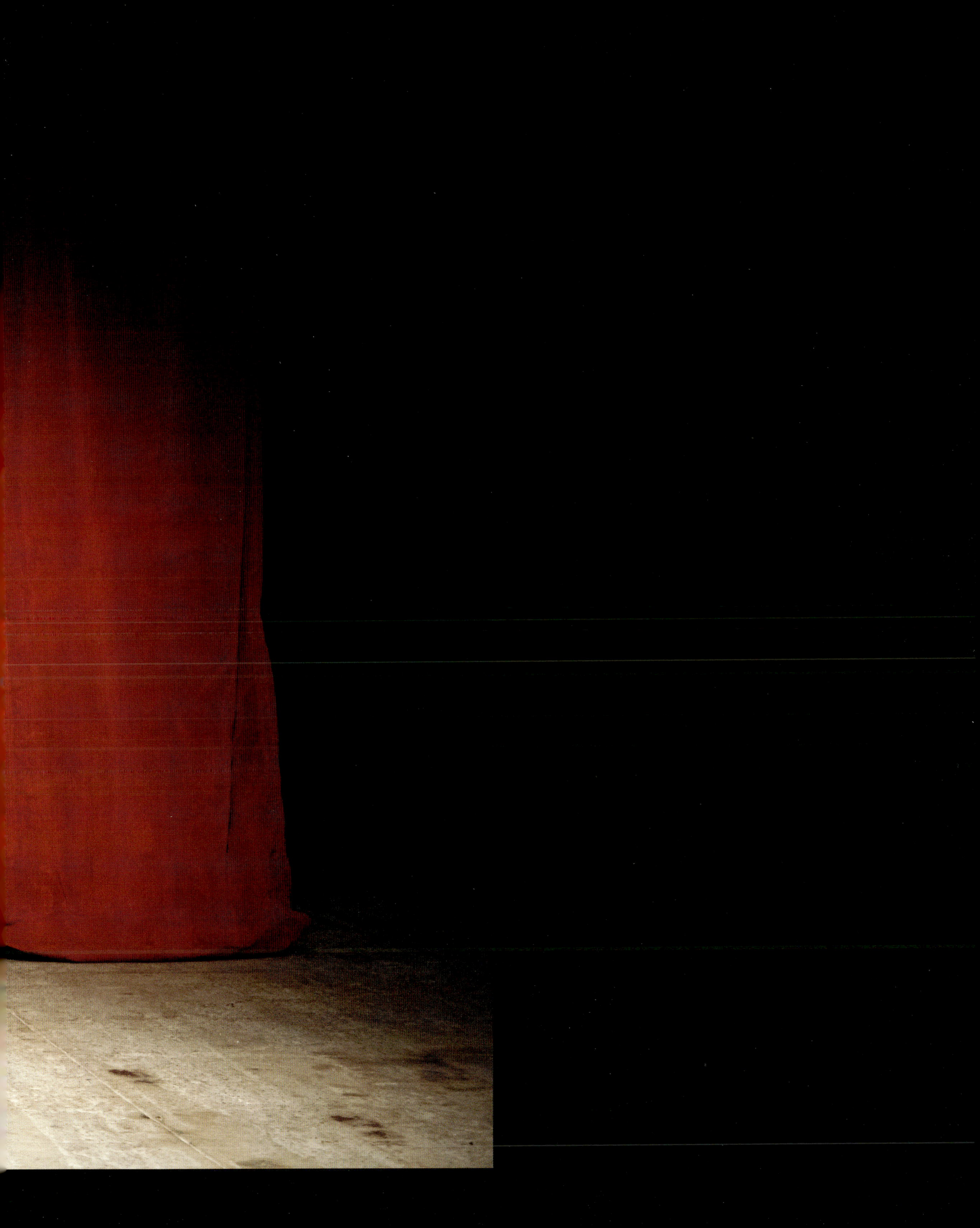

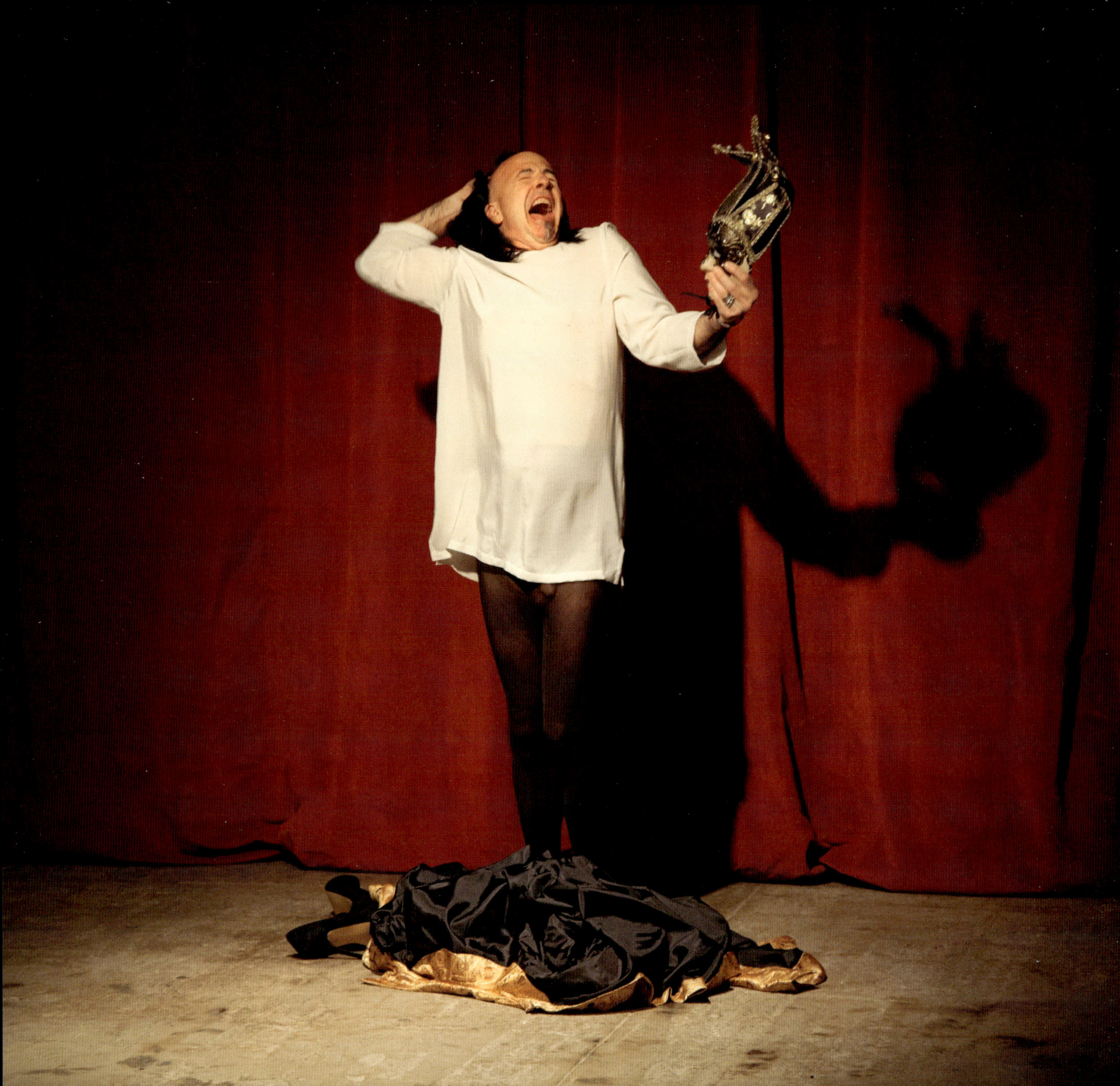

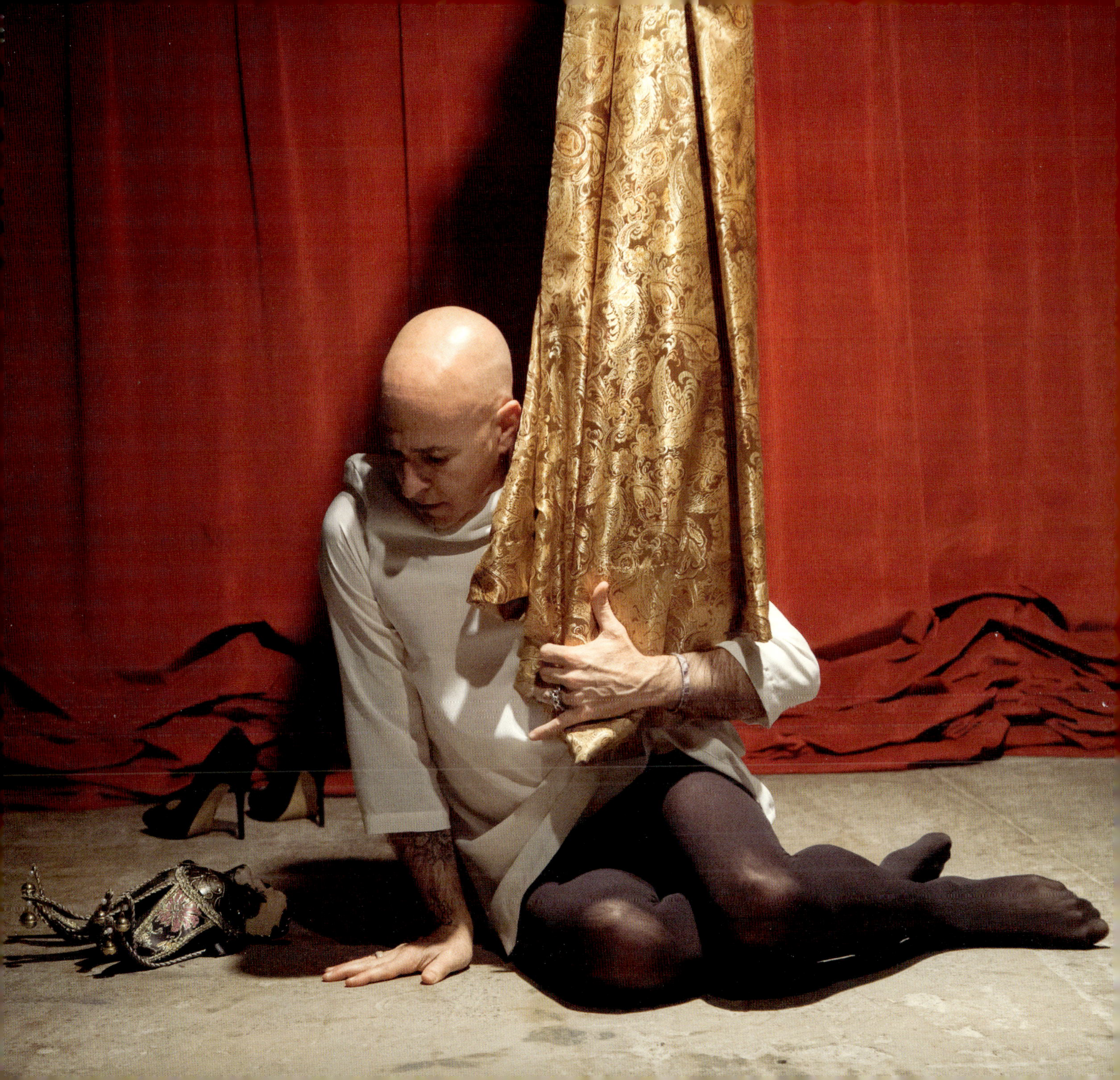

BRAIDING

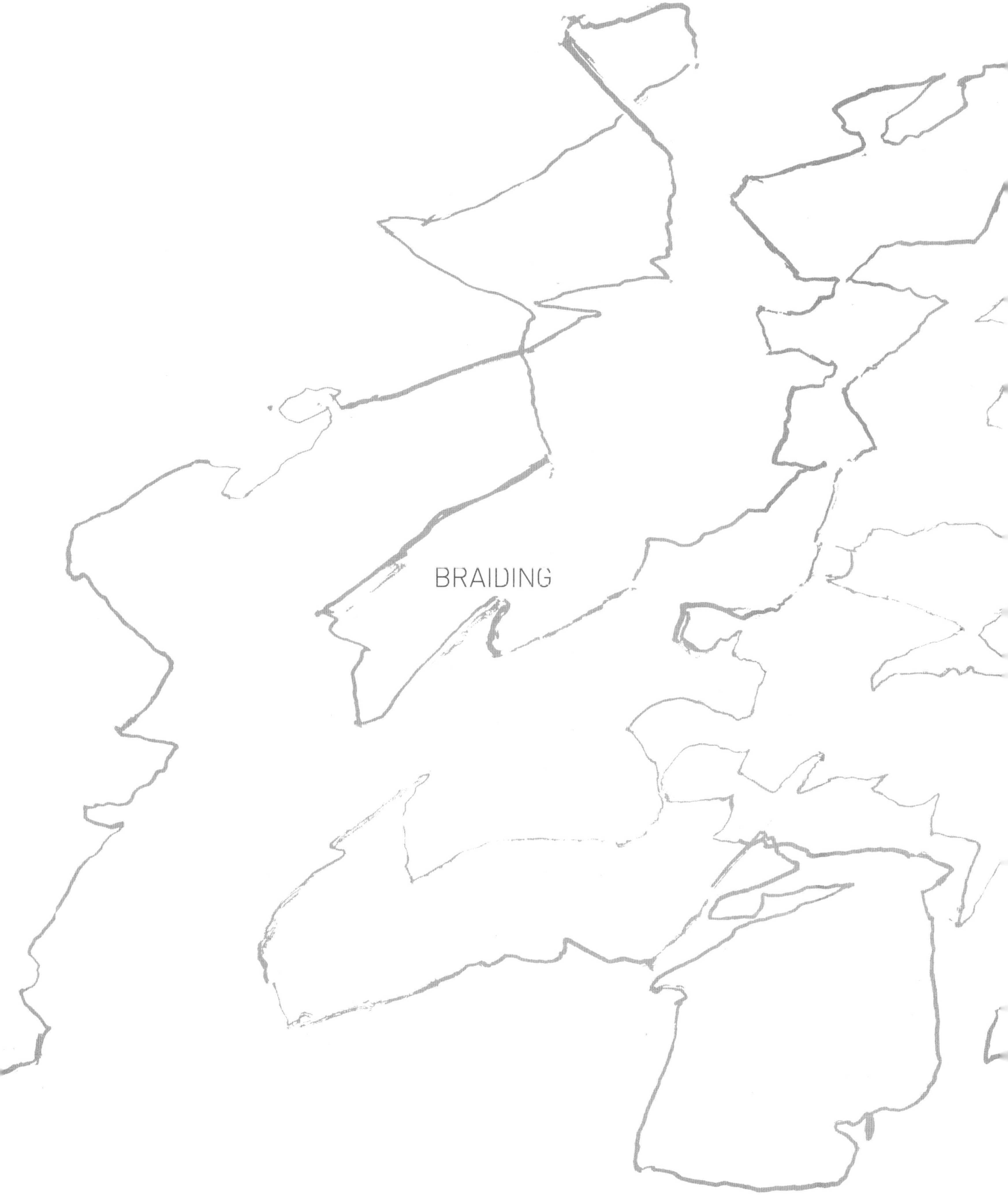

Adrian Heathfield: Thinking about the questions you are wrestling with in this moment of your collaborative process, I came across a great passage in Lawrence Halprin's *RSVP Cycles*, published in 1969 and drawn from his collaborations with Anna.

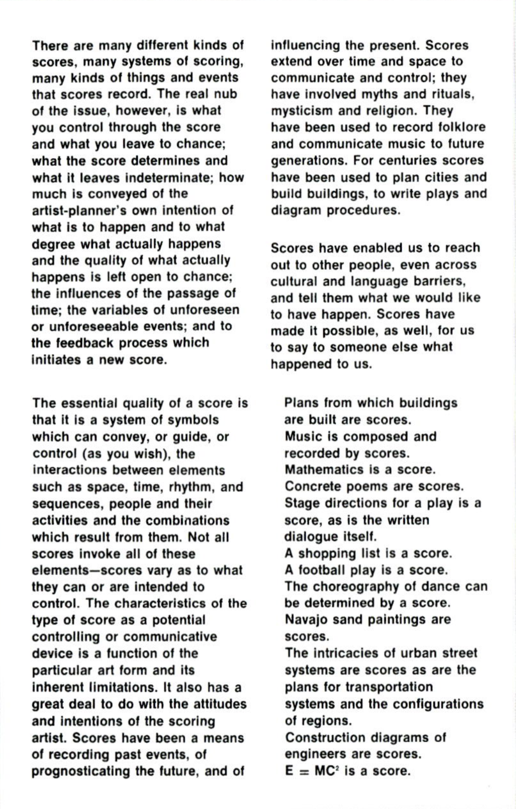

There are many different kinds of scores, many systems of scoring, many kinds of things and events that scores record. The real nub of the issue, however, is what you control through the score and what you leave to chance; what the score determines and what it leaves indeterminate; how much is conveyed of the artist-planner's own intention of what is to happen and to what degree what actually happens and the quality of what actually happens is left open to chance; the influences of the passage of time; the variables of unforeseen or unforeseeable events; and to the feedback process which initiates a new score.

The essential quality of a score is that it is a system of symbols which can convey, or guide, or control (as you wish), the interactions between elements such as space, time, rhythm, and sequences, people and their activities and the combinations which result from them. Not all scores invoke all of these elements—scores vary as to what they can or are intended to control. The characteristics of the type of score as a potential controlling or communicative device is a function of the particular art form and its inherent limitations. It also has a great deal to do with the attitudes and intentions of the scoring artist. Scores have been a means of recording past events, of prognosticating the future, and of influencing the present. Scores extend over time and space to communicate and control; they have involved myths and rituals, mysticism and religion. They have been used to record folklore and communicate music to future generations. For centuries scores have been used to plan cities and build buildings, to write plays and diagram procedures.

Scores have enabled us to reach out to other people, even across cultural and language barriers, and tell them what we would like to have happen. Scores have made it possible, as well, for us to say to someone else what happened to us.

Plans from which buildings are built are scores.
Music is composed and recorded by scores.
Mathematics is a score.
Concrete poems are scores.
Stage directions for a play is a score, as is the written dialogue itself.
A shopping list is a score.
A football play is a score.
The choreography of dance can be determined by a score.
Navajo sand paintings are scores.
The intricacies of urban street systems are scores as are the plans for transportation systems and the configurations of regions.
Construction diagrams of engineers are scores.
$E = MC^2$ is a score.

Though he was assiduous in his pursuit of systems of scoring, he noted that, "to enclose gossamer is to destroy it." So scores are seen as tools to make the logics of processes visible; they are generative, contingent and animate sharing. I wonder, coming from the formally distinct preoccupations of your previous works, how do you understand the scoring of this collaboration? How has your sense of what is determined and what is left to chance shifted in the making?

Stephen Petronio: While I began my dancing interests as an improviser, the past thirty years of my life have been dedicated to wrangling intuitive movement discovery into repeatable composed moments of choreography. While I would agree with Lawrence that the danger of "catching gossamer" is the possibility of destroying it, the methods I have learned to employ with the Judson school (particularly Paxton and Brown), led to my own research tools for corralling ether. They have proven to be enormously valuable in deepening a relationship to memorized, complex movement fields.

However, there is nothing quite like the open-ended freedom and potential for surprise that a score can offer. The score to me is a series of vectors to follow, anchors to swing off, in exploring the moment. It functions as a map to guide action, a series of directives that allow us to behave as intuitive, open and level partners.

Working with Anna's score allows Janine and I to engage on a personal level without adhering to a pre-determined language system. In my case, the Petronio lexicon is the core of my movement interest — a language that functions to free me enormously in my own work — but it can feel like an impediment in breaking new ground outside of that context. With Janine and Anna I often felt the need to inhibit that language response to feel present in a way that points to the essence of a creative motor, without digging into habits and assumptions of the system in place as a "Petronio" dancer. The score has simplified my action and opened the possibility of a raw and fresh truth to the moment.

A score can yield many results, ranging from a rote reiteration of precious research (dead moments?), re-exploration of previous discoveries and on to new territories. I have been most interested when it serves as a facilitator for problem solving and for uncovering the nature of the moment or individuals at play. How does this dancer and this artist behave in the same maze?

Janine Antoni:

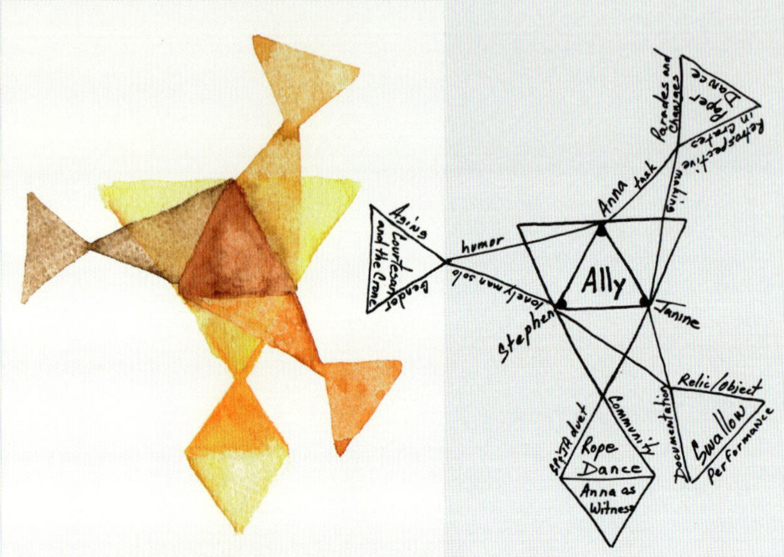

This is a map not a score although Lawrence would say a map is a score. I have been mapping my work for years. I use it as a way of locating myself when I am lost.

Can you miss someone you never knew? If so, I miss you, Lawrence. Your absence and presence is so palpable to me now. To engage Anna is to engage you. "To enclose gossamer is to destroy it." Lawrence, I hear you so loudly. In *The Spell of the Sensuous* (1996) David Abram recalls something that he saw when sheltering in a cave from the rain:

> Just in front of me, and only an inch or two to my side of the torrent, a spider was climbing a thin thread stretched across the mouth of the cave. … I lost sight of the spider then, and for a while it seemed that it had vanished, thread and all, until my focus rediscovered it. … And then, abruptly, my vision snagged on a strange incongruity … there was a *different* spider … The two spiders spun independently of each other, but to my eyes they wove a single intersecting pattern … I realized that there were *many* overlapping webs coming into being, radiating out at different rhythms from myriad centers …

I search for a score that is continually diverging in all its delicate intricacies. The "determined" is the single perspective where our webs become one, and the "chance" is the way these webs relate in time and space. The relationship between these two realities is the score.

Above left: Page from Lawrence Halprin, *The RSVP Cycles: Creative Processes in the Human Environment* (George Braziller, 1970).

Above right: Mapping/Scoring all the works in *Ally*. © Janine Antoni. Courtesy of the artist.

Opposite top: *Rope Dance* rehearsals. Photos: © Hugo Glendinning, 2015. Courtesy of the artist.

Opposite middle & bottom: Drawing and notes by Janine Antoni during the process of making *Rope Dance*. © Janine Antoni. Courtesy of the artist.

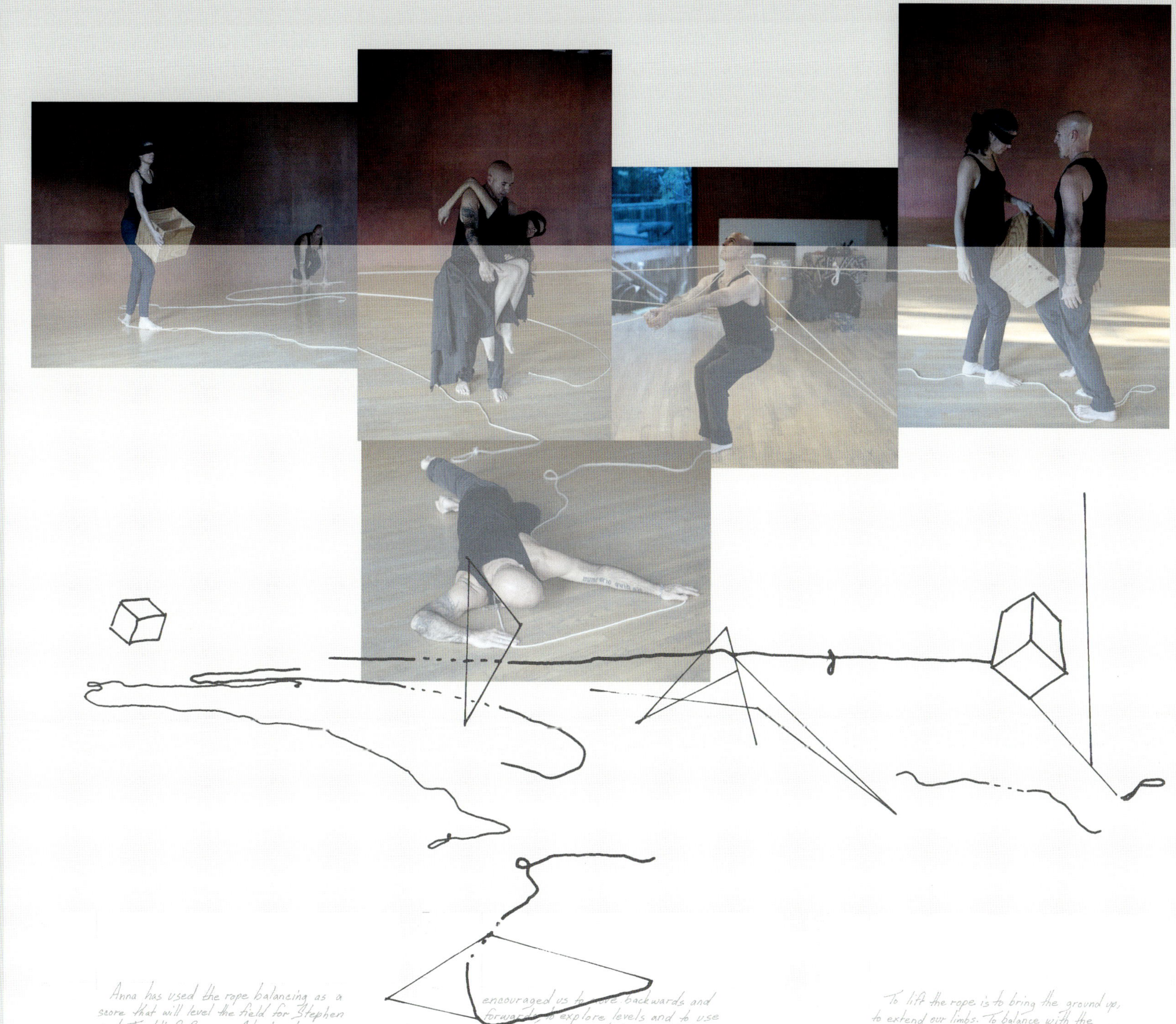

Anna has used the rope balancing as a score that will level the field for Stephen and I. Why? Because Stephen has more of an established movement vocabulary than I do: an expressive language that is formalized and deeply rooted in his body. My movement practices have all been somatic in orientation, never set, always improvisational. Faced with our different approaches to movement she decided to blindfold us and create a simple task. Just staying on the rope is a challenge and an audience will quickly understand that this is the goal. It also requires concentration from both of us that I believe is engaging from the outside.

We see the initial laying down of the rope as a graphic score. It is a drawing in space that predicts a journey. Faithfully, we follow the line with our steps staying focused on the rope under our feet as we struggle to stay steady without using our vision to help balance us. Balance is unpredictable. On any day one of us will be more in balance than the other. Anna encouraged us to move backwards and forwards, to explore levels and to use our other senses to lead us. While we stay focused on our task the audience knows something we do not know, which is when we will meet. This creates expectation, tension, a narrative. From our standpoint, meeting is always a shock especially if we are immersed in the task. Anna encouraged us to meet anew every time, to make no assumptions and to explore with curiosity. Asking, what is this thing we are encountering. There is tenderness in the meeting, in the tentative probing.

There is an exposure and vulnerability to the blind balancing and when we find each other we immediately find ourselves in space in accordance with the other, or with their body parts. We are not alone: we are together in our blind balancing. We are being witnessed in our togetherness. How do our past journeys inform this one? What do I know about him in the moment? How do we journey together? How can we help each other on our precarious path? Where are we going?

To lift the rope is to bring the ground up, to extend our limbs. To balance with the counterweight of the other. Our bodies are like the tin cans at the end of a string: its tautness and vibration communicate. This rope seems to be an extension of our veins, a line that delineates the space between. We draw together. This process, these questions prompted by "blindness" and a rope seem to enact the bigger questions of our collaboration.

pelling that just executing them would occupy the performer's full physical and emotional attention.[58]

Intuitively, Ann was pursuing a Zen-like approach, sensing that nature was the best model for human behavior and that people, if freed from arbitrary external rules and conventions, can more easily achieve a harmonious integration of themselves with the world. Perls's work, which stemmed from a fascination with Zen, also aimed at directing people to live totally in the here-and-now.[59] In his later years, Perls jokingly referred to himself

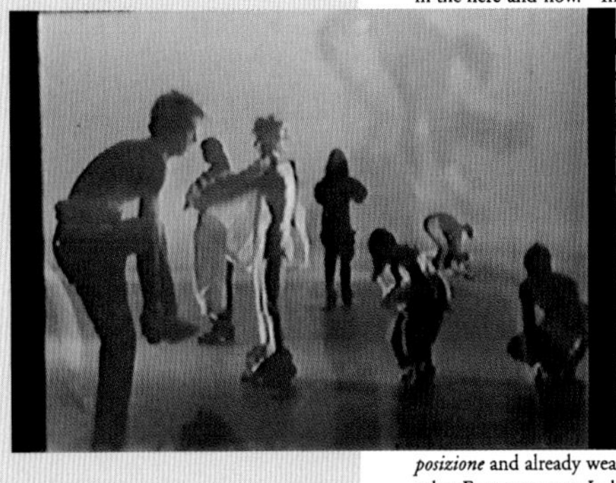

of the fusion of his German Jewish cultural her-
hilosophy of harmony and acceptance.[60]
th a model and a mentor in the sixty-nine-year-
led, balding, chain-smoking, drug-taking, sex-
After starting out as a classically trained European
spent the next thirty years radically challenging
und Freud and psychoanalysis. In 1964 Perls's
ntion on the present moment as a means of cur-
upations and encouraging the free display of emo-
oth radical and supremely simple. Two funda-
l of Gestalt therapy—that it was not therapy and
secured its appeal to Ann.
irst meeting with Perls. Baum had arranged for
cers, A.A. Leath, John Graham, and Norma Leis-
rapy session Perls was leading at the home of the
inne. Ann arrived in a combative mood. She was
an Francisco Opera's peremptory rejection of *Esposizione* and already weary at the prospect of trying to fund-raise for another European tour. In her words:

> I remember the day I came. I was really hurt. Because I felt I knew what we were doing and I couldn't understand why the critics didn't and why we weren't getting more support. I was feeling pretty upset and brazen and sort of furious with the world. We were all waiting for Fritz to come and I was sitting next to this man who was wearing a black suit, white shirt and a tie and black shiny shoes and black silk stockings. And he was sitting sort of upright in his chair.
>
> Something about the look of that man sitting there like that, wearing those kind of clothes, just freaked me. All my resentments about not being understood just triggered me off. So I stood up in front of this man (John Enright, whom I have since learned to love and appreciate), and I started to rip my clothes off. I was just staring him in the eyes as I pulled this off and that off until I stood in front of him stark naked. I stood there very brazenly and then I sat down and crossed my legs. Humph![61]

Ann hadn't noticed that Perls had arrived at the start of her spontaneous undressing, and he watched her improvisation unfold from the doorway as he stood smoking a cigarette. As Ann flung off her final piece of clothing, Enright began to sob, tears pouring down his face. This made Ann even angrier. She had expected him to at least shout at her to stop but never to react with such passivity. Then Perls entered the room, gave the group a slow, relaxed look of appraisal, and finally, looking over at Ann, he said, "*Nu?* [Yiddish for "Well?"] So why have you got your legs crossed?"

Ann felt belittled and at the same time charged with admiration. In a single sentence Perls had identified her aesthetic goal, her personal inhibitions, and the inconsistency in her performance. If this was an impromptu dance of full disclosure, then why was she hiding her crotch? "All I could think was oh, my God, he's just totally busted me. It was terrific!" Ann later said. "I was inspired, he was just so right on!" That evening began a six-year friendship between the therapist and the dancer, one in which the congruence between the task of psychotherapy and the capacity of art to remake the maker became manifest. Perls had understood immediately what Ann had been trying to do, and he told her bluntly how she had failed. It was the cruelest, and most useful, piece of criticism she could have received at that moment.

"Anybody who can see the connection between movement and another dimension of what's really going on, who you really are—that's part of art," she later commented. "I wasn't thinking of that as therapy. I was thinking of it as theater. You've got to be totally open and honest and true to be a performer."[62] Perls believed that one had to cultivate a similar pleasure and openness to the immediate present to be awake as a person. His "Gestalt prayer," which in turn became the mantra of the human potential movement of the 1960s and 1970s, was a do-your-own-thing endorsement set to loosely metered rhyme:

> I do my thing, and you do
> I am not in this world to li
> And you are not in this wo
> You are you, and I am I,
> And if by chance we find e
> If not, it can't be helped.[63]

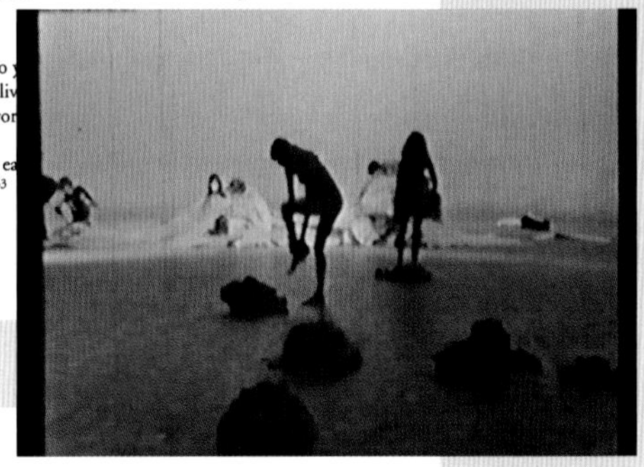

Soon after moving into the two large studios on the second floor of 321 Divisadero Street, Ann began work on her next major European commission, a full-evening work for the Stockholm Contemporary Music Festival. This dance, scheduled to premiere September 5, 6, and 7, 1965, would become the signature statement of her task performance choreography and her last work in this mode before she turned fully toward the emotional territory of Gestalt therapy in *Apartment 6. Parades and Changes* is a valedictory to

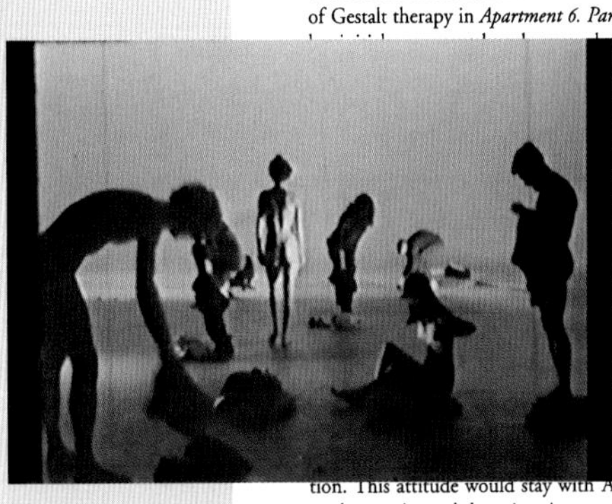

o dance and the point of departure
the dancers' and the audience's pas-
te change.
des and Changes, Ann explained to
ow the entire ninety minutes were
e dance form evolves from the very
form it; (2) the objects in the per-
d (3) time is compressed, so instead
of everyday life.[81] There is a Perls-
stead of a task serving as a means of
rves as a physical Rorschach for the
external and environmental limits
Ann, like Perls, exerts a subtle con-
r identity is etched in quiet clarity
onses.
arade of changes in which the task
r than the *depiction,* of a life situa-
tion. This attitude would stay with Ann her entire career, and only very rarely, even in workshop situations, would she offer analytic or interpretive criticism of a dance. She was abandoning a purely formalist approach to task in favor of a more Gestalt relationship—investing each action and response to an object on stage with an intense sense of the present. According to Ann, Perls used to tell the dancers, "I don't want you to rehearse. I don't want you to think about this. Whatever we do, we do what's present right now. No rehearsing, no planning, no trying to figure out, no analysis. Just deal and express what's there right now."[82]

By the spring of 1965 the Dancers' Workshop was ready to give two preview showings of *Parades and Changes,* in Fresno and in San Francisco. The centerpiece, which would become the most legendary part of *Parades and Changes,* was a seven-minute section in which the full cast serenely undressed, dressed, and undressed while coolly locking eyes with someone in the audience. Although this section derived directly from that spontaneous striptease she had done the first day of Perls's workshop, Ann now revisited removing one's clothes as a statement of art rather than of anger. It had become a post-Gestalt strip, where taking off meant inviting in, uncovering meant peeling back to the skin of the emotions. Reflecting on her initial experience with Perls, Ann explained:

> Yes, that was the beginning of *Parades and Changes.* That was the beginning of dressing and undressing, because what I learned from that was that my attitude was just totally off. There is a way of removing your clothes and appearing totally vulnerable—open and vulnerable—without this attitude. I needed to learn how to be an extension of nature, and not impose this self-righteous attitude. I had been so self-righteous, standing in front of this man and judging him and saying, "You think you're free? Look at Me!" So that's what inspired me to make *Parades and Changes.*[83]

The original cast of *Parades and Changes* consisted of only three adults (Ann, A.A. Leath, and John Graham), as well as six adolescents (Ann's two daughters, seventeen-year-old Daria and fourteen-year-old Rana; college-age Jani Novak; eighteen-year-old Kim Hahn; and two veterans from Ann's children's dance co-op, fourteen-year-old Paul Goldsmith and sixteen-year-old Larri Goldsmith, who came along mostly to help unload props but also performed some).[84] Morton Subotnick created the music score, Patric Hickey the lighting, Jo Landor the costumes and staging, and sculptor Charles Ross fashioned the scenic environment out of backstage objects, including a tall scaffold used to change lights.

Everyone who was in the September 1965 premiere of *Parades and Changes* remembers a different dance and no one can say with certainty, least of all Ann, what opening night or the subsequent two evenings actually looked like. The reasons for this are many—not the least of which is structural. Ann was ritualizing spontaneity, and this often made for a stronger memory of motivations than stage pictures. "There was no chance in *Parades and Changes,*" Subotnick recalled. "Everything was done by
choice, but there was a freedom in choice. We did e
first, working on different attitudes of space. Th
putting each section together. It was a real collab
Each element of the dance—lighting, sound sc
raphy—was divided into six discrete units that coul
orders or relationships. The choreographic sections

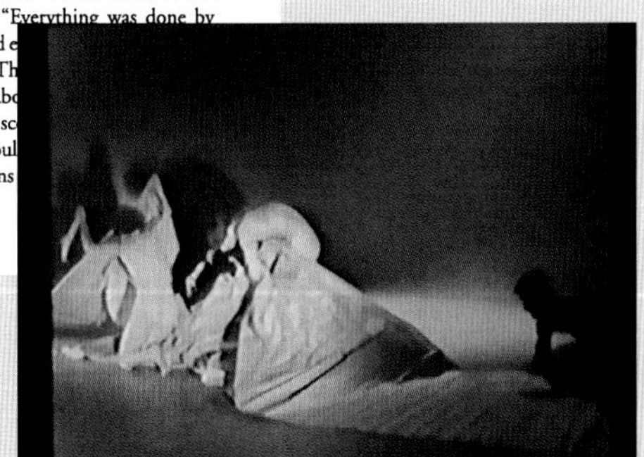

Stills from video documentation of *Parades and Changes*, 1965.
Choreographer: Anna Halprin. Sculpture: Charles Ross. Painter: J Landor.
Music: Morton Sobotnick. Lights: Patric Hickey. © Anna Halprin. Courtesy of the artist.

Pages from Janice Ross, *Anna Halprin: Experience as Dance* (University of California Press, 2009).

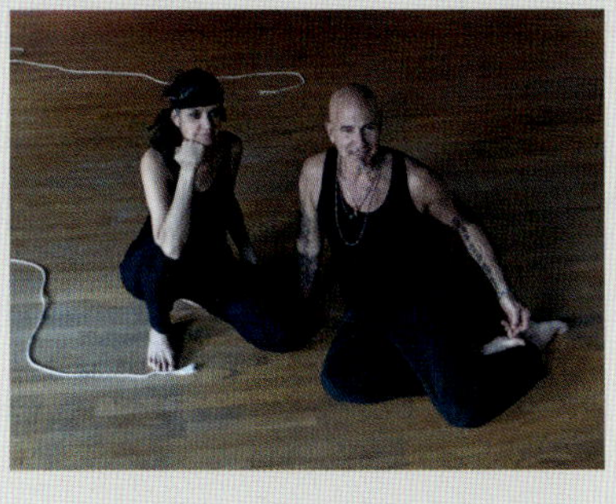

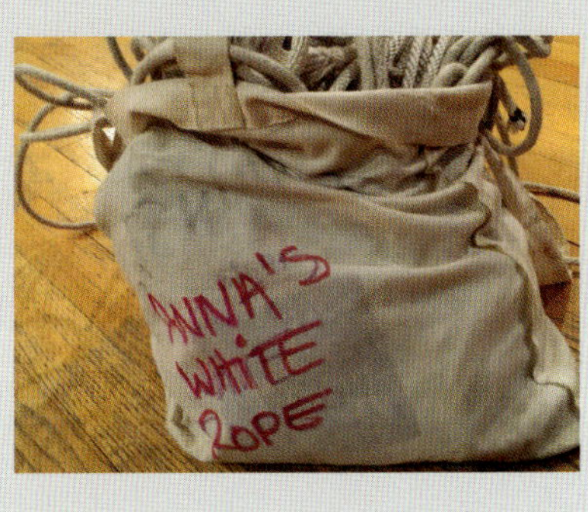

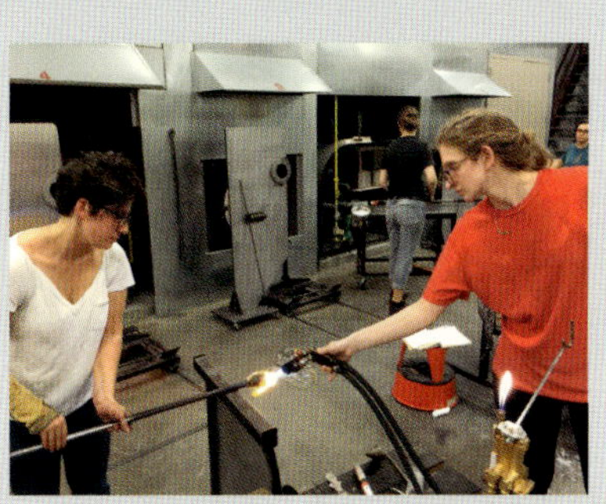

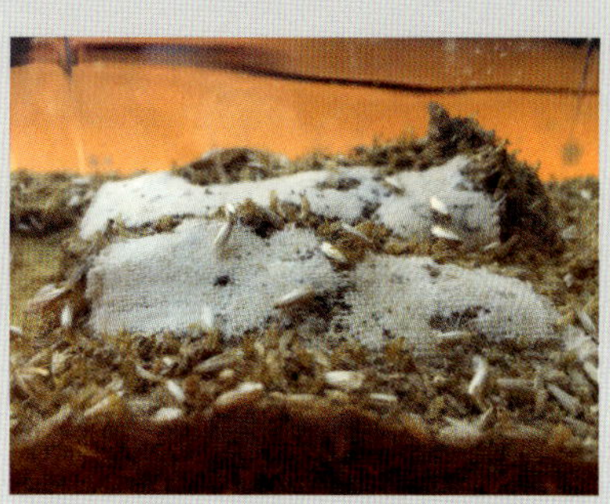

AH: So I am thinking that these tensions — between fixity and free-play, the substantial and the immaterial, or between a lasting and a transient thing — are also the prevailing tensions in the works you are conceiving for the The Fabric Workshop and Museum? How do these tensions play into the relationship between material objects and performance in the works you are making?

SP: Anna's work, which I understand as the unfolding of process through action motored by a score, will take place at several times in FWM, but what's left behind is of most interest to me and I believe Janine. While the scoring of events is the great contribution of Anna and her generation, a tool for producing endless individual responses and manifestations from a directive map, what we have been most drawn to is how the actions that result from a set of directives mark their space.

Perhaps most prominently, we leave a new work in place of our *Rope Dance*, and that is Anna as witness. The large and simple work is a close-up of Anna, the author of our score, watching us in an early enactment of that score. So even here, it's not what Janine and I are doing to bring the score to life, but the mark it leaves behind, seen in the eyes of Anna, engaged in the process of watching us.

I'm so drawn to the experience of walking into a room and lingering in the state between what's left behind in the room and what I imagine took place to form these remnants of action. The grossest examples of this kind of fascination are crime or accident scenes long after the action occurs. Or the sheets of a bed that have been freshly vacated — the smell, twist and crumple, the temperature and moisture that disclose a set of possibilities for what happened in repose or sleep. The ephemeral act is fleeting and mysterious, each one of us engages an act through the shape and quality of the clues left behind. Skid marks will never cease to fascinate me.

But there is a component of scoring of an ongoing event at FWM in that we intend to have our *Swallow* document material disappear over the course of the show. We will set up an "incubator vitrine" to grow larvae that will consume a fabric object: the documentation of our unseen act of swallowing fabric that connects Janine and I. How that erasure progresses will be dependent on a number of as yet unpredictable things: light, temperature, the nature of the fabric. We are just at the beginning of researching these possibilities, but I imagine that even with rigorous control and limitation of the situation, the actual disappearance will be as relatively unpredictable as we hope it is fascinating. In this way the score will be a set of environmental conditions set up to propel the vanishing act.

Top left to right: Janine Antoni and Stephen Petronio rehearsing *Rope Dance*.
Photo: © Hugo Glendinning, 2015. Courtesy of the artists.
Photo: Janine Antoni. © Janine Antoni. Courtesy of the artist.
Glass blowing for *Swallow* monstrance. Suzanne Peck and Naomi Mishkin.
Photo: Janine Antoni. Courtesy of the artist.
Moth colony. Photo: Suzanne Peck. Courtesy of the artist.

Bottom: A print test on wool with granite and saliva made by FWM printers Kate Abercrombie, Joy Ude and Anthony Bowers.

JA: Rope Dance (action, workshop)

How does a simple act become dramatic? What is riveting about watching a person struggle? What if the audience become the dancers? What if they are directed? Is viewing passive? Is moving active? Is being directed passive? How does the audience transition from observer to performer? What meaning is made in the decision to participate? What meaning is made in the decision not to participate? How do we create a desire to participate? How can we connect the audience to each other?

Rope Dance (documentation, film of Anna's face)

How does the choreographer hold possibilities for the dancers? What do they know about their vision that they withhold from the dancers? Why? How does the choreographer embody the audience when creating their choreography? What can be gleaned of the dance through the reaction of the witness? Could the witness be the documentation of the dance?

Swallow (action)

How is the fabric transformed by the body? How does the fabric transform the body? How can two bodies connect both literally and through shared experience? How does an object gain its power from its history?

Swallow (object, reliquary)

How can another party understand the performance through mere contact with the relic? What does the object need to help it tell its story? How do the gaps in the story make space for the audience to participate? What kind of framing device tells you of the object's significance? How do we ascribe worth? What if we relied on the material worth of the frame? What if the fabric rotted away? Would the empty space be charged?

Swallow (documentation, consumed by moths)

What if the documentation was intentionally ephemeral? What if the process of degeneration was the ongoing performance?

What if the distance between each iteration of the absent performance was palpable? Who will believe our story? Who has faith? Who will doubt? Who will empathize so deeply that they will have a visceral response?

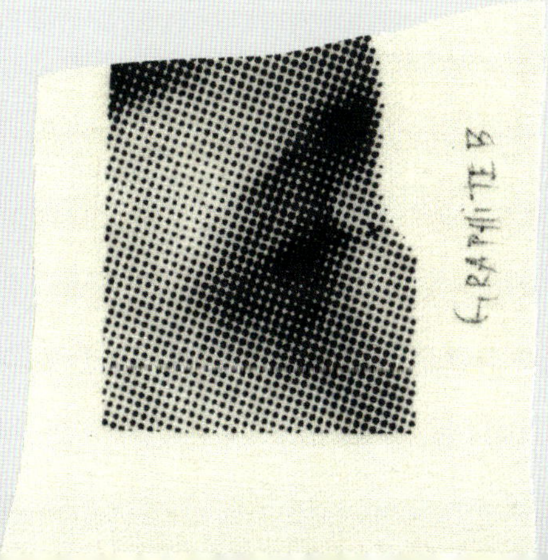

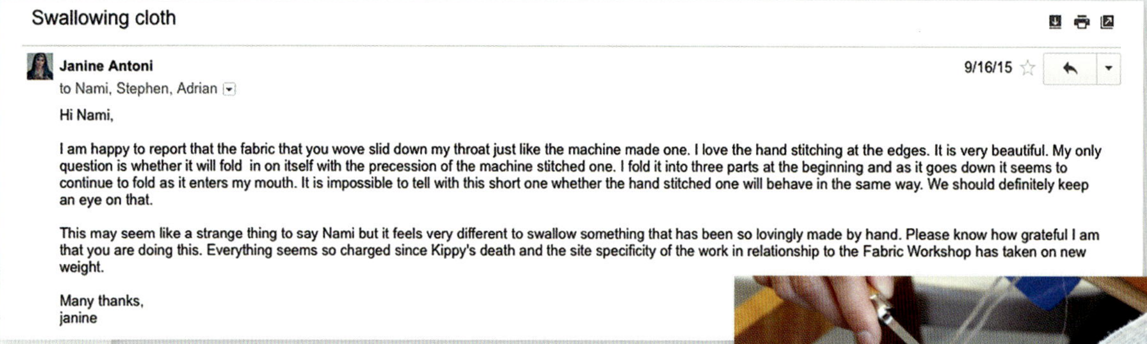

Swallowing cloth

Janine Antoni 9/16/15

to Nami, Stephen, Adrian

Hi Nami,

I am happy to report that the fabric that you wove slid down my throat just like the machine made one. I love the hand stitching at the edges. It is very beautiful. My only question is whether it will fold in on itself with the precession of the machine stitched one. I fold it into three parts at the beginning and as it goes down it seems to continue to fold as it enters my mouth. It is impossible to tell with this short one whether the hand stitched one will behave in the same way. We should definitely keep an eye on that.

This may seem like a strange thing to say Nami but it feels very different to swallow something that has been so lovingly made by hand. Please know how grateful I am that you are doing this. Everything seems so charged since Kippy's death and the site specificity of the work in relationship to the Fabric Workshop has taken on new weight.

Many thanks,
janine

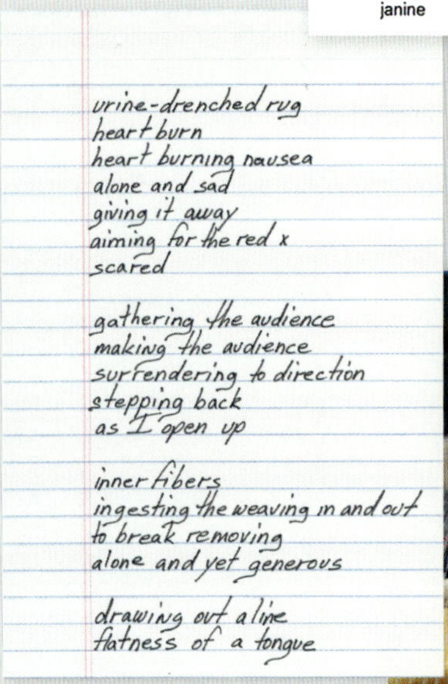

urine-drenched rug
heart burn
heart burning nausea
alone and sad
giving it away
aiming for the red x
scared

gathering the audience
making the audience
surrendering to direction
stepping back
as I open up

inner fibers
ingesting the weaving in and out
to break removing
alone and yet generous

drawing out a line
flatness of a tongue

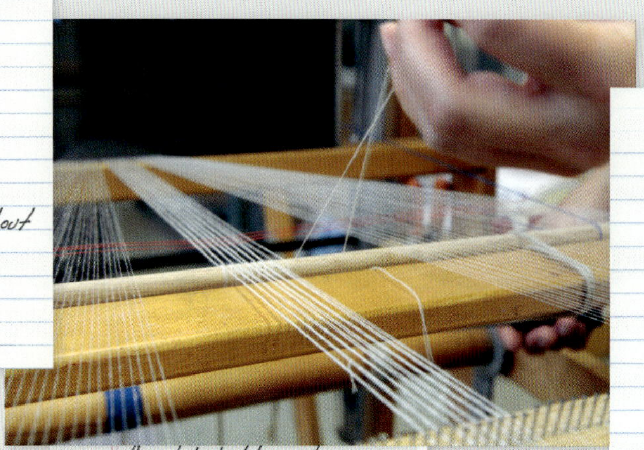

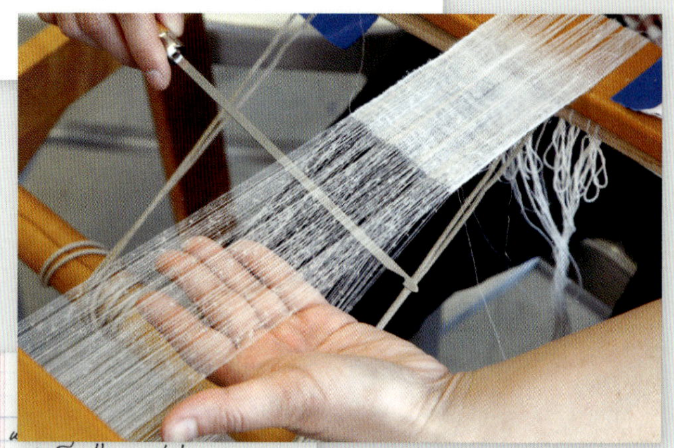

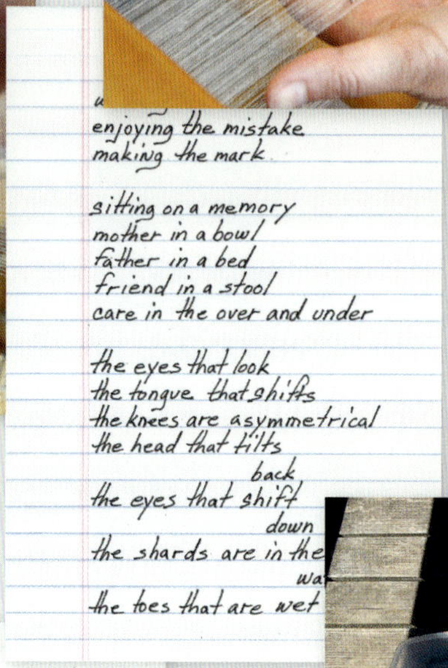

enjoying the mistake
making the mark

sitting on a memory
mother in a bowl
father in a bed
friend in a stool
care in the over and under

the eyes that look
the tongue that shifts
the knees are asymmetrical
the head that tilts
back
the eyes that shift
down
the shards are in the
wa
the toes that are wet

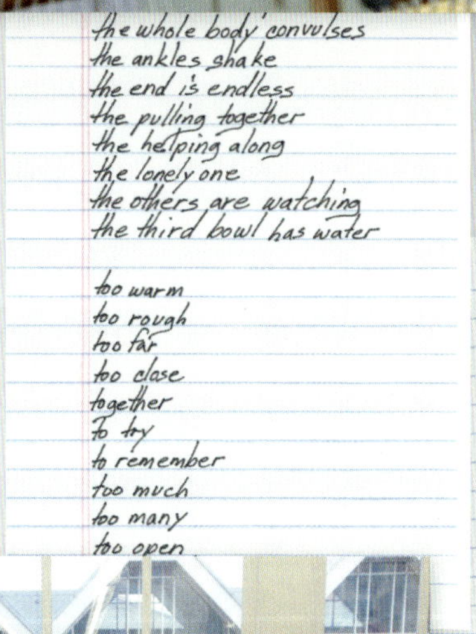

the whole body convulses
the ankles shake
the end is endless
the pulling together
the helping along
the lonely one
the others are watching
the third bowl has water

too warm
too rough
too far
too close
together
to try
to remember
too much
too many
too open

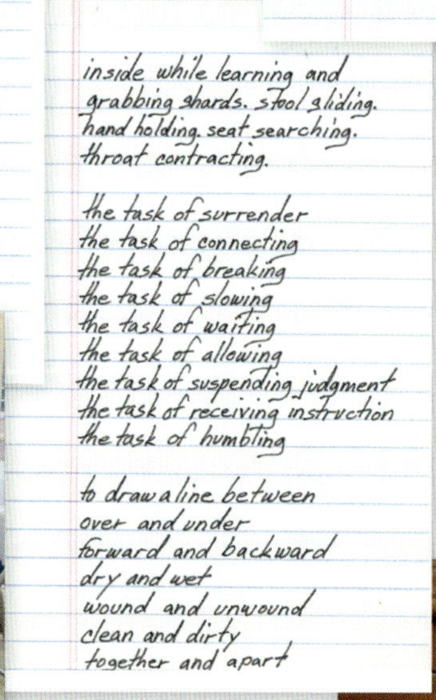

inside while learning and
grabbing shards. stool sliding.
hand holding. seat searching.
throat contracting.

the task of surrender
the task of connecting
the task of breaking
the task of slowing
the task of waiting
the task of allowing
the task of suspending judgment
the task of receiving instruction
the task of humbling

to draw a line between
over and under
forward and backward
dry and wet
wound and unwound
clean and dirty
together and apart

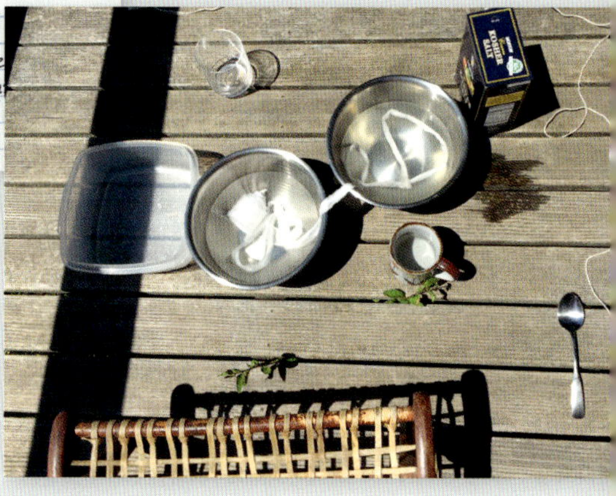

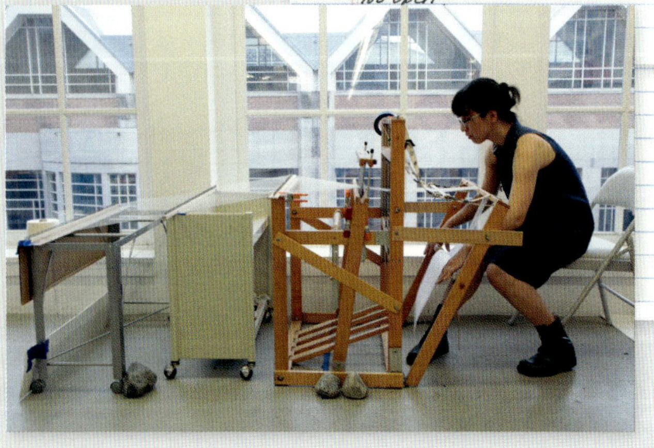

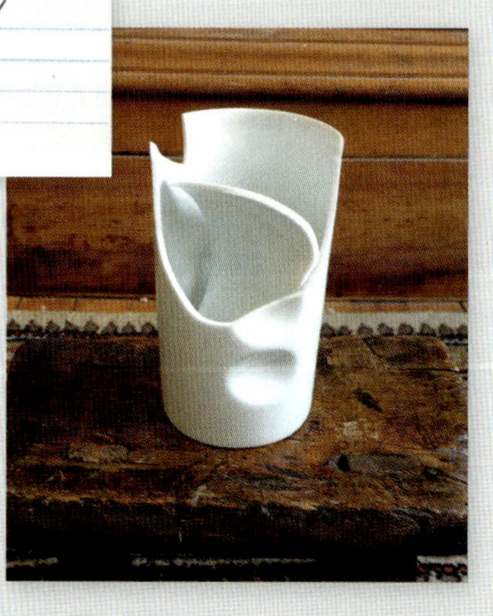

Top left, top right and above: Nami Yamamoto weaving.
Photos: Carlos Avendaño. Courtesy of the artist and FWM.

Middle right: Practicing swallowing at Kippy camp in Maine, 2015.
Photo: Janine Antoni. Courtesy of the artist.

Right: Cup broken by accident during the act of swallowing.
Photo: Janine Antoni. Courtesy of the artist.

Notebook Pages: Writing exercise – Janine Antoni describing swallowing fabric.
Courtesy of the artist.

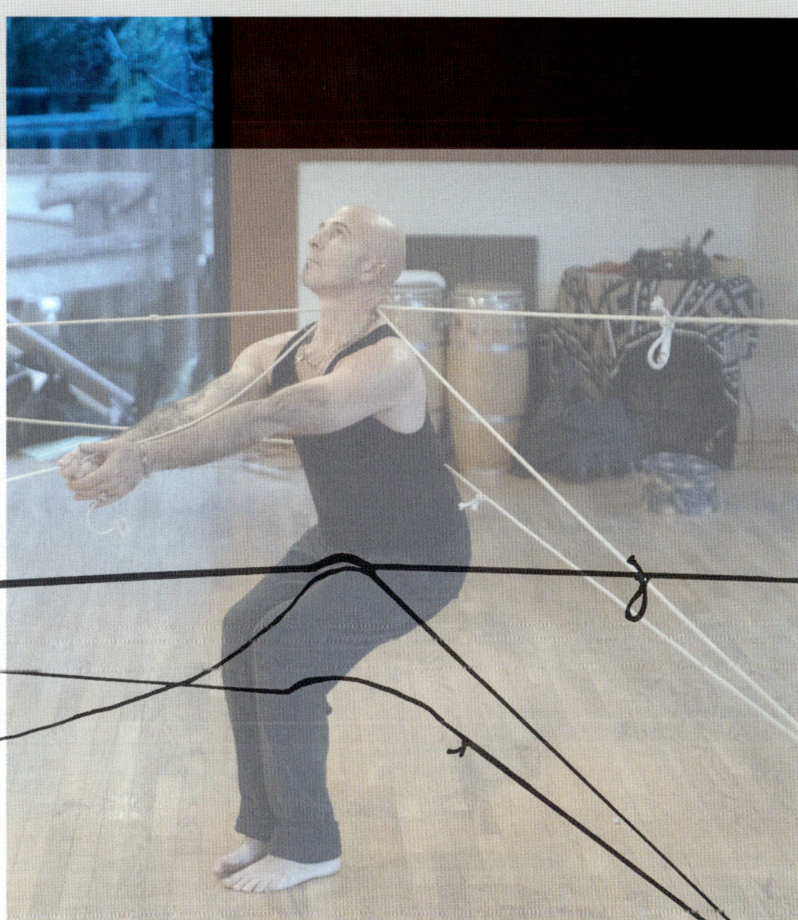

Women and men — some of them are quiet, some of them are not. My father Thomas is a good talker, easy and free. He understands some things but his opinions are certain and fierce.

My grandfather never speaks. An immigrant from the Southern Italian diaspora, he never learns English but doesn't seem to need it. His quiet is profound and his moves are small and suspended.

Robert Rauschenberg opens me to a world of visual making. His life is impossibly large and omnipotent, translucent roiling. He shows me how to see what's already there, odd and revealing juxtapositions, strangers that are related in some larger dance. The random becomes symphonic through his eyes.

Trisha Brown is a woman of power and lightness, rippling a consciousness through my maleness that cleaves me from the patterns that cage my body, my thought, my sex. I am the first male. Now I can move like that, a man can move like that. My gender is winged.

Steve Paxton is a cobra searching the desert in powdery sequences of distal reach, intense curiosity. He is the snake — I am his progeny.

Stephen Petronio rehearsing *Rope Dance*. Photo: © Hugo Glendinning, 2015. Drawing by Janine Antoni. Text by Stephen Petronio. Courtesy of the artists.

AH: There is a sense then, in all of this, that you are focusing on the relation between art making and time: not just the consideration of what is erased or dissipated and what persists or remains, but the act of inspiration in response to what has gone before. Whatever you are making together, it somewhat re-works and transforms some of your previous concerns individually. But this is a mode of retrospection that moves through and with others.

Looking at your own accumulated body of works, I wondered if you could say what has changed for you in terms of how you now perceive your artistic history as a result of this collaboration? What aspects of your work have been re-discovered, or re-activated, or seen differently? What does re-evaluating your practice through these specific collaborators bring out?

JA: My work is formed by my desire to enter the objects of my making; to have a full-blown relationship with the material in the hopes that what is left behind will hold the emotional resonance of that relationship. In *Paper Dance*, Anna asked me to show this process. She gave me a roll of paper and set me to work. It has been both a vulnerable and revealing experience to catch the inspiration at its inception, to watch myself "act on" the material, to witness my sculptural mind at work, to expose the emotional intensity of the interaction and to learn to trust my ability to respond in the moment with the support of my past work as a resource. It is in Anna's reframing of my process as dance that these things could surface and be shown.

Stephen and I are storytellers, with a taste for drama and a love of seduction. When we make, I am slow and Stephen is rapid fire. Working with him makes me realize I have been playing a game of hide and seek. My story is teased out, his intricately woven. Mine is simple and full of innuendo, his generously emotive. Our stories are driven by our deep need to connect. We constantly try to draw a line from the emotional to the physical and back. Our work together addresses the longing for connection and its impossibility.

SP: The most distinctive result of the *Ally* process in relation to the body of work that I have built as a choreographer for more than thirty years, is the highlighting and re-examination of the road that I chose to move along in terms of the construction of movement.

In many ways my entire career has been ignited by the conceptual underpinnings of score making: chart a course and pursue it, idea and instruction as map. My extreme love of motion required that the movement must be of a highly refined level of interest and sophistication born from that map, in the larger worlds I was constructing.

I came to dance quite late, without a classical education in either modern dance or ballet or music. I am a proposition of the DIY movement. I have chosen quite specifically the incorporation of vocabulary and signs from more traditional movement systems (i.e. ballet) and grafted them onto ordinary movement: pedestrian, street and other shards of information. Quite early on, I established that any shard of action was fair game to assimilate into the flowing continuum that is the base of Petronio language.

The possibility of taking a different tack in *Ally* has been quite attractive. To release the history of what I've built and to follow a notion of score set free from a goal of "movement making," has been of particular interest. For example, to follow a course that Anna has set in *Rope Dance*, simply as a set of directives to complete, outside of my preconceptions as a movement maker, as a human who lives in my present body at my present age, though challenging, has been extremely exciting. An opportunity for some kind of renewal and reassessment has appeared, and in it, the choices that I am generally prone to make have vanished.

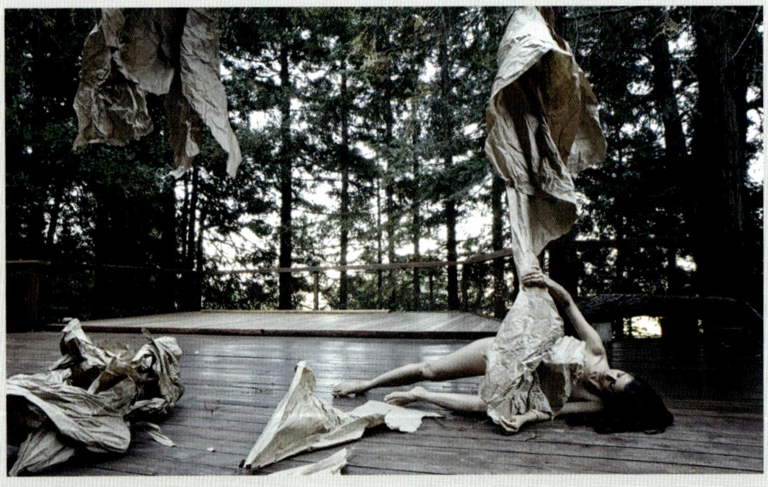

Janine Antoni in collaboration with Anna Halprin, *Paper Dance*. Photographed by Pak Han at the Halprin dance deck, 2013. © Pak Han. Courtesy of the artists.

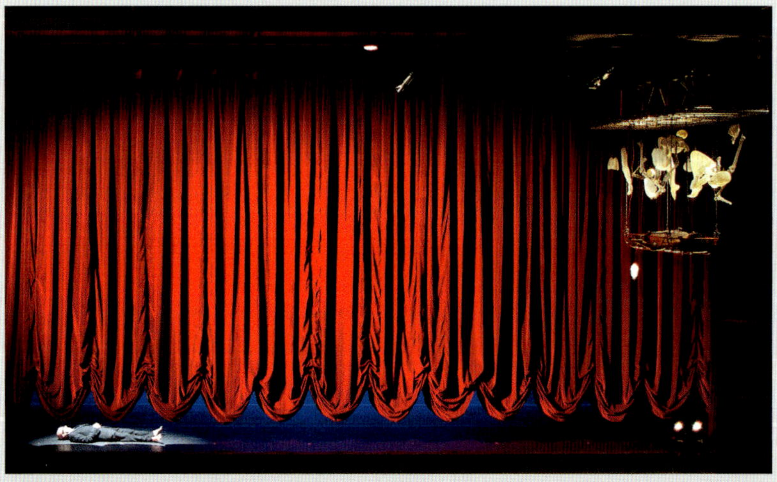

Janine Antoni hanging in her "living set" and Stephen Petronio on stage in *Like Lazarus Did*, performed by the Stephen Petronio Company, 2013. Photo: Paul Ramirez Jonas. Courtesy of the artists.

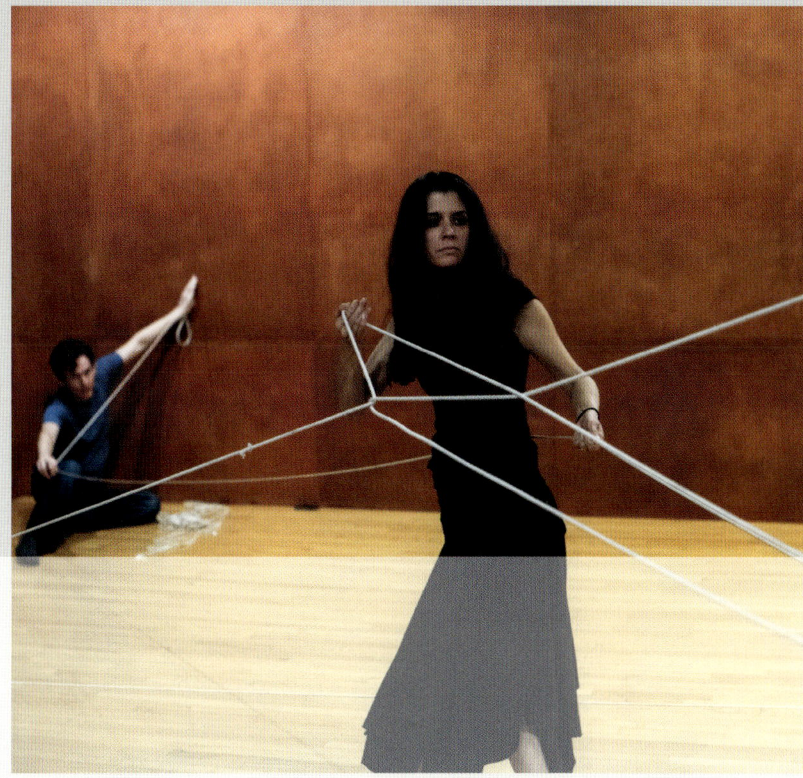

Anna Halprin: When they are not physically touching dancers very often forget that they are related in space. Being married to a landscape architect I became very aware of space as a potent force in dance. The ropes bring people's attention to their spatial connection.

Adrian Heathfield: Entwined with others, I become acutely aware that every move of the other affects me, limits me, creates new potential to move. Material resistance makes things happen. Each movement in the web of relations sends out vibrations, information of the shifting image.

Janine Antoni: The rope became an extension, not only of my hands but of my veins. I felt energy running down the line to meet another.

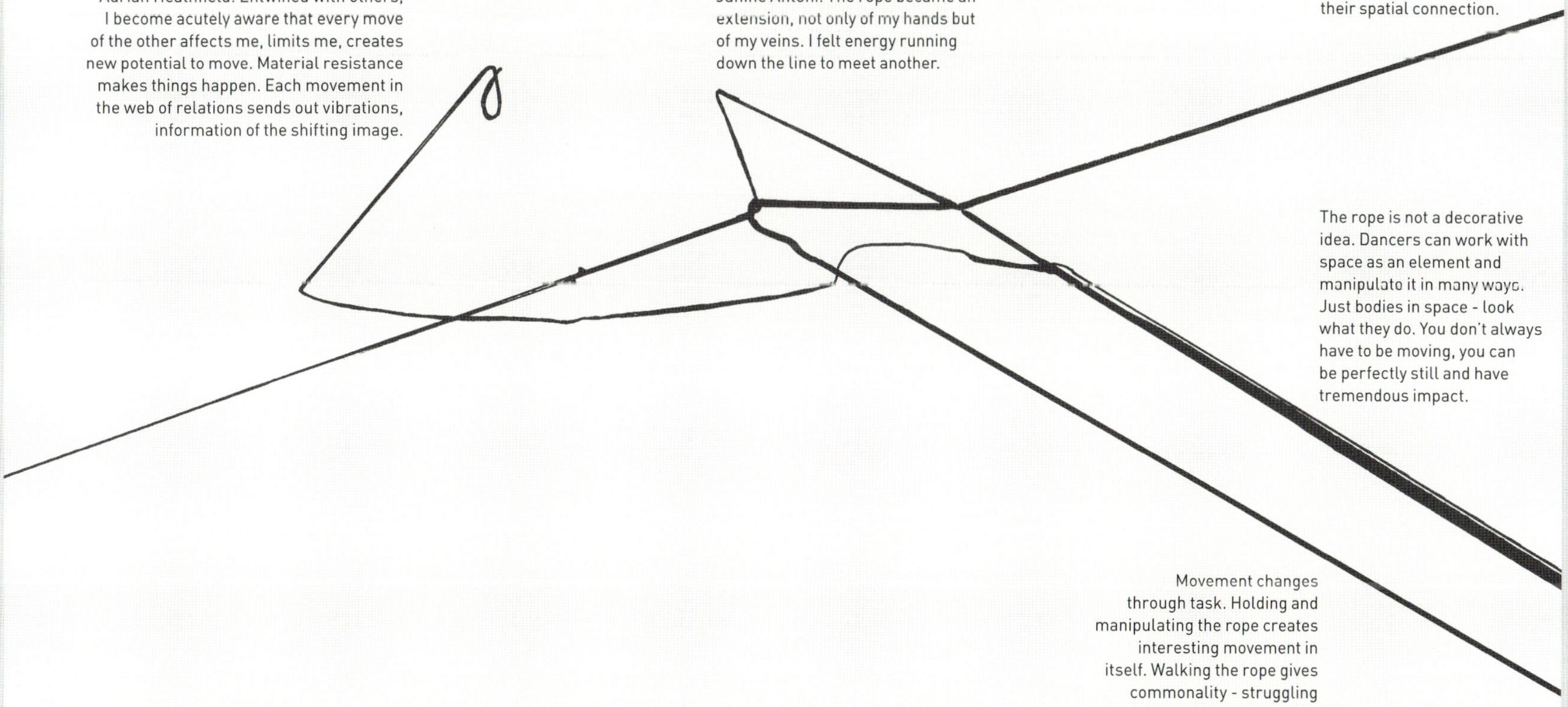

The rope is not a decorative idea. Dancers can work with space as an element and manipulate it in many ways. Just bodies in space - look what they do. You don't always have to be moving, you can be perfectly still and have tremendous impact.

Movement changes through task. Holding and manipulating the rope creates interesting movement in itself. Walking the rope gives commonality - struggling to maintain balance makes another form of movement. It can't be stylized.

Janine Antoni rehearsing *Rope Dance*. Photo: © Hugo Glendinning, 2015. Drawing by Janine Antoni.
Text by Janine Antoni, Anna Halprin and Adrian Heathfield. Courtesy of the artists.

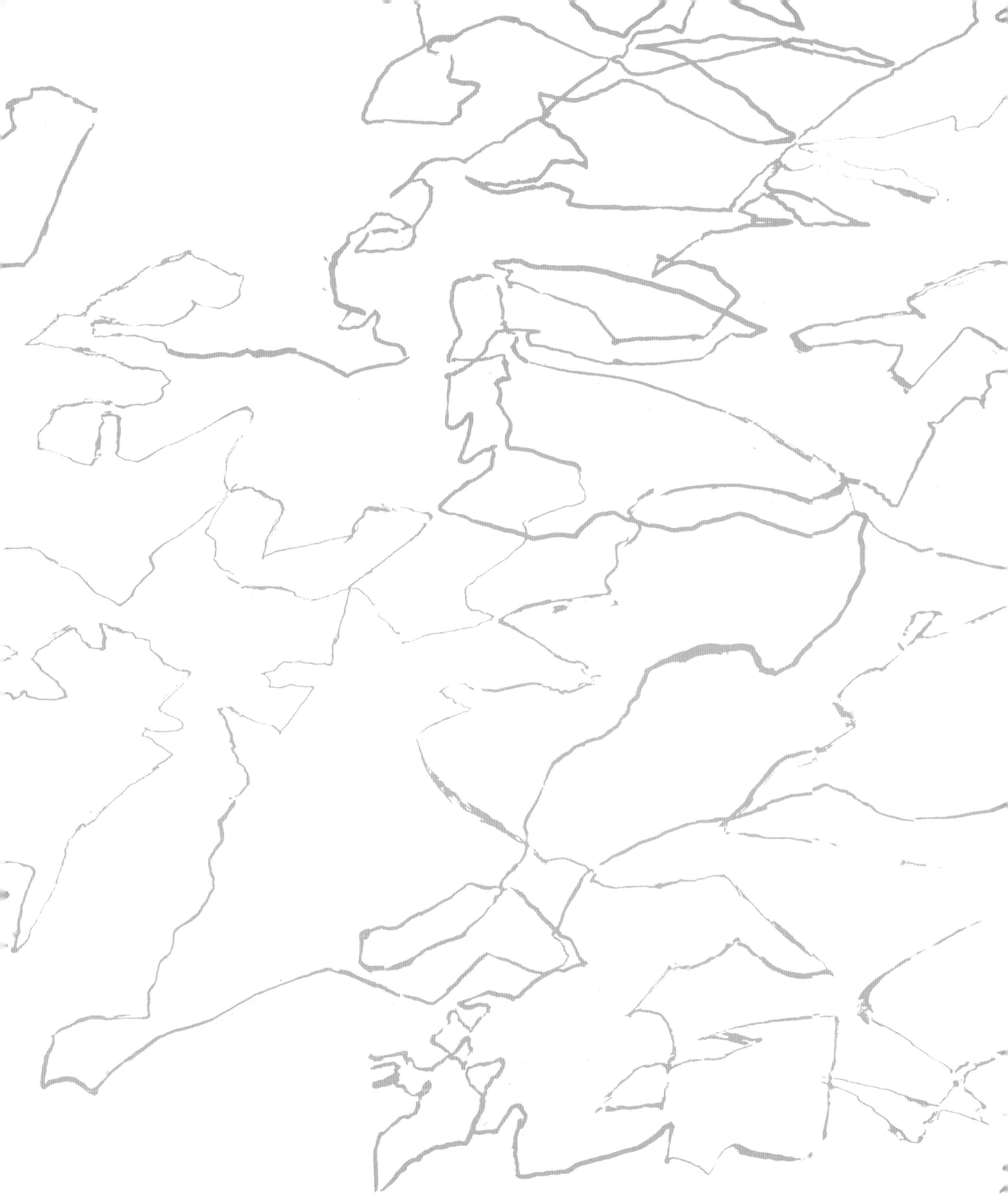

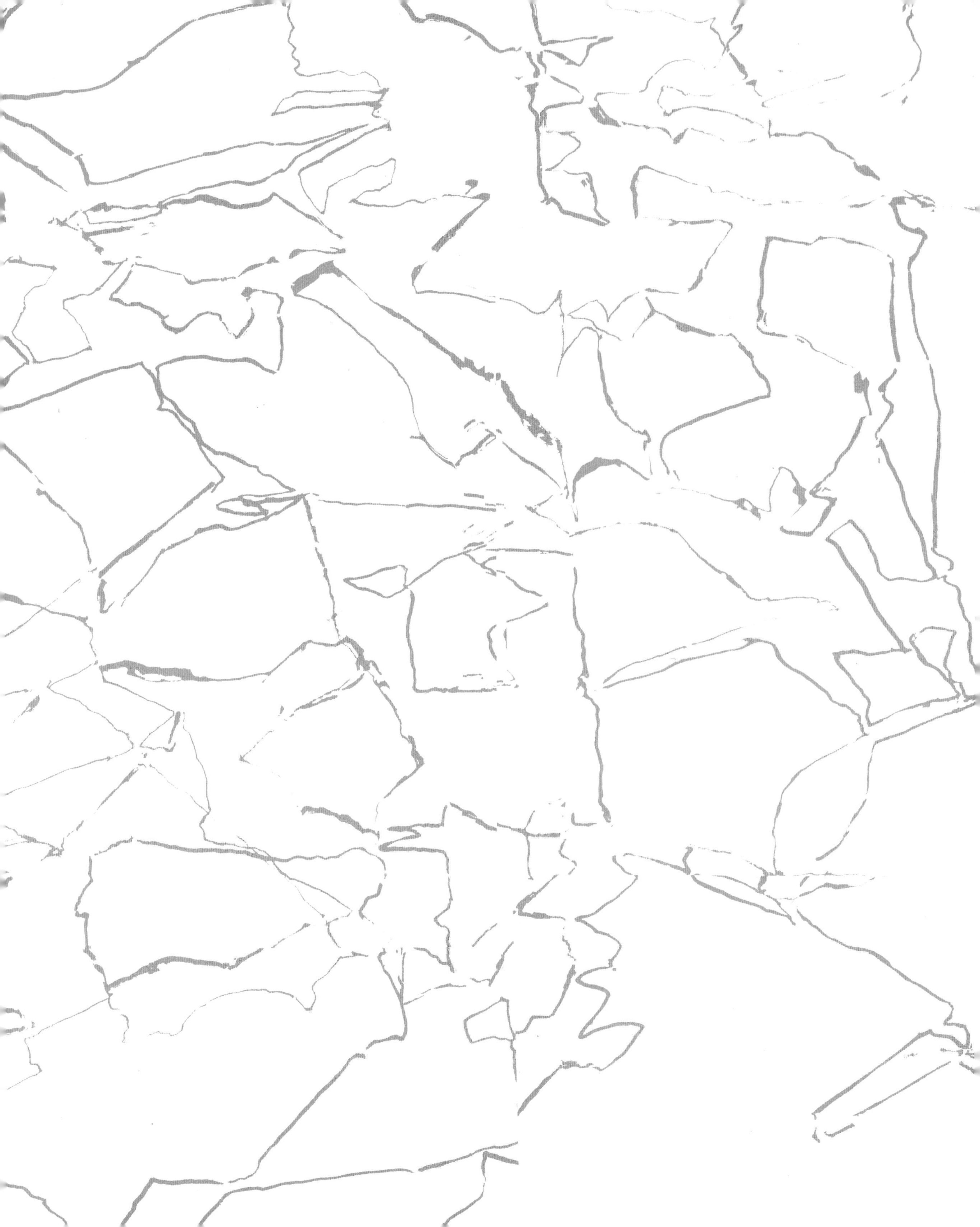

SIMPLES
THE WARBLING OF A THRUSH

Hélène Cixous
Translated by Laurent Milesi

Maman tries to get up from her bed. She rejects any assistance. It would prevent her from trying. Her ambition is astonishing, but she can see some light or other through the room's darkness. She clings to her walking stick. Puts her right foot forward. Says: either I can. Or I can't. Presses with her left hand on the edge of the bed. Musters up all her strength. She can.

How bright your place is, Eve, in the pure volume of your being, a geometry of gold, without any waste, any trace of fat, without grime, without any rotting ulterior motives; you are a museum of transparencies and joyfully restrained satisfactions, you find the soup good and the flowers beautiful, these finds delight your heart with an inexhaustible rapture; enrapture us, Eve, elevate us

we, who live in rooms cluttered with dozens, and sometimes hundreds, of quarrels perpetually hungry for meats freshly slaughtered in pigsties of rancour, we who collide with one another, we who sometimes hate those whom we love and who gnaw our thoughts with human acid, we who are irritated at the end of the morning, we look at you beaming by the window, Eve, and chirping [*piailler*] your way up, with rusty hands and feet clinging to your tree of life like some mangy squirrel. Oh! Oh! We exclaim, and at your sight, our soul is freed from its inertia and the admiration heals the blind and the palsied. We look at you. Go in front, Eve, go your own, uncertain way, forward, forward, we look at you tottering forward along a way cobbled together by each of your old gained astonished footsteps, you don't walk, you hold on, you create each yard with bits of frayed string, with old porous bones, old cracked wooden bark swollen with dropsy, no, the next footstep is far! — ooh! You're thinking, ooh! It's hard, no no — do you want to sit down, maman? — Yes — No! No! One more step, ooh, what a cliff, it's too high — and like that? — no no, too low — and like that? — it's fine. Yes. It's fine. But where am I going like that? Where are you taking me? — You're the one who's taking us and leading, Eve, you overtake us with a broken flap of your clumsy, unbalanced featherless wings.

We look at you, we're flabbergasted, you flabbergast us, Eve, you divide us deeply, you analyse us, some of us turn round and think, that's it, she's dying, she's going, and they put today's date down on the last page, and on the same today some can see far in front of you the shimmering of silks, illegible from here, of a still nameless, faceless year which you could reach after a long journey, they see themselves over there, time has made their hair turn white, P. has put on weight and F. has slimmed, everybody is sculpted otherwise, but all look at you with one single childish smile for all the different faces, thinking: this Eve, she *flabbergasts* us. *Estomaque*, that was her favourite word, eighty years ago when she began cultivating French in Paris; *estomaque* rhymes with *Andromaque* [Andromache], nobody other than her used this word, she's always been fond of words which clack and crack, when the tongue sounds like a comical turnstile. — Cut! — Let's run!

A racket from her bedroom. She is letting out big screams. — I'm coming! I shouted very loud. Let my voice be near her before me! Dim light [*pénombre*]. Has she fallen? Sitting up in bed with all those screams around her like toys. — The cats! The two cats! Came to say hello! Two cats! Two cats!

Such is the cause, such is the news, blessed be they. It wasn't death this time. The same racket greets Eros and Thanatos. We rush. — Two cats! She's laughing to high heaven, and the angels are cats that make up a beautifully symmetrical chorus for her. Hello! Hello! In my turn, hello! The velvet-furred angels are singing, hello to you, Eve! And then Eve laughs away, on and on. All of this mine? What an uproar. Now we're laughing at the uproar [*chahut*]. Uproar! Uproar! Uproar! — I'm coming, the daughter yells! I'm coming to save you! The door opens, the orifice of screams is ajar: peals of broken laughter. Cra cra cra! How good it feels when terror metamorphoses into two Carabas cats[1] at the last minute.

What a deceiver old age is, it's a disgrace how the old woman fools me, that's what old age is, the old woman thinks, it's an old woman in me who says silly things to me and the other old woman believes her. The old woman says: 'it's all over', poor her, this sentence scares me, the old woman thinks, she makes me believe it's all over. That's it. 'It's all over'? What does it mean? It scares me to think something which is scary. But all this is said by the other old woman. All over? Well, not at all! *I* am still here! Eve exclaims. Oh! What a delightful surprise! — Everything alright? She wonders. — It's ok! It's ok! That's some reassuring sentence! It's ok! Let's be reassured, everything's alright. You see? says Eve to herself. Even I didn't believe it. I was afraid it was all over. When I was told we'll leave tomorrow. We'll go to our house, to the city that's waiting for us, shall we? I said yes, the other old woman said: it's too late. She quavered throughout the whole journey lying in this big black Mercedes, therefore too black, is that all you could find, taking me in a big black car, it's a cack cack car of death [*du ca ca ca de mort*], don't tell anybody, thinking: 'a hearse, all this for me, boohoohoohoo [*ouin ouin ouin ouin*]' and when she arrived at the unhoped-for house, from one moment to the next she became a bunch of petunias, a regiment of geraniums. She claps her hands: It's beautiful! It's beautiful!

So she was still there, the house, she who didn't believe it, she who felt pity for her, the house was expecting her, she who was expecting the end. And you see, she said, I only had to come back to my ultra-resistant house, to see myself in the trees which have grown again,

1. An allusion to the Marquis de Carabas in Charles Perrault's fairy tale *Puss in Boots* (*Le Chat botté*) – Trans.

then a pink squirrel with webbed feet like a chameleon's only had to hug the bole of a pine tree and life picked itself up [*se relève*] according to a tale's fairy laws. Picked up her life [*Se relève la vie*]. She had fallen from the bed!

— How come I fell? Astonishment repeated. One can fall and rise from the dead, then. She did not grow tired of being astonished. She laughs. She laughs. She laughs. But what astonishment! I thought it was over. She laughs louder and louder.

17-7-11

'Maman fell off the bed around midnight.' More precisely the bed overturned, a wave lifted it and knocked it over right at the time when maman could see the familiar welcoming coastline advancing towards her. There was a setback [*contretemps*]. She screamed in her distressed voice which carries as far as the horizon, rescue rushed to the scene from all sides, maman came down trembling ('maman' is the mum whom necessity gave me as a present for my hundredth birthday) my grandson whose name I've forgotten, booming 'Hang-on-just-coming' [*Voilà-Voilà*] in a loud baritone, we assessed the damage: none. Maman was all in one hybrid heap with the slop pail for a chest and arms and legs sprouted into live branches around the white plastic trunk but nothing broken, the carpet's lapping up the pee, cra cra cra, maman screams, but how come? What an enormous event, a shipwreck, eh, a mute film that breaks out into onomatopoeias, the character lifts up her head with a slop pail of a hat, looking blind drunk, hey hey, dumbfounded, death fluffed its cue and turned into an angry rat in the corner behind the door. Not this time, dirty rat, move on. — I hadn't been back in India for so long! Maman thinks, what a timid happiness to arrive in this country! To find again the African landscape with tall trees like high dark green flocks. What, it's not India! I look at maman's face, not India? 'Maman' is not contrary, she is kind, if it's not India, it doesn't matter, it's India too, you have only to tell me, 'maman' says. So what is it then? I say. It's Ar —. Maman gives me a prompt. The first syllable is Ar — Arfrica, I exclaimed — No? — Arca — , says 'maman', and I: — Chat! No: — Chon! There. It's hard. Especially the tail end of the word. When my head is on the tip of my tongue, it slips on the tail[2] — Arcachon is not India? No, no. — You never wanted to go to India, 'maman' says dreamily. I thought it scared you. — Well, you see? You see? — So that's how one goes to India without going there, without having ever been there, except by wanting, while not wanting, wanting wanting, wheely wanting [*voulant voulant, en voulance*[3]], well [*voilà*]. Arcachon goes for India, you see? — Yes, I see, 'maman' says, who's laughing so much that she looks like me.

'Maman' is her mum's name for my hundredth birthday. — I do know you're not maman, maman whispers in my ear, you are my daughter, my good girl of a daughter, but may I? — But of course I am maman if you wish, maman darling, says 'maman'. It suits me and it suits you. — That's how I have my mum, maman thinks, but that's my business.

2. *Quand j'ai la tête sur la langue c'est la queue qui fourche*: the French involves a convoluted pun on *avoir le mot sur le bout de la langue*: to have the word on the tip of one's tongue, and *ma langue a fourché*: it was a slip of the tongue – Trans.
3. The last phrase is a coinage in which one may wish to hear the French for 'ambulance', hence 'wheely' (for 'really') – Trans.

My mother has always been discreet about anything having to do with emotional life [*affectivité*]. It's a courtesy. No frills. She doesn't sport lovers or darlings on her lapel. The 'intimates' are designated by light, all-purpose words. 'Friend'. 'Somebody'. It's a way of not taking over. I'm talking about her years as a woman here. This epoch ended in 2009. With her hundredth birthday in sight, as she was entering another world, she moved on to other procedures as other-human. When she had a mother, who was a strong, faithful, majestic mother, totally respected until her penultimate will (— for my mother did not respect the last will: when her mother, having had enough, said: 'do it' (trans.: kill me) she did not respect her according to her will, she respected her) otherwise my mother never did make a mum out of her mother. She refrained. She pooled her mother for all the children. Her mother was Omi for everyone as well and for my mother too.

Maman has great powers, so has 'maman', maman thinks. 'Maman' saves me. And thus she can also drop me, for everything can happen, in particular the opposite of everything. Sometimes at night, since everything can happen stealthily in the dark, I scream-scream and I scream.scream.scream and I scream scream scream scream until maman comes running. Then I have the proof: maman exists. But precisely because maman and 'maman' have such great powers one must not use them excessively. One must use them accurately, when it is necessary or inevitable. When all at once there is somebody at the very moment when I was going to moan 'maman' and didn't notice soon enough, I scribble fast and it gives miaouwman [*miaoumian*] and it sounds like I'm wittering on in mumbles and grumbles [*en grommelis*] but actually I do what cats do when they cover up their secrets by rubbing them out with their paws. I cover with sand: miaouwman.

And maman says: Yes, maman darling. Saved!

'But how come I fell?' Long after we picked her up, palpated her, put her back to bed, reassured her, maman was still in full swing [*agitait encore le branle*]. In the end my son stayed behind in the bedroom. Sitting on a night chair, he was filling in a whole segment of the room like a mound of the moon on earth. That way there's no room for sinking. Through the walls and ceilings, the tone of a song rose, sonorous, muffled and convinced, whose text was absorbed by the walls and the ceiling but not its rhythm. A distant, profound, religious, stubborn music against danger.

Alone in the world with the primordial, according to the Pithecus' ritual. The male Pithecus utters a powerful, meditative cantata. A cavity carved out of the darkness serves as a temple. This chant is so charged with emotions that nobody may or should linger in the vicinity. From a distance, however, it is as if the message of the vibrations means: I am stronger than death, sleep in peace, maternal stock, I am very strong, I keep a supremely watchful eye, I am the keeper of the finalist female monkeys. In three months' time I will be fifty, old venerated century. Now I am the one who will lead my people by your example.

He was singing a song loudly to her. She screamed: ENOUGH. He said: I love you very much, Eve. He put the words in a silent moon paper. He was happy that she had fallen and that he could pick her up. There was no witness. This scene would keep its purity

All night long from Thursday to Friday Eve asked with a twang: but how come I fell off the bed? And she had ended up with a plastic sallet [*salade*][4] across her head without knowing that she was a fabulous version of La Mancha. Sometimes she was making a drama out of it and sometimes it was a comedy, she was laughing to tears, she was afraid, her heart was beating so fast that it could have stopped, she could see herself falling again, and in the end, it was not the end. I thought: next year we'll be one hundred and two, there was no image, only the words, which were breathing, breathing

18.7.11

Then we reached the avenue lined with tall hibiscus. And nobody thought: the oak tree is one hundred and one years old, for it was in the verdant youth of its life, gallant, harmonious, frequented by tom tits and squirrels, with a fresh skin and finely-proportioned waist.

— I thought that too, my mother brooded in the tongue of the tall hibiscus. She carries on with the conversation that her fellow creatures started. — Yes yes my lovelies, I thought that you would never see me again. Yes, I thought we wouldn't see one another again and that you would forget me, how sad this avenue is without me that's how I was thinking, my mother said to the tall curly geraniums, in boohoo-speak [*en ouin-ouin*], one of her languages which she perfected over the last years. I thought, that's it, I boohoo (trans.: I'm dying) and I didn't dare say it in French, didn't dare think my thought straight in the eye, I was escaping, han han,[5] I was saying ambiguous things so that nobody could understand and I could understand nothing at all, I was acting the fool unintentionally, if I was another I can't be forced to answer. Don't recognize yourself, that's my philosophy. When I lived in Paris, I said that I was living in Berlin or the other way round, I used to say: but where do I live? I was truly lost and I knew it. It's awful but at least the minister cannot find us, when we're not where we are. Another thing I had invented, boohoo I say to you, my mother says to the hibiscus, is disgust. To be disgusting is repulsive. Offer me to watch television, I say: Idontgiveadamn. — You want this book? — Idontgiveadamn. We leave you alone.

The geraniums had never been so beautiful. A slender virility. My mother said: are these mosquito nets? She looks at me questioningly. It can't be that. We remain uncertain.

Last night she found it hard to fall asleep. Usually, no sooner is she in bed than she embarks for her night's sleep. Night is a welcoming, fertile island, where she replenishes her supplies. Tonight, we're waiting. For what? For whom? The teeth. Maman screams: My teeth! Your teeth are in the glass, the daughter says. It's not the right answer. — Where are my teeth? my mother asks with concern. — They're here, next to you, on the mirror table. Her concern gets worse. My mother looks at the teeth. The two jaws in a glass of water, inert, sleeping crabs. — Here? Why? I feel pity. — For whom? For them — I catch sight of a grief of separation. — Shouldn't I be wearing them for the night? — It seems to me that they're fine in their jar, I say. — Who's going to take care of them during the night? — They will sleep too, in their glass. Now my mother is pleading. — I feel pity *for myself*. But don't you understand? maman thinks. Can't you see that I can't sleep without teeth? I am unhappy. I don't want to

4. A medieval head-piece worn by Cervantes's Don Quixote of La Mancha – Trans.
5. A recurring onomatopoeia in the original, suggestive of grunting with effort (*à grand ahan*: with much puffing and panting) – Trans.

die without teeth, can't you hear my fear? Have I ever been out without knickers? Never. I never went out without making my bed. That you didn't understand either. You thought I was a disciplined housewife. *I* can see: I go out, I fall, maybe I die, I'm brought back, and my bed is unmade! This I can't stand. I don't want to EXIT like a toothless old woman. When one dies at night, it's pathetic, one is least fit to be seen, without eyes, without ears, without teeth. I'm very old. I've been VI SI TED several times for a month, I won't tell you about the one which one mustn't talk about. I do know that you know this, but *you* don't know that I know it, on the one hand like you, on the other hand like me. I want to be ready. On the eve of the first day of school, I was six, I went to bed all dressed between the sheets I'd even kept my shoes on I was afraid of being late to start this new life. All I'm asking for are *my teeth*. The ears Idontgiveadamn. That one can't hear over there makes no odds. But I want to have proper shoes on.

Don't tell me I'm not nearing [*touche à*] my fatal hour, you know nothing about it and nor do I. Who touches me [*me touche à*] at midnight? Boohoo

It's not until this morning that Homer[6] opened my eyes and ears. At the moment when Hector, in spite of Andromache's resistance, took his eleven-cubit-long javelin whose bronze tip, clasped within a golden ferrule, glitters in front of him, suddenly I 'saw' maman's last and only tooth glitter faintly with a steel glint on the right side in the old lightless sunken mouth and I gave a start of surprise. *I* competed with maman for her javelin!

A confession: my lack of subtlety and empathy when it comes to maman's 'teeth'. The only part of her body that I don't feel is mine. Whereas she loves her teeth and walking stick like her sturdy fingers. She is anxiously fond of her detachable parts. If her legs went away during the night, one could not even run after them. One could only shout: Maman! maman! Boohoo! (*mouin! Mouin!*)

Maman and I are living ardent times from now on. This is because the real proximity of separation throws us into each other's arms several times a day. It scares me so much that many times I believe when I open the door that I've just come to find her again after losing her. She too greets me and greets herself, with the exaltation of a fighter who has pulled through beautifully once more and who, all covered with dust and streaming with sweat, greets from the farthest distance the one who can't believe her eyes.

'I was sure she was dying', my brother said

Actions. Main action 1: to eat. To cut, prick and lift to one's mouth, snap up, chew (how is it happening in there between the two dentures?), swallow, tame, overcome, look all around the table, point the Forefinger with authority at those present then at the pieces of melon, at the salad bowl, at the cheese. The Forefinger: 'eat.' The neighbours struggle feebly. One eats under maman's finger. Maman is eating. Action, battle, trade. Very big spoonfuls containing pyramid, soup, cereals, slices of sausages. I propose a smaller-sized spoon.

6. *Homère* in French, in which one can hear *ô mère*, and which Cixous has used repeatedly to refer to her mother, as in the recently published *Homère est morte*... (Paris: Galilée, 2014) – Trans.

Again very big spoonfuls. Challenge: a matching opponent. Who's challenging whom? Part of the spoonful collapses. But maman is wrapped [*ceinte*] in a cloth which stretches from one shoulder to the other on top of which sheets of kitchen paper have been placed. The mystery remains: without trembling the hand lifts the spoonful up to the lips. Afterwards the collapse of the pyramid occurs because the opening at the top is insufficient. Probably maybe only a pyramid-shaped spoonful gives maman the assured feeling of victory or else an answer to a spiritual appetite.

After all, I say to myself, everyone must be able to 'eat' according to their secret scenario.

Maman deconstructs our routines? Eats? Hunts, fishes, harpoons mixed potatoes, pieces of chicken. Then follows a mental calculation: half a sliced banana gives ten bananas. Too much! Uncut, same half-banana, only one piece. Good. Banana finished. Next. Harpoons a chicken wing. Cuts the piece into equal segments, single-handedly. Looks at these slayed pieces with a shrewd eye. Gulps down the pieces one after the other uninterruptedly until the last one. At ease [*Repos*].

Main action 2: at the *cabinet* — a frequently used, even overused, word in Oran, designating on the one hand my father's (medical) *cabinet* or surgery, on the other hand the privy [*cabinet (d'aisances)*] for my mother. The one enhancing (uplifting [*relevant*]) the other. Something very French, frivolous, whimsical in this word appealed to her when in 1935 she discovered the charms of the city of Oran, where inhabitants conversed in a stylish language haloed with dreams of Paris. While sitting on the throne, one felt quite near the buildings baked in the ovens of familiar ruminations by Proust, Descartes and Rousseau, all these solitaries living in seclusion [*gens de poêle et de cabinet*].[7] To-go-to-the-*cabinet* now does duty for all errands, activities, initiatives, businesses. The *cabinet* is gaining ground. Half the house is gradually being devoted to the commode [*garde-robe*]. Modification of the hierarchy of our activities: the *cabinet* comes before anything else. A Sunday at the loo. A fresh, desirable Sunday like a youthful love, a flood of light on the lavatera, a lush garden visited by bees, narrow-bodied dandies, plane wings right within the reach of my hands and chest but inaccessible: I am detained, on duty at the entrance to the *cabinet*. — Where are you? Maman's voice rises. The question stabs me in the side. Am I not one metre [*mètre*] away from my master [*maître*]? — You're gone, maman complains. A little revolt gets hold of me. — Yes, I say curtly, I'm gone. — I need help, maman pleads. — Get up, I say. Hold on to the bars. — It's hard, my mother says. — You did it not long ago. — I'd rather you raised me. The little child in her insists. He's the one that throws tantrums and stamps his feet for her. One can't say that it is her nor that it is not her. Comedy, no comedy, ruse, need, she is haunted, wants to go back up earlier, dreams of being in my arms as before she learnt how to walk. Photo. A very little girl with a big ribbon on her head. Tears rush to my eyes. A true comedian! I say. The need is so strong. Maman wants 'maman' to love her and protect her against all the dangers forever [*dans les siècles*]. The child is naturally the comedian of her states. Plays out his drama of fright and weakness in order to gain maman's powerful affection [*tendresses*]. Swear! — I swear. What Proust does to maman, maman does to me. You marcellize me, I say. Marcel! I say. I stiffen. She moans. I soften. I rush. I take the child

7. A small heated 'stove room' and a study, especially associated with René Descartes (*Discourse on the Method*, Part II), and with Marcel Proust (*Swann's Way*) and Jean-Jacques Rousseau (*Reveries of a Solitary Walker*) respectively – Trans.

in my arms. I smother her face in kisses, her cheeks, her nose, her temples, her neck. A little cicalfate cream on her rash. I love you, my child, I love your scabs.

Am I living in sacrilege [*profanation*] with my mother? We act day and night, maman wails in the middle of the night, I was riding between Sodom and Gomorrah on the narrow grassy path, with maman as a pillion passenger, I crossed a level crossing plunged in darkness, we could have got run over since I couldn't see anything but I was blindly relying on good fortune, I was going to enter an even thicker night, maman's screams stopped me, I threw myself down the stairs, into the darkness maman clutching the overturned bucket, the carpet was soaking up the urine, she will never manage to climb back into her boat, I threw my dream into the maw of the abyss as a sacrifice, I put my arms around maman and *with a strength I don't have* I hoisted her up onto the mattress. I thought: one more broken night, one more day without early writing [*sans lever d'écriture*], it was raining furiously, the sky is mad, the earth has convulsions, maman is in a state of arrhythmia, let me listen to your heart, I say, she pushes my head towards her belly, the heart has gone down into the abdomen, I'm thinking: how much time already yet again will the mystery work on our side? Why do you call me, night and night? I ask my mother, I'm afraid of slipping on the stepless stairs from which one can't go up.

My little doll, I say, please sleep. But why is this word coming to me here? It's showing me a picture so old that I hadn't seen it since my Oran childhood: the old German doll came back, a foreign doll which so uncannily looked like an old lady, I never played with it, it worried me, it looked at me silently with its *real* expression, so one makes human dolls in Germany, the old doll had really broken fingers, a sharp eye. Exile and travels had aged her. She kept a dignified air. Maman on the pot casts an unflustered glance at me. You put me back to bed? The train is about to depart again [*repartir*].

If you see her going [partir] *one night, my brother says. Don't bring her round. He cuts the sentence into two halves. That way it doesn't touch. It divides into two curtains on both sides of a blind window.*

I was waiting for maman. I was waiting for the sun. I was waiting for the apparition with a violent expectation. These are prayers which do not hope, which beg, which gnash their teeth. Come! Just as one beats one's chest in order to wake up the dream which sleeps instead of coming straightaway to our rescue. Just as an exile squatting at the desert's gate expects from all his taut limbs the dream which will bring him back to his native country. The week which separates me from life was not a week, it was a mountain range whose sides were red with flayed wild animals. I was squatting at their feet and motionless like a young soldier. I was waiting for my mother to rise radiantly at the world's door. It was a long time. The sun must also climb, notching its way up in the week. I had no doubt that maman would eventually vanquish the darkness and on Sunday her head would appear, her figure would come and shine in the middle of the frame and I would stop suffering one whole day. I doubted my strengths: they were scant, weak, feverish. I was fading. Here is the last minute, here is my mother appearing up there. She feeds me. The rolled omelette is her body. I eat maman in small mouthfuls to eke her out. I cry.

Maman never cried. When she did not cry saying in as few words as possible that my father was no more, I took her for a member of another species than mine, a military, mythological soul. She was the law, she enforced it, she obeyed it: a mother is never ill. She never fell ill: in case an illness attacked, she would undo the assailant without fuss.

Sunday on a coach — D'youremember, my precious? You came to bring me back to life, I was lying in exile, on the edge of the Aïn el Turk desert, you were my only country and my hope, you loomed up between the sky's brush [*brousses*] with the powerful grace of a leopard, d'youremember? — Boohoo. No.

and all these arrivals and risings [*levers*] now reduced to a single image, a picture with fading colours, in front of which I go and collect my thoughts from time to time, to see again the time when maman was the rain to my thirst, her smile a shield, and death could not kill me. This year we're having a picnic very near the entrance to the cemetery.

Then my mother started choking. — Where is my breath? It doesn't come any more. A thick smoke emanated from life's bush. Maman with her eyes that widen in order to drink an air which eludes her. I'm giving you oxygen straightaway. — You think so? Submissive. With grey lips. The small plastic glass in maman's nostrils. Suck! Breathe in! 'My back is cold. My feet are cold.' I struggle, I rub, I quixote an enemy who's tilting from all sides and whom I can't see, I flail my arms about [*fais des moulinets*][8] like there is no tomorrow [*en veux-tu en voilà*], the main thing is to side with the oppressed. To defend the weak and the frightened.

With its big right hand, the leopard revives the diminutive [*ranime le minime*] baby baboon. One cannot imagine a more human, more naked pretty little face [*minois*], a small mask with its wide eyes hungry for solicitude. With the same front right paw which killed my mother this morning, the leopard is now playing mother to the oh-so-small being.

— Feeling better? I murmured. Maman is sucking the oxygen. The two tabbies are sitting keeping watch. Vroom, the oxygen machine throbs. Between the quiet curtains darkness has clawed its way in. The machine is suckling the old thirsty being: ran ran ran ran. Mechanical mother. Mother cats. All the mothers, industrious, bustling about, fatalistic, mobilized: it starts again, it starts again.

I shouldn't have felt reassured. I listened to the snake named tiredness: I dozed off in the guardroom. I mistook a day for a year. I thought we were out of the bad dream. We were returning 'back home', it was another year, maman was coming back from the market, the little girls had grown, they were offering maman a diamond as big as a goose egg. It's beautiful, it's beautiful, maman exclaimed.

Maman wants to get up before dawn, she is bustling about. — What are we doing? What are we waiting for? — The hour, maman. — Which hour? — The ninth. — It's not the right hour? — It is dark. It is cold. Sleep a little longer. — What a country! You've never seen so many distances creeping in everywhere. There's no landscape here. Nobody's coming with me? Even 'maman'. I don't want to sleep, no, no. No way I'm going to let

8. Literally (in sports): to do windmills; here an allusion to the windmills (*moulins*) against which Don Quixote was fighting – Trans.

myself be bamboozled. Not stupid. All night long my voice stood watch, yelped, cackled, screeched [*hié*], bleated, croaked, chittered [*chucheté*], tinkled [*grilloté*], cheeped [*piaulé*], twittered [*trissé*].[9] The proof. I'm capable. I'm incapable of stopping. — Stop, maman, I beg you, 'maman' says. — Yep, yep, I say. And now the voice countersigns, calls [*courcaille*], chirrs [*grésille*], comes close to howling, peeps [*piaille*], honks [*cacarde*],[10] heehee hanhan. 'Maman' says to me: Maman, I need to sleep, it's two hours past midnight. And me and my voice we yap we yelp, we squeak and squeal [*on ouine, on vouine, on couine*]. Nah [*nan*] nah nah. I won't sleep. I won't sleep ever again. If you don't remain seated near me, snap snap [*trac trac*] it's got to crack, my voice must make the blaze crack crack crackle, cluck cluck [*cot cot*] I did what it takes, and nobody has got to sleep in this house. Good thing I'm here with my voice and my walking stick to keep up the racket. No night for the foe, no rest for the friend.

26-7-11

What is this language? It's a blanguage [*blangue*[11]], a language before language, a forgotten language which comes back to her. An alarming language. Resounding from afar, clappering [*claquetant*][12] from nearby. Not tamed at all, it seems. It kicks out. My mother doesn't speak it, so it seems, the language chatters, whether she likes it or not. The magpies make a nest in her throat. Through I do not know what trick of telepathic understanding I manage to reconstitute her messages after a few attempts at translation. Maman makes as much noise as those buried alive, she strikes with all her might; well, there are doors in the bedroom, lids, vaults, partitions in people's heads, armies of worms and ants which crawl on the walls. She can only rely on herself. It is death and his sidekicks that she addresses mainly.

— She is ultra-resistant, the doctor says.

From my language, which she spoke admirably from 1930 to 2010, that French language of which she had made a modern-style trophy for herself in the three months following her arrival from Osnabrück to Paris, in these circumstances, she keeps only some strong terms of refusal: No! Enough! Idontgiveadamn! We are barely significant interlocutors, the neglecting, negligible infantry which has next to no idea about the battle she is waging. Nobody to confide in, just as when she was a midwife during the war, during the curfew, soldiers prevented her from acting on the pretext of protecting her. And even these interjections wither. Except for Enough. ENOUGH! Oh! She has a thundering, mightily ferocious ENOUGH at her disposal. In a scene she borrows from impotent Zeus one of his tantrums thrown at the deaf heads under the helmets, in another scene as if she was addressing it at God and she was furious like Job. Good thing there's this projectile: E-NUFF [*AHCÉ*]! She hurls it at the assailant's face with prodigious strength. The soul can't stand any longer, all the passions are in her throat: E-NUFF! We all recoil in fright at this scream. Don't forget the enormity of my irritation. I have known your language. I have thrown your sounds and your stones. When I was an ordinary mortal (like everybody) I spoke in common sentences. Now I am among the superhumans. With the moaning of hoarse owls, I bump against night's eardrums.

9. I have added between square brackets the more 'technical' cries or noises used in this series: for machinery hoisting loads, sparrows, a small bell [*grelot*], chicks and swallows respectively – Trans.
10. A similar string evocative of quails, a cricket, a small bird, and geese – Trans.
11. A portmanteau word composed of *blanc* (white, blank) and *langue* (language) – Trans.
12. The sound made by a stork – Trans.

Epitaphs.

Maman is slowly devouring a live croissant. Time passes. What does it change? It passes, it passes. It eats. And at your place? Everything's fine. I don't write anything. Nothing happens [*se passe*]. It's all past. I regret. Youth is far behind: A foreign country. — I've never been there. She was someone else. I'm still here. I'm holding on. I'm holding on. Thanks to the croissants. Can one say that this croissant is present? In two minutes it won't be any longer. Poor little one. But where has time gone [*est-il passé*]? Now where is this croissant? I haven't swallowed it? — You remember all the same, it's a form of presence. — A little. — Do you remember Oran? — It's ancient. We don't live in Oran any longer. Where is the wheely table? Gone? — Its foot was broken. — Poor little table, I mourn for it. Poor little one. — The Council will take it away. — To the hospital?

Lost, yesterday, I understood that Eve has lost all the names. All the people come before her without their names. They thus make only one person called 'Miss' or 'Mr'. Astonished: *you* have a son? One after the other, all the family members go out. We remain alone. She greets me with a joyful, springtime smile, her eyes filled with fresh wonder. 'Good morning, maman!' Looks furtively, feeling as if she had committed an offence. Corrects herself. 'Mmman'. That way she calls me maman without getting caught. She has not lost my name. Plied with questions she confesses. But 'Hélène' is a thing of the past. Now you're maman. From that moment on, a great freedom stretches around her. When I move towards her the name of a person who was and whom time has swallowed like a croissant, she puts together a fictional biography for this person, from a few elements of reality, an address, an occupation. History unfolds with unexpected twists, she plays a decisive role in it and in the end everybody heads towards a tragic death, but she stops before, poor him. Surprise: to become the author of fiction past a hundred years old. Much more ability than me, a hack always struggling to invent scenarios. I tell myself that she benefits from an exceptional release from custody.[13]

Found lost, to find lost, not found[14]

24-6-11

The Confession. I put her to bed and I draw the portrait of this speckled face, in the care of Rembrandt so that he can paint it beyond ugliness, gnawed at by death's mandibles which can only stab and crack [*larder et lézarder*], an old striated shell, a fibrous nest, attacked by nodules, scaly, inhabited by two big lively eyes, where overexcited squirrels hop about. To see the evening mug: once the dentures are out, an old narrow fish face shows up, an orifice full of darkness where the stump of a metal tooth, also known as 'The Tooth', glints feebly, where a thick slug of a meaty tongue lives. Out of the cavern a grating yet articulate voice emerges, coos [*croucoule*], hoots [*chuinte*], whirrups [*cricrisse*]:[15] 'Hélène'. A mental letter comes to Hélène. A letter breathed out, made up mostly of blanks, and words carved out thus: than   kyou. The sender looks for a way of saying without saying. Follows: I lovyou [*taime*] very much. (Lovyou barred by very much.) Thank you.

13. *levée d'écrou*: French *écrouer* means 'to imprison', by reference to the old meaning of *écrou*, designating the register where imprisonments were recorded – Trans.

14. *Trouvé perdu, trouvée perdue, trouver perdue, trou* in the original; French *trou*: hole – Trans.

15. A sequence of sounds (and portmanteau words) for the dove (*roucouler*), the owl and the wings of a (colloquial) *cricri*, or cricket (*crisser*), here rendered as whirr + chirrup – Trans.

The two squirrels race round the room like two cyclists wheel against wheel, sprinting along watching anxiously, casting looks on all sides. — Anybody there? — No. — So quick, let's hurry. Then throws in quick as a flash, running away: I love you.

That's what she's been meaning to say, for a few weeks, but it's so dangerous. One says I love you and thereupon one changes into a larva tangled up in bonds and given over to the demons of necessity, abandon and solitude.

My mother has never said to me I love you.

Maman admits defeat, overcome by the continuous storm which hits her hull shipwrecked on the last ice-bank. She emerges half-drowned from the ocean, she had docked in the land of men this morning, the island was male, the old hull worn thin cracks at the touch, I lift her, put her down on a gentle slope. She's trying to catch her breaths [*cherche ses souffles*]. The two squirrels sometimes run panic-stricken. To whom? To whom? — Oxygen? I say. — No: You. — I'm here, I say. On the armchair, beside you. — Where? Blind squirrels: Where? Where? I turn the armchair so she can see me from the front, close up. It's not enough. — Where are you? Help me. Invent a nearer proximity. — Maman! Don't go away! She looks around her: chasms. — Without you I'm lost. — I'm here, here. — It's far, far. *I* have sorrows. Big sorrows. — Where are they? — On the chest. I don't know what it is. I don't know why, sitting on my chest. Because I'm old. Nothing doing. It's too late. Any solution? She's thinking: I forget, — That I'm old — Let's try. She tries. She whispers: it's too late for me. I *am* old. What shall I do?

Me: — There is a giant staircase, very wide and beautiful. Let's take it. The staircase is majestic, it has been ascended by generations. Where will it lead us? Alas once at the top the high sea is waiting for us, a small plane flies above us looking for a place to land, I feel dizzy, a big wave is brewing, if the water keeps rising we shall perish, I'm afraid, maman says. We should go down, but is it still possible? What I don't understand is that there is this vast staircase which appears to us. This seems like an invitation to go up. Does this mean that we are at the height of danger but that then it won't go any further? We crawl back down, Maman straddling me: the weather's not nice! — You can say that, I say. We laugh. — Where are we going? — Into the dream next door. — It's a long way

The house is full of long ways.

Now I am *alone*.

I don't know what to do. I don't know what the matter is: I'm getting old. It scares me. I've just got old. Where am I going? Suddenly she loses sight of me. Screams: Hélène's going away! — I'm not going away; my voice says to her ear. Look, I'm here. — Ah, good! That's fine. She reassures me: I am here too. Now she strikes up a terrified lamentation, like a cow which fills the void left by a calf with her mooings. Nobody can stand such bawling. — Stop it! Maman dear, translate, I exclaim. — Moo moo! I can't. I'm mad. — Since when? — Since this morning. I don't know where it comes from. Dreams came. There were thieves. They stole *mein Verstand*. — How did they manage to steal your reason? — They didn't give me the recipe. *Ich hab' kein' Verstand mehr.* Where is understanding [*entendement*]? *Weg! Weg! Weg!* Understanding is no longer here. — You saw thieves? — There were several of them. They were disguised as honest men. — You saw that they were thieves? — Yes, I did, yes. I didn't know what they wanted to steal. — You were afraid?

— Oh yes! Very much. I was afraid and they were afraid. They ran away. They were afraid of the police. — You're the one who called the police? — Oh yes. But the police were afraid. — So everybody was afraid? — I didn't call because I was afraid you might be afraid. The police were afraid too. Even Fear was afraid, maman whispers. — How did you call the police? — With the phone! — But you don't know how to use the phone. — You see!!? So I called the neighbour and he came with the revolver. They all left. Then I said BIG SILLY THINGS. You can see: they stole my understanding. Now I know what they wanted to steal. — Yet you're eating your croissants *mit Verstand*, I say. I don't find that you lack understanding, I say. I hold on to the croissant. — Maybe you found it? Maman asks. She stares into my eyes with wide eyes of hope mixed with regret. She should not have been afraid that I might be afraid. She swallows her croissant. It's over. Too late.

While I'm weighing these iridescent words, — is it a farce? — No, it isn't, maman's eyes say, widening as if to drink better the potion of my words, moo moo! re-moos the cow with the raided belly, suffering in its pure state.

It's not that she lost her memory, rather nobody cares at all about it in this country, the traveller is already weighed down with his own burdens, with feet of cast iron, knees of granite, a crane to hoist himself from one cobblestone onto another, one must get rid of whatever holds and pulls one back where there is no back to cover [*pas d'arrière*], no past, one can only go forward, lifting a universe with each centimetre, one keeps only a paper handkerchief rolled up in the left hand for the right hand is steering the walking stick. This paper ball is the brilliant find of the human who tackles the limit of the possibilities of living. Multiple functions and minute weight: is a summary of mummy and daddy, mana, a sacred embryo, a handkerchief for the ceaselessly running nose, a mental spare wheel, a buffer against the void (for hands at this age cannot stand lack, they are mouths which need filling in order not to scream with terror), equivalent of a cat, of a horse, a nano-planet, a portable nest, an egg for itself. On the other hand, when one wants to cling to 'maman' in order to get up from the pot, one is torn between two grippings, one doesn't want, can't let go of one for the other a bird in the hand is worth two in the bush, maman tries and tries to hang on to my arm without releasing the hand where the little crumpled deity is housed.

'She will perhaps still be around in three months' time', my brother says.

27-7-11

The trick: When Eve replies to the male nurse who asks, a flask of blood in his hand, 'When were you born?' 'I wasn't born', then she utters piercing shrieks: 'my blood! don't take my blood!', each drop does matter and each reply has its reasons. Who knows whether we are not on the eve of the last battle. The smallest element of the body must be at its post. 'Eighty'. She stares at me: 'Is the card I'm playing fine?' she silently asks for my opinion, then, for a more realistic, more credible effect: Eighty-two. So be it, I say. She is rather pleased with herself. Screams like a peacock, which makes the male nurse shudder. Good war strategy. Military technique. Maman as an aboriginal. I join in her screams so she does not feel all alone on the front line. Later I'll take care of the disarmed nurse.

One must put oneself in the place of such a single-character army. And yet it's impossible. To 'say' to oneself, to come near the thought 'is it possible that *I* might be about a hundred years old? that "I" might be worse than a hundred, farther, more alone, more less?'

This causes a sensation of frozen desert, of infinite appalling depopulation and expulsion. One feels driven forward, far from the living, and nobody in front of you to say 'come this way, don't be afraid, there's a bench over there, under a bower of wisteria, you'll be able to rest without fearing to wake up below the earth', reunions become as rare as the rain, one doesn't dare look behind oneself, who knows what sad traces one's own broken legs will have left and nobody to whom to say, 'I'm hungry, I want my soup, it's my mother who's being kept far from my bowl, I want to lap up, I want my mother the soup to keep me company and tell my exiled body tales of the hearth surrounded by parents and protective animals.'

— My soup! Here's maman asking for her soup at any time. Well, there is no fellow creature 'over there', beyond our encampment where townless roads and bankless rivers wind along

I know nobody, in this country, nobody in all the genealogies of my families has ever sent me a postcard from this country. Nobody came close to the barrier. Nobody in the photo albums went beyond the ninety-fifth year, all sat down, they posed for the last photo, some in Osnabrück, others in Algiers, Oran, Montevideo, Johannesburg, Strasbourg, Melbourne, Manchester, Santiago, Los Angeles, London, Hamburg, Theresienstadt, Dresden, Buenos Aires, Baranovici, Berlin, Jerusalem, with the last pictures of the family's travellers maman made a necklace of cemeteries round the neck of the Earth, they stopped, they got off the train, nobody signalled to maman on the station platform, the wheelchair shakes her bones, she feels her skeleton rattling, she screams enough! I want to get off, she can't get off, the armchair train rolls past the station of the second century without stopping. Maman takes her first steps staggering along, she still doesn't know how to stand, it's the second country, the ground is spiked, but the trees are beautiful she is the one who took *the first steps* on this moon. It is sad. I am alone. Cousins, I've lost the list, ten pages disappeared. I had female cousins. There were fewer and fewer. Then Jeanne stopped last week. They remain far behind me with their names. Once dead the female cousins die more and more. Faster and faster. Poor Jeanne! I cry. Maman cries. She eats her croissant. I had a cousin. She's dead. And her husband. She hadn't one any more for a long time. *Ich weiß nicht wie sie hieß.* Jeanne, I say. Her name was Jeanne. And your female cousin in the Gurs camp? — It wasn't Irmgard, no, no. She's trying to think. There was Ilse Hauer. No. She had a sister whose name was Hilde. No. Her name was Jeanne? She's wondering. — Jeanne, I say, went a week ago. — Jeanne is gone? — There's your old friend Simone left still.

I had one left, maman says. Yes, I say. Jeanne. — A tooth, my mother says. She looks at me with round eyes. — You're lucky to have teeth. I think I had some once. I think I was born with teeth. I don't know where they're gone, my teeth. They fell into the water, I think. You've got to be careful to keep them. I *used* to have teeth. Suddenly you don't have teeth any more. You're outside, without return. You can't go back up. You know what a catastrophe is?

Song of catastrophes:

Ca ca ca ca ca tastrophe

It's an event you can't avoid (she swallows a spoonful of soup). I still had a female cousin (soup). It's a bad event (soup). It's an event which was not anticipated (soup). When you eat soup and you expect pieces of meat in it and there are none, it's a catastrophe. When you're on a train (soup) and there's a train coming from the other side with the female cousins which smashes right into it, you are invited and you wear a bunch of flowers and the people who invited you didn't want flowers, they wanted presents and then when you have a soup and you think there's some sausage and there's no sausage. When you're invited ... — and you, I say, what happened to you? (she eats five spoonfuls of soup) — when I have a husband who falls ill (a big spoonful of soup) so what? She resumes: when you go to the dentist — But your husband was ill, I say. — If the husband falls ill, it's serious. She scratches her bowl. Licks her lips. And when he died that was a catastrophe, because he didn't come back any more. God knows where he is now. Now he doesn't come back any more. At the dentist I say Sir I have toothache. So what does he do? He takes a pair of pliers and pulls out my teeth. I say: Sir you mustn't pull them out. I need them to eat. I had all my teeth pulled out. So I said it doesn't matter I have one tooth left. It is good. One tooth is a little too little. But you can't be too choosy. One tooth is better than nothing. I love my tooth. My tooth and I. Otherwise, I would be alone.

This morning, seeing maman trying to catch her breath in vain, I cry, I embrace her. She cries out tenderly: Maman! Little maman. Then confused, as if she wished she did not have to give me back to reality: Hélène! my little Hélène! No. You're not my mum. PITY. Pity resounds for a long time, gravely, like a de profundis. Maman's hands are trembling. Whereas nobody is going to pull out my tooth. It's hard to defend one's tooth. People are all dentists.

Besides, admittedly the audience is crowding on the terraces watching her move forward on the tightrope of the second century while thinking out loud and low that the acrobat is going to fall over. Some who gave her up for good [*donnait chue*] last year are following her footsteps with interest, others have already put away their things and are streaming out since the end is known.

It's hard to walk on a tightrope with feet on which you can't rely any more, maman thinks, people who hold your arms with lobster claws, supposedly to prevent you from falling but who absolutely never put themselves in your place, one walks along surrounded by barely concealed natural death wishes, some have already put the lid back on the dustbin of your character, maman thinks, but her thought unravels, sets out in search of a handkerchief, the handkerchief grows, opens, fills the whole screen of desire. On the screen the little girls' diamond casts animated prisms, little scraps of rainbow scud hither and thither, there are some on the floor also and all the way to the window on the other side of the room traversed by a needle of sun. It's beautiful, it's beautiful. However, the dentists feast on the day's News, minced meat is soaking in a bed of blood, every day somebody's story is taken to bits [*désossée*] what's odd is that the dentists' appetite for steak tartare seems to be insatiable. And yet it's always the same flesh that has been swallowed since the dawn of time.

It is the other childhood. On 4 February, she takes up drawing. She successively draws all the beings, adults, creatures, household friends. The drawings are graceful and extremely small. The characters are one centimetre tall on average. Maman's technique is the following: you start with the chest. You draw a circle. Secondly you line up a vertical row of dots, in the middle of the circle: the buttons. All humans are created with clothes and buttons. When the person is 'big', you draw a big circle in which you sketch two big round breasts very well, with a button in the centre. To draw a cat, start with a curve: the spine, place two small open triangles on the left: ears; put a U tail on the right; add a row of four paws J J J J. The mouth is an upturned Σ. That's it. The cat is a cross between a pig and a fish. Eve draws Eve: 'Eve' is one centimetre tall and she puts a foot forward towards the right-hand side of the page: L. And now where do I go? Eve asks me. Me: You're coming with me. Eve indicates the direction to 'Eve'. She follows God's order: animals, humans.

Eve is going.

And now, where do I go? When the past is too far and the future is much too near, one no longer knows what to do with this life and in this life. It's ridiculous. I give her green beans and pink scissors. Top them. It's long, it's tiring. It's useful. You can't prepare green beans every day. And now? She is no longer a midwife. She is no longer born. She is no longer old. One is old. Old is older in the masculine than in the feminine.[16] Thoughts pass; they are not thoughts. Dreams? Flown away. Cities? Turned to salt and ashes. Remain the names. Osnabrück, Oran, Algiers, Paris, Manchester, defrocked names of incinerated places. — Where are we? — We're in Paris, I say. But I'm not so sure myself. This Paris can hold in one room.

I've got all my teeth, I can't imagine my life without them, without my smile. But nostalgia, in the bathroom, pain, mourning alive and writhing, is the veiled figure of the pitiful promise: she stands up hesitantly, when there is no hope yet. Far beyond despair, but in the not-yet-to-be-hoped, the world stumbles under an eyeless night. Nevertheless, this pain, this phantom cry (for one cries sitting on the ground in the soul's cellar but the cellar already has a window [*soupirail*]) are what is sharpest. I am cooped up, under lock and key, incarcerated outside myself, I dream of my inner forests with tall trunks between which stirs the long snake with the many ocean blues, I do not have the time for what is within, all my time to maman, except for three minutes during which, thoughtful, I brush my teeth. Between my reflection and myself, between my image and my appearance writing creeps in: it is on its way but as invoked, absent like a god. It can and it cannot, may and may not, is wholly in a maybe. And yet, in this barely [*dans l'à peine*], already it is here, a blind deaf mute larva.

In the bathroom where I brush my teeth, just as one sharpens a nib, preparations by a running angel and lover, a sign passes in front of the mirror and I'm looked at. Oh I recognise it so well! It is a word. The word which the forest of words keeps hidden. Invisible but stable. *Death*. Its word is death. I saw it. As one *sees* the invisible murderer: by a slight undeniable shiver which ruffles the soul. It is calm and I am calm. At this moment in time, it is inactive, not unleashed, no firing away [*pas de mitraille*]. Enveloped in a thick sleep and without any dream. Not hurried. I can say it, 'look at' it, write it, with all its stupefying monumental motionless letters, now. It is digesting. Its harmful, contorted period is right behind me. At ease.

For a few weeks, since the stroke on 15 May, I had declared a ban on it. It is a tactic. One acts as if one was not afraid. Its spectre was wandering, seeking to materialise in the house. My soul and myself, and my whole animal being, this little nervous brigade which speaks to itself constantly, we were emitting powerful repulsive rays. Who can say whether it is fear or courage which galvanises us. One makes the other, for it is war. Sometimes the house is a warship and the murderer sneaks into the passageways, in order to go and pierce

16. In the original: *Vieux est plus vieux que vieille* – Trans.

the hull. I note that I can still *see* it at the moment when it has just gone past, these are dark humid waves, the tips of ghostly wolves' paws which scratch in dreams, I can also see the cats seeing these traces below the surface of the visible. They are seated on their behinds, side by side, and their eyes follow something imperceptible in the top right-hand corner. Ruses, understatements, insinuations, the medical staff's sentences are fringed with little silvery viscidities. One moves along, edging forward in preteritions. On 15 May I became a feline prophet. All my hair, standing on end, detects. I went off the road of time and I slipped through the crack into the cave of the present. Squatting near maman, I keep the fire going, with my eye at the loophole [*meurtrière*]. I can sense the coming and going of the Darkness without, true I don't have the moment or the lightness to cast a glance from the corner of my eye at the enemy's manoeuvres, there's way too much to do around the bed. Besides, under the canopy of our shelter, there is nothing but life. This life is as new for me as the island on which one emerges after being shipwrecked. It all changed during the plunge. The short spell in the hospital has the abnormal force and duration of a dream, one comes out of it a *different* person, *on the other side*, still one lives at the same address, but the 'same' does not exist any more, a thin film of mud from the Acheron lines the walls of the house from now on.

Maman moves away, while moving away trembles at being separated from her teeth, my teeth! my teeth! while moving away causes writing to move away.

It's not that I couldn't write, rather it is that two mothers fight for my body, maman and writing, both need all my strengths, my beloved has enormous needs, she devours me, at each moment she threatens to sink and I must hoist her on-board, I don't choose, I am devoted to her, it means hauling her, raising her, restoring, washing, introducing my smile between her pale lips, the need for me to give her my soul to sip, to pour my breaths back into her breathlessness, calls me, my name hisses five hundred times a day, five hundred, that's correct. And I answer: yes yes, a smithy, one saws up silence.

There is no more silence in the house. Boohoo. Hélène! Hélène! Han! Han! And yet writing feeds on the air of silence. I dream about the silences of silence, of their unhurried depths, of the coolness of their foliage which throbs under the sun's burning caresses. Then I dream of cruel abductions by executioners, of bodies pierced with wounds which pour out black blood ceaselessly. Then I wake up and I hear maman's shrill, high-pitched screams. She yells like a woman in labour. The child will be dead. The child whom she announces while yelling: dead. My mother's roar: she fights against the advance of silence, making as many noises as possible in order to frighten it: with the help of cracking, twitching, creaking noises, and especially stridulations. And this braggart's ruction is effective, just as Quixote's sword thrusts rout regiments, the flourishes are struck with surprising strength for somebody whose head is half cardboard. At the top of her voice. Come! Come! Hélène! This means: go away, death! For when I am sitting beside her, she still keeps calling me to frighten the thieves that steal old women. It is the stratagem of her grandmother Helene Meyer, a very impotent, very intelligent old woman. Sitting inertly at the window that looks out onto Nicolaiort (central Osnabrück), for she no longer comes down and lives mentally through this window, she hears someone coming in: The Thief. It is a frightening light touch, on the stairs. Immediately this headstrong woman but with a bound body orders all the generals to charge: Andreas! Moritz! Oscar! Hans! Salo! And all these generals dash forward like one single ghost so that The Thief scampers away. I am maman's five phantom knights. As soon as The Thief brushes past, maman screams five times Hélène! Hélène! Hélène! Hélène! Hélène!

In our story The Thief puts his foot on the step every ten minutes, at least this is what Eve believes. A magic belief. But according to me involuntarily Eve calls the one whom she abhors. Then she throws my name in front of the enemy.

I am mobilized. The others mobilized in the family: Michael Klein, Eve's father. Her husband. Photos of somewhat sad-looking young men who seem to have a premonition that they are going to be killed.

War. And quite as incomprehensible as a 'battle field', amorphous, senseless space, where events succeed one another in a most random fashion, white smoke with indistinct depths, sudden diarrhoeas. Alarms without content.

— What's the matter? Whazzamatter [*Quèsquispasse*]? maman asks. One would like to know. We are being sniped at. Bleeded. Thick black sticky blood. The following day: an ideal spring all over the earth, sheaths of bright-yellow dwarf ginestra, one thinks the strafing [*mitraillage*], the end was but a dream, one lives while laughing, whole, I look at maman lapping up her soup. One does not understand. At that moment a shell [*obus*] falls on the table.

It is a fight whose rules I do not know. My ignorance weakens me: I am fought, at night dream attacks cause infamous damage to my image, my body is taken as a target as if I were guilty of maman. I resist blindly. Only at the end of the bombardment do I reconstruct the event. Slowly I make out: 'somebody' (but it is a being as vast as night's formlessness, which is everywhere) is trying to abduct maman. A big limp muscular force snatches her and drags her downwards. Maman thrashes about, her body partly inside time's thick-lipped, slobbery maw which gulps her down very slowly, a crafty, frightening slowness.

Panic terror in the lift and in whatever has the shape of a small box moving down, and what if it was going to sink below the earth?

In the evening I put up barricades around her bed, I pile up chairs.

She was always Courage itself, but here no Courage has the means to oppose the Threat. Monstrous movements of slimy sands suck away at her.

— I am lost, she says. — Therefore it means you're not lost, I say. But I slowly understand that one can be lost otherwise: separated from all times and weathers. One never manages to be in a dry place.

8-7-11

Morning truce. She's asleep. Still here. Around the bed a chaos of chairs and cans. There was a ghost last night. At least as long as she is not awake, the enemy sleeps too. The two camps restore their strengths.

I am *always* afraid. I sleep only in short naps of half an hour. Sometimes I start to shake. This gives the moments of peace an intoxicating flavour. Even a happiness, detached, ahuman.

Everybody is waiting.

For what?

One can't say. One is waiting for what one doesn't want to expect.

Eve says: No! No, no! No. — What do you say No to?

She says: No! Forcefully. That's all. Everybody is waiting. Eve is the main character. The verdict has been pronounced. One doesn't know exactly which one, which day. She received the notice. Not in a hurry to open the envelope. Not obliged. Not tempted. Not signed.

Everybody is waiting.

Sitting on the bowl, her bare legs stained with dark blotches of old blood, vast areas of dark countries on a crumpled world map, says: I'm lost.

— I see and there's nothing. I see nothing.

She sees, separately. Things do not speak to her — Flowers? I say. Even flowers, sometimes, lost [*perdue, perdues*]. However, sometimes flowers wave their bright red flags, she sees them, and they are flowers.

State of being lost: one is outside, there is no outside, there is no way in, no inside, no home of one's own, the tongue is in the mouth, feels [*tâte*]. The world is far, it goes on, illegible. Some red flowers signal. The brioche too, allows one to get near, all the rest attacks you. In the toilet: it's locked! Eve complains. The lavatory lid, another locked door, illegible face. — Where are you taking me? We walk towards the bedroom. West-South-West. Three more steps. Planes fly low towards us. Eve attempts slowly to run. We surrender. Too hard. — Where do I sit? I show the embankment of the sofa with my hand: over there. She stumbles. We wait.

Eve empty inside. Desert inner landscape: a bowl Beckett style. Main, central and unique furniture.

To fill the void with dry bitter little noises, monotonous pecks at the white earthenware. Han! Han! Han! Regular. Not to take your mind off while looking at memories. Eve lodges a complaint. Complaint! Complaint! Complaint!

Three cities

— I'm lost, here. I can't see the cats any more. The books? No. She holds the books upside down. Dead fish. Lost! — Where? In a city? In a forest? — In a city, in a forest. Can you help me? — To do what? — I must come back, maman says. *Come back*. My head is far. She explains to me: *me*, I am lost.

I begin to understand. — Do not forget *me*.

I look for the eyes of *me*: — Can you see me? I say. I'm here, in front of you. — You are *here* and *I* am *elsewhere*. My head is upside down.

So I set off in search for her. Let's sum up, I say: — In which city were you born? — Koenigsberg, says maman. — Koenigsberg? Then that means we're really totally lost. I get worried. She sees how distraught I look. Tries to get back on track. — Koenigsberg, is it not? Then Osnabrück? — If you wish, I say. After all, if I whispered Strasbourg to her, it would be as worrying as Koenigsberg. — Where do you live? I dared. — Berlin. No? that's not it.

— At least you know a little what isn't, I say. However, she would leave Berlin regretfully; or else that's because she's held back there. We therefore live in Berlin for some time. A feeling of detention breaks out like a fever. — What am I doing in Berlin? Help me.

Don't leave me alone in Berlin. I'm afraid you might forget me. — I'll go with you, I say. But that would not calm her down. To bring her back to Paris? I hold her hand firmly. I pull. We clamber up a dark slope which leads to 'Paris'. — It's hard. — A few more steps, I say. Paris doesn't come. When we reach the top the landscape is but a vast bowl devoured by storms. The sight of this non-landscape frightens me. I ask the passers-by who seem at home to take us back down. If only they could drop us off at rue Bab Azoun in Algiers, maman would perhaps find our way back. I could buy a paraffin lamp to light the way all along the dark boulevard.

— Prague? — No. — New York? — No — London? No.

Me — Pa- …? — Ris! she says triumphantly. You see? You can see that I'm lost without you, I only have the end. Bring me back nearer you, hold me back! You tell me I'm not lost since I know that I'm lost, you don't see that I'm all the more lost since I lose everything but the experience of loss, I am in distress [*en perdition*], the river is swallowing me up slowly while I'm getting a mouthful [*bois la tasse*] of the Lethe, I drink and it drinks me [*je suis bue*].

My teeth! Give me back my teeth, without my teeth I am without oars, rudderless, without me. Fo, fo, fo, fo, Forgetting drinks me, I'll soon be totally drowned. If you forget me, I'll never be any more.

— Put me to bed. Lying in bed saved lost, the reassuring bed but under the bed the demons ponder their dirty tricks, the hull floats on the side, I pull up maman just in time, she does not know whether she will come back from this journey, in what state, perhaps never. Perhaps never. She is keen on dislodging her fears:[17]

— It's over, she says severely. — What is over? I question, insistent, serious. It's over. Itsover [*Séfinie. Céfini*]. Erect, the small sentence, slim, closed, open, mocking, snaps shut in the nondescript near-open country where I sink endlessly into a sandy soil which bears no indication. I am in a distraught state which develops cruelly, I move forward helplessly, I have nothing to sustain me [*pour tout viatique*] but my glasses and seven pages of an exercise-book.

Explain to me, I say. I look at the very old woman being gnawed, shrivelled, furrowed toothless, whose right eye darts an indisputable force. It can't be life that is over. The worn-out recumbent being is still emitting. So what is?

Life's plan? Without which no life, Kleist asserts violently. Life would be life truly alive only if it was *led* into battle, conquering, towards a sovereign goal.

Then this recumbent furrowed life this pure goalless stubbornness of a life, which stays, is perhaps nothing more than the sloughed, empty skin of what was once an unbeatable, glorious life? And yet she is hungry. Hunger and the healing of hunger would be another plan? What's there to eat?

— What is over? I say. — Nothing, says maman. Coffee with milk.

17. In the original, the French *déposer crainte* puns on *déposer plainte*: to lodge a complaint, hence the translation – Trans.

It is midnight. The man who comes to pick up the midwife my mother is shaking. What if she were to refuse? It is forbidden to go out in wartime. The woman in labour yells in the distance in a lightless waterless cubbyhole. Eve gets up, arms herself, bag, shoes [*godasses*], pocket lamp, the man is shaking beside Eve at the wheel of his 4 CV. On the way back, my mother says, I was completely in the dark, I was driven around in this streetless district for an hour without finding my way, under curfew reality has all the features of my horrendous dreams, the road is not a road, in the middle of time a cardboard box appears stuffed full of explosives, that was long ago, but finally maman is lying in bed [*couchée*], the delivery [*accouchement*] went fine.

It's eight o'clock. The light shines across six planes of different foliage. A painter is needed, straightaway, to preserve this glistening pink colour which washes the hands with the magnolia leaves. I kiss her hand lightly. 'Maman's hand'. Who will paint this? A disproportionate, grown limb, a wide grip gloved in bruised tissue. Patches of congealed blood speckle what used to be a skin. The face is pockmarked with dozens of brownish growths over the whole surface, except the forehead. Old age weaves its small dark-brown flags. Primacy of earthen colours. Bluish sienna scabs. The fungal wins, its kind neither animal nor vegetable, face of another reign. You are already mine, says the earth. I kiss the earthy cheek; I introduce the breath [*haleine*] of love below the earth. The eye opens: 'it's time?' The eye shines towards me. An eye towards light. An eye below the earth. The stocky, grown, wide and shapeless tongue fills in the sagging opening of the mouth [*embouchure*], stirs, an agile gastropod. Distinctly: 'I'm afraid'.

— What makes you afraid? Where shall I place the fear-driver [*chasse-peur*]? Maman's mind crumples an old smile: 'I'm not afraid'.

August 2011

Opposite: Janine Antoni, *eve*, 2017. © Janine Antoni. Courtesy of the artist and Luhring Augustine, New York.

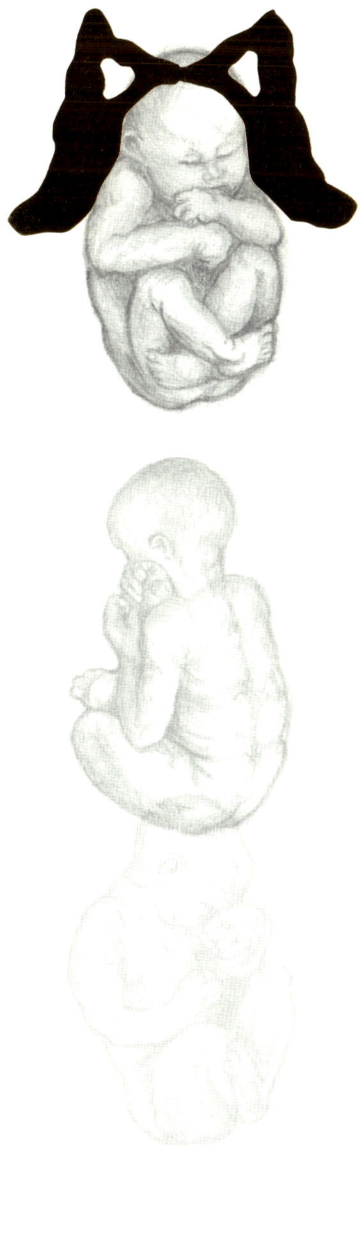

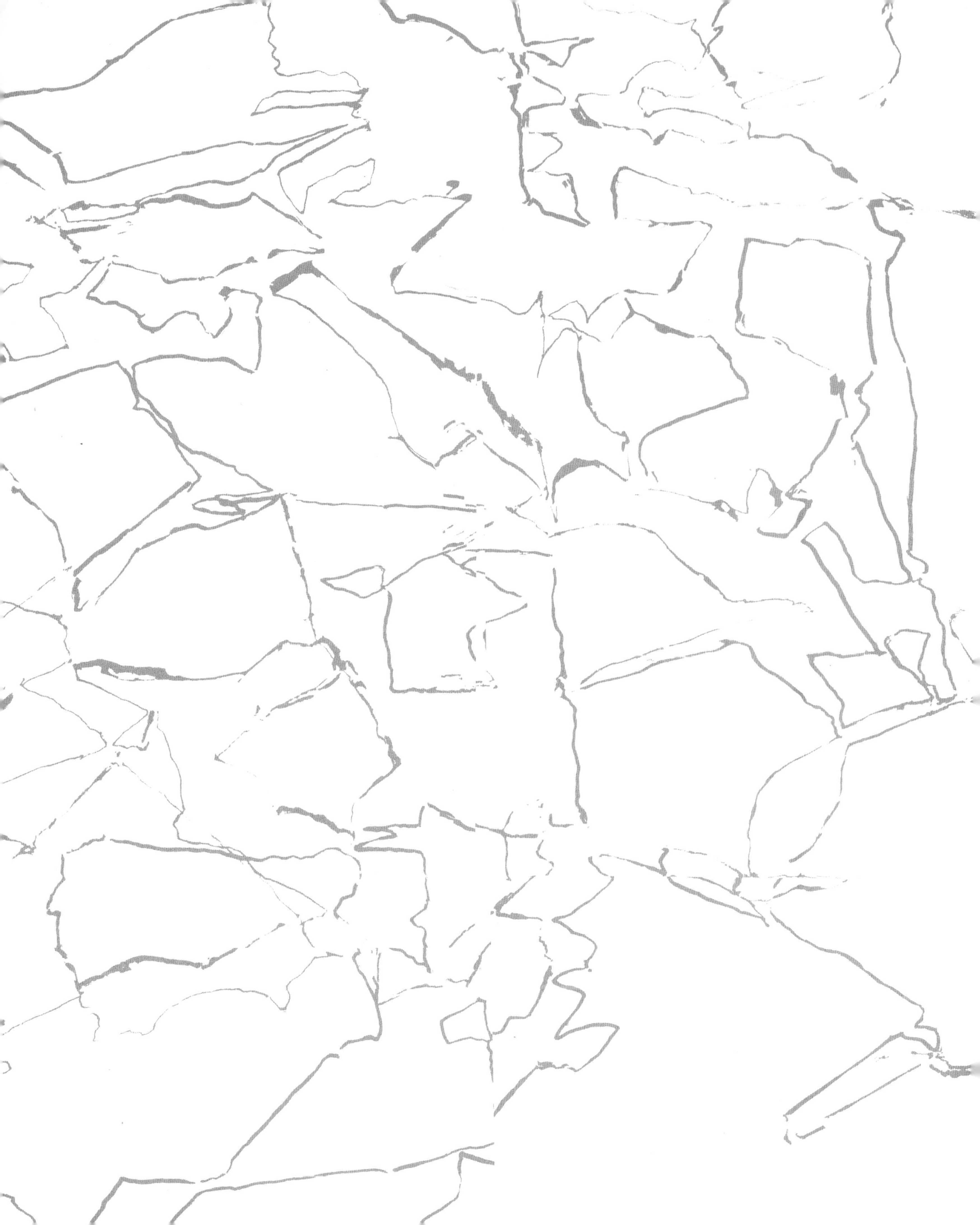

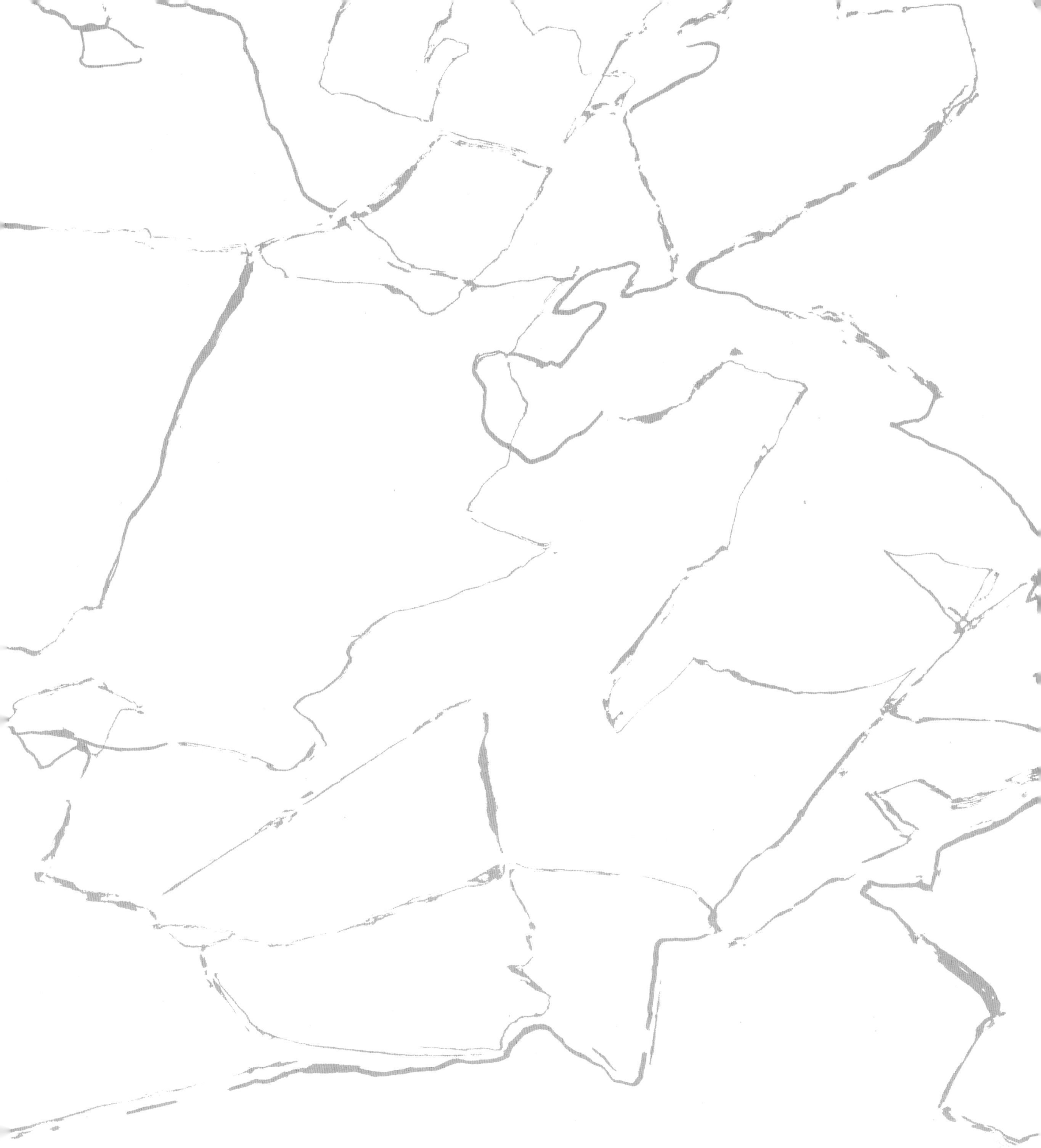

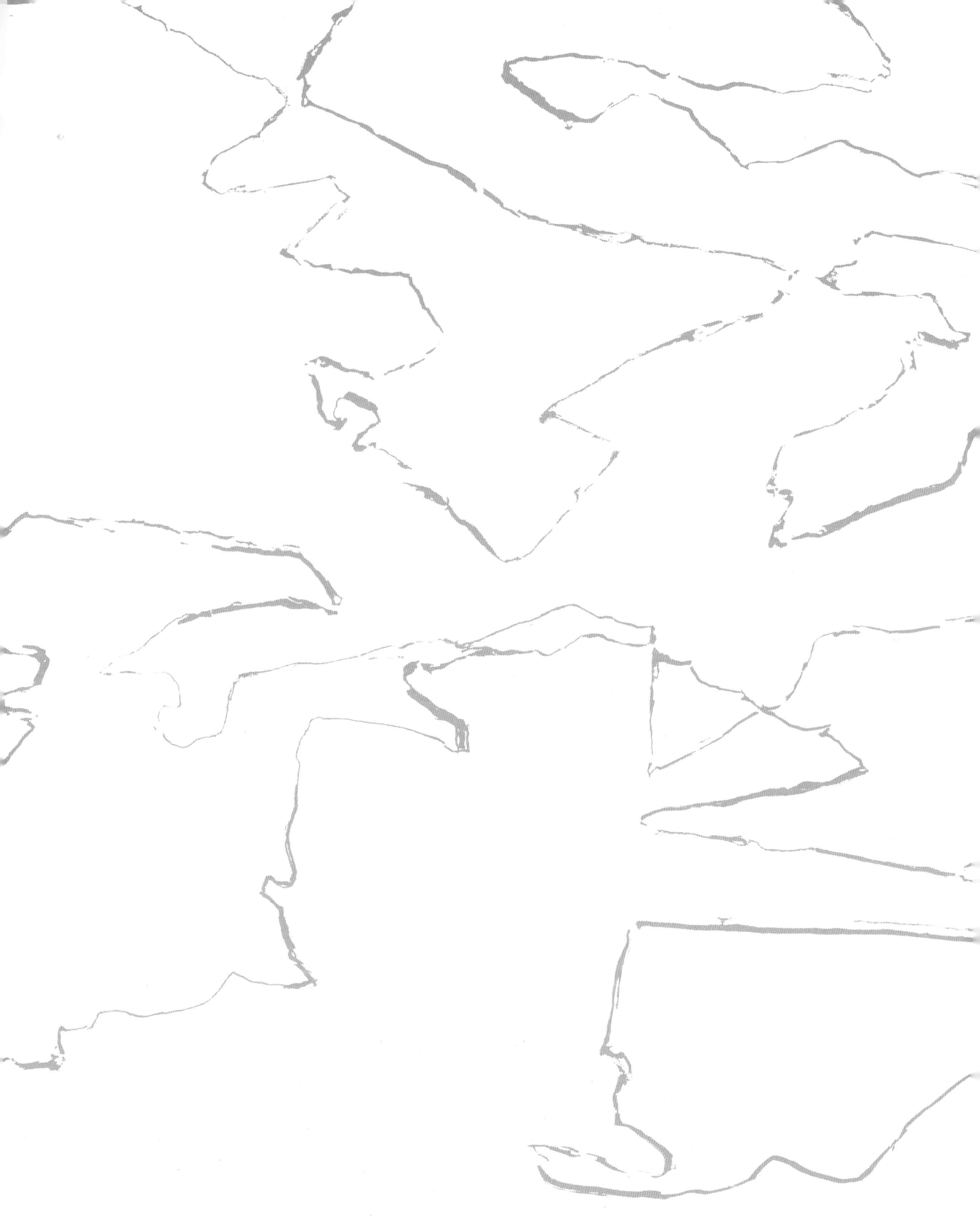

BIOGRAPHIES

Janine Antoni

Janine Antoni is a sculptor and performance artist who was born in Freeport, Bahamas in 1964. She received a BA from Sarah Lawrence College and an MFA from the Rhode Island School of Design. She is known for her unusual processes. Her body is both her tool for making and the source from which her meaning arises. Antoni's early work transformed materials like chocolate and soap, and used everyday activities like bathing, eating, and sleeping as sculptural processes. She carefully articulates her relationship to the world, giving rise to emotional states that are felt in and through the senses. In each piece, no matter the medium or image, a conveyed physicality speaks directly to the viewer's body.

Her work shows nationally and internationally. Antoni has exhibited at numerous major institutions including documenta 14, at the Fridericianum, Kassel, the Venice Biennale, the Whitney Biennial, the Johannesburg Biennial, the Istanbul Biennial, the Kwangju Biennial and the SITE Santa Fe Biennial.

Her work is included in the collections of the National Gallery of Art, Washington, DC; Museum of Modern Art, New York; The Whitney Museum of American Art, New York; The Israel Museum, Jerusalem; Guggenheim Museum, New York; The San Francisco Museum of Modern Art, San Francisco; Art Institute of Chicago, Chicago; Hirshhorn Museum and Sculpture Garden, Washington, DC; Magasin 3 Stockholm Konsthall, Stockholm; Sammlung Goetz, Munich; Astrup Fearnley Museet for Moderne Kunst, Oslo; and The Museum of Contemporary Art, Los Angeles.

Antoni is the recipient of several prestigious awards, including the Irish Museum of Modern Art/Glen Dimplex Artist Award in 1996, a John D. and Catherine T. MacArthur Fellowship in 1998, the Larry Aldrich Foundation Award in 1999, The John Simon Guggenheim Memorial Foundation Fellowship in 2011, a 2012 Creative Capital Artist Grant, and Anonymous Was A Woman Grant in 2014. In 2016, Antoni collaborated with Anna Halprin and Stephen Petronio on *Ally*, an exhibition presented by The Fabric Workshop and Museum, Philadelphia, with major support from The Pew Center for Arts & Heritage.

Antoni currently resides in New York and is represented by Luhring Augustine, NY, and Anthony Meier Fine Art, San Francisco.

Anna Halprin

For over seventy years Anna Halprin has created revolutionary directions for dance, inspiring artists in all fields. Richard Schechner, editor of *The Drama Review*, calls her "one of the most important and original thinkers in performance." Through her students Trisha Brown, Yvonne Rainer, and Simone Forti, Halprin strongly influenced New York's seminal Judson Dance Theater. She also collaborated with such innovative musicians as Terry Riley, La Monte Young, and Morton Subotnik, and poets Richard Brautigan, James Broughton, and Michael McClure. Other artists who have studied with her include Chip Lord, Meredith Monk, Eiko and Koma, Wanda Coleman, Carrie Mae Weems, and Dohee Lee.

Defying traditional notions of dance, Halprin has extended its boundaries to address social issues, build community, foster physical and emotional healing, and connect people to nature. She formed the first U.S. multiracial dance company and highlighted social justice themes. Diagnosed with cancer in the early 1970s, she used dance to aid her healing and then created innovative dance programs for cancer and AIDS patients. An early pioneer in using expressive arts for healing, she cofounded the Tamalpa Institute with her daughter Daria in 1978, and today it fosters dance as a healing and peace-making force worldwide. Increasingly, Anna's performances moved out of the theater into the community. Her *Planetary Dance* — open to everyone — has promoted peace among people and peace with the Earth for over thirty-six years in countries worldwide.

Her many honors include the Doris Duke Impact Award and Isadora Duncan Dance Award in 2014. In 2017 her work was shown at the 57th International Art Exhibition of La Biennale di Venezia and at documenta 14, as well as in the exhibit *Radical Bodies: Anna Halprin, Simone Forti, Yvonne Rainer*, in Santa Barbara and New York. Her work has also been featured in shows at MoMA PS1, Centre Pompidou, and ZKM Museum, among other venues.

Stephen Petronio

For over thirty years, Stephen Petronio has honed a unique language of movement that speaks to the intuitive and complex possibilities of the body informed by its shifting cultural context. He has collaborated with a wide range of artists in many disciplines over his career and considers the integration of multiple forms as fundamental to his creative drive and vision. Petronio was born in Newark, New Jersey, and received a B.A. from Hampshire College in Amherst, Massachusetts, where he began his early training in improvisation and dance technique. He was greatly influenced by working with Steve Paxton and was the first male dancer in the Trisha Brown Dance Company (1979–1986). He has gone on to build a unique career, receiving numerous accolades, including a John Simon Guggenheim Fellowship, awards from the Foundation for Contemporary Performance Arts, the New York Foundation for the Arts, an American Choreographer Award, a New York Dance and Performance "Bessie" Award, and most recently a 2015 Doris Duke Performing Artist Award.

Petronio, whose training originated with leading figures of the Judson era, performed *Man Walking Down the Side of a Building* in 2010 for the Trisha Brown Company at the Whitney Museum, and performed his 2012 rendition of Steve Paxton's *Intravenous Lecture* (1970) in New York, Portland, and at the TEDMED-2012 conference at the Kennedy Center Opera House in Washington, DC. His numerous collaborators have included composers Son Lux, Lou Reed, Laurie Anderson and Nico Muhly, visual artists Anish Kapoor and Cindy Sherman, lighting designer Ken Tabachnick, and commissions outside his company with Serj Tankian and Atticus Ross, director Diane Paulus, writer and lyricist Steven Sater, photographer Matthew Brandt.

Petronio has been entangled with visual artist Janine Antoni in a number of discipline-blurring projects, including the video installation *Honey Baby* (2013), created in collaboration with composer Tom Laurie and filmmaker Kirsten Johnson. Petronio and Antoni were the 2017 McCormack Artists in Residence at Skidmore College. In 2014, Petronio published his memoir, *Confessions of a Motion Addict* (CreateSpace, 2014).

Adrian Heathfield writes on, curates and creates performance. His books include *Out of Now* (Live Art Development Agency & MIT Press, 2009), a monograph on the Taiwanese-American artist Tehching Hsieh, and the edited collections *Perform, Repeat, Record* (Intellect Books & University of Chicago Press, 2012), *Live: Art and Performance* (Tate Publishing, 2004), *Small Acts* (Black Dog Publishing, 2000) and *Shattered Anatomies* (Arnolfini Live, 1997). His numerous essays have been translated into eight languages. He co-curated the *Live Culture* events at Tate Modern, London (2003) and a number of other performance and durational events in European cities over the last eighteen years. He was a curatorial adviser and attaché for the 20th Biennale of Sydney, an artistic director with the collective *freethought* of the 2016 Bergen Assembly, Norway, and curator of Taiwan's exhibition, *Doing Time*, at the Biennale Arte 2017, Venice. He was President of Performance Studies international (2004–2007) and is Professor of Performance and Visual Culture at the University of Roehampton, London.

Hélène Cixous' experiments in writing, including the development of *l'écriture féminine* for which she is renowned, have had wide-ranging influence on the fields of cultural theory, feminism, philosophy, literary criticism and theater practice. She was Andrew D. White Professor-at-Large at Cornell University, New York from 2008–2014 and is currently Professor Emerita of English Literature and Women's Studies at the Université Paris 8.

Carol Becker is Professor of the Arts and Dean of Columbia University School of the Arts. Previously, she was Dean of The School of the Art Institute of Chicago. She is author of *The Invisible Drama: Women and the Anxiety of Change* (Macmillan, 1987; CreateSpace, 2013); *The Subversive Imagination: Artists, Society and Social Responsibility* (Routledge, 1994); *Zones of Contention: Essays on Art, Institutions, Gender, and Anxiety* (State University of New York Press, 1996); *Surpassing the Spectacle: Global Transformations and the Changing Politics of Art* (Rowman & Littlefield, 2001); *Thinking in Place: Art, Action, and Cultural Production* (Paradigm, 2009); and *Losing Helen* (Red Hen Press, 2016). Among other publications, she has written for *Art in America*, *Huffington Post*, *Time* magazine, *Performing Arts Journal*, *Truthout*, and the World Economic Forum blog. She travels widely, often lecturing on the evolving role of art in society.

Jacquelynn Baas is Emeritus Director of the University of California Berkeley Art Museum and Pacific Film Archive, having served as Director (1988–99). Previously, she served as founding director of the Hood Museum of Art, Dartmouth College (1982–88). In 2000 Baas co-founded the arts consortium, Awake: Art, Buddhism, and the Dimensions of Consciousness, which over the course of its five-year existence generated some fifty exhibitions, educational programs, artist residencies, and two books: *Buddha Mind in Contemporary Art* (University of California Press, 2004) and *Smile of the Buddha: Eastern Philosophy and Western Art from Monet to Today* (University of California Press, 2005). She has organized over thirty exhibitions, including *The Independent Group: Postwar Britain and the Aesthetics of Plenty* (1990) and *Fluxus and the Essential Questions of Life* (2011, voted Best Show in a University Gallery by the International Association of Art Critics). Baas has published, lectured, and conducted numerous workshops on subjects ranging from the Mexican muralists, to Asian perspectives in European and American art, to modern and contemporary art and architecture. Her most recent essay, "Agnes Martin: Readings for Writings," appears in the catalogue for the exhibition, *Agnes Martin* (Tate Modern, 2015).

Richard Move is Artistic Director of the interdisciplinary performance collective, MoveOpolis! He is a TEDGlobal Oxford Fellow and Assistant Professor of Drama, Theatre and Dance at Queens College, CUNY. Move's commissions include productions for Mikhail Baryshnikov and the White Oak Dance Project, Martha Graham Dance Company, American Festival of Paris, Florence Opera Ballet of Italy, European Cultural Capitol, Guggenheim Museum, Deborah Harry and Blondie, Dame Shirley Bassey, Isaac Mizrahi and New York City Ballet's Helene Alexopolous. His films include: *Bardo*, Jury Prize nominee at Lincoln Center's Dance on Camera Festival, *BloodWork – The Ana Mendieta Story*, National Board of Review Award/ Directors Guild of America, *GhostLight*, Tribeca Film Festival premiere and *GIMP – The Documentary*, Lincoln Center Dance on Camera Festival premiere. *Martha@...*, Move's performance as 20th Century icon, Martha Graham, received two New York Dance and Performance Awards ("Bessies") and tours internationally. His scholarly publications include a chapter for the *Oxford Handbook of Dance and Reenactment* (Oxford University Press, 2017). Move received his M.F.A. in Media Arts Production from The City College of New York, CUNY and he is completing his Ph.D. in Performance Studies at New York University in 2018.

Laurent Milesi is Tenured Professor of English Literature and Critical Theory at Shanghai Jiao Tong University and a member of the ITEM-CNRS Research Group on James Joyce's manuscripts in Paris. He has written extensively on Joyce and related aspects of modernism, 20th-century (American) poetry, postmodernism and poststructuralism, especially on Jacques Derrida and Hélène Cixous. His edited collection, *James Joyce and the Difference of Language*, was published by Cambridge University Press in 2003. He has translated several works by Jacques Derrida: (with Stefan Herbrechter) *H. C. pour la vie, c'est à dire...* (Stanford University Press, 2006) and by Hélène Cixous: *Le Voisin de zéro* (Polity, 2010), *Philippines* (Polity, 2011), *Tombe* (Seagull Books, 2014). He is currently completing a monograph titled *Jacques Derrida and the Ethics of Writing*. He is one of the general editors for the *Theory, Culture and Politics* book series at Rowman and Littlefield International and Editor in Chief for the international journal *Word and Text - A Journal of Literary Studies and Linguistics*.

Kirsten Johnson (The Mother) is a filmmaker and cinematographer, whose most recent film *Cameraperson* is distributed by the Criterion Collection. *Cameraperson* was named One of the Ten Best Films of 2016 by the *New York Times* and the *Washington Post*. It was shortlisted for an Academy Award, won the National Board of Review Freedom of Expression Award and won the Cinema Eye Outstanding Nonfiction Feature Award. Viva and Felix (The Twins) are now five years old and about to begin kindergarten.

Gregory Pardlo (The Poet) is the author of *Digest* (Four Way Books, 2014), winner of the 2015 Pulitzer Prize for Poetry, and *Air Traffic*, a memoir forthcoming in 2018.

Tim Kilker (The Mole) was born in 1967 to Thomas and Katherine Kilker. He grew up in the town of Mahopac where he and his wife of twenty years raise their five children. He is a sandhog (a construction worker on underground excavation projects, including tunneling in the New York City Subway system).

Michael Vincent Miller (The Listener), PhD, is a psychotherapist who practices in New York City. He is the author of *Intimate Terrorism* (W. W. Norton & Co., Inc., 1995) and *Teaching a Paranoid to Flirt* (Gestalt Journal Press, 2011).

Winston T. Cheng (The Mender), MS, CCC-SLP, BCS-S is a speech-language pathologist and a Board-certified specialist in swallowing disorders. He specializes in managing patients with voice and swallowing disorders in New York City.

Stephanie Berger (The Framer) has been photographing performance and cultural events for over twenty-five years for cultural centers such as Lincoln Center, the Brooklyn Academy of Music, Carnegie Hall, Park Avenue Armory, Met Museum, Dia Art Foundation, Baryshnikov Arts Center and The Kitchen. Her photographs appear regularly in a wide range of publications, including the *New York Times*, *Artforum* and the *Wall Street Journal*. She recently published her first book of photographs, *Merce Cunningham: Beyond the Perfect Stage* (Damiani Press, 2016).

Susan Klein (The Healer) is founder and developer of Klein Technique™, a movement practice aimed at teaching dancers/people how to use their bodies correctly to increase efficiency, power, and excellence in movement, while diminishing injuries. Susan is also a Worsley Style 5 Element Acupuncturist, a faculty member of the Zero Balancing Health Association and a practitioner of Zero Balancing. She teaches groups and private sessions at the Susan Klein School of Movement and Dance in NYC.

Sam Gregory (The Defendant) is a criminal defense attorney in New York. Sam is also the director of The Brooklyn to Alaska Project, a nonprofit that takes urban youth to the wilderness of Alaska on a two-week adventure.

The Fabric Workshop and Museum (FWM) was founded in 1977 with a visionary purpose: to stimulate experimentation among leading contemporary artists and to share the process of creating works of art with the public. Providing studio facilities, equipment, and expert technicians, FWM originally invited artists to experiment with fabric and later with a wide range of innovative materials and media. From the outset, FWM has also served as an education center for Philadelphia's youth who, as printing apprentices, learn technical and vocational skills along with approaches to creative expression.

Today, FWM is recognized as an internationally acclaimed contemporary art museum, distinguished as the only institution in the United States devoted to creating work with textiles and new media in collaboration with artists from diverse artistic backgrounds including sculpture, installation, video, painting, ceramics, and architecture. Research, construction, and fabrication occur on-site in studios that are open to the public, providing visitors an opportunity to see art being made from conception to completion. In fact, FWM's permanent collection includes not only complete works of art but also material research, samples, prototypes, and photography and video of artists making and speaking about their work. FWM seeks to bring this spirit of artistic investigation and discovery to the wider public and to area schoolchildren in particular, to ensure and broaden their access to art and to advance the role of art as a catalyst for innovation and social connection. FWM offers an unparalleled experience to the most significant artists of our time and to students and the general public.

ACKNOWLEDGMENTS

For work on the exhibition, the artists would like to thank:

The Fabric Workshop and Museum and the following staff members

Marion Bolton "Kippy" Stroud, Founder and artistic director (1977–2015)

Susan Lubowsky Talbott, Executive Director

Kate Abercrombie, Printing Production Manager/Master Printer

Carlos Avendaño, Photographer / Photo Archivist

Tracey Blackman, Director of Facilities & Museum Shop

Paige Fetchen, Project Technician (Stage Manager for all performances, Seamstress for *The Courtesan and the Crone* robe)

Stephanie Alison Greene, Associate Director for Administration

Justin Hall, Registrar

Brittany Rafalak, Former Visual Media Production Coordinator/Videographer (Sound editor for *Swallow*)

Patrick Smith, Former Manager of Technology and Visual Media

Alec Unkovic, Exhibitions Manager

Nami Yamamoto, Director of Studio Operations (Weaver of the fabric swallowed by the artists)

Creative Capital
Sean Elwood, former Director, Programmes and Initiatives
Ruby Lerner, Founder and former Executive Director and President

The Pew Center for Arts & Heritage
Bill Bissell, Director of Performance
Paula Marincola, Executive Director

The National Endowment for the Arts

LLWW Foundation

The Shipley Miller Foundation

The John Simon Guggenheim Memorial Foundation, Guggenheim Fellowship 2011

Independent Curation and Dramaturgy
Adrian Heathfield

***Rope Dance* (audio and visual)**
Hugo Glendinning, editing
Richard Neill, filming
Claudia Katayanagi, sound recording

***Paper Dance* (crates)**
Art Crating Inc.
Atelier 4, Inc.
Red Hook Crating

***Paper Dance* (dance floor)**
Joy Feasley and Paul Swenbeck, Wormwood and Haze

***Swallow* (Witnesses)**
Stephanie Berger
Winston Cheng
Sam Gregory
Kristen, Viva, and Felix Johnson
Tim Kilker
Susan Klein
Dr. Michael Vincent Miller
Greg Pardlo

***Swallow* (object)**
Yogi Charu, instructor
Shane and Julia Stratton, reliquary fabricators, Stratton Sculpture Studios
Marcia L. Weiss, weaving mentor, Associate Professor, Textile Design, University of Philadelphia

***Swallow* (chairs)**
Scott Currie, carpenter

***Swallow* (document)**
Pat Kelley, moth expert, Insects Limited
Thomas A. Parker, PhD, entomologist, moth expert, Pest Control Services, Inc.

Studio of Janine Antoni
Holli McEntegart
Naomi Mishkin
Suzanne Peck
Amanda Valdez

Stephen Petronio Company
Yvan Greenberg

Anna Halprin Studio
Stephanie Earle
Sherri Mills

Luhring Augustine
Roland Augustine
Lawrence Luhring
Natalia Sacasa

Anthony Meier Fine Art
Anthony Meier

Paul Ramirez Jonas
Indra Ramirez Antoni
Brian Pinkney
The Halprin family
Jean-Marc Flack

For work on this publication, the artists would like to thank:

Editor: Adrian Heathfield
Designer: David Caines
Editorial Assistant: Emma Leach
Photographic Documentation of *Paper Dance*, *Swallow*, *Rope Dance* and *The Courtesan and the Crone*: Carlos Avendaño
Photographic Advice: Hugo Glendinning
Proofreader: Lawrence Wells
Writers: Carol Becker, Richard Move, Jacquelynn Baas, Hélène Cixous

The editor would like to thank the artists and essayists, David Caines, Hugo Glendinning, Bill Bissell, Paula Marincola, Emma Leach, Lawrence Wells, Branislava Kuburović and Noémie Solomon for their support in the making of this publication.

Adrian Heathfield's editorial and curatorial work on *Ally* was supported by a Marie Curie International Fellowship held at Columbia University School of the Arts, funded by the European Union's Seventh Framework Programme for research, technological development and demonstration under grant agreement no 329451.

This book was published in relation to the exhibition *Ally*, organized by
The Fabric Workshop and Museum, April 21, 2016–July 31, 2016.

Published in 2017 by The Fabric Workshop and Museum
and Hirmer Publishers

The Fabric Workshop and Museum
1214 Arch Street, Philadelphia, PA 19107

www.fabricworkshopandmuseum.org

Hirmer Verlag GmbH
Nymphenburger Str. 84
D-80636 Munich Germany

www.hirmerverlag.de/eu/

Designed by David Caines
Cover and endpaper photographs © Hugo Glendinning
Documentary photographs of *Paper Dance*, *Swallow*, *Rope Dance* and
The Courtesan and the Crone are copyright and courtesy of the artists and FWM.
Premiered in collaboration with The Fabric Workshop and Museum, 2016.

Printed and bound in Italy.

Library of Congress Control Number: 2017954258

A CIP catalogue record for this book is available from the British Library.

ISBN: 978-3-7774-2952-6

Major support for *Ally* has been provided by The Pew Center for Arts & Heritage. Initial support for this project was provided by Creative Capital. This project was supported in part by an award from the National Endowment for the Arts, with additional support from the LLWW Foundation and Harvey S. Shipley Miller, The Shipley Miller Foundation.

Major support of FWM is provided by the Marion Boulton "Kippy" Stroud Foundation. FWM receives state arts funding support through a grant from the Pennsylvania Council on the Arts, a state agency funded by the Commonwealth of Pennsylvania and the National Endowment for the Arts, a federal agency. Additional operational support is provided by the Philadelphia Cultural Fund, Agnes Gund, and the Board of Directors and Members of FWM.

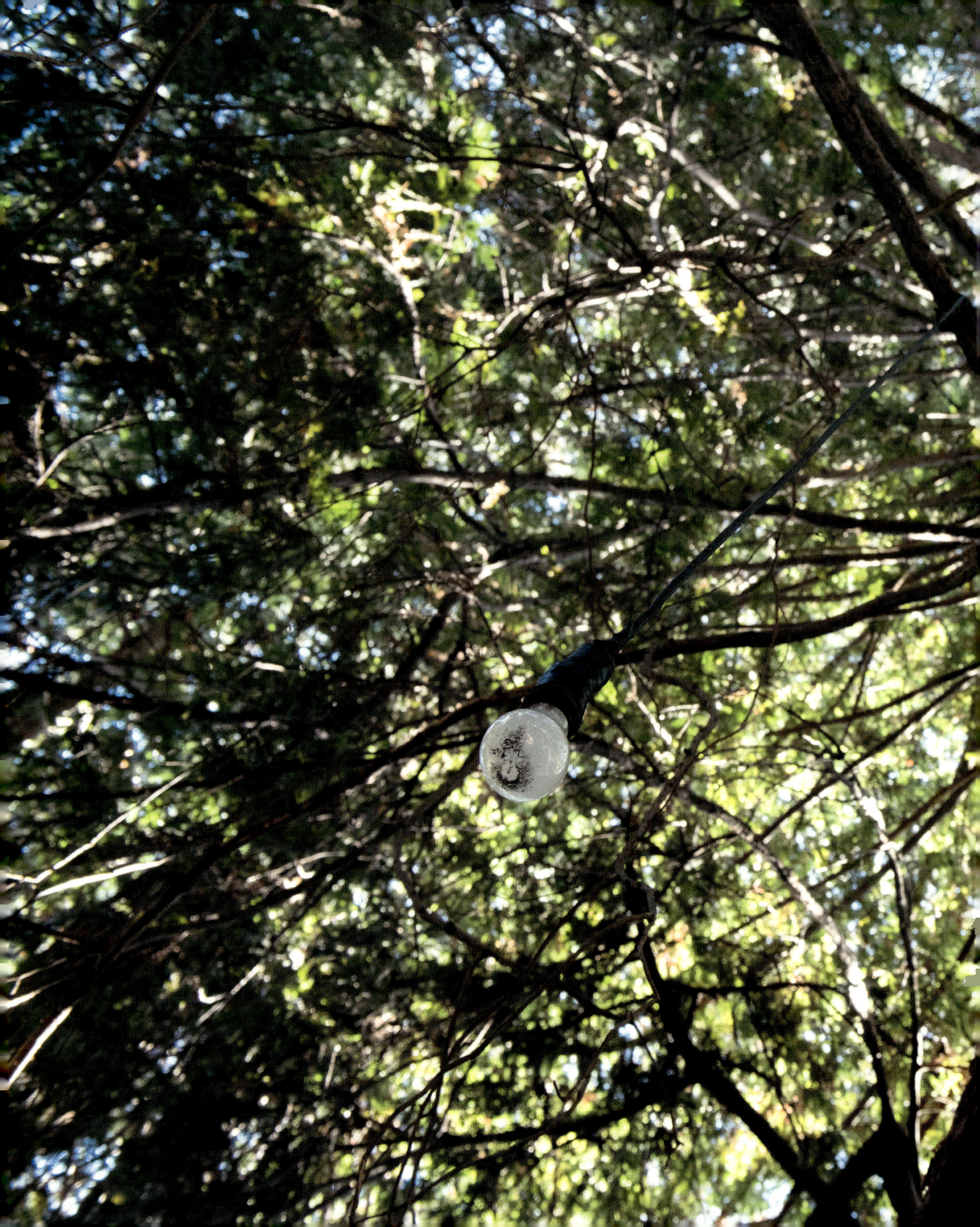

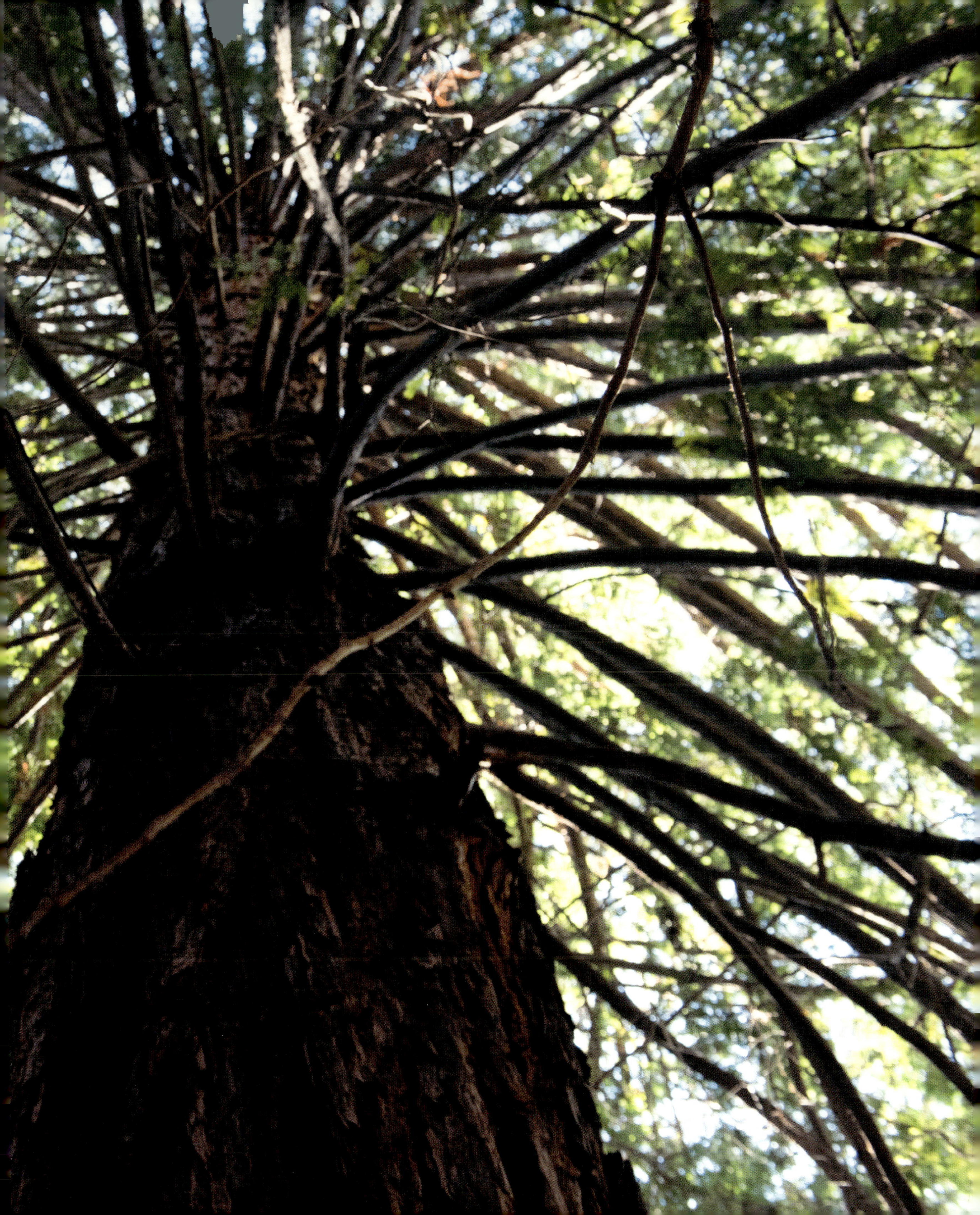

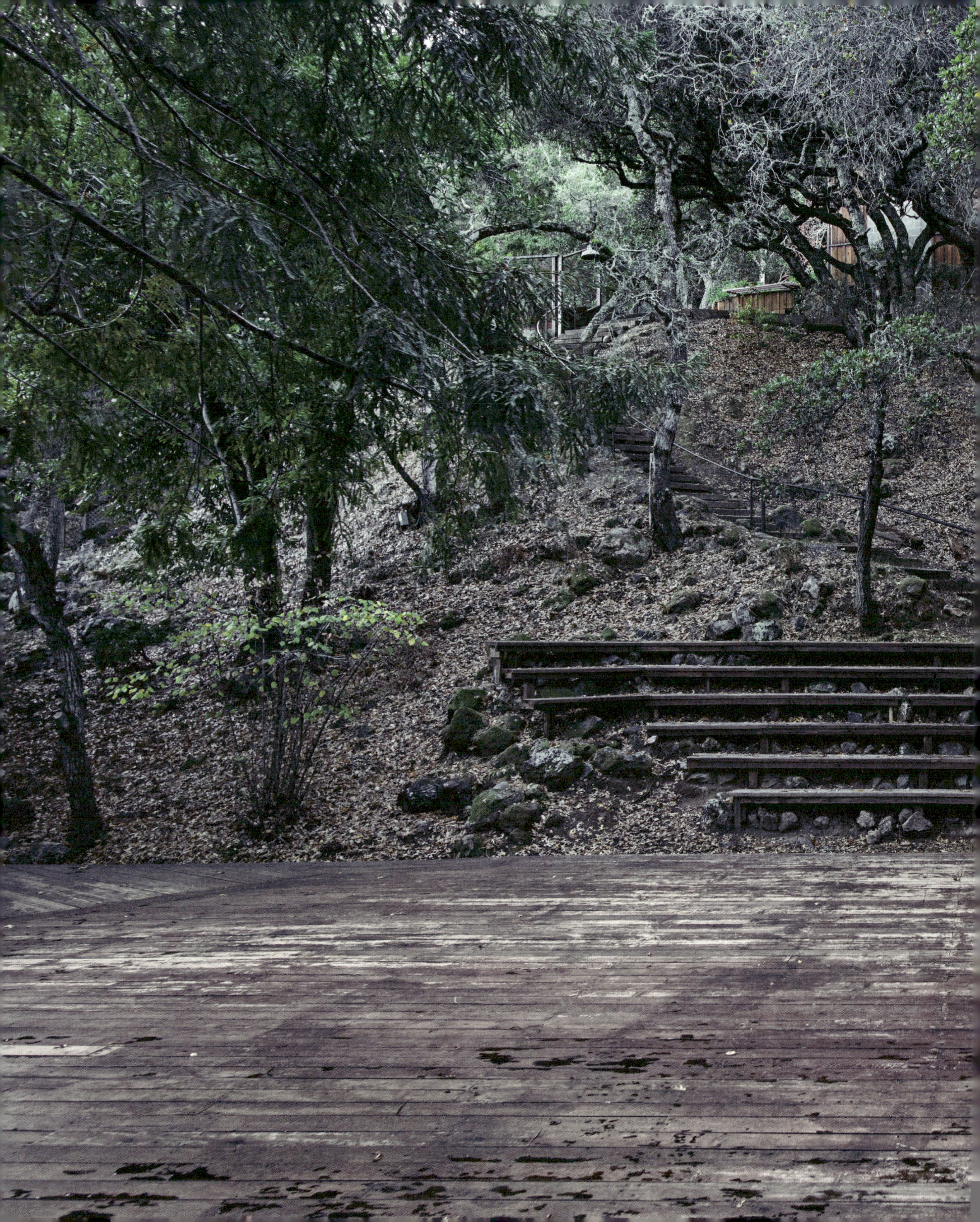